W9-BYX-554

Peripheral Visions

# Peripheral Visions

## Deterrence Theory and American Foreign Policy in the Third World, 1965–1990

Ted Hopf

Ann Arbor

THE UNIVERSITY OF MICHIGAN PRESS

Copyright © by the University of Michigan 1994
All rights reserved
Published in the United States of America by
The University of Michigan Press
Manufactured in the United States of America
∞ Printed on acid-free paper

1997   1996   1995   1994     4   3   2   1

*A CIP catalogue record for this book is available from the British Library.*

Library of Congress Cataloging-in-Publication Data

Hopf, Ted, 1959–
    Peripheral visions : deterrence theory and American foreign policy
in the Third World, 1965–1990 / Ted Hopf.
        p.   cm.
    Includes bibliographical references and index.
    ISBN 0-472-10540-X (acid-free paper)
    1. International relations.   2. United States—Foreign
relations—1945–1989.   3. Soviet Union—Foreign
relations—1945–1991.   4. Developing countries—Politics and
government.   5. Deterrence (Strategy)   I. Title.
JX1391.H65   1994
327.730172′4′09045—dc20                              94-21495
                                                        CIP

# Contents

# Preface

Deterrence theory probably has had more success than any other social science product in influencing postwar American foreign policy. Its deductive rigor looks impressive; its simple propositions appear intuitively sensible; and its prescriptions seem straightforward to implement. Moreover, for two generations of policymakers whose most salient historical lesson was World War II, the theory had historical resonance. The lessons of Munich gave life to the theory. The theory, in turn, offered a scientific pedigree to a set of memories.

Unfortunately, both the theory and the lessons of history have proven so powerful to U.S. policymakers and scholars that the assumptions, predictions, and prescriptions of the theory have rarely been seriously analyzed. In this book I investigate three of the central assumptions that have determined U.S. policy in the Third World over the last forty-five years. Each of these assumptions concerns the effects of U.S. behavior on the perceptions of potential challengers to the status quo, in this case the Soviet Union.

Deterrence theory tells us that three sets of concerns matter in the Third World: U.S. credibility, allied behavior, and regional dynamics. If the United States were to suffer a loss somewhere in the Third World, it was assumed that the Soviet leadership would infer from that defeat that the United States lacked the will and capacity to defend its interests elsewhere: the United States lacks credibility. American allies around the globe would begin to question the reliability of U.S. security guarantees: U.S. allies bandwagon with the Soviet Union. Finally, the Soviets would feel that their victory had set off dynamics in the region that would lead to further U.S. losses there: local U.S. allies and neutrals fall like dominoes.

These assumptions combine to require a U.S. policy of interventionism in the Third World in order to teach the Soviets the right lessons. For forty-five years, the United States pursued precisely such a policy. In the twenty-five-year slice of cold war history examined in this book, deterrence theory largely failed to achieve the desired results.

As the evidence shows, the policy of military intervention demanded by the theory was unnecessary to achieve the desired ends. It was, in fact, counterproductive to such a task. The United States expended far too much blood and treasure over the last forty-five years in conflicts that yielded negligible returns in its cold war competition with the Soviet Union.

By now the reader may be asking, why should I want to read a book that looks at cold war history? Hasn't the Soviet Union disappeared and been replaced by a Russian state with a fundamentally different foreign policy? Though the cold war is over and the Soviet Union has disintegrated, it is hard to exaggerate the historical and contemporary importance of deterrence theory. There are three major reasons why the arguments of this book are still highly relevant to the concerns of the academy, policymaking circles, and broader public.

First, it is vital that we learn from our own history. The most disruptive event in postwar U.S. history, the Vietnam War, was the product of the assumptions of deterrence theory. In looking at the history of the cold war, we need to identify which policies were effective and which were misguided, so that we may not only avoid future mistakes but also repeat past successes.

Some might argue that the latter task is irrelevant now, for there are no Soviet Unions in our future. To those critics, I would answer that while the cold war is over with the Soviet Union, history has not ended just yet. While Russia may not present a military challenge to the United States for the foreseeable future, the lessons of the cold war are useful regardless of who the future challenger might be. It is not hard to imagine a resurgent Japan or Germany, a united Europe, or a modernized China, any of which might vie for hegemonic leadership of the international system. In such an event, this book counsels that the United States should not be too quick to dissipate its scarce resources in conflicts in the periphery, as it did against the Soviet Union.

Second, deterrence theory remains applicable in dealing with indigenous threats to the status quo in the Third World. Iraq's Saddam Hussein is not unique. There are other potential aspirants to regional hegemony, India for instance. In such cases, this book urges that our responses to such events should depend entirely on our material, not our reputational, interests in the region. So, while we might want to confront Saddam because of Persian Gulf oil reserves, we could be indifferent to the fate of the Indian subcontinent.

Finally, the August 1991 coup attempt against Mikhail Gorbachev and the electoral success of Vladimir Zhirinovsky's Liberal Democratic Party in December 1993 should remind us that new thinkers are not the only possible rulers of Russia. His successor(s) need not be so disengaged from competition in the Third World. Again, this book advises that the United States should act in the Third World only if Russian or other behavior threatens strategic U.S. stakes. Let the Russians and others learn the futility of expending resources in that most unrewarding of games. In addition, U.S. policy in the Third World could have some effect on the attitudes of current and prospective Russian leaders. Restraint in U.S. third world policy could provide support for "new thinkers" in the Russian foreign policy elite, ensuring that benign Russian behavior continues. Conversely, an adventuristic U.S. policy could cultivate the interests of any of several variants of Russian imperialists.

Beyond its prescriptive value, this book contributes by its empirical findings to the further erosion of deterrence theory. It builds upon the works of Alexander George and Richard Smoke, Robert Jervis, Richard Ned Lebow, and Stephen Walt. It reveals the danger of a social science theory whose deductive rigor and elegance have allowed it to divert attention from its lack of validity for far too long. By establishing that Soviet lessons from their experiences in the Third World over the last twenty-five years are not unique to Soviet Marxist-Leninists, I show that the propositions underlying deterrence theory are invalid for a far more general population of foreign policy decision-makers and thus need to be fundamentally revised.

Anyone who writes a book always owes a great deal of gratitude to those who offered so much support over the years. My work is certainly no exception. I am especially indebted to Jack Snyder for being the one who introduced me to the study of international relations theory and Soviet foreign policy at Columbia University. Not only was Jack a great inspiration as a scholar, but far more important, he was an inspiration as a teacher, mentor, and friend. He also impressed upon me the need for rigorous thinking; contrary instances in this book remain despite his interventions. I was also blessed with the continual advice and encouragement of four colleagues, Jon Mercer, Sue Peterson, Elizabeth Kier, and Mike Desch, each of whom not only waded through numerous drafts but was always ready to be supportive, no matter what the hour and no matter under which stage of dissertation writing they themselves were buried. My arguments also benefitted greatly from discussions with and comments from Rick Herrmann, Robert Jervis, Chaim Kaufmann, Janice Gross Stein, Naomi Kirshner, Doug Blum, Robert Legvold, Rick Erickson, and Marc Trachtenberg.

In terms of institutions, I am very grateful for the three years of support received from the International Security Fellowship of the Carnegie Endowment for International Peace, while at Columbia University. I also enjoyed three summers of support from the Ford Foundation's Project on Superpower Competition in Rimland Asia. The Social Science Research Council's Joint Committee on Slavic Studies provided me with one year of dissertation research support. Finally, I owe the Olin Institute for Strategic Studies at the Center for International Affairs at Harvard University and its director, Sam Huntington, great thanks for the two years I spent there as a fellow in an enriching intellectual environment.

All translations from Russian are mine unless otherwise noted.

# Abbreviations

| | |
|---|---|
| *AIAS* | *Aziya i Afrika Sevodnya* (Asia and Africa Today) |
| *IA* | *International Affairs* |
| *JPSP* | *Journal of Personality and Social Psychology* |
| *KP* | *Komsomolskaya Pravda* (Komsomol Truth) |
| *KVS* | *Kommunist Vooruzhenykh Sil* (Communist of the Armed Forces) |
| *KZ* | *Krasnaya Zvezda* (Red Star) |
| *LA* | *Latinskaya Amerika* (Latin America) |
| *LG* | *Literaturnaya Gazeta* (Literary Gazette) |
| *MEIMO* | *Mirovaya Ekonomika i Mezhdunarodnye Otnosheniya* (World Economics and International Relations) |
| *NAIA* | *Narody Azii i Afriki* (Peoples of Asia and Africa) |
| *NINI* | *Novaya i Noveishaya Istoriya* (New and Newest History) |
| *NT* | *New Times* |
| *PDV* | *Problemy Dalnevo Vostoka* (Problems of the Far East) |
| *RKISM* | *Rabochii Klass i Sovremennyi Mir* (Working Class and the Contemporary World) |
| *SR* | *Sovetskaya Rossiya* (Soviet Russia) |
| *SShA* | *SShA: Ekonomika, Politika, Ideologiya* (USA: Economics, Politics, Ideology) |
| *VF* | *Voprosy Filosofii* (Questions of Philosophy) |
| *VI* | *Voprosy Istorii* (Questions of History) |
| *VIZ* | *Voenno-Istoricheskii Zhurnal* (Military-Historical Journal) |

# CHAPTER 1

# Introduction

> We lost thirty thousand dead in Korea to save face for the United States, not
> to save South Korea for the South Koreans, and it was undoubtedly worth
> it. Soviet expectations about the behavior of the United States are one of the
> most valuable assets we possess in world affairs.
>
> —Thomas C. Schelling

Was Schelling right? Did the United States really have to fight in Korea and
Vietnam, overthrow governments in the Dominican Republic and Guatemala,
and send arms to the Contras in Nicaragua and the mujahideen in Afghanistan? Deterrence theorists would have us believe that a failure to intervene
would have mortally damaged Washington's reputation for strength and will.
American policymakers, imbued with the lessons of Munich, believed that if
they did not demonstrate American military might in these intrinsically unimportant areas of the globe, the Soviet Union, just like Hitler, would have been
encouraged to challenge American interests in far more valuable parts of the
world, such as Europe or the Middle East.

To the contrary, I show that deterrence theorists, and the policymakers
who followed their prescriptions, were fundamentally misguided. The American military interventions in Vietnam and Grenada were unnecessary for
deterrent purposes. Instead, the United States taught its most powerful deterrent lessons through policies—for instance, diplomacy in the Middle East and
the maintenance of military capabilities for defending Europe—that are not
the primary policies prescribed by deterrence theory. Moreover, Soviet defeats that were not the result of any American actions, for example, Kwame
Nkrumah's overthrow in Ghana in 1966, taught the Soviets deterrent lessons
that the theory ignores. In sum, establishing a reputation as a nation able and
willing to defend its interests is a much easier task than deterrence theorists
and Munich analogists have maintained.

This chapter reviews the predictions that deterrence theory makes based

---

The epigraph is taken from Thomas Schelling, *Arms and Influence* (New Haven: Yale
University Press, 1966), 56.

upon Soviet victories and defeats in the Third World. It describes the lessons Soviets would have had to learn in order to validate or disconfirm the assumptions of deterrence theory.[1] It shows why some kinds of lessons are more powerful evidence than others and suggests that different kinds of explanations for these lessons should have different evidentiary weight. The more general the explanations for Soviet perceptions, the more confidence we should have in accepting such evidence as applicable to deterrent cases beyond the Soviet experience. If, however, the explanation for Soviet inferences rests on decision-making processes peculiar to Soviets, then this evidence is of little use beyond Soviet cases.

## The Predictions of Deterrence Theory

At its core, deterrence theory assumes that a potential aggressor is a rational calculator of costs and benefits. Faced with costs that are greater than its prospective gains, the opponent will be deterred. These probable costs are a combination of the defender's capability and its willingness to use that capacity. In other words, in order for an aggressor to be deterred, it must be convinced of the credibility of the defender.[2] Concern for credibility was the mainspring of U.S. foreign policy in the Third World throughout the cold war. Regardless of the trivial nature of a given piece of territory, it was assumed that the United States must act in that part of the world if it was to maintain a reputation for defending its interests elsewhere.[3]

---

1. Hereafter in the text, I often use the phrase *deterrence theory* as shorthand for the three assumptions of traditional deterrence theory that I am in fact testing. Please accept that if I write that deterrence theory has been invalidated by this case, it does not mean that all aspects of the theory have been disconfirmed, but only those assumptions with which I am concerned in this work.

2. It should be stressed at the outset that a challenger being convinced of the "credibility" of a defender is only a *necessary* condition for deterrent success, but not at all *sufficient*. Consequently, in this book, I make no claims whatever about whether in fact the Soviets were deterred or not deterred by particular American victories and defeats, but only that Soviets believed that the United States, its allies, and regional actors were more or less capable and resolute.

3. It should be noted that these assumptions about one's opponent are not at all peculiar to the American experience. As Jack Snyder's work on imperial overexpansion shows, British and German statesmen in the nineteenth century were very anxious about maintaining their countries' reputations for resolve. See Jack Snyder, *Myths of Empire: Domestic Politics and Strategic Ideology* (Ithaca, N.Y.: Cornell University Press, 1991). Thucydides recorded how the Athenians, in their negotiations with the Melians, argued that an Athenian failure to subordinate the island of Melos would create the impression that "we are afraid to molest" even those weaker than us. See *The Peloponnesian War* (New York: Modern Library, 1982), 352. Machiavelli advised Renaissance Italian princes to respond to any "injury" done to them, so as to prevent future challenges, in *The Discourses of Niccolo Machiavelli*, trans., L.J. Walker (London: Routledge

As Schelling argued:

> The main reason why we [the United States] are committed in many of these places is that our threats are interdependent. Essentially we tell the Soviets that we have to react here [in the periphery] because, if we did not, they would not believe us when we say that we will react there [in strategic areas]. The loss of face that matters most is the loss of Soviet belief that we will do, elsewhere and subsequently, what we insist we will do here and now. Our deterrence rests on Soviet expectations.[4]

The critical argument is that U.S. interests are not to be equated with the strategic value of a piece of territory but are to be expanded to include the protection of the reputation of the United States. Schelling eloquently expressed this logic:

> It is often argued that "face" is a frivolous asset to preserve, and that it is a sign of immaturity that a government can't swallow its pride and lose face. . . . [But] a country's "image," consisting of other countries' beliefs (their leaders' beliefs, that is) about how the country can be expected to behave . . . relates . . . to its reputation for action. . . . If the question is raised whether this kind of "face" is worth fighting over, the answer is that this kind of face is one of the few things worth fighting over. Few parts of the world are intrinsically worth the risk of serious war by themselves, . . . but defending them may preserve one's commitments to action in other parts of the world and at later times.[5]

Deterrence theory assumes that American credibility to defend central, strategic values in Europe, Japan, and the Middle East depends not only on its manifest capacity to defend those areas, but also on its willingness to confront perceived aggression in areas with little or no intrinsic importance to the United States. Glenn Snyder developed a taxonomy of interests relevant to this work. There are three kinds of American interests in the world— strategic, deterrent, and political. Strategic interests comprise the elements of war-making potential of a piece of territory—its military machine, economic resources, manpower, and so on. George Kennan, for example, in speeches in

---

and Kegan Paul, 1950), 1: 442–44. In sixteenth-century Europe, the Habsburg emperor Charles V was often worried about attacks on areas peripheral to his empire, lest his enemies be encouraged and his allies disheartened. See Ted Hopf, "Polarity, the Offense-Defense Balance, and War," *American Political Science Review* 85, no. 2 (June 1991): 475–94.

4. Thomas Schelling, *Arms and Influence* (New Haven: Yale University Press, 1966), 55–56.

5. Ibid., 124–25.

the government in late 1947, argued for such a calculation of American interests. Those areas of the world with industrial and war-making potential—Europe and Japan—must be given top priority in American security considerations, as their loss to the Soviet Union immediately and directly would threaten American economic and military security.[6]

Deterrent interests are those discussed by Schelling—the value the United States puts on losing face in a conflict. Snyder takes concern for reputation to its logical extreme, suggesting that "for deterrent reasons it might be desirable to try resistance against a limited enemy attack even though we know in advance that we will fail. The purpose would be to inform the enemy that gains could be had only at a price which he would not want to pay."[7] According to this rationale, even American losses, if sufficiently costly to the United States and for stakes of sufficiently low strategic value, can create the correct deterrent image.

This logic found its expression in the official thinking of Washington during the Vietnam War. As Undersecretary of Defense John McNaughton stated in 1964, it was "essential that the United States emerge as a 'good doctor.' We must have kept promises, been tough, taken risks, gotten bloodied, and hurt the enemy very badly."[8]

Political interests are the effect of a response or nonresponse on the alignment or attitudes of third countries—American and Soviet allies and neutrals. American allies lose confidence in the United States when it tolerates Soviet victories in the periphery;[9] Soviet allies, whether radical states or national liberation movements, are encouraged to act more aggressively; and neutrals shy away from any U.S. efforts to obtain even their "positive" neutrality. Arnold Wolfers wrote that "there is danger that failure to live up to a commitment to defend [one ally] may have the much-feared [effect] of driving other allies into the arms of the Soviets."[10]

The rationale for U.S. interventions in the Third World had three elements: concern for Soviet perceptions of U.S. credibility; concern that U.S. allies would bandwagon with the Soviets if the United States did not respond

---

6. In John Lewis Gaddis, *Strategies of Containment* (New York: Oxford, 1982), 40–41. See also George F. Kennan, *Memoirs, 1925-1950* (Boston: Little, Brown, and Co., 1967).

7. Glenn Snyder, *Deterrence and Defense* (Princeton: Princeton University Press, 1961), 38.

8. Quoted in Gaddis, *Strategies of Containment*, 267.

9. I use the word *periphery* and the term *Third World* interchangeably in this book. Both refer to all parts of the world other than North America, Europe, the Soviet Union, Japan, and East Asia. The only potentially confusing area is the Middle East, which is part of the Third World, but not of the periphery, since the United States has strategic interests in the oil-bearing areas of that region. I will make this distinction clear whenever necessary in the text.

10. Arnold Wolfers, *Discord and Collaboration* (Baltimore: Johns Hopkins University Press, 1962), 221.

to Soviet aggression in the Third World; and fear that nations would fall like dominoes in a pro-Soviet direction in the region of a recent Soviet victory.

Hence, deterrence theory makes three broad predictions about Soviet perceptions of its international surroundings after its victories and defeats in the Third World.

1. After a victory, the Soviets should express disbelief in the American willingness and ability to defend U.S. interests elsewhere in the world—both in the Third World and in strategic areas of the globe. Conversely, a Soviet loss should result in gains for U.S. credibility.[11]

2. After a victory, the Soviets should advance the argument that U.S. allies now fear that the United States cannot provide reliable security guarantees, and so accommodation to, or bandwagoning with, the Soviet Union is the best policy. Conversely, a Soviet defeat should result in Soviet perceptions of U.S. allies who are increasingly confident in their alliance relationship with the United States.

3. After a victory, the Soviets should talk about how other victories in the region and beyond are just a matter of time, about how dominoes will fall in their favor both in the area and around the globe. After a defeat, however, they should express pessimism about the prospects for further gains.[12]

---

11. Deterrence theory makes no determinate predictions about credibility because of the logical tension between resolve and capacity. At one logical extreme, the theory would predict that if the United States fought for a decade to subdue Belize, losing one hundred thousand lives in the process, the United States would gain in credibility, because it has demonstrated high resolve, if little capability. This is the position of John MacNaughton and Glenn Snyder. This would mean that losses to weak powers are equal in importance to high credibility as victories against powerful states. The latter position can hardly withstand any test for prima facie common sense.

Given the theory's lack of logical clarity on this point, I have chosen the categories of victories and defeats, or gains and losses, as measures of credibility. If the United States wins a war, overthrows a government, or turns a country's foreign policy away from Moscow, it is assumed the United States gains in credibility because it has demonstrated both resolve and capacity. If the United States loses a war, watches an allied government get overthrown, or loses a friend to Moscow, it is assumed the United States loses credibility, because it has shown a lack of capability, even if it has shown resolve.

12. Note that I am investigating *Soviet* perceptions of allied reactions and regional dynamics, rather than the lessons and behavior of these American allies and that of governments and other actors in the area. I do this because deterrence theory assumes that a challenger's calculations about the costs and benefits of expansionism are based, in large part, on its assessments of the credibility of its opponent, the probable behavior of its adversary's allies, and the most likely policies of the actors in the region being considered.

However, work has been done in this area to test deterrence theory's predictions about the behavior of allies and neutrals after defeats are suffered by their "protectors." It has been found,

**TABLE 1.   Soviet Inferences and Deterrence Theory's Assumptions about U.S. Credibility after a Soviet Victory**

| Soviet Lessons | |
| --- | --- |
| Confirming | Disconfirming |
| The United States will not defend its strategic interests. | The United States will attack the Soviet Union. |
| The United States will not defend its peripheral interests. | The United States will attack members of the socialist alliance. |
| The United States will negotiate on third world conflicts. | The United States will resist detente and arms control. |
| The United States will continue detente and arms control. | The United States will not negotiate on third world conflicts. |
| The United States will not attack members of the socialist alliance. | The United States will defend its peripheral interests. |
| The United States will not attack the Soviet Union. | The United States will defend its strategic interests. |

*Note:* Lessons are listed in order of decreasing strength as evidence.

Tables 1 and 2 propose a continuum of Soviet lessons from their victories and defeats. The lessons are arranged in two columns. Lessons in the left-hand column validate deterrence theory's assumptions about U.S. credibility after a Soviet gain, while lessons in the right-hand column invalidate those assumptions. Read from top to bottom, the lessons are arranged from the strongest possible evidence for and against the theory to the weakest such evidence.

Thus, deterrence theory's assumptions about U.S. credibility after a

contrary to the theory, that these states opt to balance with any available allies, rather than bandwagon with the ascendant aggressor. On American allies in the postwar period, see Stephen Walt, "Alliance Formation and the Balance of World Power," *International Security* 10, no. 1 (Spring 1985): 3–43; *The Origins of Alliances*, (Ithaca, N.Y.: Cornell University Press, 1987); and "Alliance Formation in South Asia," in *Dominoes and Bandwagons: Strategic Beliefs and Superpower Competition in the Eurasian Rimland*, ed. Robert Jervis and Jack Snyder (New York: Oxford University Press, 1991). Jonathan Mercer found that allies' views of their own allies are unrelated to the behavior of the latter in conflicts. "Attribution Error and The Credibility of Threat and Promise," Columbia University, 1989, typescript; and "Broken Promises and Unfulfilled Threats: Resolve, Reputation, and Deterrence Theory," Ph.D. diss., Columbia University, 1992.

**TABLE 2.   Soviet Inferences and Deterrence Theory's Assumptions about Regional Dynamics after a Soviet Victory**

| Soviet Lessons | |
|---|---|
| Confirming | Disconfirming |
| Dominoes will fall in areas of strategic interest to the United States. | Countries contiguous to the region of the victory will effectively resist any further revolutionary change in the region. |
| Dominoes will fall in other peripheral areas of the globe. | Other third world countries around the globe will balance effectively against any regional revolutionary threats. |
| Dominoes will fall in countries contiguous to the region of the Soviet victory. | United States strategic allies will balance effectively against any threats of revolution in their area. |

*Note*: Lessons are listed in order of decreasing strength as evidence.

Soviet gain (or U.S. loss) would be most strongly confirmed if Soviet inferences clustered in the upper left boxes of table 1 and if there were no disconfirming lessons. For example, after the U.S. loss in Vietnam, Soviets would have inferred that the United States was neither capable nor willing to defend its allies in Western Europe, or its interests elsewhere in the Third World. Likewise, the most powerful disconfirmation of deterrence theory's assumptions about credibility would be a concentration of Soviet lessons in the upper right quadrant of the table with no confirming inferences. For example, after the Soviet victory in Angola, Soviets would suggest that the United States was intent on undermining the security of the Soviet Union and its socialist allies and was opposed to any arms control or detente with Moscow. The same interpretation applies to the kinds of lessons about regional dynamics, as shown in table 2.

After Vietnam, for example, deterrence theory would be most strongly confirmed if Soviets expected American allies in Western Europe and the Middle East to feel threatened by the victory in Southeast Asia. Likewise, if the theory's predictions were to be strongly invalidated, then Soviets would have to infer from a U.S. loss in Vietnam that Laos, Kampuchea, Thailand, Malaysia, and others, would redouble their efforts to prevent any destabilizing effects from reaching their countries.[13]

---

13. In each of the case-study chapters, I provide these continua of lessons for each of the cases.

## The Alternatives to Deterrence Theory

Academic criticism of these particular assumptions of deterrence theory has rarely gone beyond merely questioning their merits. There have been only two empirical studies that even partially tested these propositions.[14]

### Prevailing Criticisms of Deterrence Theory

Given the decisive influence deterrence theory has had on American foreign policy since World War II, it is quite surprising that there has been no effort to test these three critical assumptions against the empirical record, especially since there is an impressive literature examining the conditions for successful deterrence.[15] However, the concern here is not so much with whether communicating one's resolve and capability results in an aggressor backing down, but rather in a prior question: whether in fact a strategy based on deterrence theory is necessary in the first place. If the Soviets did not make the kinds of inferences ascribed to them by American decision makers and deterrence theorists, then postwar American foreign policy in the Third World was seriously misguided. And if these unpredicted Soviet lessons can be explained by universal or general models of decision making, then the assumptions deterrence theory makes are invalid.

A number of theorists have questioned these traditional assumptions about how states learn about another state's credibility after the latter suffers a defeat. It is rare, however, for these arguments to go from informed speculation to empirical testing. Glenn Snyder and Paul Diesing, for example, object to the assertion that a state's passive behavior in one crisis is used by its foe in the next crisis to measure its credibility.

---

14. Paul Huth and Bruce Russett, "What Makes Deterrence Work," *World Politics* 35, no. 4 (July 1984): 496–526; and Paul Huth, *Extended Deterrence and the Prevention of War* (New Haven: Yale University Press, 1988).

15. A representative sample includes Alexander L. George and Richard Smoke, *Deterrence in American Foreign Policy: Theory and Practice* (New York: Columbia University Press, 1974); Chihiro Hosoya, "Miscalculations in Deterrent Policy: Japan-U.S. Relations, 1938-41," *Journal of Peace Research* 5, no. 2 (1968): 97–115; Robert Jervis, "Deterrence Theory Revisited," *World Politics* 31, no. 2 (January 1979): 289–324; Robert Jervis, "Deterrence and Perception," *International Security* 7, no. 3, (Winter 1982/83): 1–34; Robert Jervis, Richard Ned Lebow, and Janice Stein, eds., *Psychology and Deterrence* (Baltimore: Johns Hopkins University Press, 1985); Richard Ned Lebow, *Between Peace and War* (Baltimore: Johns Hopkins University Press, 1981), Bruce M. Russett, "The Calculus of Deterrence," *Journal of Conflict Resolution* 7, no. 2 (March 1963): 97–109; Bruce M. Russett, "Pearl Harbor: Deterrence Theory and Decision Theory," *Journal of Peace Research* 4, no. 2 (1967): 89–106; and Glenn Snyder and Paul Diesing, *Conflict among Nations* (Princeton: Princeton University Press, 1977).

Perhaps the most reasonable hypothesis is that a state's resolve reputation is most likely to be undermined for future crises in the same geographical area or the same type of issue on which it has backed down before, and least likely for those in other areas over distinctly different issues. Thus the U.S. refusal to play the "end-game" in South Vietnam probably damaged its resolve image in Southeast Asia, but not with respect to crises in the Middle East.[16]

The problem with this argument is that Soviet decision makers might differ from Snyder and Diesing and American decision makers about what made the Middle East "distinctly different" from Southeast Asia. It is possible that Soviet leaders saw the Middle East in terms of national liberation movements, rather than in terms of the relative importance of oil in the Middle East to the West and the absence of any commensurate material interests in Indochina. If this were the case, then the Soviet Union should have been emboldened by the American defeat in Vietnam to act more aggressively in the Middle East.

Stephen Maxwell also claims that states overemphasize the importance of standing firm for the sake of maintaining credibility. Unfortunately, without any supporting evidence, he argues that "the only conclusions the Russians could confidently draw from an American retreat from Berlin [in this case] was that Berlin was not a vital national interest to the Americans."[17] This assertion is reasonable, but it is equally logical to assume that an American retreat in Berlin would lead the Soviets to believe that the United States was also willing to relinquish its positions in all of West Germany, or even Western Europe.

Jervis devotes a book to the problem of how statesmen try to manipulate the images of their country to create the appearance of a state ready and willing to resist aggression. He suggests several tactics a state can use if it wishes to retreat in a conflict without losing credibility. In general, a leader must find ways to "decouple" the current conflict from future ones by stressing the special circumstances that surround the current retreat and how such circumstances would not obtain in subsequent confrontations. Jervis warns, however, that it is very difficult to succeed in such operations.[18]

In a later work, Jervis argues that cognitive psychological biases may work in favor of maintaining an image of high credibility. Given the fact that

---

16. Snyder and Diesing, *Conflict among Nations*, 187.

17. Stephen Maxwell, *Rationality and Deterrence*, Adelphi paper no. 50 (London: International Institute for Strategic Studies, 1969), 19.

18. Jervis, *The Logic of Images in International Relations* (Princeton: Princeton University Press, 1970), 198–99.

beliefs change very slowly and strongly resist information that conflicts with them, a state "with a reputation for standing firm will not only be able to win disputes by threatening to fight, but has the freedom to avoid confrontations without damaging its image." Jervis adds, however, that "these propositions still lack empirical evidence."[19] Moreover, belief perseverance can work in the reverse direction as well—a state with a reputation for retreating is going to have a hard time convincing its enemies that it will stand firm the next time.

The historical record also appears mixed on this count. While Hitler commented after British and French appeasement at Munich that "our enemies are little worms. I saw them at Munich,"[20] the "never-again syndrome" also exists. For example, Russia's humiliation at the hands of Germany over Bosnia in 1908–9 and 1912 ensured Russian resistance in the summer of 1914.[21] As Alexander George and Richard Smoke suggest, "deterrence is a policy which, if it succeeds, can only frustrate an opponent who aspires to changing the international status quo. The consequences of continued frustration, however, are not easily predictable and are not necessarily benign."[22]

However, two works test the proposition that past defeats influence future perceptions of credibility. Paul Huth and Bruce Russett found that in twenty-three cases of failed deterrence, there was no correlation between a previous victory by the attacker and its decision to challenge the deterrer in subsequent cases.[23] Since they do not perform case studies on any of their twenty-three episodes, they establish only the lack of a correlative relationship between victories and future challenges, without establishing whether or not there is any causal significance to their findings.

In a later work, Huth does perform case studies to determine the conditions for successful deterrence. One of his independent variables is the past behavior of the present defender. Two of Huth's findings are relevant for this study. First, he finds that if either the defender or the potential attacker has been forced to retreat in a previous military conflict with the other, deterrence success in the future is less likely. In the postwar world, however, there were

---

19. Jervis, "Deterrence and Perception," 11.

20. Quoted in Fred Ikle, *How Nations Negotiate* (New York: Harper and Row, 1964), 82.

21. Even these two seemingly clear-cut examples are problematic. The Munich case might not qualify as an example of weakness in the periphery leading to a challenge of deterrence, as Hitler's plans for conquest after the March 1936 remilitarization of the Rhineland were not contingent on whether he was resisted or not. Moreover, Czechoslovakia hardly qualifies as a peripheral area of Europe. (I owe the former point to Robert Jervis.) With respect to the Russian case, it can be argued that had Russia stood firm in either event, but especially in 1912, the question of Russian credibility would not have arisen in the first place for German decision makers, for the latter would have seen Russia as both capable and willing to use that power to defend its interests in the Balkans.

22. *Deterrence*, 5.

23. Huth and Russett, "What Makes Deterrence Work," 517.

no direct military clashes between the two superpowers, so Huth's findings do not bear directly on the question of Soviet perceptions of the outcomes of conflicts in the periphery.

A second finding, however, does support the critics of traditional deterrence assumptions. Huth finds that the past behavior of a defender in conflicts with a state other than the present attacker has no effect on that attacker's decision making calculus.[24] This implies that American defeats at the hands of enemies other than the Soviet Union would not affect Soviet views of American credibility.[25]

## Explaining Soviet Lessons: From the Universal to the Peculiar

Establishing whether Soviet inferences confirm or disconfirm deterrence theory's predictions over the last twenty-five years is very important to testing the validity of the theory's assumptions. It is not sufficient, however, to the task of testing the theory's more general validity. In order to mount a challenge to deterrence theory in general, it must be demonstrated that Soviet inferences from U.S. losses or victories are not unique, that any decisionmaker in any nation-state would have drawn the same conclusions from these events. Soviet lessons lie on a continuum from universal to peculiar, with general in the middle. (See table 3.)

Deterrence theory would be most strongly validated if Soviet lessons were concentrated in the "universal" and "general" confirmation columns in the table. If, instead, confirmatory Soviet lessons were mostly in the "peculiar" column, then all we could say is that deterrence theory was accurate only in the case of the Soviet Union and in cases of challengers with similar belief systems. Likewise, the theory would receive its most powerful disconfirmation if Soviet lessons were concentrated in the left and middle columns. If the theory were mostly invalidated as a consequence of peculiar Soviet beliefs, then this disconfirmation of the theory would be restricted to a rather small universe of challengers to deterrence in the world. Even if this were the case, however, it would show that deterrence theory was misapplied to the Soviet Union during the forty-five years of the cold war. The three kinds of explanations for Soviet lessons are discussed in what follows.

---

24. Paul K. Huth, "The Dilemma of Deterrence: Credibility versus Stability, Escalation and Conflict Resolution in Crises from 1885-1984," Ph.D. diss., Yale University, 1986, 109–29 and 228–77. Also published as *Extended Deterrence*.

25. This assumes, however, that Soviet policymakers do not see national liberation movements and other allies in the Third World as proxies in conflicts with imperialism, an assumption requiring empirical investigation.

**TABLE 3.   The Power of Different Explanations for Soviet Lessons from Victories and Defeats in the Periphery**

| Types of Explanations | | |
|---|---|---|
| Universal (most powerful) | General (strong) | Peculiar (weak) |
| Rational attribution model/ logical indeterminancy | Bounded rationality/cognitive economy | Belief systems |

## Universal Explanations: Logical Indeterminancy and Rational Attribution Theory

Several of the assumptions of deterrence theory are logically indeterminant. In other words, their logical *opposites* have just as much a priori theoretical standing to be underlying principles. Neither set of assumptions is logically superior or prior to the other. In cases of logical indeterminancy, the assumption that receives overwhelming *empirical* support should be adopted as the most valid. So, if Soviet lessons tend to confirm one assumption at the expense of the other, then we should be confident that the disconfirmed assumption is invalidated in general.

If Soviet lessons are the product of rational attribution processes, then we should accord them universal status because rationality is assumed by deterrence theory, and because the assumption of rationality is so widely distributed throughout all social sciences.

### Logical Indeterminancy

Deterrence theory assumes that U.S. credibility is interconnected across issues and events. It is equally logical, however, to assume that a continuum exists in this interconnectedness. If credibility is linked only across *similar* issues and events, then United States behavior in a particular region or with respect to a certain issue will be used by Soviets to diagnose future U.S. behavior only in that region or on that kind of issue. But Soviets will not use U.S. conduct in some area of the periphery to generate predictions about U.S. resolve or capability to defend its strategic interests in Europe, Northeast Asia, or the Persian Gulf.

Deterrence theory predicts that United States strategic allies will reassess continuing their alliance with the United States if Washington fails to respond to challenges in the periphery. However, the alternative hypothesis, derived from balance of power theory, that such allies, when assessing the U.S. commitment to their security, would *ignore* U.S. behavior in unimportant areas of the globe has equal if not far greater plausibility. Hence, Soviets also would not expect bandwagoning American allies after U.S. losses in the Third World.

Deterrence's assumption that local actors will fall like dominoes into the lap of the local victor and its Soviet patron can also be challenged. It is equally plausible, and again consistent with the tenets of balance of power theory, that in the face of this new and enhanced threat, local states would mount a resistance to this local threat.[26]

Deterrence theory further assumes that the United States must deal the Soviet Union *military* defeats in the Third World; the theory ignores the possibility of using nonmilitary instruments to obtain the same results.[27] The theory also assumes that Soviet defeats that occur without any U.S. involvement would have no effect on Soviet views of U.S. credibility, allied behavior, or regional dynamics. Similarly, Soviet defeats that come as a result of *non-American* efforts are also assumed to be less effective than direct U.S. military actions.

On each of these counts, it is at least, if not more, logically compelling to hypothesize the opposite. If the Soviets are rational deterrence theorists themselves,[28] then direct U.S. military involvement in delivering defeats to the Soviets should be the *least* effective strategy for convincing them not to challenge the status quo in the future. This is so because a military defeat dealt directly to them by the United States engages Soviet reputational interests and should impel them to find an opportunity to regain their credibility. Soviets would be less likely to have concerns about credibility if the defeat was dealt to them by the United States by nonmilitary instruments. Being outmaneuvered diplomatically or outbid economically is less likely than a loss in a

---

26. These logical alternatives to the theory's assumptions about allies and regional dynamics have received empirical validation in the works of Stephen Walt cited in footnote 12 above.

27. The theory ignores, but does not preclude, the use of nonmilitary instruments to deter a potential challenger. One of the major findings of this book is that, despite the theory's assumption that one deters a challenger by confronting it with a high probability for high costs for any attempts at expansion, the theory omits the entire range of costs that could be imposed by the defender, beyond direct military force. Deterrence theory's current assumptions about costs, benefits, and probabilities very comfortably could capture the expanded category of instruments elaborated here.

28. This has to be one of most peculiar omissions of deterrence theory. It assumes the adversary is rational but does not assume that the adversary also is motivated by deterrent concerns. What makes this even more striking is that a theory whose historical roots are in the lessons of Munich ignores *Soviet* lessons from Munich. After all, except for Czechoslovakia, no single state suffered more than the Soviet Union from the appeasement of Hitler at Munich. Moreover, the Soviets also learned from the lessons of Stalin's appeasement of Hitler, from the Molotov-Ribbentrop Pact of August 1939 until the June 1941 German attack, that credibility matters . . . a great deal.

contest of arms to trigger Soviet anxieties about other states' perceptions of their capabilities. And Soviets would be very *unlikely* to feel the need to respond for reputational reasons if the United States was not involved at all in their defeat because they have not suffered a defeat at the hands of the other superpower.

Finally, deterrence theory assumes that a challenger's assessment of a defender's credibility ceases as soon as an event ends. If the United States loses in, say, Vietnam, then Soviets will infer lessons of reduced U.S. credibility, at least until the next case. But this is an oddly truncated view of rationality. A rational challenger would not use a single outcome alone to assess the probability of a future response from the defender. It would instead closely assess what kinds of steps, if any, the defender takes subsequent to its defeat to enhance its capacity to meet the next challenge. It would be an extremely reckless challenger indeed that did not go through this kind of analysis. And yet deterrence theory assumes this kind of challenger.

In sum, deterrence theory has a number of assumptions that lack any exclusive logical standing. These include the propositions that (a) there is interconnectedness of credibility across issues and events; (b) strategic allies pay attention to events in the periphery when making their alliance choices; (c) dominoes fall; (d) military defeats are the best communicators of deterrent lessons; and (e) credibility is based only on the behavior manifested in the event, not on any ensuing behavior. Each of these assumptions has an equally logical opposite. Whichever assumption receives overwhelming empirical support in the case studies of this book should be included in a revised theory of deterrence.

### Rational Attributions

The rational attribution model is a combination of conventional rational actor assumptions and "first wave" attribution theory. Since traditional deterrence theory is based on the assumption of rationality, it is necessary to develop a model of rationality appropriate to Soviet inferences from its third world experiences, and then test it against the empirical record.[29] The two most widely employed models of rationality are either too spare or too elaborate for my purposes here. The rational choice requirement that an actor's preferences be stable and transitively ordered is a necessary component of any rational model, but insufficiently rich to capture the dynamics of Soviet learning.[30] And the procedural rationality characteristic of Janis and Mann's vigilant

---

29. On the centrality of the rationality assumption to deterrence theory, see Christopher H. Achen and Duncan Snidal, "Rational Deterrence Theory and Comparative Case Studies," *World Politics* 41, no. 2 (January 1989): 143–69.

30. For descriptions of the assumptions of rationality in rational choice models, see George Tsebelis, *Nested Games: Rational Choice in Comparative Politics* (Berkeley and Los Angeles:

information processor is too detailed to be used in its entirety.[31] So, in the rational attribution model developed below, I borrow central elements of both rational models and combine them with the findings of the first wave of attribution theorists. The resultant model yields predictions for how a rational Soviet decision maker would learn lessons from U.S. victories and defeats in the periphery.

Early attribution theory claimed individuals operated like "naive scientists," employing crude models of Mill's method of difference. A decision maker observes some outcome and determines its antecedents. In order to predict whether or not the same outcome will appear in the future, she looks to see whether the same antecedents are present; if they are, she predicts the presence of the outcome. If she is correct in her forecast, the story ends there. She is satisfied with her causal model and does not inquire whether some other, as of yet unidentified variable may have caused the outcome in both cases. If her prediction is inaccurate, she will add an antecedent that she had previously ignored, restoring her confidence level. Given a sufficient number of cases, the naive scientist becomes quite certain of her causal beliefs.[32]

One body of experimental psychology investigates the attributions individuals make about people who fail or succeed at some task. These attributions are divided into two broad categories: situational and dispositional. Situational attributions refer to transient or contextual factors; dispositional attributions refer to characteristics of the actor. Exertion of effort by the actor is seen as an indicator of intent, or resolve. If an actor fails at a difficult task, she is not necessarily seen as incapable. However, an actor who makes a great effort and fails, though perceived as highly resolute, is seen as incapable.[33]

---

University of California Press, 1990), 24–31; Bruce Bueno de Mesquita, *The War Trap* (New Haven: Yale University Press, 1981), 29–33; and William H. Riker, "Political Science and Rational Choice," in *Perspectives on Positive Political Economy*, ed. James E. Alt and Kenneth A. Shepsle, (Cambridge: Cambridge University Press, 1990), 172–74.

31. Irving L. Janis and Leon Mann, *Decision Making: An Analysis of Conflict, Choice, and Commitment* (New York: Free Press, 1977), esp. 45–80. See also Graham T. Allison, *Essence of Decision: Explaining the Cuban Missile Crisis*, (Boston: Little, Brown, and Co., 1971), 10–38.

32. Harold H. Kelley, "Processes of Causal Attribution," *American Psychologist* 28, no. 2 (February 1973): 107–28.

This "first wave" of attribution theory has been superseded in the literature by what might be called "irrational" attribution theory. Experimental psychologists have discovered that people do not behave like naive scientists, but rather make a number of attribution errors. For an excellent review of this "second wave" of attribution theory, see Richard Nisbett and Lee Ross, *Human Inference: Strategies and Shortcomings of Social Judgment* (Englewood Cliffs, N.J.: Prentice-Hall, 1980); and Lee Ross and Richard Nisbett, *The Person and the Situation: Perspectives of Social Psychology* (Philadelphia: Temple University Press, 1991). Many of these second-wave insights are incorporated into my second set of learning models that follow below.

33. David L. Ronis, Ranald D. Hansen, and Virginia E. O'Leary, "Understanding the Meaning of Achievement Attributions," *JPSP* 44, no. 4 (April 1983): 702–3.

One of the most critical, if intuitively obvious, findings is that observers who believe a particular cause for a success or failure is likely to be stable across cases are very confident in their ability to predict future behavior. For example, belief in the stability of, say, capability is created by observing instances of capability both across a number of cases and, more important, across a number of cases with different characteristics.[34] In the contrary instance, Soviets who learned from Vietnam that public opinion was merely a temporary constraint on an executive branch committed to interventionism would not treat low American capability as a stable variable.

Soviet lessons that follow this pattern are the most powerful evidence for testing deterrence theory. If Soviets process information like naive scientists using causal models that follow the method of similarity and difference, then it is reasonable to assume that the universe of challengers to deterrence do likewise. In sum, either if Soviet lessons provide overwhelming empirical support for one logically indeterminant assumption over another, or if Soviets arrive at their lessons through rational attribution processes, these are evidence for the *universal* validity of these findings.

### General Explanations: Cognitive Economizing

General explanations for Soviet lessons are those that imply that most decision makers most of the time use the kinds of shortcuts identified below. Cognitive economizing comprises the process of mental shortcuts and the array of simplifying mechanisms that individuals employ to make sense of a world that is simply too complex to fathom in a purely rational way. Since these economizing devices are not fully rational, they do not have the same theory-confirming and disconfirming status as the universal explanations above. But, since they are not at all peculiar to Soviets, they do not have the more limited applicability attached to belief systems and various motivated biases. Consequently, deterrence theory in general is only moderately confirmed or disconfirmed by Soviet lessons with general explanations.

Bounded rationality, a form of cognitive economizing, assumes that decision makers are mentally unable to perform the kinds of tasks required by rational attribution theory. Instead of developing complete causal models of reality, cognitive misers rely on a limited number of crucial variables to

---

34. Bernard Weiner, "Achievement Motivation as Conceptualized by an Attribution Theorist," in *Achievement Motivation and Attribution Theory*, ed. Bernard Weiner (Morristown, N.J.: General Learning, 1974), 6–21.; Valerie A. Valle and Irene H. Frieze, "The Stability of Causal Attributions as a Mediator in Changing Expectations for Success," *JPSP* 37, no. 5 (May 1976): 579–87; John P. Meyer, "Causal Attributions for Success and Failure," *JPSP* 41, no. 5 (May 1980): 704–17; and Edward E. Jones and Daniel McGillis, "Correspondent Inferences and the Attribution Cube," in *New Directions in Attribution Research*, ed. John H. Harvey, William John Ickes, and Robert F. Kidd (Hillsdale, N.J.: Erlbaum, 1976), 1: 393–94.

explain phenomena. They monitor only these variables to assess whether it is advisable to change policy. If the values of variables appear to remain little changed, then the person's predictions about what he or she is observing will stay unchanged. For example, if a Soviet identifies the U.S. Congress as the main factor explaining American propensity for interventionism, he will not change his prediction about future American conduct in the Third World, unless Congress manifestly alters its position on the policy. If, however, either Congress gains or loses power vis-à-vis the executive, or Soviet policy fails dramatically due to the effects of some factor that had been ignored by Soviet policymakers, then economizing decision makers will reassess the policy and behavior and construct a new causal model to account for American interventionism.[35]

If Soviets employed this model when reaching their assessments about the world, we should have less confidence in the overall power of the evidence than if they were making rational attributions. This is so because different decision makers choose different factors to monitor when constructing their causal models, and it is a priori impossible to predict precisely which variables will be chosen by any given decision maker. This limits the generalizability of the findings because presumably one's choice of variables will significantly affect one's lessons from any given event.

Nevertheless, general psychological explanations for Soviet lessons do have validity beyond the Soviet case. The process by which people choose which critical variables to monitor bounds the range of possible choices with some degree of predictability. People may select these factors according to various decision making heuristics: availability, vividness, concreteness, representativeness, and personal salience.[36] Each one of these heuristics implies that a person will have a predictable preference for information that easily comes to mind, stands out from a dull background, is presented as an actual event rather than a statistical abstraction, appears to share characteristics that

---

35. For discussions of bounded rationality, see John Steinbruner, *The Cybernetic Theory of Decision* (Princeton: Princeton University Press, 1974); Charles Lindblom, "The Science of Muddling Through," *Public Administration Review* 19, no. 2 (Spring 1959): 79–88; and Richard Cyert and James March, *A Behavioral Theory of the Firm* (Englewood Cliffs, N.J.: Prentice, 1963).

36. For a general review of the role of heuristics in decision making, see Daniel Kahneman, Paul Slovic, and Amos Tversky, eds., *Judgment under Uncertainty: Heuristics and Biases* (Cambridge: Cambridge University Press, 1982); and Nisbett and Ross, *Human Inference*. For a speculative application of heuristics to foreign policy decision making, see Nancy Kanwisher, "Cognitive Heuristics and American Security Policy," *Journal of Conflict Resolution* 33, no.4 (December 1989): 652–75. For an impressive effort by a political scientist to apply heuristics, in the form of analogical reasoning, to international politics, see Yuen Foong Khong, *Analogies at War: Korea, Munich, Dien Bien Phu, and the Vietnam Decisions of 1965* (Princeton: Princeton University Press, 1992).

are similar to the event under consideration, or resonates with the individual's salient historical experience.

While this model of decision making is certainly not as generalizable as rational attribution processes, it constrains sufficiently the realm of possible lessons an individual can draw from an event to qualify as a general set of propositions. Assessing Soviet lessons in this way does, however, require paying attention to individual Soviet's menus of critical variables, and the model's application to other, non-Soviet, deterrent relationships would require a similar level of analysis. In sum, if the assumptions of deterrence theory are invalidated by Soviet lessons that are arrived at through cognitive economizing, then this is a significant strike against the *general* validity of the theory's assumptions. Likewise, lessons that support the theory through this process are of general importance.

*Peculiar Explanations: Belief Systems*
If Soviet lessons are caused as much by their beliefs as by the world they are observing, then these are not valid indicators for assessing deterrence theory in general. Belief systems may operate in either of two ways. They may determine which critical variables Soviet cognitive misers choose when constructing their causal models, or they may directly predetermine how Soviets analyze events. In the former case, it is critical to distinguish causal models whose set of variables has been reduced because of some general heuristic from variables whose selection is driven by the need to maintain the cognitive consistency of a belief system. In the former case, it is an example of a general cognitive model; in the latter, it is an instance of a peculiar belief system.

Once an individual establishes a system of beliefs about the international arena, that belief system remains virtually impervious to disconfirmation. While the first priority of the bounded rational decision maker is to economize on cognitive resources, the decision maker with a belief system seeks to maintain the internal psychological consistency of these beliefs. A belief system is "a configuration of ideas in which elements are bound together by some form of functional interdependence." Interdependence is the probability that a change in the status of one belief will psychologically require some compensating change(s) in the status of other beliefs. Belief systems are hierarchically organized with central, intermediate, and peripheral beliefs. A belief that is more likely to change in the face of discrepant information is less central than the beliefs that are maintained.[37] The centrality of a belief may also be defined as the degree to which other beliefs follow from it. The less

37. Philip E. Converse, "The Nature of Belief Systems in Mass Publics," in *Ideology and Discontent*, ed. David E. Apter (New York: Free Press, 1964) 207–8.

productive a belief is in terms of its role in giving rise to subordinate beliefs, the less central it is.[38] For example, one's beliefs about the nature of human-kind are more central than one's beliefs about scientists, and the latter are more central than beliefs about paleontologists. The more coherent, well-articulated, and internally consistent the belief system, the more resistant it is to change.[39]

Beliefs are inconsistent with one another to the degree that the opposite of one belief follows from the other.[40] For example, one has a friend who robs a bank. These beliefs are in conflict, as presumably the characteristics of one's friend would not predict felonious behavior. A number of conditions are generally considered necessary or at least conducive to feelings of cognitive dissonance and hence the need to deal with apparent belief inconsistencies. A decision maker must have expressed her beliefs publicly; she should have chosen one explanation of reality over competing options; and her decision should have tangible consequences for the success or failure of its implied policy outcome. Moreover, if that decision maker defends her choice against those of others or that choice has irreversible policy consequences, it is more likely that she will feel a need to protect her original beliefs from dissonant information.

The principle of least effort defines a clear hierarchy of devices that people use to maintain consistency among their beliefs. By definition, a belief system's central and intermediate elements will be more resistant to revision than peripheral ones. One protects a belief system even before one perceives a possible challenge to its consistency through the method of selective attention to the available evidence. The belief system in effect directs the search process to look only for information that bolsters existing beliefs. If, however, this does not work, the denial of the inconsistency itself is the easiest response. One simply refuses to believe that one's friend robbed the bank. The second tactic is to distort the incoming information in a way so as to render it consistent with the prior belief. One determines that the friend was coerced into robbing the bank, or that she only robbed the bank because she had to pay her mother's hospital bills.

---

38. William J. McGuire, "The Current Status of Cognitive Consistency Theories," in *Cognitive Consistency,* ed. Shel Feldman (New York: Academic Press, 1966), 15.

39. Shelley Chaiken and Suzanne Yates, "Affective-Cognitive Consistency and the Effect of Salient Behavioral Information," *JPSP* 46 (1985): 1470-81. This fits nicely with the findings of cognitive psychologists that the more theory-driven their subjects, the more resistant they are to discrepant information about their beliefs. See Craig Anderson and Eliza S. Sechler, "The Effects of Explanation and Counterexplanation on the Development and Use of Social Theories," *JPSP* 47, no. 1 (January 1986): 29.

40. Elliot Aronson, "Dissonance Theory: Progress and Problems," in *Theories of Cognitive Consistency,* ed. Robert P. Abelson et. al. (Chicago: Rand McNally, 1968), 5–6.

A third mechanism is to bolster one's beliefs about the good character traits of one's friend. She is generous, intelligent, sensitive, and so on, so this particular felonious action is only an aberration. The last choice is to actually change one's beliefs about that friend. This is so because one's beliefs about that friend are connected to one's general rules for choosing friends in the first place. One must ask how did this felon become a friend anyway, leading to a reevaluation of one's decision rules for all one's friends, which of course is quite cognitively onerous as well as psychologically and socially uncomfortable.[41]

Since belief systems are generally uniquely associated with an individual or society, Soviet lessons based on such principles are not valid evidence for a general theory of deterrence. However, this is not to say that the findings from the Soviet case are irrelevant to predicting the kinds of lessons a challenger will infer from its victories. It is possible to construct a general typology of belief systems that varies along two dimensions: its assumed universality and its assumptions about its opponents. The four ideal types are in table 4.

There are two types of ideologies, universalistic, whose adherents believe their ideas are transferrable to the rest of the world, and exclusionary, whose adherents think their beliefs are inappropriate for most of the rest of the world. Ideologies may be further defined on the basis of their assumptions about their adversary's resolve and capability. For the deterrer, the worst possible opponent to face is the one who considers its ideology universally exportable to the rest of humankind and who thinks its main opponents are weak and irresolute. This is the box (lower left) where deterrence theory assumes one's opponents reside. When faced by a challenger with a universalistic ideology, but a high regard for the defender's credibility (upper left), the deterrer need not act as aggressively to defend its reputation as would be demanded if the challenger were at the lower left. But the deterrer cannot afford to do nothing since the challenger has an unfalsifiable conviction that its ideology will ultimately triumph on a global scale.

If a state faces a country with an exclusive ideology convinced of its adversary's credibility (upper right), then no deterrent relationship exists, and so no effort is necessary in the periphery to convince any opponent of one's commitment to the status quo. Challengers with exclusionary ideologies, but with low regard for a defender's credibility (lower right), require a stronger deterrent policy than those in the upper left, but less than their universalist neighbors to the left. Just how vigorous a deterrent strategy depends critically

---

41. Robert P. Abelson, "Psychological Implications," in Abelson et. al., *Theories*, 116; Karl E. Weick, "Processes of Ramification among Cognitive Links," ibid. 516; Bernard Kaplan and Walter H. Crockett, "Developmental Analysis of Modes of Resolution," ibid., 667; Paul D. Sweeney and Kathy L. Gruber, "Selective Exposure: Voter Information Preferences and the Watergate Affair," *JPSP* 45, no. 6 (June 1984): 1208–20; and Robert A. Wicklund and Jack W. Brehm, *Perspectives on Cognitive Dissonance* (Hillsdalem, N.J.: Erlbaum, 1976), 1–10.

**TABLE 4. Deterrence Theory and Belief Systems**

| | Types of Ideologies | |
|---|---|---|
| Opponent's Credibility | Universalistic | Exclusionary |
| High | Quite easy to deter | No deterrence required |
| Low | Hardest to deter | Quite hard to deter |

on the value of the territory that the challenger threatens. The more strategic the interest in the territory, the more forceful a policy is required.

In sum, unless Soviet belief systems are in one of the two lower boxes, deterrence theory's assumptions are inaccurate. This is so because deterrence theory assumes a challenger who is unconvinced of the credibility of its opponent. So, even though particular Soviet belief systems may never be encountered again, it is still possible to draw general conclusions about different types of belief systems and the relevance of deterrence theory to them.

*Summary*
The evidence provided by Soviet lessons for and against deterrence theory should be evaluated according to how these lessons can be explained. If they provide overwhelming empirical support for a logically indeterminant assumption of the theory, or are the product of rational attribution processes, then they are of *universal* value in testing the theory. If the lessons are the product of Soviet belief systems, then they are applicable only to those challengers who hold simliar sets of beliefs. If Soviets are cognitive economizers, then their lessons are only moderately powerful indicators of the theory's general validity.

## Soviet Victories and Defeats in the Third World, 1965–90: Case Selection

Lessons learned by the Soviets from their experience in the Third World over the last twenty-five years provide a particularly fertile source for testing deterrence theory. First, there are thirty-eight cases in which to assess Soviet inferences. They vary according to level of U.S. involvement, outcome for the Soviets, geographical region, and value of the area to both powers. There are a number of crucial cases among the thirty-eight that provide easy tests for deterrence theory: if the theory fails under these favorable conditions, the presumption is that the theory is severely weakened. The Soviets themselves should be an easy case for the theory, since Western Sovietologists believed that the Soviets were driven by an expansionist ideology, or "operational code," that would be very hard to deter. There is also variance in the Soviet leadership: from Brezhnev, through Andropov and Chernenko, to Gorbachev. Moreover, many of the individuals who were mere academics and journalists during the 1960s and 1970s became major players in Gorbachev's foreign policy circle. There is also a purported variance in the level of Soviet activism in the Third World.

Many American analysts argue that there was a secular increase in Soviet adventurism in the Third World from the late 1960s until 1980, with a secular decline thereafter. These deterrence theory adherents assert that Soviet activism was a consequence of detente in general and, in particular, the U.S. loss in Vietnam. These academics and policymakers attribute the decline in Soviet activism to the effective application of the postulates of deterrence theory by the Reagan administration. By increasing the costs of Soviet adventurism in Afghanistan, Nicaragua, Angola, and Kampuchea, the United States compelled the Soviets to retrench. This book systematically assesses these arguments.

From 1965 to 1990, the Soviet Union experienced thirty-eight gains and losses in the Third World. The eighteen victories involved the ascension to power by some group committed to Soviet positions on fundamental questions of foreign and domestic policy, the maintenance of such a group in power despite attacks by anti-Soviet groups, or the removal from power of some group committed to policies consistent with U.S. policy preferences. The twenty losses involved either the removal of pro-Soviet governments, failed efforts to remove or destabilize pro-U.S. governments, the coming to power of groups committed to foreign and domestic programs desired by the United States, or the same government abandoning its pro-Soviet positions for policies favored by the United States. The level of U.S. involvement in these Soviet gains and losses varied from direct military involvement to no involvement at all. The United States was also indirectly involved in many cases, providing military, economic, or political support to its allies who were pursuing policies preferred by the U.S. government. Table 5 lists the universe of cases and the various levels of U.S. involvement.

A comprehensive test of the assumptions of deterrence theory requires assessing Soviet lessons from each of these thirty-eight cases. This book, however, concentrates only on a representative sample of cases, not only because presenting evidence on each of the thirty-eight cases would require a book two to three times its present length, but also because having already performed such a comprehensive test, I need not provide the reader with redundant findings.[42] Moreover, the selected cases illuminate the one primary

---

42. For the reader who is interested in an analysis of each case, please see Theodore G. Hopf, "Deterrence Theory and Soviet Foreign Policy: Soviet Lessons from Their Victories and Defeats in the Third World," Ph.D. diss., Columbia University, 1990.

**TABLE 5.　Soviet Losses and Gains in the Third World, 1965–90**

| Direct | | Indirect | | None | |
|---|---|---|---|---|---|
| | | Nature of U.S. Involvement | | | |

| Direct | | Indirect | | None | |
|---|---|---|---|---|---|
| **Losses** | | | | | |
| | | Middle East | 1967 | | |
| | | Jordan | 1970 | | |
| | | Chile | 1973 | | |
| | | Middle East | 1973 | Indonesia | 1965 |
| | | Egypt | 1976 | Ghana | 1966 |
| Dominican Republic | 1965 | Zaire | 1977 | Mali | 1968 |
| Grenada | 1983 | Somalia | 1978 | Sudan | 1971 |
| | | Zaire | 1978 | Bolivia | 1971 |
| | | Zimbabwe | 1980 | Peru | 1975 |
| | | El Salvador | 1981–88 | | |
| | | Mozambique | 1984 | | |
| | | Nicaragua | 1990 | | |
| **Gains** | | | | | |
| | | | | Peru | 1968 |
| | | | | Sudan | 1969 |
| | | | | Somalia | 1969 |
| | | Angola | 1975–90 | Libya | 1969 |
| Vietnam | 1973–75 | Ethiopia | 1977–78 | Bolivia | 1969 |
| | | Afghanistan | 1979–90 | Chile | 1970 |
| | | Nicaragua | 1981–90 | Afghanistan | 1973 |
| | | | | Ethiopia | 1974 |
| | | | | Mozambique | 1975 |
| | | | | Afghanistan | 1978 |
| | | | | Iran | 1979 |
| | | | | Grenada | 1979 |
| | | | | Nicaragua | 1979–81 |

independent variable being tested: level of U.S. involvement. Representative cases from each of the six possible categories allow for clear tests on the competing hypotheses. In addition, some cases had so little salience for Soviet observers that their prolonged assessment here would be pointless. Of course, the relative salience of these thirty-eight cases has important theoretical significance, and appendix A discusses this at some length. Finally, these particular cases offer an opportunity to execute tests in *crucial cases*, that is, cases where deterrence theory propositions should have an easy time demonstrating their validity, while the alternative hypotheses should have a hard time. As a consequence, if my hypotheses prove correct, my alternatives have passed a hard test, while deterrence theory assumptions have failed an easy test.[43]

The string of Soviet gains from 1975 to 1979 (Vietnam 1975, Angola 1975–76, Ethiopia 1977–78, Nicaragua 1979, Iran 1979, and Afghanistan 1979) offers a valuable set of crucial cases for deterrence theory because if Soviet views are not of reduced U.S. credibility, bandwagoning allies, and falling dominoes, as predicted under these easy conditions for the theory, then deterrence theory cannot logically be expected to obtain under more difficult circumstances. The overthrow of the shah in Iran in 1979 is a crucial case for one particular proposition of deterrence theory. If Soviets did not infer from that U.S. loss in a strategic area of the globe that the United States had lost its credibility to protect its interests in other strategic parts of the world, then U.S. losses in peripheral areas of the globe could hardly generate Soviet lessons of reduced credibility in strategic areas.

The cases discussed herein are as follows: chapter 2, the U.S. withdrawal from Vietnam and the fall of Saigon; chapter 3, Soviet gains in Angola from 1975 to 1990, in Ethiopia in 1977–78, and in Afghanistan from 1975 to 1990, where U.S. involvement was indirect; chapter 4, the overthrow of Somoza in Nicaragua and the shah in Iran in 1979, Soviet gains with no U.S. involvement; chapter 5, the Soviet loss suffered through the direct U.S. military intervention in Grenada in 1983; chapter 6, Soviet losses in the Middle East from 1973 to 1980; and chapter 7, the Soviet loss in Ghana in 1966 without U.S. involvement.

## Soviet Lessons from 1965 to 1990: Selection of Soviet Observers

To fairly test the theory, I have selected a group of Soviets who reasonably represent Soviet perceptions of international developments over these twenty-five years. Because deterrence theory focuses on decision makers as the critical group, I have included all politburo members with foreign policy responsiblities, all defense ministers, and several individuals who can be considered members of the Soviet foreign policy elite, among them high-ranking officials at the Central Committee's International Department, as well as academics and journalists who had close relationships with Soviet decision makers.

Including academic experts on American foreign policy or particular regions in the Third World reflects these scholars' important role in policy

---

43. On the value of crucial cases for theory disconfirmation, see Harry Eckstein, "Case Study and Theory in Political Science," in *Handbook of Political Science*, ed. Fred Greenstein and Nelson Polsby (Reading, Mass.: Addison-Wesley, 1975), 7:113–20.

formation. Many of these individuals provided advice to Soviet policymakers on foreign affairs. Often, the content of the speeches by Soviet party leaders is more fully elaborated on in the scholarly literature. And in some cases, Soviet academics discuss events about which the leadership has remained silent. Table 6 lists the Soviet observers whose perceptions are used as evidence for testing the alternative theories.

**TABLE 6. Soviet Observers**

| Foreign Policymakers | | |
| --- | --- | --- |
| Party Leadership | Military Elite | Foreign Policy Elite |
| Iurii Andropov | Sergei Gorshkov | Georgii Arbatov |
| Leonid Brezhnev | Andrei Grechko | Karen Brutents |
| Konstantin Chernenko | Nikolai Ogarkov | Boris Ponomarev |
| Mikhail Gorbachev | Sergei Sokolov | Evgenii Primakov |
| Andrei Gromyko | Dmitrii Ustinov | Rostislav Ulyanovsky |
| Alexei Kosygin | Dmitrii Yazov | Valentin Falin |
| Nikolai Podgorny | | |
| Edvard Shevardnadze | | |
| Mikhail Suslov | | |
| Aleksandr Yakovlev | | |

| Academics | |
| --- | --- |
| Third World Economists | Third World Historians |
| Elena Bragina | Georgi Kim |
| Viktor Sheinis | Georgi Mirsky |
| Glerii Shirokov | Nodari Simoniya |
| Latin Americanists | Middle East Specialists |
| Anatolii Glinkin | Igor Belyaev |
| Iurii Korolev | Robert Landa |
| Sergo Mikoyan | |
| Anatolii Shulgovsky | |
| Petr Yakovlev | |
| Irina Zorina | |
| Americanists | Africanists |
| Aleksandr Kislov | Arkadii Butlitsky |
| Andrei Kokoshin | Valentin Gorodnov |
| Viktor Kremeniuk | Vladimir Iordansky |
| Genrikh Trofimenko | Anatolii Khazanov |

Obviously, my choice of scholars is not the universe of available Soviet academics. I selected them on the basis of specialty and quantity of publications. In order to get a sample of Soviet lessons after the thirty-eight cases, we must have Soviets who specialize in particular regions of the Third World, and who study American foreign policy. Once I established the required areas of specialization, I chose those scholars who wrote the most on the cases being investigated.[44] By using this simple rule, I not only generated the maximum number of lessons to be evaluated, but also avoided any particular "liberal" or "conservative" bias in Soviet scholarship. I do not analyze the lessons of each of the forty-five Soviet observers in the chapters that follow. Like the method of selection I use for focusing on certain cases, I spare the reader by focusing only on a representative sample of Soviet perceptions.[45] However, when calculating a case's salience, or concluding what the general lessons were from any given case, I draw on the evidence produced by all forty-five Soviet observers.

## The Reliability and Validity of Using Soviet Sources to Test Deterrence Theory

Establishing confidence in the reliability of these findings is a far easier task than convincing readers of their validity. Their reliability rests on whether any other researcher, using the same body of evidence, will arrive at the same conclusions about the assumptions of deterrence theory. In fact, the reader of this book can assess for him- or herself the reliability of my conclusions. First, there is the clarity of the hypotheses themselves. I have listed the explicit kinds of lessons Soviets should have learned if deterrence theory assumptions are correct and the sorts of inferences that Soviets should have drawn if my alternatives are accurate. In the discussion of these cases, numerous examples of evidence for and against the theories are given to allow the reader to determine whether this evidence really points in the direction claimed.[46]

Second, there is the character of the sources. If the reader is convinced of both the representativeness and randomness of the forty-five sources of perceptions that constitute this sample, then there should not be a problem with

44. This operation was performed by looking through the tables of contents of Soviet journals specializing on Latin America, Asia, Africa, the United States, and international affairs in general and simply counting the number of articles published since 1965 by the universe of Soviet authors. Those who wrote the most are in table 6.

45. Again, for the reader who would like to read a comprehensive account of each Soviet observer, please see Hopf, "Deterrence Theory."

46. Given the space constraints of this book, I have omitted far more evidence than I have included. For those interested in a more comprehensive display of the raw data that underlie my arguments, please see Hopf, "Deterrence Theory." See appendix B for a representative list of evidence for each hypothesis tested in this book.

reliability. A reader who selects his or her own sample of Soviet observers, as long as it is both representative and not skewed, should be able to replicate my results.

Establishing the validity—as opposed to the reliability—of my findings, however, is a more demanding task. The question boils down to whether public Soviet statements and articles are a measure of genuinely held Soviet beliefs, and if so, whether we should accept this as evidence against which to test deterrence theory.

Admittedly, the method used in this book is a second-best approach. The best method would be one that combined archival research in Moscow with interviews of the foreign policy principals. Unfortunately, this best method is not feasible for the period of Soviet foreign policy under review here. The Russian government has adopted a thirty-year rule that precludes access to any of the documents one would need to establish the validity of public Soviet speeches and articles. Only the most scattered documentary record is now being made available on an ad hoc basis by Russian archivists and librarians.[47] While it would be possible to interview a fair number of the authors and policymakers cited in this book, such a method has as many questions about its validity as relying on open written and oral sources. Historians and political and other social scientists agree that interviewees often recall events in ways designed to advance particular interests, other than a faithful reproduction of their past intentions. Often, people cannot even remember their motives, let alone reconstruct their prior beliefs at various points in time. Indeed, most of us are hard-pressed to reconstruct our motives even for current behavior.[48]

---

47. Patricia Kennedy Grimsted, the foremost American authority on post-Soviet archives, has spoken and written about both the promise and problems of access to Russian documents. The more contemporary the documents, the greater the obstacles, both in terms of higher monetary outlays for "admission" to the archives, and in terms of cultivating the appropriate contacts. See, for example, Grimsted, *A Handbook for Archival Research in the USSR* (Washington: Kennan Institute for Advanced Russian Studies, 1989) and Robert H. Davis, Review of Grimsted, "Archives and Manuscript Repositories in the USSR, Ukraine and Moldavia," *Slavic and East European Journal* 34 (Winter 1990): 520–22. Grimsted also delivered a lecture on this topic in April 1992 at the University of Michigan's Center for Russian and East European Studies in Ann Arbor.

48. See, for example, Shelley E. Taylor and Susan T. Fiske, "Salience Attention and Attribution: Top of the Head Phenomena," in *Advances in Experimental Social Psychology*, ed. Leonard Berkowitz, vol. 11, (New York: Academic Press, 1978); Richard Nisbett and T. D. Wilson, "Telling More Than We Can Know: Verbal Reports on Mental Processes," *Psychological Review* 84 (1977): 231–59; G. R. Goethals and R. F. Reckman, "The Perception of Consistency in Attitudes," *Journal of Experimental Social Psychology* 9 (1973): 491–501; Michael Ross and Michael Conway, "Remembering One's Own Past: The Construction of Personal Histories," in *Handbook of Motivation and Cognition*, ed. R. M. Sorrentino and E. Tory Higgins, (New York: Guilford, 1986), 122–44; and Robert W. Pearson, Michael Ross, and Robyn M. Dawes, "Per-

Since this book relies on a second-best method, it is only fair to acknowledge that its findings can only be tentative until tested by future researchers against the archival record that seems likely to become available in Moscow in coming years. In the meantime, we can be encouraged by the fact that the very best books and articles that have tested deterrence theory over the last twenty years also relied on second-best methods.[49] Let me now turn to a defense of the second-best method itself.

Perhaps the most frequently raised objection to using public Soviet sources is that all of them are simply propaganda. For propaganda to be effective, however, it must adhere to some general line on a particular issue. If it does not, it risks confusing its audience, both domestic and foreign. Its recipients will not be certain as to which position they should adopt on this topic. So, if I find that different Soviets advance different arguments before the same or similar audiences, this is prima facie evidence against their arguments being merely propaganda. The case against propaganda becomes even stronger if it is possible to establish an institutional interest that is consonant with the person's argument. In this case, it is most probable that the argument is not being advanced for propagandistic reasonings, but rather in order to defend the interests of the institution with which this individual is affiliated.

Another instance of a prima facie presumption against a propaganda explanation is when a Soviet advances an argument that fundamentally contradicts the interests of the audience before which the argument is being presented. Similarly, Soviet arguments that contradict current Soviet foreign policy positions are also very unlikely to be instances of a propaganda strategy. Contrariwise, if I find that the same argument is being advanced by all Soviets before all kinds of audiences, then it is strong evidence for a propaganda explanation.

We can also determine the veridicality of Soviet beliefs by looking at the temporal relationship between the presentation of some argument on an issue and Soviet foreign policy action on that issue. If there is a change in some Soviet policy, and subsequently a Soviet advances an argument that justifies that policy, we must assume that this is simply a rationalization for that policy. If, however, we can establish that a Soviet's arguments preceded this policy

sonal Recall and the Limits of Retrospective Questions in Surveys," in *Questions About Questions: Inquiries into the Cognitive Bases of Surveys*, ed. Judith M. Tanur (New York: Russell Sage Foundation, 1992).

49. For example: George and Smoke, *Deterrence*; Huth and Russett, "What Makes Deterrence Work?"; Janice Gross Stein, "Calculation, Miscalculation, and Conventional Deterrence I," and "Calculation, Miscalculation, and Conventional Deterrence II," in Jervis, Lebow, and Stein, *Psychology and Deterrence*; and Walt, *Origins of Alliances*.

change, then we should assume that his or her arguments are genuine and may have in fact influenced the adoption of the new policy.

A less satisfactory way to establish the validity, but not the veridicality, of Soviet beliefs, is to correlate public Soviet statements with Soviet foreign policy behavior. In this procedure, we make absolutely no claims that Soviet arguments reflect genuinely held beliefs, but only that we can predict future Soviet behavior on the basis of the high correlation between an argument that is formulated in a particular way and the consistent association of that argument with a particular Soviet behavior.[50] So, in the crudest terms, if deterrence assumptions are accurate, we should expect aggressive Soviet behavior after they learn a given set of lessons following a Soviet victory, and Soviet retrenchment based on another set of lessons following a Soviet defeat. This kind of test should be generally true except in the event that there are some exogenous explanations for deviant Soviet behavior.

My use of psychological models to explain Soviet learning provides yet another validity check. If the evolution of a particular Soviet's beliefs follows a course predicted by a psychological model (whether of rational attribution, bounded rationality, or belief system), then this is good evidence that this individual genuinely holds these views. It is very improbable that a person could deliberately manipulate his or her arguments in such a way as to maintain consistency with a psychological explanation for these views. This validity check gains added power with each additional Soviet observer I am able to model in this manner.

Yet another important way to establish the validity of using Soviet beliefs to test deterrence theory is to continually deal with competing explanations for how Soviets appear to be learning from their victories and defeats. In the case-study chapters that follow, I make a sustained effort to consider the most obvious alternative explanations for the findings I present. These alternative explanations most commonly include propaganda, domestic politics, the context of the audience, institutional interests, and Soviet foreign policy considerations.

Finally, independent of Soviet lessons entirely, one can compare Soviet behavior to the kind of behavior predicted by deterrence theory. After Soviet victories, the theory's assumptions would predict additional Soviet efforts at

---

50. Alexander George describes how, during World War II, U.S. intelligence became very adept at predicting future German military actions and responses to various Allied military strategies by simply correlating various kinds of Nazi propaganda with subsequent German behavior. This was done without ever presuming to know the true beliefs of Nazi decision makers. See his *Propaganda Analysis: A Study of Inferences Made from Nazi Propaganda in World War II* (Westport, Conn.: Greenwood, 1959). I thank Deborah Larson for bringing this much underutilized study to my attention.

making gains at American expense; after Soviet defeats, deterrence theory would predict Soviet quiescence. I perform such a test in each case-study chapter.

## A Reader's Guide

In this section I provide the reader with a map to the rest of this volume, summarizing my findings in the process. Chapters 2–7 contain the set of case studies. I conclude in chapter 8 with a version of deterrence theory that is modified in accordance with the findings of these case studies.

I analyze Soviet lessons from their victory in Vietnam in chapter 2. This is the easiest case for deterrence theory in the book, since the United States exerted the most effort here and still lost. Even so, its assumptions only gain partial verification. For example, Soviets inferred contradictory lessons about U.S. credibility: Washington is resolved to resist future revolutionary change in the Third World, but its attempts will be ultimately futile. Contrary to the most extreme deterrence assumptions, there were no Soviet inferences about reduced U.S. credibility in areas of strategic interest to the United States. Deterrence theory received its strongest validation in the area of regional dynamics, but even here that validation was not clear-cut. Soviet observers did see dominoes fall, but they were limited geographically to Kampuchea and Laos. They did not even mention Thailand as a prospective target, let alone places farther afield. However, the success of these Indochinese national liberation movements were seen as inspirations to other such movements elsewhere in the world. Soviets saw the outcomes of these struggles as dependent on their particular context.

The cases in chapter 3—Angola, Ethiopia, and Afghanistan—constitute a crucial case for deterrence theory in that they are a string of Soviet victories that follow on the heels of the biggest postwar U.S. defeat—Vietnam. The theory does not pass this test. Soviet perceptions of American credibility after these victories are not consistent with the predictions of deterrence theory. Soviets saw the United States as both capable and resolute. Deterrence theory assumptions are disconfirmed also in the area of regional dynamics. Soviets saw regional actors balancing against the gains in the three countries, rather than accommodating themselves to these events.

Chapter 4 includes the ouster of Somoza in Nicaragua in 1979 and the overthrow of the shah in Iran the same year. The latter case yields two crucial cases for deterrence theory. On the one hand, it is like the cases of chapter 4, occurring during a string of U.S. defeats. On the other hand, Soviet lessons derived from a U.S. loss in a strategic area of the globe—the Persian Gulf. Deterrence theory does not pass these crucial tests. Soviets continued to see a highly credible United States and inferred no lessons about reduced U.S.

credibility in strategic areas of the world. Soviet observers paid virtually no attention to the American loss but instead concentrated their attention on what measures the United States took to compensate for these losses.

Deterrence theory received partial confirmation in the area of regional dynamics. The evidence depends on the case. Soviet observers were encouraged about regional revolutionary prospects after the Sandinista victory in Nicaragua but were not encouraged by the overthrow of the shah in Iran, as they saw that local states were inclined to balance against the Khomeini revolution and that American military assets were being deployed to the region.

In chapter 5, I discuss Soviet lessons from their loss in Grenada in 1983, effected by a direct U.S. military intervention. Consistent with deterrence theory, Soviets did see a credible America as a consequence of U.S. actions. However, this finding implies only that such direct military actions are sufficient, but not necessary. Moreover, deterrence theory was disconfirmed in the realm of regional dynamics, since Soviet observers saw regional actors rise up in opposition to the American intervention, rather than rally in support of U.S. actions.

Chapter 6 deals with a set of Soviet losses about which deterrence theory is silent, those in which there was no U.S. military effort. This lack of coverage seriously weakens the general validity of the theory, especially since Soviet lessons about American resolve and capability were as powerful from the Middle East cases as they were from American military intervention in Grenada. This shows that direct American military involvement in a Soviet loss is not necessary to demonstrate American credibility to Soviet observers. Moreover, Soviet lessons about the regional dynamics set off by the Middle East losses were far more pessimistic than the lessons inferred from the loss in Grenada. Direct American military involvement is an obstacle to teaching some kinds of deterrent lessons, rather than a necessary condition.

Chapter 7 contains a case, the overthrow of Kwame Nkrumah in Ghana in 1966, that is representative of another class of events unremarked by deterrence theory. These are cases of Soviet losses with no U.S. involvement at all. Despite the fact that the United States had nothing whatever to do with the removal of Nkrumah, Soviet observers still attributed responsibility to Washington. In this way, the United States received a credibility bonus. Deterrence theory's focus on the need for *American* actions to impart the right kinds of lessons to Soviet observers ignores the possibility that perhaps the external environment, independent of American behavior, can impart deterrent lessons to the Soviet audience. In fact, Soviet lessons from Ghana demonstrate that this is precisely the case. Because the United States was *not* involved in this Soviet defeat, Soviet observers were forced to search for explanations for the loss within Ghana itself. And what they discovered increased their pessimism about the prospects for revolutionary changes elsewhere in the periphery.

In the concluding chapter, I summarize the results of this study with an eye toward developing a *revised* theory of deterrence that avoids the traditional theory's logical indeterminism, lack of empirical fit, and failure to consider the possibility that challengers to the status quo may not process information according to the assumptions of the theory. I highlight the word *revised*, however, because I want to stress that this book does not invalidate deterrence theory wholesale, but only argues for the fundamental alteration of three of its most central assumptions. The conceptual framework animating the theory remains intact.

# Soviet Gains

CHAPTER 2

## Soviet Lessons from the Vietnam War: A Crucial Case for Deterrence Theory . . . Which It Does Not Pass

If South Vietnam went, [the way would be open for] a guerilla assault on Malaya, [and it would] give the impression that the wave of the future in Southeast Asia was China and the Communists.

—President John F. Kennedy

If you let a bully come into your front yard one day, the next day he'll be up on your porch, and the day after that he'll rape your wife in your own bed.

—President Lyndon B. Johnson

If we leave Vietnam with our tail between our legs, the consequences of this defeat in the rest of Asia, Africa, and Latin America would be disastrous.

—General Maxwell Taylor

The American people, our allies and our enemies alike, are increasingly uncertain as to our resolution to pursue the war to a successful conclusion.

—The Joint Chiefs of Staff

The U.S. withdrawal from South Vietnam in 1973 and the subsequent military victory of the North Vietnamese in 1975 are crucial cases for deterrence theory because U.S. policymakers explicitly based their rationale for intervening in Vietnam in 1965 on the propositions of deterrence theory being tested in this book. Moreover, the United States expended $150 billion, lost over fifty thousand lives, and incurred serious domestic economic, political, and social costs and yet still lost the war. Such enormous effort, when combined with such a total defeat, is a textbook example of a most easy test for the assumptions of deterrence theory.

---

The epigraph from President Kennedy is taken from a television interview with NBC anchors Chet Huntley and David Brinkley, as quoted in George Kahin, *Intervention: How America Became Involved in Vietnam* (New York: Anchor, 1987), 166. Each of the other three quotes are from Stanley Karnow, *Vietnam: A History* (New York: Penguin, 1984), 321, 399, and 501.

If deterrence theory and its advocates were accurate, Soviets should have learned three sets of lessons from their victory in Southeast Asia. At the very least, the Soviets should have concluded that the United States was both incapable and unwilling to intervene in the future to stop revolutionary change in the Third World. At the most, they should have inferred that the United States had lost its credibility to defend its vital interests in strategic areas of the world—Western Europe, Northeast Asia, and the Persian Gulf. Second, the Soviets should have learned from the U.S. defeat that American allies around the globe were uncertain about whether the United States could be trusted to honor its commitment to these countries' security. Finally, at a minimum, Soviet observers should have believed that the rest of Southeast Asia was going to follow the path of South Vietnam. At the most, they would think that dominoes would fall beyond the region itself, in the rest of Asia, through the Indian subcontinent, to the Middle East, Africa, and beyond.

Deterrence theory does not pass its crucial test here. While Soviet lessons from Vietnam are more supportive of the theory than those from any of the other thirty-seven cases, they still provide only ambiguous confirmation. In a case as easy for deterrence theory as the U.S. defeat in Vietnam, we should expect unequivocal results. Instead, the evidence disconfirms the theory's assumptions about allied behavior and provides only qualified confirmation for deterrence propositions on U.S. credibility and regional dynamics.[1]

While no Soviet doubted a continued U.S. commitment to defend strategic American interests, most were also convinced that the U.S. ability to prevent future revolutionary change in the Third World had been weakened; no doubt, Washington would continue to make such efforts, even if they were ultimately futile. Finally, Soviet visions of falling dominoes were limited to Kampuchea and Laos. They did not even mention Thailand as a prospective target, let alone places farther afield. However, they did argue that the success of the Vietcong, Khmer Rouges, and Pathet Lao had inspired revolutionary movements elsewhere in the Third World.

Furthermore, if deterrence propositions were accurate, the Soviet lessons that confirmed the theory would be based on either rational explanations or general psychological models. Perceptions that disconfirmed deterrence theory assumptions would be the product of peculiar Soviet belief systems. After all, a theory that assumes rationality cannot receive general validation from lessons generated by *non-rational* processes. Likewise, Soviet lessons that disconfirm the theory should be exclusively irrational. In fact, the picture is mixed. Soviet perceptions of a highly credible America are generated rationally. But, Soviet lessons of falling dominoes are the product of both general psychological models and peculiar Soviet belief systems, though not the

---

1. See appendix A for evidence on Soviet lessons about American allies.

category of belief system assumed by deterrence theory. Instead, the predominant Soviet ideology, while universalistic, axiomatically assumed a highly credible United States.

Below I describe the range of lessons Soviets learned about U.S. credibility and regional dynamics from their victory in Vietnam. I explain why they inferred the lessons they did and how the nature of the explanations relate to the general (in)validity of deterrence theory, and I consider alternative explanations for these perceptions.

## Soviet Lessons about U.S. Credibility

Soviet views of U.S. credibility after the Vietnam War were on a continuum ranging from disconfirmation of deterrence theory to merely ambiguous support for the theory's propositions. Disconfirmatory and validating evidence are also arranged on a continuum. In table 7 I show the relationship between Soviet lessons from Vietnam and the relative evidentiary power of these lessons. The numbers in parentheses refer to the number of times that a particular kind of lesson appeared in Soviet speeches and articles from 1973 to 1976.

**TABLE 7. Soviet Inferences and Deterrence Theory's Assumptions about Credibility**

| Soviet Lessons (*N*) | |
| --- | --- |
| Confirming | Disconfirming |
| The United States will not defend its strategic interests (0). | The United States will attack the Soviet Union (4). |
| The United States will not defend its peripheral interests (6). | The United States will attack members of the socialist alliance (0). |
| The United States will negotiate on Third World conflicts (4). | The United States will resist detente and arms control (1). |
| The United States will continue detente and arms control (8). | The United States will not negotiate on third world conflicts (0). |
| The United States will not attack members of the socialist alliance (2). | The United States will defend its peripheral interests (6). |
| The United States will not attack the Soviet Union (2). | The United States will defend its strategic interests (0). |

*Note*: Lessons are listed in order of decreasing strength as evidence.

If the assumptions of deterrence theory are accurate, Soviet lessons from Vietnam should be concentrated in the upper left-hand corner of table 7. In descending order of validation for the theory, the Soviets should have learned from Vietnam that the United States would (1) not defend its interests in Europe, Northeast Asia, and the Persian Gulf; (2) not protect other third world allies; (3) negotiate on other third world conflicts; (4) continue strategic detente with the Soviet Union; (5) not attack socialist Soviet allies; and (6) not attack the Soviet Union itself.

In descending order of disconfirmation of the theory, the Soviets should have inferred from Vietnam that the United States would (1) attack the Soviet Union; (2) attack its socialist allies; (3) resist strategic detente; (4) defend its interests in the Third World; (5) not negotiate on Third World conflicts; and (6) defend its strategic interests.

Soviet lessons from Vietnam can be interpreted as either very weak support for or equally weak disconfirmation of deterrence theory's assumptions about U.S. credibility. On the whole, members of the Soviet party, military, and foreign policy leadership and Americanist community learned neither fundamentally confirming nor disconfirming lessons about U.S. credibility after Vietnam. While the United States would not abandon its strategic or peripheral interests, it also would not attack the Soviet Union or its socialist allies. While the evidence clearly cannot sustain the argument that the United States *gained* credibility by losing in Vietnam, it also is not consistent with the position that the United States *lost* much credibility. Given the latter, it is clear that deterrence theory has not performed well in this crucial test. If the theory is not strongly confirmed by Soviet lessons from the U.S. debacle in Vietnam, then it is very unlikely it could be validated in any other case in the Third World. The conditions of enormous U.S. effort, coupled with utter defeat, create the easiest possible conditions for deterrence theory's predictions to be unambiguously confirmed. Instead, these received only the weakest support.

The strongest evidence for deterrence theory—Soviet inferences that the United States is unlikely to intervene in the Third World in the future—is also ambiguous. Such lessons were short-lived. They were soon replaced by contrary predictions. Georgii Arbatov, for example, argued soon after the Paris accords that the United States was unlikely to engage in third world adventurism any time soon, since U.S. business interests thought it too expensive and the majority of the American people preferred more spending on the domestic social agenda.[2] But not nine months later, he raised doubts about his own recent conclusions, writing that it was not at all certain that the U.S. govern-

---

2. See, for example, Arbatov, "O Sovetsko-Amerikanskikh Otnosheniyakh" (On Soviet-American Relations), *Kommunist*, 1973, no. 3, 101–13.

ment had internalized the true "lessons of Vietnam."[3] Not only were views of an irresolute America ephemeral, but they moved in a direction precisely opposite to the one that deterrence theory would predict. If deterrence theory were accurate, Soviets should have been *increasingly* convinced of low U.S. credibility from the signing of the Paris accords in January 1973 to the aftermath of the fall of Saigon in April 1975. Instead, Soviets were initially optimistic about U.S. credibility immediately after the peace agreement but then became *less* confident about the pacific nature of American foreign policy in the Third World in subsequent months and years.

The most frequent Soviet lesson from the U.S. defeat in Vietnam was that the United States was committed to pursuing detente with the Soviet Union. This lesson was hardly a product of Vietnam alone, what with strategic arms control talks (SALT I), meetings on settling the question of Berlin, and a European detente in general all being discussed at the time. But Soviets interpreted the U.S. decision to seek a negotiated settlement in Southeast Asia as additional evidence that Washington would move forward on strategic nuclear arms control, security-enhancing measures in Europe, and bilateral economic ties.[4] Americanists, such as Arbatov and Trofimenko, had bifurcated views of U.S. credibility. On the one hand, they agreed that Washington was committed to strategic detente; on the other hand, they ultimately concluded that the United States would continue to compete in the Third World.[5]

The weakest piece of confirming evidence is Soviet expressions of confidence that the United States no longer had aggressive designs on the Soviet Union itself.[6] But, as is evident from table 7, some Soviets did not even feel confident that the United States had learned that minimal lesson from Vietnam. However, these beliefs were expressed only by members of the Soviet military leadership.[7] It is quite likely that such threat assessments were ad-

---

3. Arbatov, "Vneshnyaya Politika SShA v Nauchno-Tekhnicheskaya Revoliutsiya" (U.S. Foreign Policy in the Scientific-Technological Revolution), part I, *SShA*, October 1973, 3–11. A similar evolution of views is apparent in the writings of Genrikh Trofimneko.

4. For representative examples of this line of reasoning, see Foreign Minister Gromyko's speeches at a conference on Vietnam held in Paris, *Pravda*, February 28, 1973, 4; a meeting of the Conference on Security and Cooperation in Europe in Helsinki, *Pravda*, July 4, 1973, 5; and the opening of the Geneva conference on the Middle East, *Pravda*, December 23, 1973, 4. At the latter event, Gromyko suggested that the Paris accords on Vietnam boded well for U.S. willingness to reach a negotiated settlement between Israel and Arab countries. On the connection between Vietnam and the Middle East, see sources in note 25.

5. For this combination of views, see Arbatov, "Vneshnyaya Politika"; and Trofimenko, "Uroki Vietnama" (Lessons of Vietnam), *SShA*, June 1975, 76–80.

6. General Secretary Brezhnev advanced this argument at a Central Committee plenum, *Pravda*, October 26, 1976, 2–3.

7. For representative examples, see Navy Minister Gorshkov, "Okeanskii Shchit Rodiny" (Ocean Shield of the Motherland), *KVS*, 1975, no. 14, 9–16; then–army general and first deputy defense minister Sergei Sokolov, "Vo Imya Mira na Zemle" (In the Name of Peace on Earth), *SR*,

vanced in order to argue for budgetary considerations and to heighten morale within the armed services. This interpretation is further supported by the fact that each member of the military elite makes this argument, and no one other than a member of the armed forces expresses similar concerns about U.S. intentions.

In summary, Soviet lessons about U.S. credibility after the Vietnam War were not what deterrence theory predicts in a crucially easy case. Soviets did not infer the strongest confirmatory lessons, and the most powerful validating inferences they did make were both evanescent and replaced by disconfirming lessons on the same issue.

## Soviet Lessons about Regional Dynamics

If the assumptions of deterrence theory are correct, Soviets should have learned from their victory in Vietnam that dominoes would fall in a pro-Soviet direction elsewhere in the world. If my alternative propositions are accurate, Soviets instead should have inferred from the U.S. loss in Vietnam that other potential targets of subversion or insurgency would redouble their efforts to avert the fate of the Thieu government in Saigon. The perceptual evidence that counts for and against the alternatives is in table 8.

As in the case of credibility, different Soviet lessons provide more and less powerful empirical support for the two contending theories. Deterrence theory would be most robustly validated if Soviets learned from Vietnam that the governments of France, Japan, or Iran were now vulnerable to overthrow. It would be least validated if they saw Laos, Kampuchea, and Thailand (in that order) as dominoes on the brink of revolution. The theory would receive significant support if Soviets expected increased prospects for the success of revolutionary movements elsewhere in the Third World. In turn, deterrence theory would receive powerful disconfirmation if Soviets did not foresee falling dominoes even in the region of Southeast Asia. The validity of the theory would only be trivially affected by Soviet perceptions of Japanese balancing. However, the theory's assumptions would be markedly undermined if Soviets expected balancing behavior by other third world governments.

The assumptions of deterrence theory receive more support from Soviet lessons about regional dynamics after Vietnam than from any other event covered in this book. Members of the party, military, and foreign policy elite, and of the Americanist community did not infer a single positively disconfirming lesson from Vietnam about the prospects for revolutionary gains else-

---

May 9, 1974, 2; and then-defense minister Andrei Grechko's speech at a conference of party workers in the armed forces, reprinted in *KVS*, 1973, no. 8, 13–20.

**TABLE 8.  Soviet Inferences and Deterrence Theory's Assumptions about Regional Dynamics**

| Soviet Lessons (*N*) | |
| --- | --- |
| Confirming | Disconfirming |
| Dominoes will fall in areas of strategic interest to the United States. | Countries contiguous to Vietnam will effectively resist any further revolutionary change in the region. |
| Dominoes will fall in other peripheral areas of the globe (12). | Other third world countries around the globe will balance effectively against any regional revolutionary threats. |
| Dominoes will fall in countries contiguous to Vietnam (2). | U.S. strategic allies will balance effectively against any threats of revolution in their area. |

*Note*: Lessons are listed in order of decreasing strength as evidence.

where in the world. Instead, many Soviets concluded from the victory in Vietnam that national liberation movements around the world could be far more confident that "no kind of force is able to smash people fighting for freedom and independence."[8]

However, before declaring this proposition of the theory validated (even if only in this case), a few qualifications are in order. First, no Soviet ever inferred from Vietnam that dominoes would fall in strategic areas of the world.[9] Hence, deterrence theory is not strongly validated in this crucially easy case. Second, while Soviets were in agreement that revolutionary movements around the globe would be greatly encouraged by the gains in Southeast Asia, they simultaneously expected continued U.S. resistance to these challenges in the Third World. So, Soviets learned from Vietnam that future victories in the periphery would occur, but not with ease.

Finally, we should consider the cases where "dogs did not bark," that is, where context demanded a Soviet to declare his enhanced confidence in revolutionary gains, but he failed to do so. It is a truism that the more often Soviets make arguments that validate deterrence theory, the greater the valida-

8. Gromyko's speech at a conference on Vietnam in Paris, *Pravda*, February 28, 1973, 4. For further examples of this common refrain, see Brezhnev's speech on the fortieth anniversary of the surrender of Germany in World War II, *Pravda*, May 9, 1975, 2; then–prime minister Kosygin's speech in Libya, *Pravda*, May 14, 1975, 4; Podgorny in Kabul, *Pravda*, December 10, 1975, 4; and, Rostislav Ulyanovsky, "Razryadka Mezhdunarodnoi Napryazhennosti i Razvivaiushchiesya Strany" (Detente and Developing Countries), *Pravda*, August 30, 1973, 4–5.

9. In this instance, I am speaking not only of the elites and Americanists being analyzed in this chapter, but of the inferences drawn by *all* forty-five Soviets included in my dissertation.

tion for the theory. However, we should not hold the theory to an unreasonable standard of frequency; we should not judge the theory as weakened if Soviets do not make validating inferences before *all* audiences. There are three kinds of audiences, each of which should generate different expectations for the theory. The first, or demanding, audience, is a group of people whose character implies the need for a Soviet speaker to tell them that future revolutionary gains are more certain given the victory in Vietnam. These audiences would include Vietnamese and other Indochinese officials, members of other national liberation movements in the Third World, other third world allies, and to a lesser extent, domestic party members, military officers, and ideological workers.

If Soviets make arguments consistent with deterrence theory in these cases, they should not be taken as strong evidence for the theory's assumptions. If, however, in front of these *demanding* audiences, Soviets do *not* assert that revolutionary prospects have been improved by the victory in Vietnam, or even more, assert the opposite proposition, this is strong evidence against the theory.[10]

At the opposite pole are *deterrent* audiences. These comprise people who would react negatively to Soviet expressions of heightened optimism about revolutionary prospects in the world. Such audiences would include U.S., West European, and Japanese leaders and representatives, and delegations from pro-Western governments in the Third World. If Soviets do express such optimistic beliefs before these groups, this is very strong evidence in favor of this deterrence theory assumption. Failure to make such arguments, however, is not disconfirming evidence.

Finally, there are neutral audiences. These groups have either a mixed membership, with some demanding and some deterrent listeners, or a membership with indeterminate effects on the Soviet speaker. The net effect of the former instance is that whatever the Soviets say is likely to offend large parts of these audiences. Groups such as the United Nations General Assembly, or the Non-Aligned Movement are in this category. The second audience exerts no clear demand or dissuasion on the Soviet speaker. Examples include groups gathered to hear election or anniversary speeches. In both cases, Soviet arguments either consistent with, or contrary to, the assumptions of deterrence theory yield strong evidence for testing the theory. However, the absence of any Soviet expressions count neither for nor against the validity of the theory.

---

10. It should be stressed that the standard of evaluation used here is a mild one. I do not code as "no inference" cases where a Soviet does not mention Vietnam at all, only cases where the Soviet notes the victory in Vietnam and then does not go on to outline that victory's implications or significance. This system of coding, if anything, understates instances of disconfirming Soviet statements.

**TABLE 9. Inferences about Regional Dynamics with Audience Effects[11]**

| Type of Inference for Deterrence Theory | Type of Audience | | |
|---|---|---|---|
| | Demanding | Deterrent | Neutral |
| Confirming | 1 | 0 | 13 |
| Disconfirming | 0 | 0 | 0 |
| None | 19 | 20 | 12 |

In table 9, I show how the Soviet party, military, and foreign policy elite and Americanist community behaved before audiences that varied along these dimensions.

The data in table 9 reinforce the point that Soviet lessons from Vietnam about regional dynamics are not unambiguous evidence for either the assumptions of deterrence theory or my suggested alternative. If deterrence theory were completely validated, all Soviet inferences would be in the Deterrent-Confirming and Neutral-Confirming cells. Soviet assertions of low U.S. credibility, for example, would come before such audiences as the visiting French president or agricultural workers in Sverdlovsk. There would be no lessons in the Disconfirming row, which is the case, and there would be no inferences in the None row, which is most decidedly not the case. There should not be a speech on Vietnam where the speaker draws no conclusions at all about the victory's consequences for world affairs. The theory's assumptions also failed to attain the strongest validation, which would appear in the Deterrent-Confirming cell.

However, there is only ambiguous support for the competing set of hypotheses. There was not a single instance of a disconfirming Soviet lesson. However, deterrence theory's assumptions were strongly invalidated by the nineteen lessons in the Demanding-None cell. Vietnam also went unmentioned a dozen times before neutral audiences. Nineteen times Soviets made no mention of the revolutionary effects of the victory in Vietnam before audiences who would have wanted to hear such encouragement and twelve times before audiences providing no incentives one way or the other.

In summary, Soviet lessons about the consequences of its victory in Vietnam for further revolutionary gains in the world do not provide the kind of unambiguous evidence that would be necessary to claim that the theory has

11. The total number (65) in table 9 refers to the number of times members of the party and military leadership, foreign policy elite, and Americanist community had opportunities between 1973 and 1976 to speak or write about the consequences of Vietnam. This means that if Brezhnev gave a speech on agricultural production in which he did not mention Vietnam, it is not included as a data point in the table.

performed well under crucially easy conditions. While these lessons came far closer to supporting the theory than did Soviet inferences about U.S. credibility, they still were not as optimistic and far-reaching as the propositions of deterrence theory posit.

### Explaining Soviet Lessons from Vietnam

Why didn't Soviet observers see an irresolute and weak America after the U.S. defeat in Vietnam? Why didn't they see bandwagoning U.S. allies and falling dominoes? In other words, why weren't the predictions of deterrence theory strongly borne out in this case? As has been suggested earlier, there are two broad sets of explanations for why the assumptions of deterrence theory are likely to be wrong: rational and psychological. The theory's validity is most undermined by either rational or general psychological explanations for its failure, for these are most aptly generalizable to any other state challenging the global status quo. Table 10 shows the three possible kinds of explanations for Soviet lessons and their implications for deterrence theory.

The broad applicability of Soviet lessons weakens as one reads from left to right across the columns. We should have the strongest confidence that deterrence theory is generally (in)valid if Soviet lessons were all products of rational information processing. We should be far less impressed, except in terms of the Soviet cases and other challengers who share their type of belief system, by Soviet lessons that are the consequences of Marxist-Leninist belief systems. We should have moderately high confidence that Soviet lessons based on bounded rationality and cognitive shortcuts are generally applicable to the universe of deterrent cases.

We should have less confidence in the middle case because it is impossible to establish a priori which aspects of reality any given decision maker will omit from his or her analysis of an event. Even though we know that it is most common for individuals to simplify reality, we also know that different individuals ignore different aspects of reality. A person assigns causal weight to a

TABLE 10.   The Power of Different Explanations for Soviet Lessons of Vietnam

|  | Types of Explanations | | |
| --- | --- | --- | --- |
|  | Universal | General | Peculiar |
| Lessons confirming deterrence theory |  | Regional dominoes | Regional and global dominoes |
| Lessons disconfirming deterrence theory | High U.S. credibility |  | High U.S. credibility |

particular characteristic of an event based on a number of considerations: the person's own lessons of history; the characteristic's seeming availability, representativeness, vividness, and concreteness; the individual's prior causal theory for this class of event. Consequently, if Soviet lessons can be explained by any general psychological models, it is reasonable to use these inferences as evidence for or against the general validity of deterrence theory. But we cannot impute the same power to these lessons as we do to those that are the product of rational attribution processes. In the case of belief systems that are peculiar to the Soviets, we, of course, cannot make any general statements.

I show below that the results for general deterrence theory are mixed. In the case of U.S. credibility, disconfirming Soviet lessons are the product of both rationality and peculiar beliefs. Soviet lessons that confirm deterrence theory's assumptions about regional dynamics, however, are the product of both general psychological models and peculiar belief systems. Hence, the theory is generally invalid in its assumptions about the credibility of a defender after a loss, but generally valid in its assumptions about the effects of a loss on regional dynamics.

## Universal Rational Explanations for Soviet Lessons of Vietnam

Soviets maintained images of high U.S. credibility after Vietnam by two rational processes. First, they rationally inferred lessons from Vietnam that refute several of the logical inconsistencies of deterrence theory's assumptions. And they also made rational attributions.

### Soviet Images of High U.S. Credibility in Strategic Areas of the Globe

Deterrence theory in extremis, and its many practitioners in unanimity, assume that as a consequence of the Vietnam defeat Soviet observers would doubt American will and capability to resist Soviet expansionism in Europe, Northeast Asia, and the Persian Gulf. As I suggested in chapter 1, this assumption is based on flawed logic; an equally logical, and rational, assumption would be that Soviets assess U.S. credibility in strategic areas based on U.S. behavior in these areas, not in peripheral areas of the world, such as Southeast Asia. The fact that there is not a single example that confirms deterrence theory in this, a crucially easy case for the theory, demonstrates that the theory's assumption is wrong and should be replaced by the empirically validated alternative.[12]

---

12. The evidence from the case of Vietnam refutes only one-half of this assumption. The other half, that defenders' victories in the periphery teach potential challengers that the defender

Another general reason for continued Soviet views of high U.S. credibility in strategic areas was the fact that the periphery was indeed peripheral to Soviet observers. It is both illogical and, as table A-1 in appendix A shows, empirically incorrect to assume that policymakers equally divide their attention between marginally and critically important areas of the world. For example, Brezhnev made forty-one speeches on foreign policy from 1973 to 1976. In only eight of them did he draw any inferences based on Vietnam; in *all* of them he made inferences based on U.S. behavior on issues of strategic importance.

### Soviet Images of High U.S. Credibility in Peripheral Areas of the Globe

U.S. credibility in the Third World did not suffer greatly because Soviets learned lessons from Vietnam as if they were making rational attributions.[13] They attributed various causes for the U.S. defeat and assigned probabilities for future U.S. adventurism based on their assessment of the value of these variables. These Soviets, primarily Americanists, were generally encouraged at first to believe that perhaps the United States would foreswear third world adventurism for some time. But the values of the variables on which their cautiously optimistic projections depended changed. As a consequence, these Soviets reversed their predictions about probable U.S. behavior.

Georgii Arbatov, for example, based his view of U.S. resolve on the expressed preferences of three groups in the United States: the "ruling elite," Congress, and public opinion.[14] He assessed U.S. capability, the second element of credibility, by looking at U.S. economic performance and military expenditures and deployments. Arbatov wrote that the only guarantee of an end to U.S. adventurism in the Third World would be if the ruling elite would recognize that economic issues were the bedrock of U.S. security, not global gendarmerie, a truth that he felt the American people had already grasped and that an increasing number of elected representatives were advancing. He similarly noted a split between the government and the people on the issue of nuclear stability. He argued that the American people had come to recognize the danger of nuclear escalation posed by the war in Vietnam, and consequently raised by all third world conflicts in which the United States was

---

will protect its strategic interests, is tested in the cases of the Dominican Republic and Grenada, chapter 5. Deterrence theory fails that test too, as such U.S. victories, while sufficient to generate Soviet perceptions of high U.S. credibility in strategic areas, are completely unnecessary.

13. In fact, U.S. credibility in the Third World was also protected by belief systems peculiar to certain Soviets. I deal with this topic below.

14. The "ruling elite" generally comprises all members of the Executive branch, but with decided emphasis on the individuals who are responsible for national security and foreign policy.

involved. Arbatov again denied that the ruling elite had learned such sobering lessons.

In fact, by the time of the 1976 presidential primaries, Arbatov wrote about an ominous new trend in American domestic politics: the rise of the Right. These "attacks from the Right by Ronald Reagan, George Wallace, George Meany, James Buckley, and Barry Goldwater are shaking the Realists." As a consequence, the defeat in Vietnam, instead of being seen as evidence that military force does not yield rewards, is "causing a reversion to cold war thinking." Conservative politicians are making the argument that the war could have been won, if only the United States had used more force.[15]

In the writings of Arbatov we can see how a rational response to the evidence from the American political scene is to revalue the currency of U.S. credibility. The views of Genrikh Trofimenko followed very similar patterns, though he chose to rely on different variables in his evaluation of U.S. credibility. Trofimenko, for example, argued that the American ruling elite had been compelled to end the war in Vietnam in spite of its preference to continue fighting. The public turned against the war because of its fear of nuclear escalation and its realization that in paying for the war, critical domestic needs were going unmet.[16] Trofimenko separated the two elements of American credibility: capability and resolve. While the United States remained resolute, its capabilities were temporarily undermined by public opinion. The ruling elite, in his view, would engage in third world adventurism as soon as it could find some capability that was not thwarted by public resistance.[17]

Less than a year after the fall of Saigon, Trofimenko identified how the ruling elite was evading these public constraints. The U.S. government was relying more on the navy, improving the quality of reserve and national guard

---

15. These quotes are from Arbatov, "O Sovetsko-Amerikanskikh," *Pravda*, April 2, 1976, 4–5. For a recapitulation of the foregoing arguments, see his "Vneshnyaya Politika," "Sovetsko-Amerikanskie Otnosheniya na Novom Etape" (Soviet-American Relations at a New Stage), *Pravda*, July 22, 1973, 4, and "Sovetsko-Amerikanskie Otnosheniya v 70-e Gody" (Soviet-American Relations in the 1970s), *SShA*, May 1974, 26–40.

16. See Trofimenko, "Uroki Vietnama," "Evoliutsiya Voenno-Politicheskoi Strategii SShA Posle Vtoroi Mirovoi Voine" (The Evolution of American Military-Political Strategy Since World War II), *VI*, March 1976, 64–65 and 80–90, and "Vneshnyaya Politika SShA v 70-e Gody: Deklaratsii i Praktika" (American Foreign Policy in the 1970s: Words and Practice), *SShA*, December 1976, 17–28.

17. This division of credibility into its two necessary components reproduces the findings of numerous psychological experiments. In assessing the kinds of attributions people make from cases where someone has made a great effort but nevertheless failed, people attribute low capability to the actor, but continued high resolve. For a summary of the literature, see Ronis, Hansen, and O'Leary, "Achievement Attributions," 702–3.

detachments, and continuing to increase real military expenditures "not related to Vietnam." Trofimenko interpreted the Guam Doctrine as yet another clever way for the American ruling elite to resist revolutionary change in the Third World without provoking domestic discontent. By relying on local forces to bear the burden of any military action on the ground, while holding U.S. naval and air power in reserve, Washington had developed a strategy designed to advance adventurist foreign policy goals while avoiding effective domestic opposition.[18]

By the end of 1976, Trofimenko's analysis of the domestic political situation in the United States implied that the ruling elite no longer had to design around any domestic constraints on its preference for adventurism. Citing the advent of Reagan and Wallace, he argued that the "antiwar sentiments of the late 1960s have waned" and so the "needs of the Pentagon are again on the top of the agenda."[19]

In summary, Soviets saw the United States as continuously resolved to, and ultimately capable of, resisting revolutionary change in the Third World because Soviets were rational attribution theorists. They developed causal models of the American defeat in Vietnam and watched as their predictions were disconfirmed by evidence of an increasingly credible America.

### General Psychological Explanations for Soviet Lessons of Vietnam

Many Soviets inferred lessons from Vietnam that can be explained by psychological models with general validity. These observers used a menu of critical variables that was so truncated that one could reasonably argue that they were applying the "representative heuristic," or a very spare version of bounded rationality. These Soviets saw only one or two features of the Vietnam case as key predictors for future U.S. behavior and for revolutionary change elsewhere in the world. What is critical here is *how* Soviets selected the characteristics of the Vietnam case that they considered to be necessary and/or sufficient for predicting the future behavior of the United States and the prospects for future gains in the Third World. If variables are selected on the

---

18. Trofimenko, "Evoliutsiya Voenno-Politicheskoi." He also suggested in this article that the American decision to end the draft and begin voluntary military service was not a sign of weakness, but rather a tactical "concession to prosperous strata" in the United States (83). Also see Trofimenko, "Vneshnyaya Politika," for more on new American military tactics to get around post-Vietnam obstacles.

19. Quote from Trofimenko, "Vneshnyaya Politika," 23. See also "Traditsiya Realizma i Borba Vokrug Razryadki" (A Tradition of Realism and the Struggle Around Detente), *SShA*, July 1976, 26–28.

basis of some underlying belief system, then we can reasonably assume that the lessons generated by this analysis have no generality.[20] If it is impossible to establish that a biased selection process occurred, then the more general models of bounded rationality and the representative heuristic likely are applicable.

### Soviet Images of High U.S. Credibility

The Soviet party leadership and military elite maintained views of a highly credible America primarily because they evaluated U.S. resolve and capability as a function of absolute U.S. military capabilities. Reliance on this single element to determine U.S. credibility ensured that these Soviets would perceive the United States as always highly credible given the size of U.S. defense expenditures, even as they declined after their peak during the war.[21] U.S. military capability was identified in various ways: the size of the overall military budget,[22] construction of foreign military bases,[23] and particular deployments.[24]

### Soviet Images of Falling Dominoes

Many Soviets inferred lessons from Vietnam about the prospects for future victories by national liberation movements that can be explained by psychological models with general validity. These Soviets saw only one or two features of the Vietnam case as the key predictors for revolutionary change elsewhere. If they perceived these critical elements as present in another context, they were then encouraged about the prospects for gains there. What

---

20. I discuss these kinds of peculiar lessons in a subsequent section.

21. U.S. military expenditures and deployments were used very frequently by members of the party leadership and military to assess U.S. credibility. For example, Brezhnev evaluated U.S. credibility in twenty-nine speeches from 1973 to 1976; in fully twenty-six of these addresses, he used U.S. military programs as at least partial evidence. There are similar figures for Podgorny: twelve of fifteen; Gromyko: eight of ten; Suslov: four of eight; Kosygin: three of six; Sokolov: five of six; Grechko: eleven of seventeen; Gorshkov: three of three; and Ponomarev: sixteen of seventeen.

22. For example, see Suslov's Supreme Soviet election speech, *Pravda*, June 12, 1974, 2; Kosygin's message to the World Peace Council, *Pravda*, February 16, 1974, 1; Sokolov, "Na Strazhe Mira i Sotsializma" (In the Defense of Peace and Socialism), *Izvestiya*, February 23, 1973, 1, 3; Gorshkov, "Podvig Naroda" (Feat of the People), *Trud*, May 9, 1974, 1.

23. For example, see Brezhnev's plenum speech, *Pravda*, October 26, 1976, 2–3; and Kremeniuk, "Strategiya SShA v Zone Indiiskovo Okeana" (U.S. Strategy in the Indian Ocean Region), *SShA*, May 1973, 6–17.

24. See, for example, Ponomarev's Supreme Soviet election speech, *Pravda*, June 5, 1975, 2; Kremeniuk, "Regionalnye Napravleniya vo Vneshnei Politike SShA" (Regional Directions in U.S. Foreign Policy), *SShA*, May 1974, 44–51; and Kokoshin, "American Foreign Policy Strategy for the 1970s," *IA*, October 1973, 67–73.

is critical here is *how* Soviets selected the characteristics of the Vietnam case that they considered to be necessary and/or sufficient for the replication of the victory elsewhere.

The kinds of dominoes Soviets expected to fall as a consequence of the victory in Vietnam depended on which variables they deemed to be most important to that triumph. Some used geographical propinquity, so limiting future revolutionary victories to Laos and Kampuchea.[25] For others, the most salient feature of the victory was the fact that it had been reached through a negotiated peace treaty. These Soviets agreed that the victory in Vietnam should lead to similar negotiated settlements elsewhere in the Third World, but particularly in the Middle East.[26] Trofimenko found the single sufficient explanation for the victory in the instability of the Thieu government. While not identifying other U.S. allies in the Third World that lacked domestic support, he implied that similar regimes could be expected to fall to the forces of national liberation.[27]

In summary, it is reasonable to argue that this proposition of deterrence theory was validated by the lessons Soviets inferred from Vietnam. While it is impossible to predict how far and what kinds of dominoes a victorious challenger will see fall, it is sensible to assume that it will be encouraged to expect future victories somewhere in the periphery.

## Peculiar Psychological Explanations for Soviet Lessons from Vietnam

Many Soviets, but especially the party elite and several members of the foreign policy establishment, maintained their views of a highly credible America through the operation of Marxist-Leninist belief systems. While such beliefs are hardly peculiar to Soviets, they are held by only a small, and seemingly ever-dwindling, subset of the universe of challengers. If deterrence theory assumptions about credibility are invalidated by lessons that are the product of Leninist beliefs, this is not an invalidation of the theory more generally. Similarly, many Soviets were greatly encouraged about the pros-

---

25. For example, Brezhnev's report at the Twenty-Fifth Party Congress, *Documents and Resolutions, Twenty-Fifth Congress of the CPSU* (Moscow: Novosti, 1976), 9.

26. This lesson does not clearly support deterrence theory, since these Soviets did not argue that the Palestinians could now confidently expect to gain national liberation through *military* means, only that the chances of reaching an acceptable resolution of the Arab-Israeli dispute via negotiations were now enhanced. See, for example, Ulyanovsky, "Razryadka Mezhdunarodnoi" (International Detente), *Pravda*, August 30, 1973, 4–5; Arbatov, "O Sovetsko-Amerikanskikh"; and Kislov, "Arabskaya Neft, Israel i Politika SShA" (Arab Oil, Israel, and U.S. Policy), *SShA*, November 1973, 46–50.

27. Trofimenko, "Uroki Vietnama."

pects for revolutionary change throughout the Third World on the basis of this same set of peculiar beliefs. This validation of deterrence theory is also not generalizable to a larger universe of cases.

### Soviet Images of High U.S. Credibility

A Marxist-Leninist belief system assumes axiomatic U.S. hostility to any events in the world that threaten the interests of American ruling classes. The latter, representing the interests of the bourgeoisie, pursue a foreign policy aimed at preventing any changes in the international arena that could undermine continued U.S. economic domination and exploitation of the Third World and extraction of economic surplus from its strategic allies in Western Europe and Japan. In advancing this strategy, the narrow ruling elite ignores or manipulates the American people, their elected representatives, and the media. The consequence of such a set of beliefs is that the level of U.S. credibility is not a variable; those who adhere to these beliefs see the United States as constantly capable and willing to defend its interests anywhere in the world.

For example, Podgorny told his Bulgarian audience several months after the Paris accords that "we do not harbor any illusions that the forces of aggression and oppression have been so squeezed that they cannot undertake efforts to upset the political life" of third world countries.[28]

Hence, despite their victory in Vietnam, Soviets with these beliefs continued to see a highly resolute and capable America. Soviets who developed and applied rational attribution models at least entertained the possibility that the U.S. government might be compelled by domestic constraints to renounce adventurism in the Third World. Marxist-Leninist ideologues, on the other hand, were psychologically unable to admit that any societal forces could influence, let alone constrain, the choices of the ruling elite in an imperialist state. Such an admission would have challenged a fundamental, core belief, necessitating the very painful rearrangement of the entire system of beliefs. Instead of initiating this very costly process, Brezhnev, Podgorny, Grechko, Gorshkov, Ulyanovsky, and Ponomarev perceived a more credible America than they would have had they processed information rationally.

### Soviet Images of Falling Dominoes

A Marxist-Leninist belief system assumes that victories by national liberation forces in the Third World are inevitable. At the heart of this belief system is the "world revolutionary alliance" that comprises the international working

---

28. *Pravda*, July 8, 1973, 4. For other expressions of confidence that the United States was both willing and capable of intervening in the Third World in the future, see Brezhnev's speech in India, *Pravda*, November 28, 1973, 2, and his comments at a Central Committee plenum, *Pravda*, October 26, 1976, 2–3.

class, the national liberation movement, and the socialist community. As the most powerful and original member of the latter group, the Soviet Union is the leading force of this alliance. The struggle against imperialism proceeds along two avenues: working-class agitation within the imperialist powers themselves and national liberation movements whose victories detach third world countries from the imperialist zone of exploitation. Since the maintenance of social peace within the imperialist metropole depends on suborning the working class with superprofits extracted from third world economies via multinational corporate investment, every country that leaves the capitalist development path in the periphery is another blow at the soft underbelly of imperialism.

This set of beliefs psychologically implies a *need* for its adherents to see continual successes for revolutionary movements in the Third World. If they were to believe that such victories were not inevitable, their entire system of beliefs would have to endure fundamental restructuring. For example, they might have to accept that imperialism would exist forever, since it would always have third world economies to exploit. But this would mean that socialism was not the necessary future for the world and would demonstrate that the Soviet Union, as leader of the socialist community, was not an effective promoter of the interests of the world revolutionary alliance. These would be very painful admissions for any orthodox Marxist-Leninist. Assuming the ultimate success of national liberation movements would restore psychological balance.

Driven by this need for consistency, many Soviet observers seized on the victory in Vietnam as demonstrating the inevitability of future triumphs for the forces of liberation in the Third World. As Brezhnev told the visiting Vietnamese prime minister, Le Duan, the victory in Vietnam showed that "peoples fighting for the just cause [of national liberation] are invincible."[29] Moreover, the victory proved that the Soviet Union was an effective leader of this revolutionary movement, providing "powerful support [to] its allies" and "demonstrating the power of international solidarity."[30]

In summary, it is generally inappropriate to apply either the Soviet lessons from Vietnam that disconfirm deterrence theory propositions about U.S. credibility or those that are consistent with its assumptions about regional dynamics to the universe of deterrence relationships, since these lessons are products of a belief system peculiar to Soviet Marxist-Leninists. Other challengers to deterrence may, however, have belief systems that systematically

---

29. *Pravda*, October 29, 1975, 1–2.

30. The first quote is from Kosygin in Libya, *Pravda*, May 14, 1975, 4. The second is from Suslov's speech at the Fourth Congress of the Worker's Party of Vietnam in Hanoi, *Pravda*, December 16, 1976, 4.

exaggerate the defender's credibility and the cumulativity of its own victories. This is an empirical question to be verified.

In table 11, I place the orthodox Marxist-Leninist belief system of many Soviets into its proper context.

For the defender, the most dangerous opponent is at the lower left. This opponent assumes both that its gains will cumulate and that the defender is irresolute and weak. This is also the box in which deterrence theory incorrectly placed the Soviet Union, ideologically at least. In fact, Marxist-Leninists, while convinced of the universality of their creed, were equally convinced of high imperialist/U.S. credibility. The task of deterring those at upper left is far less demanding than the imperialists at lower left. But the defender cannot afford to do nothing against Marxist-Leninists, given their chiliastic assumptions about inevitable global victory.

An isolationist challenger is an oxymoronic entity requiring no deterrent strategy. Those challengers at lower right require a more vigorous stance by the defender than if they were Marxist-Leninists, but not as much as if they were the imperialists to their left. The strategic value of the territory at risk is the determining factor here. For example, Hitler's location in the heart of Europe made any expansionism by him very threatening, even though it was limited by his racialist ideology. But if a challenger with such a belief system were located in central Africa, there is little reason for a Great Power defender to adopt a very ambitious deterrent strategy.

In summary, Marxism-Leninism is not the kind of ideology that deterrence theory assumes is held by a challenger to the status quo. Marxist-Leninists' beliefs in the inherent hostility of imperialism makes establishing one's credibility much easier than the theory assumes. Selecting an appropriate deterrent strategy depends on the ideology of the potential challenger. Moreover, despite the unique distortions of reality that are the product of Marxism-Leninism, it is still part of a more general class of ideologies. Consequently, the arguments in this book that rely on "peculiar" explanations for Soviet lessons are not irrelevant to a broader, though of course still limited, universe of possible challengers.

**TABLE 11.  Deterrence Theory and Belief Systems**

| Opponent's Credibility | Types of Ideologies | |
| --- | --- | --- |
| | Universalistic | Exclusionary |
| High | Marxism-Leninism | Isolationism |
| Low | Nineteenth-century British, French, and U.S. imperialism. *Deterrence theory's assumed challenger* | Nazi Germany Imperial Japan Khomeini's Iran |

## A Scorecard for Deterrence Theory

In this crucially easy case for the assumptions of deterrence theory, Soviet lessons from Vietnam should both confirm these propositions and be explained either rationally or by general psychological models. Any lessons that disconfirm the theory should be the product of peculiar belief systems unique to the Soviets. Rational and general psychological explanations for lessons that invalidate the theory's assumptions are very strong disconfirming evidence. Deterrence theory's assumptions about U.S. credibility do not pass this crucial test. They receive no confirmation, and lessons that disconfirm the theory are generated rationally. Its propositions about regional dynamics, however, are partially confirmed. These validating lessons are both the product of psychological models with general applicability and peculiar Soviet beliefs. I combine the explanations for Soviet lessons and their implications for deterrence theory in this scorecard:

1. Universal explanations that confirm deterrence theory: *None*
2. General explanations that confirm deterrence theory: Many Soviets felt that dominoes would fall elsewhere in the region and the world based on their invocation of "representative heuristics" to explain the victory in Vietnam.
3. Peculiar explanations that confirm deterrence theory: Those Soviets with orthodox Marxist-Leninist belief systems, especially the party leadership, predicted future victories for national liberation movements around the world based on this set of beliefs.
4. Universal explanations that disconfirm deterrence theory:
   a. All Soviets continued to attribute high credibility to the United States in strategic areas of the globe because they saw no logical connection between U.S. behavior in areas of negligible interest and its future conduct in places with critical stakes.
   b. All Soviets derived their images of U.S. strategic credibility almost exclusively from its behavior on strategic issues because U.S. behavior in the Third World was of only peripheral salience to Soviet analysis of this question.
   c. The community of Americanists was always convinced of U.S. resolve to resist revolutionary changes in the Third World and was shortly convinced of its capability because its members were rational attribution theorists.
5. General explanations that disconfirm deterrence theory: Many Soviets, including virtually the entire party leadership and military and foreign policy elite, maintained images of a highly credible America because they operated with a very restricted menu of critical variables in their analyses, namely, military spending and deployments.

6. Peculiar explanations that disconfirm deterrence theory: Most members of the party leadership and military and foreign policy elites considered high U.S. credibility to be axiomatic, given their adherence to orthodox Marxist-Leninist belief systems.

## Considering Alternative Explanations for Soviet Lessons of Vietnam

### A Soviet Bias to Perceive the United States as Inherently Aggressive

It could be argued that the reason Soviets saw U.S. credibility as undamaged after the Vietnam War was that Soviets were uniquely biased to see the United States as always hostile to the Soviet Union and its allies. While such an argument does not undermine the fact that Soviet lessons from Vietnam were contrary to those predicted by deterrence theory about U.S. credibility, acceptance of this position would preclude generalizing the Soviet experience to the universe of deterrent cases. There are a number of problems with this argument.

Not every Soviet observer saw equal levels of U.S. credibility.[31] The party leadership, while consistently expecting the United States to defend its interests in the Third World with whatever means necessary, simultaneously expected the U.S. government to behave reasonably in negotiations on strategic nuclear arms control, bilateral relations, and the Conference on Security and Cooperation in Europe. Members of the military elite, while acknowledging an American commitment to detente in general, also spoke of a continuing U.S. predilection to resolve issues by military force.

The lessons inferred by Soviet Americanists were contrary both to the argument that all Soviets had the same view of an inherently credible United States and to the argument's implication that U.S. credibility is a constant, not a variable. Their lessons reflected an understanding both that different levels of credibility were appropriately attributed to different areas of U.S. behavior and that credibility was a product of many factors affecting American resolve and capabilities.

In summary, there was no bias among Soviet observers that would account for their perceptions of a credible United States after the Vietnam War.

### A Soviet Lulling Strategy

It could be argued that the Soviets deliberately downplayed how much they

---

31. All the claims I make below are based on the empirical evidence presented earlier in this chapter. Please refer to the first three sections of this chapter for specific citations.

thought U.S. credibility had been damaged by Vietnam. They may have realized that overly enthusiastic and optimistic expressions of their beliefs about U.S. irresoluteness and weakness would have triggered a hostile reaction within the United States and its government. Wanting to maintain American support for detente, the Soviets would not have wanted to humiliate the United States just as the new relationship was getting under way. Given this strategy, Soviets would have continued to credit the United States with high credibility, while privately believing otherwise.

This explanation, if true, would reverse my findings about Soviet perceptions of U.S. credibility, confirming the assumptions of deterrence theory. It does not, however, fit well with the evidence. The first problem with this argument, as with all alternatives that depend on the existence of a single Soviet line, is that different Soviets inferred different lessons about the state of U.S. credibility. I noted this variety in my consideration of the first alternative explanation.

More important is the fact that a Soviet lulling strategy cannot account for the many Soviets who argued that the victory in Vietnam demonstrated the inevitability of future successes of revolutionary forces around the Third World. Certainly, Soviets could not have expected American support for detente if the U.S. ruling elite was convinced that its Soviet counterpart would be enjoying a string of victories in the periphery. In trying to save this alternative, it might be argued that the Soviets had different messages for different audiences. They told the United States and the West that U.S. credibility was not affected by its loss in Vietnam, while telling third world allies that national liberation victories were assured in the future. One can be quite confident, however, that Soviets were not so obtuse as to believe that no American official, academic, or reporter paid attention to the messages they gave to third world audiences. Indeed, some of these audiences, such as the UN General Assembly, had U.S. representatives present.

## An Insoluble Foreign Policy Dilemma

One could argue that the frequent Soviet lesson that Vietnam showed only that the United States was committed to detente was advanced in order to justify Soviet foreign policy before third world audiences. The Soviet Union, this argument goes, risked alienating its revolutionary allies in the Third World by its commitment to detente with the United States, because these allies perceived this commitment as implying a diminished Soviet commitment to their causes. In order to square this foreign policy circle, Soviets had to argue that detente had made the victory in Vietnam possible; detente would make other victories possible; and the United States was committed to detente. The contradiction here of course is that these same Soviets were simultaneously asserting that the United States would continue to resist revolutionary change in the Third World, even if such change was inevitable. The problem with this alternative explanation is that the dilemma is not insoluble and the paradox can be adequately explained as a product of the peculiar belief system of orthodox Marxist-Leninists.

First, the Soviets could have resolved their dilemma by tailoring their messages to different audiences. While telling the United States and its allies that Vietnam signified a commitment to detente (which they did), they could have simultaneously told their third world allies that national liberation victories were inevitable (which they did) *and* that U.S. willingness and capacity to thwart these victories had proved wanting in Vietnam (which they did not). The fact that they did not take this route out of the dilemma strongly suggests that Soviets held genuine convictions of a highly credible United States in the Third World and that this alternative explanation for the pattern of Soviet lessons is not compelling. Moreover, this contradictory set of Soviet lessons can be explained as the product of the core Soviet belief in an axiomatically hostile United States, the infallible leadership of the world revolutionary process by the Soviet Union, and the ultimate triumph of national liberation movements around the world.

In summary, each of these alternative explanations provides a plausible account for certain Soviet lessons from Vietnam, but none of them is able to explain the entire set of lessons in a logically coherent manner.

## Soviet Behavior after Vietnam

If deterrence theory assumptions are accurate, then Soviet foreign policy in the Third World should be marked by greater activism after the American withdrawal from Vietnam and the fall of Saigon. In fact, such enhanced activism did not occur, as is evident from the following chronology of Soviet gains and losses in the Third World, 1973–77.

| | | |
|---|---|---|
| Vietnam | 1973 | Gain |
| Afghanistan | 1973 | Gain |
| Chile | 1973 | Loss |
| Middle East | 1973 | Loss |
| Ethiopia | 1974 | Gain |
| Vietnam | 1975 | Gain |
| Angola | 1975 | Gain |
| Mozambique | 1975 | Gain |
| Peru | 1975 | Loss |
| Egypt | 1976 | Loss |
| Zaire | 1977 | Loss |
| Ethiopia | 1977 | Gain |

While the Soviet Union did benefit from the overthrow of the monarchy in Afghanistan in April 1973, not five months later, Salvador Allende was ousted from power in Chile by a pro-American military junta led by Augusto Pinochet. Only a week after the overthrow of Allende, Israel scored military victories over Egypt and Syria in the October War. Far more importantly, Washington began its successful efforts to exclude Moscow from the Middle East peace process and to turn Egypt, the most important Arab military power, into an American ally.[32]

This ongoing loss in the Middle East is accompanied by the overthrow of Emperor Selassie in Ethiopia, and his replacement with the pro-Soviet government of Mengistu Mariam. The fall of Saigon is followed by a successful Soviet-Cuban intervention on behalf of the Popular Movement for the Liberation of Angola (MPLA) in its war against the National Union for the Total Independence of Angola (UNITA), headed by Jonas Savimbi, and supported by China, South Africa, and the United States. While the MPLA was fighting in Angola, Portugal was granting independence peacefully to the National Front for the Liberation of Mozambique. But in Latin America, the anti-Western government of Juan Velasco was the victim of a coup by right-wing military officers. The fifth year after the American withdrawal from Vietnam began with the successful Western suppression of an uprising in Shaba Province against the Mobutu government in Zaire and ended with the successful Ethiopian defense of Ogaden from Somali invaders.[33]

This cluster of cases shows that there is no clear pattern of Soviet behavior after its dramatic victory in Vietnam. While Moscow provided military support to ensure gains in Angola and Ethiopia, it stood by and did nothing to prevent the loss of its most powerful strategic ally in the Middle East—Egypt. The other gains it achieved, in Afghanistan, Ethiopia, and Mozambique, were not at all the product of any Soviet activism. Indigenous forces caused the two revolutions, and Portugal "caused" Mozambican independence.

In sum, the behavioral record does not support the assumptions of deterrence.

## Conclusion

The conditions of the U.S. defeat in Vietnam are precisely those circumstances—enormous effort combined with total failure—that create the easiest possible test for deterrence theory to pass. If it cannot gain unambiguous support in this crucial case, then the theory's validity is in serious doubt. The actual Soviet lessons from Vietnam are such that deterrence theory does not

---

32. See my discussion in chap. 6.
33. See chap. 3 for the cases of Angola and Ethiopia.

pass this crucial test. While Soviets expected dominoes to fall, they also expected U.S. resistance to continue.

In terms of a general theory of deterrence, the predominantly universal and general explanations for Soviet views of high U.S. credibility after Vietnam imply that the theory's assumption about resolve and capability is wrong. However, the fact that Soviet images of dominoes can be explained, at least in part, by general psychological models, implies that the theory's assumption about regional dynamics is correct. Finally, the theory has miscategorized the opponent's ideology, with the consequence of an excessively ambitious deterrent strategy by the defender.

CHAPTER 3

# Soviet Lessons from Angola, Ethiopia, and Afghanistan: The "Arc of Crisis" as a Crucial Case

A challenge not met today will tempt far more dangerous crises tomorrow. If the United States is seen to emasculate itself in the face of massive, unprecedented Soviet and Cuban intervention [in Angola], what will be the perceptions of leaders around the world as they make decisions concerning their future security?

—Henry Kissinger

[The Soviet invasion of Afghanistan] was a vindication of my concern that the Soviets would be emboldened by our lack of response over Ethiopia.
—Zbigniew Brzezinski

The Soviet victory in Angola came only months after the U.S. evacuation of Saigon. This success was shortly followed by more gains in Ethiopia, and then Afghanistan. Nonetheless, the Soviets did not see a weak and irresolute United States after this string of losses. Nor did Soviets see dominoes falling in their direction. Deterrence theory does not pass a crucial test, since Soviets saw both a capable and resolute America and effective regional balancing following their series of victories.

Soviet perceptions after these three victories contradict the predictions of deterrence theory. In the case of Angola, Soviets saw even an abortive effort to resist the MPLA victory as evidence of American resolve to prevent revolutionary change in southern Africa and farther afield. This lesson was reinforced by American diplomatic efforts on Zimbabwe and its aid to the Mobutu government in Zaire in 1977 and 1978 after uprisings in Shaba Province. Moreover, Soviet views of American credibility did not change appreciably

---

The first epigraph is taken from the Senate Foreign Relations Committee, *Angola: Hearings before the Subcommittee on African Affairs,* 94th Congress, 2d session, 1976, 15. It is of note here that Kissinger explicitly denied any *strategic* American interests in Angola or southern Africa, despite being pressed by conservative Senators who wanted to justify their support for UNITA and the FNLA on this basis. The second epigraph is taken from *Power and Principle* (New York: Farrar, Straus, Giroux, 1983), 429.

toward images of a stronger America after the United States resumed aid to UNITA in August 1985. Soviets were also impressed by the power and resolve of South Africa.

Soviet perceptions after their victory on the Horn of Africa in 1977–78 also are inconsistent with the assumptions of deterrence theory. No Soviet saw the United States as weak and irresolute as a consequence of Washington's failure to support Somalia's bid to detach the Ogaden from Ethiopia. Instead, the American alliance switch to Barre in Mogadishu, combined with Saudi, Egyptian, and Sudanese support for Somalia, convinced Soviet leaders that the United States was a powerful competitor in Africa and the Third World in general.

Deterrence theory's assumptions are also confounded by Soviet lessons from Afghanistan. Soviets saw both a highly credible United States and a large group of countries, in the region and beyond, that had committed themselves to reversing the gains Moscow had made in Afghanistan.

While deterrence theory assumptions are invalidated empirically in these three cases, the question remains as to whether this empirical disconfirmation is a *general* indictment of the theory. If the contrary Soviet lessons were arrived at rationally, or as the product of general cognitive economizing efforts, or if these lessons confirmed a counterassumption of equal logical standing, then general deterrence theory has been invalidated. If, however, this disconfirmation is the product of belief systems, then the theory is invalidated only within the domain of decision makers who share these kinds of ideologies. In fact, Soviet lessons of high American credibility after these three cases were the product of rationality, while Soviet images of global dominoes set off by these victories were derived from Leninist belief systems. Deterrence theory receives universal and general disconfirmation, and only peculiar validation.

Below I provide a short historical description of the cases and discuss the range of lessons Soviets learned about U.S. credibility and regional dynamics from their victories in Angola, Ethiopia, and Afghanistan. I explain why they learned what they did, how the character of these explanations affects the general (in)validity of deterrence theory, and evaluate competing explanations for Soviet perceptions.

## Soviet Lessons about U.S. Credibility

During the Angolan civil war in 1975–76, the United States provided covert military assistance to two groups—Jonas Savimbi's UNITA and Holden Roberto's National Front for the Liberation of Angola (FNLA)—both of which were fighting for control of Angola with Agostinho Neto's MPLA. The

MPLA enjoyed military aid from the Soviet Union and the support of Cuban ground troops in Angola.

With the passage of the Clark Amendment in the Senate in late January 1976, American aid to UNITA and the FNLA ceased. With the withdrawal of South African troops from southern Angola in March 1976, the MPLA was recognized as the only legal government of Angola. From 1977 to 1989 the MPLA government in Luanda was compelled to fight a counterinsurgency war against UNITA, the latter receiving covert support from Pretoria and also timely military interventions by the South African Defense Forces. Meanwhile, the U.S. government refrained from providing any assistance to UNITA until Congress repealed the Clark Amendment in August 1985. The December 1988 agreement between South Africa (RSA), Angola, and Cuba resulted in South Africa renouncing any further support for UNITA, though American aid continued for another two years.

In the winter of 1977–78, the Ethiopian armed forces, with the assistance of Cuban ground troops and Soviet military aid, succeeded in driving invading Somali forces from the Ogaden area of Ethiopia. As a consequence of this successful defense, the Mengistu government in Addis Ababa was then able to use its military resources to suppress the insurgencies that were reaching critical proportions in Eritrea and Oromo Province. For the next thirteen years, until the removal of Mengistu and an Eritrean military victory in May 1991, the Mengistu government fought against Eritrean guerillas. While there was no American military support for Barre's invasion of the Ogaden, nor for the Eritrean separatists, various American allies, including Saudi Arabia, Egypt, and the Sudan, bankrolled this challenge to the Ethiopian regime.

Since the Soviet invasion of Afghanistan in December 1979 to prevent the overthrow of its ally in Kabul, the United States, along with the allied governments in Beijing, Islamabad, Cairo, and Riyadh, provided military aid to the Afghani mujahideen who were committed to overthrowing the government in Kabul. Despite the Soviet withdrawal in 1989, the mujahideen continued their resistance, and both the Soviet Union and the United States provided military aid to their respective allies. The Kabul government finally fell in 1992.

Each of these Soviet victories is a crucial test of deterrence theory's predictions of U.S. credibility. According to the theory's assumptions, Soviets should have seen the United States as unwilling and unable to resist revolutionary change in the Third World as a consequence of its defeat in Vietnam. Not a year after the evacuation of Saigon, the United States failed to prevent the Soviets from providing vital aid in the establishment of their allies in power in Luanda. Less than two years after this defeat, the United States was unable to prevent the Soviets from playing a critical role in defending the besieged Mengistu government in Ethiopia. Less than two years after the end of the Ethiopian war with Somalia, the United States failed to prevent the successful Soviet intervention to maintain the People's Democratic Party of Afghanistan's (PDPA) power in Kabul.

This string of defeats provides the *easiest* test for deterrence theory to pass. If the Soviets did not see the United States as incapable and irresolute after this run of Soviet success, then just what are the conditions under which we should expect the theory's predictions to be validated?

One aspect of the Angola case further contributes to its crucial nature. Deterrence theory predicts that the United States can establish its credibility through a demonstration of the military capacity and will to defeat the Soviets in the Third World. From 1976 to August 1985, the United States did not provide military support to UNITA in Angola, though the Pretoria government both supplied such aid and intervened several times militarily. Washington then resumed direct military aid to Savimbi's forces. Deterrence theory predicts different Soviet inferences about American credibility in these two periods. Soviets should see a weaker and more irresolute America from 1976 to 1985 than from 1985 to 1991.

Deterrence theory propositions about American credibility do not pass their tests in these crucial cases. In the case of Angola, Soviets saw even the failed U.S. effort as evidence that Washington would continue to resist revolutionary change in southern Africa and farther afield. This lesson was reinforced by American diplomatic efforts on Zimbabwe and U.S. aid to the besieged Mobutu government in Zaire. Moreover, Soviets did not attribute greater credibility to the United States after its resumption of aid to UNITA in August 1985. Presumed American support for the RSA's destabilization campaign was sufficient to teach the Soviet leadership that the United States was both able and willing to resist revolutionary changes in the world.

Soviet perceptions of American credibility after the Soviet victory on the Horn in 1977–78 also contradict the assumptions of deterrence theory. No Soviet saw the United States as weak and irresolute. Instead, American support for Somalia convinced Soviet leaders that the United States was a powerful competitor in Africa and the Third World in general.

Soviet inferences from the intervention in Afghanistan do not clearly support either deterrence theory or my alternative hypotheses. On balance though, they provide stronger validation for the latter than for deterrence theory. Soviets saw a highly credible America based on Washington's support for the mujahideen in Afghanistan. This image wavered only slightly after the Soviet Union began to withdraw from Afghanistan. Soviet observers temporarily raised their hopes that the United States might respond by cutting off aid to the rebels.

This pattern of inferences provides only ambiguous support for deterrence theory propositions, since credibility comprises both resolve and capabilities. While the United States demonstrated the will to overthrow the government in Kabul, it never demonstrated the capacity, as the Najibullah government remained in power until 1992.[1] Despite this clear instance of American impotence, Soviets still inferred lessons of a highly credible America. This finding contradicts deterrence theory insofar as it demands Soviet defeats to teach deterrent lessons, rather than simply increased costs for the Soviets to hold on to their gains. Instead, it appears that even manifestations of American inability were sufficient, through the agency of demonstrations of resolve, to convince these Soviets that the United States was credible.[2]

The obvious counter to this interpretation is that the forced withdrawal of the Soviet army dealt the Soviets a defeat. Hence, Soviet inferences of high American credibility subsequent to that event validate the theory. There are three problems with such an analysis. First, Soviets saw a highly credible America *before* Washington began to aid the mujahideen.[3] Second, they saw an equally committed America while Soviet troops were fighting in Afghanistan, not just after their withdrawal. Finally, as long as a government dominated by the PDPA remained in power in Kabul, it is not reasonable to call the Soviet intervention in Afghanistan a loss—neither in terms of the taxonomy I use in this study, nor with respect to the strategic-military advantages the Soviets gained from having an ally in Afghanistan versus having a government dominated by the mujahideen. This latter conclusion is supported by the fact that the United States continued to provide military aid to the mujahideen even after Soviet troops had left Afghanistan.

Finally, one fact that undermines the predictions of deterrence theory is common to each of the three cases. Soviet observers, with the predictable exception of those Soviet regionalists whose specializations direct them to study a particular area of the globe, did not generate their images of American credibility on the basis of American behavior in the Third World. Instead, Soviets assessed American resolve and capabilities in terms of American military programs, its attitude toward detente with the Soviet Union, and the

---

1. It could be that the United States had the capacity but declined to use it. In this case, the United States was irresolute, but capable.

2. Deterrence theory itself is very ambiguous on this point. While there is agreement that resolve plus capabilities are necessary ingredients for credibility, there is no clear position on whether one can establish credibility by establishing either one's will *or* capability. Nor is there any consensus as to which of these two elements of credibility is more important to demonstrate in order to deter a challenger. In this book, I treat deterrence theory as if it assumes the United States, as the defender, must manifest both the will to deal the Soviet Union defeats and the capacity to effect that will.

3. See, for example, Ponomarev, "Imperializm i Osvobodivshiesya Strany" (Imperialism and Liberated Countries), *AIAS*, January 1980, 5-9, 15. This article was sent to press before the Soviet invasion of Afghanistan.

activities it undertook in Western Europe, Japan, and China to compete with the Soviet Union.[4] U.S. actions in Afghanistan or elsewhere in the periphery were not a factor in Soviet assessments of American credibility in strategic areas of the world.

The data in table 12 show how Soviet views of U.S. credibility after these three victories contradict the predictions of deterrence theory.

### Angola

Table 12 shows that of the fifty-five lessons about U.S. credibility that the Soviets inferred from Angola, only one confirmed deterrence theory's predictions.[5] Instead, Soviets consistently assessed the United States as both capable and willing to intervene in the Third World to advance its interests, even after Washington's failure to prevent the MPLA victory in Angola. Moreover, in the years prior to the repeal of the Clark Amendment, Soviets still saw the United States as highly credible based on their conviction that the United States was still arming UNITA or using the Pretoria government as a proxy for destabilizing the Luanda government. Soviet images of high American credibility after the United States resumed aid to UNITA, while consistent with deterrence theory's predictions, are not convincing evidence for such predictions, since the same images were generated in the absence of any American aid to UNITA.

Soviet lessons from Angola disconfirm deterrence theory. Soviets learned a range of lessons about U.S. credibility, though they all fit into the category of "peripheral interests." They range from the entire Third World, to Africa, to Angola proper. With respect to southern Africa, many interpreted American actions after the MPLA victory as signifying an enhanced commitment to prevent the MPLA from enjoying the fruits of its victory in Angola or to ensure that there would not be any more "Angolas" in Zimbabwe, Namibia, and the RSA. At the level of the Third World in general, many felt that

---

4. From 1975 to 1988, over 90 percent of the inferences drawn by members of the Soviet party leadership, military and foreign policy elite, and Americanists about American credibility were based on American behavior in strategic areas of the globe. The figures for the four cases here follow. From 1975 to 1988, these four groups of Soviet observers inferred 616 lessons about American credibility. In only 51 of these instances, or 8 percent, did they base these lessons on American behavior in Angola. The figures for Ethiopia from 1977 to 1979 are 12 of 191 inferences, or 6 percent; and for Afghanistan, 83 of 485, or 17 percent.

5. Butlitsky wrote in April 1976 that Angola had shown that American presidents were no longer so free to intervene whenever they wanted. Congress constrained their efforts. "Angola— Sryv Proiskov Imperialisticheskoi Reaktsii" (Angola—Thwarting the Intrigues of Imperialist Reaction), *MEIMO*, May 1976, 84–90. It should be noted that two years later Butlitsky credited the United States with restored credibility as a consequence of its actions on the Horn and in Zaire. "Vokrug Zairskovo Piroga" (Around the Zairean Pie), *MEIMO*, September 1978, 116–22.

**TABLE 12.   Soviet Lessons and Deterrence Theory's Predictions**

| Soviet Inferences from Angola, Ethiopia, and Afghanistan (*N*) | |
| --- | --- |
| Confirming | Disconfirming |
| The United States will not defend its strategic interests. | The United States will attack the Soviet Union. (Afghanistan: 7). |
| The United States will not defend its peripheral interests. (Angola: 1). | The United States will attack members of the socialist alliance. |
| The United States will negotiate on third world conflicts. | The United States will resist detente and arms control. |
| The United States will continue detente and arms control. | The United States will not negotiate on third world conflicts. |
| The United States will not attack members of the socialist alliance. | The United States will defend its peripheral interests. (Angola: 54, Ethiopia: 16, Afghanistan: 78). |
| The United States will not attack the Soviet Union. | The United States will defend its strategic interests. |

*Note*: Lessons are listed in order of decreasing strength as evidence.

American actions after Angola evinced a renewed American commitment to resist progressive change throughout the periphery. In addition, the United States was accusing the Soviets of violating the "rules of the game" in Angola in order to justify buying the military hardware necessary to pursue its own interventionist course.

Only eighteen months after the South African withdrawal from Angola, Brezhnev accused imperialism of besieging that country, as the United States took "the very existence of the PRA [People's Republic of Angola] as a threat to the bulwark of racism and neocolonialism [the RSA and Rhodesia]."[6]

As evidence of American resolve to prevent any future Angolas, Brezhnev argued that "now that Africa has shown that it itself can deal with the remnants of colonialism and racism, some, under the banner of helping this process, have begun to try to replace the true liberation of southern Africa with fictitious liberation; essentially to preserve the positions of imperialism in the region and to support the stronghold of racism—the RSA."[7]

---

6. Speech at a dinner for Neto, *Pravda*, September 29, 1977, 1, 2.

7. *Pravda*, October 8, 1976, 2. See also Kremeniuk, "Neokolonializm i Afrika" (Neocolonialism and Africa), *SShA*, July 1976, 97–99; Butlitsky, "Angola"; and Iordansky, "Spasaiut Rasistov: Manevry Amerikanskoi Diplomatii na Iuge Afriki" (They are Saving the Racists: Maneuvers of American Diplomacy in Southern Africa), *KZ*, September 25, 1976, 3.

Brezhnev was referring to the diplomatic efforts undertaken by Kissinger in the summer of 1976 to work out a peaceful transition to majority rule in Zimbabwe and Namibia. Brezhnev feared that the Soviet Union's only possible entree into the region—providing arms to the last remaining liberation fighters—was about to be closed. This fear was picked up again by Brezhnev after the Carter administration embarked on its diplomatic efforts in the region. "The notorious plans of the Western powers aimed at, in their words, the transfer of power in Namibia and Rhodesia to the African majority, in fact does not bring closer, but puts off, the achievement of genuine independence for the peoples of the region. The affair is reduced to preserving the previous essence of the racist regimes behind new facades."[8] At the level of the Third World in general, imperialism simply could not reconcile itself to the existence of any progressive "countries of socialist orientation" in the Third World.[9]

Moreover, Soviet observers did not see Washington as any more credible after the United States lifted the Clark Amendment's prohibitions on American military aid to UNITA. Gromyko, for instance, still spoke only of American "indulgence of the RSA's aggressive policy" toward Angola.[10]

Gorbachev also assessed American credibility as highly before the United States began arming UNITA as after the repeal of the ban on such aid. Over three years prior to the repeal of the Clark Amendment, Gorbachev

---

8. Speech at a dinner for Ethiopian leader Mengistu, *Pravda*, November 18, 1978, 2. See also Aleksandr Kislov, "Nyneshnii Etap Politiki SShA v Afrike" (Present U.S. Policy in Africa), *AIAS*, September 1978, 2–6; Valentin Gorodnov, "Iuzhno-Afrikanskaya Respublika: Uglublenie Krizisa i Obstrenie Borby" (RSA: Deepening of Crisis and Aggravation of Struggle), *MEIMO*, April 1977, 123–28; and Kim, "The Successes of the National Liberation Movement and World Politics," *IA*, February 1979, 85–89.

9. Brezhnev's speech on the sixtieth anniversary of the October Revolution, *Pravda*, November 3, 1977, 3. This is a theme maintained throughout by Brezhnev, namely, that the very existence of progressive regimes and movements is sufficient to evoke American resistance. See, for example, his greetings to a Tashkent meeting of writers of Afro-Asian countries, *Pravda*, October 11, 1978, 1 or his speech during a visit of the Congolese president Denis Sessu-Ngesso, *Pravda*, May 13, 1981, 2. Many other Soviets agreed with this assessment. See, for example, Gromyko, "Radi Mira na Zemle" (For the Sake of Peace on Earth), *Kommunist*, 1982, no. 18, 19–30, his UN General Assembly speech, *Pravda*, September 28, 1984, 4–5, and his speech at a breakfast for Madagascar's President Ratsiraka, *Pravda*, October 1, 1985, 4; Shevardnadze's speech on Lenin's birthday, *Pravda*, April 23, 1986, 1–2; Primakov, "Nekotorye Problemy Razvivaiushchikhsya Stran" (Some Problems of Developing Countries), *Kommunist*, 1978, no. 11, 81–91; Arbatov, "Militarizm i Sovremennoe Obshchestvo" (Militarism and Contemporary Society), *Kommunist*, 1987, no. 2, 104–15; Kremeniuk, "SShA v Regionalnykh Konfliktakh" (The U.S. in Regional Conflicts), *SShA*, June 1986, 23-33; and Kislov, "Novoe Politicheskoe Myshlenie i Regionalnye Konflikty" (New Political Thinking and Regional Conflicts), *MEIMO*, August 1988, 40-47.

10. Speech at a dinner for Benin's president Kerekou, *Pravda*, November 25, 1986, 4.

noted American support for South African attacks on Angola.[11] Even after the August 1985 repeal, Gorbachev still identified "Washington's encouragement for the aggressive policy of the RSA," and not support for UNITA, as evidence of American efforts to prevent "the free and independent development" of third world countries in general.[12] And even when he did explicitly note that the United States had begun to arm UNITA again, he described it only as "a new escalation of this criminal policy," rather than as some significant departure from a previous policy of American weakness.[13]

In sum, virtually unanimous Soviet views of a highly credible United States after the MPLA victory in Angola are not consistent with the assumptions of deterrence theory.

## Ethiopia

Soviet lessons from Ethiopia follow a pattern similar to those from Angola. There are no confirming lessons for deterrence theory, as is evident from table

---

11. At Vietnamese Communist Party Congress, *Pravda*, March 29, 1982, 4. Many other Soviets also commented on American support for UNITA, prior to the resumption of aid to the rebels, as evidence of an America ready and willing to resist revolutionary change in the Third World. See, for representative examples from among numerous such cases, Ustinov, speech at the Eighteenth Party conference of the General Staff, *KZ*, January 7, 1981, 2; Sokolov, "Pobeda, Obrashchennaya v Nastoyashchee i Budushchee" (A Victory Addressed to the Present and the Future), *Pravda*, May 9, 1986, 2; Ogarkov, "Na Strazhe Mirnovo Truda" (In Defense of Peaceful Labor), *Kommunist*, 1981, no. 11, 80–91; Ulyanovsky, "Sovetskaya Sotsialisticheskaya Federatsiya i Osvobodivshiesya Strany" (The Soviet Socialist Federation and Liberated Countries), *NAIA*, 1982, no. 6, 17; Brutents, "Mezhdunarodnaya Napryazhennost i Razvivaiushchiesya Strany" (International Tension and Liberated Countries), *Pravda*, June 22, 1983, 4–5; Dobrynin's speech at an Asian-African People's Solidarity Organization (AAPSO) meeting in Moscow, *Pravda*, May 15, 1986, 4; Kremeniuk, book review of Anatoly Gromyko's "Africa: Problems, Difficulties, and Prospects," *SShA*, October 1981, 99-100; Khazanov, "TsRU Protiv Afriki" (CIA Against Africa), *AIAS*, March 1983, 10–12; Iordansky, "The Policy of Neocolonialism in Action," *IA*, June 1981, 85–90; Simoniya, "The Struggle for Social and National Liberation: A People's Inalienable Right," *IA*, March 1984, 107–14; and Petr Yakovlev, "Ot Dekreta o Mire k Programme Mira" (From the Decree on Peace to the Peace Program), *LA*, December 1982, 40–53.

12. At a dinner for Ethiopian president Mengistu, *Pravda*, November 2, 1985, 3. See also his answers to questions by the editor of *Revolution Africaine*, *Pravda*, April 3, 1986, 1–2.

13. Speech at a dinner for Angolan president Dos Santos, *Pravda*, May 7, 1986, 1. See also his speech at a factory in East Berlin, *Pravda*, April 22, 1986, 1–2. Ulyanovsky also explicitly noted the resumption of American aid to UNITA, but he also described the United States as subverting the MPLA government long before August 1985. See "K Kharakteristike Sovremennovo Neokolonializma" (Toward Characterizing Contemporary Neocolonialism), *NAIA*, 1987, no. 4, 86–92. Kremeniuk's views fit the same pattern. See Kremeniuk, "'Doktrina Reagana'—Kurs na Eskalatsiiu Vmeshatelstva" (The "Reagan Doctrine"—A Course of Escalating Interference), *SShA*, November 1985, 63–67.

12, and the disconfirming lessons cluster in the category of U.S. capabilities and resolve to defend its interests in the Third World. The most limited inference drawn by Soviet observers was that the United States was committed to reinforcing reactionary tendencies in its Somali ally and undermining the Mengistu regime in Ethiopia.[14] Shevardnadze, before the UN General Assembly in September 1986, even cited ongoing American efforts to undermine Mengistu in an "undeclared war" as one of many such wars paid for by the United States in the Third World.[15] Soviets saw American actions on the Horn as also indicative of a wider offensive against the African national liberation movement. Support for Somalia showed that the United States would use "collective colonialism" to advance its interests in Africa.[16]

Some saw American behavior on the Horn in the context of Washington's efforts to bring independence to Zimbabwe, but only under conditions that "preserve the previous essence of the racist regime behind new facades." American policy toward Zimbabawe and the Horn was part of a general American strategy of preventing revolutionary change and undermining progressive regimes in Africa. A clear manifestation of this strategy was American support for the Mobutu government in Zaire during the two Shaba incursions.[17] Most broadly, American behavior on the Horn was adduced as evidence of a renewed American strategy aimed against progressive forces all over the periphery.[18]

---

14. See, for example, Brezhnev's speech at a dinner for Mengistu, *Pravda*, November 18, 1978, 2; Kosygin's speech at a dinner for the general secretary of the Libyan General People's Congress, Major Jelloud, *Pravda*, February 17, 1978, 4; Podgorny's speech at a dinner for Mengistu, *Pravda*, May 5, 1977, 4; and Khazanov, "Problema Mezhgosudarstvennykh Konfliktov v Afrike i Sobytiya na Afrikanskom Roge," (The Problem of Interstate Conflicts in Africa and Events on the African Horn), *AIAS*, July 1978, 21–22.

15. *Pravda*, September 24, 1986, 4. I have seen no evidence that the United States has ever provided any aid to the Eritrean resistance movement, not least of all because the Eritrean People's Liberation Front is widely regarded as an even more orthodox Leninist-Stalinist group than Mengistu's Ethiopian Workers' Party. American allies, however, such as the Sudan, Saudi Arabia, and Egypt have given aid to the EPLF. Kremeniuk also erroneously accused the United States of supporting the Eritrean resistance in "'Doktrina Reagana.'" Kislov made the same charge in "Nyneshnii Etap."

16. Kislov, "Nyneshnii Etap."

17. Brezhnev, *Pravda*, November 18, 1978, 2. See also Gromyko's speech before the Supreme Soviet, *Pravda*, July 7, 1978, 2; Kosygin's speech at a dinner for Algerian president Boumedienne, *Pravda*, January 13, 1978, 4; Kremeniuk, "Washington i Razvivaiushchiesya Strany: Rol Kontseptsii 'Politicheskovo Razvitiya'" (Washington and Developing Countries: The Role of the Concept of "Political Development"), *SShA*, January 1979, 9–21; and Butlitsky, "Vokrug 'Zairskovo Piroga.'"

18. See, for example, Primakov, "Nekotorye Problemy"; Brutents, "Neokolonializm na Poroge 80-x Godov: 'Modernizatsiya' Strategii" (Neocolonialism on the Eve of the 1980s: Modernization of a Strategy), part 2, *MEIMO*, July 1979, 81–94; and Kremeniuk, "Oktyabr, Natsionalno-Osvoboditelnoe Dvizhenie i Politika SShA" (October, the National Liberation Movement and U.S. Policy), *SShA*, November 1977, 52–58.

## Afghanistan

Soviets learned far more serious lessons about U.S. credibility from their experience in Afghanistan. Like the Angola and Ethiopia cases, U.S. credibility for defending its interests in the periphery was strengthened, rather than weakened, by the Soviet gains in Afghanistan. Unlike the two previous cases, however, Soviets inferred that U.S. actions in Afghanistan demonstrated that the United States was also aiming to undermine the security of the Soviet Union itself.

The propositions of deterrence theory are contradicted by Soviet perceptions in this case. Overall, Soviets never inferred that the United States was weak and irresolute from Washington's failure to overthrow the Kabul government with the aid of the mujahideen. Moreover, while the Soviet army was fighting directly against the rebels and Western observers were fearful of an outright Soviet military victory, Soviet observers still saw a highly credible America. But during the Soviet withdrawal from Afghanistan, that is, when many Westerners were speaking of imminent Soviet defeat, some Soviets began to speak of an American leadership that was becoming committed to the pursuit of detente and the resolution of other regional conflicts.

Neither the overall view of high American credibility nor the views generated during the Soviet intervention and withdrawal are consistent with the predictions of deterrence theory. Deterrence theory implies Soviet perceptions of a weak and irresolute America throughout the period. By dividing the case into two periods, one where the Soviet victory appeared to be more secure, the other where it appeared far less certain, the predictive inaccuracy of deterrence theory propositions becomes more stark. The empirical record of Soviet inferences is precisely the reverse of that predicted by the theory in the two periods. Instead, Soviet images are of a highly credible America when the Soviets are winning and of a more conciliatory America when they are less certain of victory.

Deterrence theory is most strongly disconfirmed by Soviet assertions that U.S. actions in Afghanistan are evidence of an American commitment and capacity to undermine Soviet security. Brezhnev, for example, argued that the United States, as part of its policy toward Afghanistan, "is creating a network of military bases in the Indian Ocean, Near and Middle East, and Africa" not for use against forces of national liberation only, but also "against the socialist world."[19] Kislov saw the American reaction to the Soviet intervention as a pretext not only to build up U.S. military forces in the region, but also "as a possible springboard for subversion and espionage against the Soviet Union." Citing an article in the January 29, 1980, *Washington Post*, he commented that

---

19. Supreme Soviet election speech, *Pravda*, February 23, 1980, 1–2. See also Suslov's Supreme Soviet election speech, *Pravda*, February 21, 1980, 2.

the Carter administration regarded "Afghanistan as manna from heaven."[20] In a slightly different vein, Belyaev wrote that the United States was trying to "stoke a 'Moslem bonfire' on the Soviet border."[21]

Soviets also learned from Afghanistan that the United States was willing and able to intervene throughout the Third World to protect its interests. Gromyko was one of the Soviets who expressed the most benign view of American intentions after the introduction of troops into Afghanistan. The United States would only "continue its interference in Afghani internal affairs and its aggression against Afghanistan."[22] Belyaev argued that American aid for the mujahideen was a way to get at the "backdoor to Iran."[23]

A few Soviets saw American aid to the mujahideen as evidence that the United States was "trying to use Moslem fundamentalism to destabilize some progressive Afro-Asian states with Moslem populations."[24] Primakov also noted the reverse side of the strategy: stressing the common interests of conservative Islam and imperialism in opposing the Soviet Union and Communism in the region. [25] More broadly, Soviets interpreted events in Afghanistan as evidence of a far more aggressive American posture in Asia. The "main new element" in this strategy was Washington's "abandonment of the containment of China" and its alliance with China and Japan against the Soviet Union.[26]

---

20. "Blizhnii Vostok i Strategiya SShA" (The Middle East and U.S. Strategy), *SShA*, June 1980, 18.

21. "Kogda Chernoe Vydaetsya Belom" (When Black Is Passed Off as White), *LG*, March 12, 1980, 14. See also his "Islam i Politika" (Islam and Politics), part 2, *LG*, May 20, 1987, 12.

22. Gromyko's speech at a breakfast for Polish foreign minister E. Voitashek, *Pravda*, January 16, 1980, 4. See also Primakov, "Novaya Filosofiya Vneshnei Politiki" (A New Foreign Policy Philosophy), *Pravda*, July 10, 1987, 4; Falin, "Politicheskoe Bezdorozhe" (Political Impasse), *Pravda*, January 20, 1982, 4; Arbatov, "Ne Ot Khoroshei Zhizni" (Not By Choice), *Pravda*, November 21, 1986, 5; Belyaev, "Kogda Chernoe."

23. "Ne Otkryvat 'Vtoroi Front' Vsemirnoi Katastrofy" (Don't Open a "Second Front" for Worldwide Catastrophe), *LG*, March 18, 1987, 14.

24. Primakov, "Volna 'Islamskovo Fundamentalizma': Problemy i Uroki" (The Wave of Islamic Fundamentalism: Problems and Lessons), *VF*, June 1985, 64. See also his "Islam i Protsessy Obshchestvennovo Razvitiya Stran Zarubezhnovo Vostoka" (Islam and Processes of Social Development in Countries of the Foreign East), *VF*, August 1980, 60–71.

25. Primakov, "Kogda Chernoe Vydaetsya Belom" (When Black is Passed Off as White) *LG*, March 12, 1980, 14. See also Gromyko's speech at a dinner with Syrian foreign minister Haddam, *Pravda*, January 28, 1980, 4.

26. Trofimenko, "Aziatskaya Politika Washingtona" (Washington's Asian Policy), *AIAS*, November 1981, 11. See also Gromyko's speech at a breakfast for Bulgarian foreign minister P. Mladen, *Pravda*, January 25, 1980, 4; Ustinov, "Istochnik Velikoi Sily" (A Source of Great Power), *Pravda*, February 22, 1980, 2–3; Ogarkov, "Zavetam Lenina Verny" (True to Lenin's Precepts), *Izvestiya*, February 24, 1980, 2; Trofimenko, "Washington: Kurs na Napryazhennost" (Washington: Course Toward Tension), *SShA*, June 1980, 3–14; Kremeniuk, "Razvivaiushchiesya Strany i SShA: Usilenie Protivoborstva" (Developing Countries and the U.S.: Increasing Antagonism), *SShA*, February 1981, 5–14; Iordansky, "Policy"; and Kim, "Sovetskii Soiuz i

Finally, Soviets inferred from Afghanistan, as they had from Angola and Ethiopia, that the United States had recommitted itself to mounting resistance to progressive change all over the Third World.[27] Soviet observers continued to include Afghanistan in their bill of particulars against the United States in the Third World after Gorbachev came to power, seeing such interference as one facet of the Reaganite policy of "neoglobalism."[28]

After the Soviets had begun to explore seriously the possibility of quitting Afghanistan, Shevardnadze initially saw continued American support for the rebels as evidence that the United States still intended to establish its dominance in that country.[29] With time, however, both Gorbachev and Shevardnadze, albeit with a great deal of skepticism, concluded that the Soviet withdrawal from Afghanistan would result in a greater American commitment to resolve outstanding regional disputes and to redouble its efforts to reach arms control agreements and realize the promise of a deeper detente.

After the Intermediate Nuclear Forces (INF) treaty was signed, for example, Shevardnadze expressed some hope that the United States would forsake its support for the mujahideen, as the "treaty creates a propitious background for solving regional problems."[30] Shortly thereafter, however,

---

Voprosy Mira i Bezopasnosti v Azii" (The Soviet Union and Questions of Peace and Security in Asia), *AIAS*, September 1982, 2–6.

27. For a representative sample of many examples, see Brezhnev's speech at a dinner for Libyan leader Gadhafi, *Pravda*, April 28, 1981, 2; Gromyko, "Leninskaya Vneshnyaya Politika v Sovremennom Mire" (Leninist Foreign Policy in the Contemporary World), *Kommunist*, 1981, no. 1, 13–27; Chernenko's speech awarding Chelyabinsk an Order of Lenin, *Pravda*, May 30, 1980, 2; Kosygin's Supreme Soviet election speech, *Pravda*, February 22, 1980, 1–2; Suslov's speech at the Polish Communist Party Congress, *Pravda*, February 13, 1980, 4; Gorbachev's speech at the Party Congress of the People's Revolutionary Party of Mongolia, *Pravda*, May 27, 1981, 4; Ustinov, "Delu Partii Verny" (True to the Cause of the Party), *Pravda*, February 21, 1981, 2; Sokolov, "Pod Rukovodstvom Partii, Vmeste s Narodom" (Under the Leadership of the Party, Together with the People), *Kommunist*, 1981, no. 4, 21–30; Ogarkov, "Nadezhnyi Oplot Sotsializma i Mira" (Reliable Bastion of Socialism and Peace), *KZ*, February 23, 1983, 1–2; Ulyanovsky, "Sovetskaya Sotsialisticheskaya," *NAIA*, 1982, no. 6, 17; Brutents, "Mezhdunarodnaya Napryazhennost"; Falin, "Imperskaya Spes" (Imperial Arrogance), *Izvestiya*, June 19, 1983, 5; Kremeniuk, "Sovetsko-Amerikanskie Ontosheniya: Nekotorye Problemy Osvobodivshchikhsya Gosudarstv" (Soviet-American Relations: Certain Problems of Liberated States)," *SShA*, June 1982, 7–18; and Simoniya, "The Mighty Tide of National Liberation," *NT*, 1980, no. 50, 22–23.

28. See, from among numerous examples: Shevardnadze's speech on Lenin's birthday, *Pravda*, April 23, 1986, 1–2; Gorbachev's speech on the fortieth anniversary of the end of World War II, *Pravda*, May 9, 1985, 1–3; Primakov, "Breeding Local Conflicts," *NT*, 1986, no. 21, 2, 18, 19; Ulyanovsky, "K Kharakteristike," *NAIA*, 1987, no. 4, 86–92; Dobrynin's speech in Moscow, *Pravda*, May 15, 1986, 4; and Kremeniuk, "'Doktrina Reagana.'"

29. For example, Shevardnadze's interview with Bakhtar correspondent in Kabul, *Pravda*, January 8, 1987, 5.

30. Speech before Supreme Soviet session on ratification of INF treaty, *Pravda*, February 10, 1988, 2. One might discount this expression of optimism by the foreign minister as simply an

Shevardnadze abandoned this mild optimism in the wake of Washington's announcement of continued military aid for the resistance.[31] Shevardnadze subsequently concluded from such American behavior that other regional conflicts would not be resolved, because the United States could not be trusted to fulfill its obligations.[32]

By the autumn of 1988, however, Shevardnadze concluded that the ongoing Soviet withdrawal would impel the United States to make a new commitment to both detente and arms control with the Soviet Union. The Soviet withdrawal was "destroying the mutual 'enemy images'" and "an image of a partner ready for cooperation" was forming.[33]

Gorbachev, however, was less sanguine about the positive influence of Soviet actions in Afghanistan on American foreign policy. He initially expressed an appreciable level of optimism, arguing that

> when the Afghani knot is untied, it will exert the deepest influence on other regional conflicts. A political settlement [there] will be an important breach in the chain of regional conflicts. After the political settlement in Afghanistan, the question already looms: which conflict will be overcome next? And there definitely will be a next one. All regional conflicts could be done away with in several years.[34]

He remained quite optimistic about these prospects into the autumn of 1988.[35] At that time, however, he accused the United States of a "dangerous lack of responsible" behavior with respect to Afghanistan and cited continued American arms supplies to the mujahideen as evidence that "new approaches to international affairs do not come easily to the United States."[36]

---

effort to convince skeptical Soviet deputies of the additional importance of a treaty that required asymmetrical reductions by the Soviets in their nuclear arsenal.

31. In an interview with the Bulgarian newspaper, *Rabotnicheskoe Delo*, *Pravda*, April 1, 1988, 6. Gorbachev expressed very guarded optimism about the salutary effects of the Soviet withdrawal from Afghanistan on American attitudes toward detente and regional conflicts in his speech at the Nineteenth Party Conference, *Pravda*, June 29, 1988, 3–4.

32. At the UN General Assembly special session on disarmament, *Pravda*, June 9, 1988, 4–5.

33. Address before the UN General Assembly, *Pravda*, September 28, 1988, 4. He expressed similar confidence in his speech at UNESCO in Paris, *Pravda*, October 13, 1988, 4.

34. Statement on Afghanistan, *Pravda*, February 9, 1988, 1.

35. See, for example, his speech before the Yugoslavian parliament, *Pravda*, March 17, 1988, 2; and at the Nineteenth Party Conference, *Pravda*, June 29, 1988, 3–4.

36. Speech at a breakfast for general secretary, People's Revolutionary Party of Laos, Phomvihan, *Pravda*, September 28, 1988, 2, and speech at receipt of Indira Gandhi Prize, *Pravda*, November 20, 1988, 2, respectively. For a foreboding of trouble ahead with Washington on regional issues, see his warning at a press conference at the conclusion of the Washington summit, *Pravda*, June 2, 1988, 2–4. For an equally cautious appraisal, see Primakov, "Vzglyad v Proshloe i Budushchee" (A Look into the Past and the Future), *Pravda*, January 8, 1988, 4.

## Credibility: Deterrence Theory Fails a Crucial Test

Despite the fact that Soviet victories came one after the other in Angola, Ethiopia, and Afghanistan and were preceded by the most devastating loss in U.S. history, Vietnam, Soviet observers did not infer lessons of low U.S. credibility. Instead, they continued to see a resolute America, capable of resisting progressive change elsewhere in the Third World. This view of Washington is at variance with the predictions of deterrence theory. More critically, these lessons were generated under the most hospitable circumstances for the theory.

### Soviet Lessons about Regional Dynamics

If the assumptions of deterrence theory are accurate, Soviet observers should have forecast a cascade of revolutionary dominoes after these victories. After the MPLA's victory in Angola, they should have predicted national liberation movement victories in Namibia, Zimbabwe, and South Africa and revolutionary upheavals in countries such as Zaire. After Ethiopia's successful defense against the Somali invasion, Soviets should have perceived greater opportunities for progressive changes in the Sudan and other states in the area. After their intervention in Afghanistan, Soviets should have seen pending revolutionary eruptions in Pakistan and Iran.

Deterrence theory should also predict a strong negative correlation between Soviet optimism about regional dominoes and the level of American involvement in these cases. So, they should have seen a lower probability of revolutionary successes in southern Africa after the United States resumed aid to UNITA, and less opportunity for progressive developments in Southwest Asia after they committed themselves to withdraw from Afghanistan.

The predictions of deterrence theory are largely falsified in the case of Soviet lessons from Angola. With the exception of Suslov, no Soviet learned the kinds of lessons about the regional effects of the Angolan victory that deterrence theory would predict. Those who were initially encouraged about the prospects for revolutionary change in the region abandoned such hopes within eighteen months. Many never saw any revolutionizing influence in the first place, and many more saw nothing but South African and Rhodesian resistance both to future changes in the region and to the changes in Angola and Mozambique that had already occurred.

In addition, there is no correlation between the resumption of American support for UNITA in August 1985 and Soviet perceptions of dynamics in the region. Soviets were unanimous in seeing a credible South African threat to Angola and its regional revolutionary allies years before the American government even contemplated the repeal of the Clark Amendment.

Soviet lessons from its victory on the Horn of Africa neither confirm nor disconfirm predictions of deterrence theory. The few Soviets who drew conclusions about the effects of the Ethiopian victory were split in their evaluations. Soviet views of the regional effects of the victory in Afghanistan are not at all consistent with the predictions of deterrence theory. With the exception of two Soviet observers—Ogarkov and Kremeniuk—no Soviet wrote or spoke about any dynamic other than broad regional opposition from Pakistan to East Africa to China.

One finding common to each of the three cases is that no Soviet ever saw any dominoes falling beyond the Third World. This disconfirms deterrence theory's assumption that a string of dominoes leads from the Third World to strategic areas of the globe. Deterrence theory's predictions about Soviet perceptions about regional dynamics and the actual evidence from the three cases are in table 13.

## Angola

The data in table 13 unfortunately may mislead the reader to believe that deterrence theory's predictions are validated in the case of Angola. But this is not the case, as the Soviet lessons that confirm the theory are short-lived, and either replaced with disconfirming inferences, or simply not repeated. Moreover, a large number (six of thirteen, or over 40 percent) of the expressions of Soviet optimism came before audiences who contextually demanded such rosy assessments.

**TABLE 13.   Soviet Inferences and Deterrence Theory's Assumptions about Regional Dynamics**

| Soviet Lessons (N) | |
| --- | --- |
| Confirming | Disconfirming |
| Dominoes will fall in areas of strategic interest to the United States. | Countries contiguous to Angola, Ethiopia, or Afghanistan will effectively resist any further revolutionary change in the region (Angola: 17, Ethiopia: 4, Afghanistan: 10). |
| Dominoes will fall in other peripheral areas of the globe (Angola: 8, Ethiopia: 3, Afghanistan: 1). | Other third world countries around the globe will balance effectively against any regional revolutionary threats (Afghanistan: 1). |
| Dominoes will fall in countries contiguous to Angola, Ethiopia, or Afghanistan (Angola: 5, Ethiopia: 1, Afghanistan: 2). | U.S. strategic allies will balance effectively against any threats of revolution in their area. |

*Note*: Lessons are listed in order of decreasing strength as evidence.

Soviets who inferred lessons from Angola ranged widely from those who expected dominoes to fall throughout southern Africa to those who perceived only South African and Rhodesian efforts to undermine the revolutionary gains in Angola and Mozambique. The group in between comprised those Soviets who were initially optimistic about revolutionary prospects in the region but soon reversed their opinions. There were no instances of initially pessimistic Soviets adopting a more optimistic view.

Only one Soviet, Suslov, consistently adhered to an image of falling dominoes long after the MPLA victory in 1976. All other Soviets who had been initially encouraged by Angola either stopped inferring optimistic lessons or soon adopted more pessimistic assessments. Suslov did not limit the effects of Angola only to southern Africa, arguing that the MPLA victory "strikingly testifies to the constant growth of revolutionary processes in the world" in general.[37] Several other Soviets who at first saw only falling dominoes in the region after the MPLA victory simply did not infer any more lessons from Angola.[38]

For a great many Soviet observers, including Brezhnev, Angola initially caused increased optimism about the prospects for a Patriotic Front victory in Zimbabwe and a Southwest Africa People's Organization (SWAPO) victory in Namibia and the elimination of apartheid in the RSA.[39] However, Brezhnev's expectations were soon dampened. He recognized that the Pretoria government was fiercely defending itself and its position in Namibia by destabilizing the frontline states of Angola, Mozambique, and Zimbabwe.[40] Perhaps the

---

37. Speech in Bryansk, *Pravda*, September 19, 1979, 2. It is important to note here that this is a context, a speech before a group of industrial workers in the Soviet Union, that definitely does not demand this kind of expression of revolutionary optimism.

38. For example, Podgorny's speech at a dinner with Mozambican president Machel, *Pravda*, March 31, 1977, 4. Two factors undermine the validity of this speech as an indicator of a true belief in dominoes. The first is the context, an audience who definitely requires encouragement that the region where his revolution exists will become more hospitable in the future. The second is the fact that Podgorny disappeared from the Soviet political scene two months after this speech. Hence, he did not get a chance to change his assessment to a more pessimistic one. For initial optimism, then no comment, see also Ulyanovsky, "The Paths and Prospects of National Democracy," *NT*, 1978, no. 14, 19–20. Ulyanovsky did not comment on the effects of Angola again after this spring 1978 article. Mikoyan was also initially encouraged (see "Mezhdunarodnaya Politika Partii" (The Party's International Policy), *LA*, 1976, no. 4, 7–12), but then made no subsequent inferences. See, for example, "Vremya Velikhikh Peremen" (A Time of Great Changes), *LA*, 1978, no. 1, 8.

39. See, for example, his report to the Twenty-fifth Party Congress, *Pravda*, February 25, 1976, 2, speech at dinner for Angolan president Neto, *Pravda*, October 8, 1976, 2, and his message to Angolan president Dos Santos on the PRA's fourth anniversary, *Pravda*, November 11, 1979, 1. One should discount the latter two examples, as the audience demands a positive appraisal of the effects of the MPLA victory.

40. See, for example, his message to the World Conference of Actions against Apartheid in Lagos, *Pravda*, August 22, 1977, 1, and his speeches at dinners for Ethiopian president

turning point came in a Brezhnev speech at a dinner for Angolan president Neto in November 1977, that is, a mere eighteen months after the Organization of African Unity (OAU) recognized the MPLA as the only legitimate government of Angola. Here, for the first time, he spoke only of how the Angolan revolution was secure, not mentioning any revolutionizing effects of this victory on the region.[41]

Several Soviets made no inferences about regional dynamics deriving from the MPLA victory. Kosygin, for example, even in a speech at a dinner for the Angolan prime minister Lopo do Nascimiento, failed to mention any consequences of the progressive gains in Angola.[42]

Another group of Soviets initially saw a very capable and resolute South Africa in a battle with the forces of progressive change in the region, but ultimately spoke only of South African resistance, and no longer of inevitable victory for revolutionary forces. For example, only six months after the MPLA's victory, Gromyko declared that the "rulers of the RSA and Rhodesia are doing everything to restrain the struggle of the peoples of the RSA, Rhodesia, and Namibia." Moreover, American and British diplomatic efforts, "by means of political tricks and financial bribes," were sidetracking the armed struggle in Zimbabwe. He suggested, however, that the forces of liberation are an "irresistible stream."[43] However, five years later, Gromyko commented only on the "aggressive, bandit actions of the RSA against Angola."[44]

Finally, a significant number of Soviet observers saw exclusively balancing dynamics in the region. Gorbachev, for example, consistently spoke of South Africa not only as a barrier on the path to further progressive change in the region, but also as a threat to progressive regimes in the region that had

Mengistu, *Pravda*, November 18, 1978, and October 13, 1982, 2. These audiences, if anything, militate against expressions of pessimism and so are examples of convincing evidence of genuine lack of optimism about the prospects for revolutionary change in southern Africa.

41. *Pravda*, September 29, 1977, 2. Brezhnev made the same omission before audiences who should have demanded a more sweeping assessment. For example, see his speech on the sixtieth anniversary of the November revolution, *Pravda*, November 3, 1977, 3, his message to President Dos Santos on the fifth anniversary of the PRA, *Pravda*, November 11, 1980, 1, and his speech at a dinner for the president of Congo-Brazzaville, Angola's northern neighbor, *Pravda*, May 13, 1981, 2.

42. *Pravda*, May 25, 1976, 4. Another case of a striking omission was Ponomarev's speech to a meeting devoted to the national liberation movement in East Berlin, *Pravda*, October 21, 1980, 4.

43. UN General Assembly address, *Pravda*, September 29, 1976, 4. In subsequent years, Gromyko spoke only of the inevitability of Namibian, not South African, liberation. See his UN General Assembly addresses, *Pravda*, October 2, 1982, 4–5, and *Pravda*, September 28, 1984, 4–5. One should discount these assurances, since the UN was responsible for bringing independence to Namibia.

44. UN General Assembly address, *Pravda*, September 23, 1981, 4–5. See also his speech at dinner for Portuguese president Soares, *Pravda*, November 24, 1987, 4.

already been established in Angola, Mozambique, and Zimbabwe. Indeed, he implied that the MPLA victory in Angola would not be secure until apartheid, which is inevitably "doomed," is eliminated.[45]

In sum, if we consider how long Soviet optimism lasted after the MPLA victory (rarely longer than eighteen months), in what direction Soviet perceptions evolved (from optimism to pessimism, never the reverse), and how often audiences demanded expressions of Soviet encouragement (40 percent of the time), then we can conclude that deterrence theory's predictions about Soviet perceptions of regional dynamics do not receive strong empirical support from the Angola case. Again, it is important to recall that this is a crucially easy test for deterrence theory. Such a test should yield unequivocally validating results. The theory is not confirmed here.

## Ethiopia

Few Soviets made any inferences about Ethiopia at all, but those few who did split in their evaluations. Kosygin saw the gains in Ethiopia as evidence that the national liberation movement's triumph was assured either in Africa or globally. And he made this onetime statement before an audience that does not demand such an assessment. He told the Thai prime minister that events in Ethiopia "convincingly show in which direction the development of events in the world are going."[46] Marshal Ogarkov cited Ethiopia as evidence that "positive processes are continuing in developing countries." While consistent with deterrence theory, this is not very powerful language.[47] Suslov was far more expansive, referring to Ethiopia as a sign of the "constant growth of revolutionary forces in the world."[48]

Other Soviets who considered the consequences of Mengistu's victory in Ethiopia saw nothing but regional actors balancing against this victory. Primakov, for example, identified Egypt as committed to the destabilization of the new revolutionary regime.[49] In sum, Soviet views of the effects of its

---

45. See his speech at dinner for Mozambican president Chissano, *Pravda*, August 4, 1987, 1, and his message to the participants of an anti-apartheid conference, *Pravda*, December 1, 1987, 1. Chernenko also spoke only of balancing dynamics in southern Africa. See his speech at dinner for Ethiopian president Mengistu, *Pravda*, March 30, 1984, 2. See also Shevardnadze's speech in New York on the UN's fortieth anniversary, *Pravda*, October 25, 1985, 4.

46. *Pravda*, March 22, 1979, 4. He later told Mengistu presumably what the latter needed to hear: that his victory in Ethiopia represented an example for the rest of Africa. In Addis Ababa on the fifth anniversary of the Ethiopian revolution, *Pravda*, September 13, 1979, 4.

47. In a speech at a conference of the armed forces political staff, *KZ*, June 5, 1980, 2.

48. In a speech awarding Bryansk an Order of the October Revolution, *Pravda*, September 19, 1979, 2.

49. See, for example, "A Dead-End Middle East Settlement," *IA*, February 1979, 38–46, and "Zakon Neravnomernosti Razvitiya i Istoricheskie Sudby Osvobodivshikhsya Stran" (The Law of Unequal Development and the Historical Fates of Liberated Countries), *MEIMO*, Decem-

victory in Ethiopia on the prospects for revolutionary developments provide neither clear support for nor unequivocal disconfirmation of deterrence theory assumptions.

## Afghanistan

With the exceptions of Marshal Ogarkov and Viktor Kremeniuk, no Soviet inferred any encouraging lessons from the successful Soviet defense of the Kabul regime against the mujahideen.[50] The overwhelming majority of Soviet observers saw regional actors and countries outside the immediate region allying to destabilize the Kabul government.

However, the most important consequence of the successful Soviet effort to preserve the PDPA government in Kabul was this action's complete negation of whatever progressive regional dynamics Soviets thought would be provoked by the overthrow of the shah in Iran.[51] The overwhelming majority of Soviet observers quickly noted that the dynamics in the "arc of crisis" from Pakistan to the Horn of Africa were marked by the efforts of these states to resist this Soviet victory.

One consequence of the Soviet victory in Afghanistan was an exacerbation of relations with Iran itself, where "lies about the unfriendly intentions of the Soviet Union with respect to Iran are being circulated and [where] they apparently enjoy some demand."[52] This victory has also led to Pakistan "assuming the role of a direct accomplice in this imperialist adventure" against Afghanistan. In general, Islamic countries in the world are not "promoting a reduction of tensions in the region" around Afghanistan.[53] Belyaev singled

---

ber 1980, 28–47. Kislov added the Sudan and Saudi Arabia to his list of regional balancers against Ethiopia in "Blizhne-Vostochnaya Politika SShA: Starye Tseli, Podnovlennye Metody" (U.S. Middle East Policy: Old Goals, Renovated Methods), *AIAS*, June 1978, 11–14. Khazanov identified Egypt, Saudi Arabia, and Iran as states that were involved in undermining the revolution in Ethiopia in "Problema Mezhgosudarstvennykh."

50. Ogarkov's speech to a meeting of political officers in the Soviet armed forces command, *KZ*, June 5, 1980, 2. Kremeniuk "SShA-Afganistan: Proiski Prodolzhaiutsya" (U.S.-Afghanistan: The Intrigues Continue), *SShA*, January 1983, 56–59.

51. For a discussion of the regional dynamics set off by the Soviet gain in Iran in 1979, see chap. 5.

52. Gromyko's speech at breakfast for Bulgarian foreign minister, *Pravda*, January 25, 1980, 4. See also Belyaev, "Islam i Politika" (Islam and Politics), *LG*, January 16, 1980, 14.

53. Gromyko's speech at a breakfast for Indian foreign minister Rao, *Pravda*, June 4, 1980, 4. On the balancing effects in the Islamic world, in particular in Egypt and Iran, caused by events in Afghanistan, see also Primakov, "Kogda Chernoe," "Blizhnii Vostok: Dalneishaya Militarizatsiya Politiki SShA" (The Middle East: The Further Militarization of U.S. Policy), *Kommunist*, 1980, no. 9, 105–15, and "Strany Vostoka v Sovremennom Mire" (Countries of the East in the Contemporary World), *Pravda*, August 11, 1982, 4–5. On Pakistan, see, for example, Simoniya, "The Struggle"; and Zorina, "Razvivaiushchiesya Strany v Politicheskoi Strukture

out Saudi Arabia and the United Arab Emirates (UAE) in particular, as during his visit to the Gulf, when he raised the question of why these countries had no diplomatic relations with the Soviet Union, the Saudi foreign minister and the UAE information minister "began to speak of Afghanistan."[54]

Kim saw balancing dynamics going beyond either Afghanistan's neighbors or members of the Islamic Conference. He noted how even members of the Association of Southeast Asian Nations (ASEAN) are "being pushed toward militarization and the conversion of the association into a military-political bloc" by the deft American use of the Soviet victory in Afghanistan.[55] Perhaps Simoniya saw the most far-reaching balancing efforts of any Soviet, remarking on how even the last meeting of the Non-Aligned Movement had been the scene of "negative tendencies" with respect to events in Afghanistan.[56]

In sum, the vast preponderance of Soviet observers did not see dominoes set off by the successful defense of the Kabul regime. Instead, in this crucially easy case for deterrence theory, Soviets learned that their victories set off balancing dynamics in the region and around the Islamic countries and the Third World, in general.

## Deterrence Theory Predictions:
## Failing Another Crucial Test

As in the case of Vietnam, deterrence theory fares much better in the area of regional dynamics than in the area of U.S. credibility. But Soviet predictions about the revolutionizing effects of Angola, Ethiopia, and Afghanistan do not give deterrence theory a passing grade in a crucially easy test. After Angola, initial Soviet optimism about the MPLA victory's influence on events in southern Africa quickly gave way to a recognition of South African staying power. Soviets were split on the consequences of Ethiopia's successful Ogadeni war with Somalia. A theory being tested under easy conditions requires more than a split decision for confirmation. Finally, lessons from Afghanistan were not only mostly pessimistic, but Soviet observers identified balancing behavior by states far removed from Afghanistan's borders, among states in the Middle East and members of the Islamic Conference, and around

Sovremennovo Mira" (Developing Countries in the Political Structure of the Contemporary World), *MEIMO*, August 1982, 80–91.

54. Belyaev, "Viza v Emiraty" (A Visa to the Emirates), *LG*, June 19, 1985, 14.

55. Kim, "Osvobodivshiesya Strany na Rubezhe 70-x i 80-x Godov: Faktory Stabilizatsii i Destabilizatsii" (Liberated Countries on the Eve of the 1980s: Stabilizing and Destabilizing Factors), *AIAS*, June 1980, 4.

56. Simoniya, "Dvizhenie Neprisoedineniya na Novom Etape" (The Non-Aligned Movement at a New Stage), *AIAS*, March 1980, 6–8, 21.

the Third World in general. These three cases provide a friendly environment for deterrence theory predictions. Despite these easy circumstances, the empirical record is not supportive of the theory.

## Explaining Soviet Lessons from Angola, Ethiopia, and Afghanistan

Demonstrating that deterrence theory fails in these three cases is only the first, though of course very important, step in testing the general validity of the theory's assumptions. By failing in a crucial case, the general validity of deterrence theory is put into question. Nevertheless, we can go one step farther by analyzing not just what lessons Soviets learned, but *how* they arrived at them. If these disconfirming lessons are derived through universal or general information-processing procedures, we can be highly confident that the theory's overall validity has been discredited. (See table 14.) If, however, such contrary evidence is the product of belief systems peculiar to Soviets, then the general validity of the theory is not undermined. The latter findings are still applicable, however, to the category of belief systems of which Soviet Marxism-Leninism is only one example. Similarly, we should regard universal or general *confirming* evidence as far more powerful support for deterrence theory than lessons produced by belief systems.

If deterrence theory assumptions were strongly validated, all Soviet lessons would appear in the upper left quadrant of table 14. Instead, this is the only quadrant that remains empty; and this is a crucially *easy* set of cases for the theory. Moreover, the general confirmation of the theory's assumptions about falling dominoes is very conditional, since these lessons were, one, short-lived, and, two, replaced by the disconfirming lessons in the lower left quadrant, which are of universal validity. Furthermore, Soviet lessons of dominoes falling throughout the Third World were the product of peculiar belief systems, severely bounding the general applicability of that confirmatory finding. On the other hand, Soviet images of high U.S. credibility are the

**TABLE 14.  The Power of Different Explanations for Soviet Lessons**

|  | Types of Explanations | | |
| --- | --- | --- | --- |
|  | Universal | General | Peculiar |
| Lessons confirming deterrence theory |  | Dominoes in south-ern Africa | Global and regional dominoes |
| Lessons disconfirming deterrence theory | High overall U.S. credibility<br>Regional balancing | High overall U.S. credibility | High overall U.S. credibility |

product of both universal and general rationality, a very powerful disconfirmation of the theory.

## Universal Explanations for Soviet Lessons from Angola, Ethiopia, and Afghanistan

Universal explanations come in three varieties. The first is the discovery that the empirical record overwhelmingly confirms one assumption over its equally logical competitor. For example, while deterrence theory assumes that U.S. interests in strategic areas of the globe are tightly interconnected to its interests in the Third World, by dint of reputation, it is at least as logical to assume that only similar interests are so interconnected. If we find, for example, that the vast preponderance of empirical evidence supports one of these propositions at the expense of the other, then we should conclude that the unsupported proposition should be replaced by its empirically validated competitor.

The second variety of universal explanations is Soviet lessons that are the product of a rational attribution process. For example, if Soviets conclude from Angola that revolutionary victories are inevitable elsewhere in southern Africa because the political and military conditions in, say, Zimbabwe, are similar to those in Angola, then deterrence theory's proposition about a victor's perceptions of regional dynamics receives general validation.

The third variety comprises Soviet lessons that are simple empirical conclusions. These are lessons that are not the product of any kinds of cognitive shortcuts or decision-making heuristics. Information search should not be directed obviously by any kinds of representativeness, vividness, or availability criteria. Instead, all relevant evidence should appear to be treated with equal attention and care by the observer.

In the three cases being considered in this chapter, we have instances of each of these varieties of universal explanations. Deterrence theory illogically assumes that strategic and peripheral interests are interconnected and illogically ignores nonmilitary deterrent assets. These inaccurate assumptions cause an underestimation of U.S. credibility by deterrence theorists and practitioners. Moreover, Soviet images of high U.S. credibility are generated through rational attribution processes and Soviet lessons about regional balancing are simple empirical conclusions.

### *Soviet Images of High U.S. Credibility in Strategic Areas of the Globe*

As noted above, deterrence theory assumes that U.S. losses in the periphery will result in Soviet inferences of reduced U.S. credibility to defend its interests in strategic areas. As the evidence from Vietnam showed, this is not the case. The evidence here reinforces that finding. Despite American losses in Angola, Ethiopia, and Afghanistan, Soviets never concluded from these events that the United States was any less willing or able to defend its interests in Europe, Northeast Asia, or the Persian Gulf. This is an example of where the vast preponderance of empirical evidence requires the replacement of one logical assumption with its competitor. There simply is no credibility continuum that acts as a connector between the periphery and central strategic areas of the globe.

### Soviet Images of High U.S. Credibility in Peripheral Areas of the Globe

Soviets continued to see the United States as both resolute and capable in the Third World, despite American losses, because they recognized the effectiveness of Washington's nonmilitary assets and because they assessed the state of U.S. credibility as rational attribution theorists.

As I suggested in chapter 1, deterrence theory wrongly assumes that only military defeats can impart lessons about credibility. In the aftermath of Angola, it was U.S. *diplomatic* efforts in southern Africa that convinced many Soviets that the United States would be able to prevent additional revolutionary victories in Zimbabwe, Namibia, and South Africa.[57]

As I showed in chapter 2 on the effects of the Vietnam War, rational Soviet observers who had initially considered greater American restraint in the periphery a possible outcome of the U.S. loss in Southeast Asia, raised doubts about their own predictions very soon after the fall of Saigon. They did so on the basis of changed perceptions of a number of causes of American foreign policy. American behavior in Angola and the effects of this victory on American domestic politics were major factors in this Soviet reevaluation. I use Arbatov as a general example of this process.

Arbatov had interpreted the U.S. loss in Vietnam as a function of successful public and congressional pressure against a ruling elite who would have preferred to have continued the war but was domestically constrained. The American people and its elected representatives no longer would countenance the diversion of economic resources from pressing domestic needs. The Nixon and Ford administrations had to submit to these imperatives.[58] The U.S. loss in Angola, while partly caused by the forces that caused the loss in Vietnam, ironically evoked domestic forces that reversed this temporary American renunciation of adventurism in the Third World. Moreover, the events in Angola caused Arbatov to consider an additional cause for American behavior abroad: Soviet foreign policy in the Third World.

---

57. See the sources listed in notes 7 and 8 above.
58. For Arbatov's lessons from Vietnam, see chap. 2.

Soon after the Soviet victory in Angola, Arbatov assessed the variables he considered critical for predicting American foreign policy, and found that the American public and congress were turning against detente and were supporting a harder American line in the Third World. Moreover, the economy had recovered from its doldrums in the early 1970s; this would permit a less painful trade-off between military and social spending. While Arbatov by the mid-1980s identified a reversal in public and congressional attitudes in the area of arms control and detente with the Soviet Union, he did not identify the same softening of domestic support for adventurism in the Third World.

In late 1976 Arbatov remarked on how that year's presidential campaign had showed the power of right-wing forces that opposed detente with the Soviet Union.[59] Arbatov's articles in the rest of the 1970s documented the erosion of American public and congressional support for detente.[60] He described an ongoing struggle for the minds of those people in the United States who support detente. They are opposed by "the military-industrial complex, the present leadership of the AFL-CIO, the leadership of the Zionist wing of the American Jewish community, emigre organizations from Eastern European countries, and the extreme right wing of the Republican Party."[61]

Arbatov also saw tougher days ahead for detente as a consequence of the disappearance of three situational factors that had constrained the ruling elite earlier in the 1970s. The "sociopolitical crisis," caused by the Vietnam War and the civil rights movement, the "constitutional-political crisis," caused by Watergate, and the "economic crisis," caused by the Nixon shocks and the 1973 oil embargo, had all passed, and a "certain stabilization in the country has occurred that could not but exert significant influence on American foreign policy. In the United States they have begun to speak anew of a global role, and of new opportunities for a more active and expansionist policy." Moreover, the "resistance to growing military spending has become somewhat weaker."[62] As if he were following a textbook on first-wave attribution theory, Arbatov wrote that "many in the United States saw detente as something forced on them by the extraordinary conditions created by these shocks, and so, as something temporary. Some in the United States call this the period

---

59. Arbatov, "Sovetsko-Amerikanskie Otnosheniya Sevodnya" (Soviet-American Relations Today), *Pravda*, December 11, 1976, 4–5.

60. See, for example, Arbatov, "Bolshaya Lozh Protivnikov Razryadki" (The Big Lie of Detente's Opponents), *Pravda*, February 5, 1977, 4–5.

61. Arbatov, "S Pozitsii Realizma: Zametki ob Odnoi Amerikanskoi Knige" (From a Position of Realism: Notes on One American Book), *Izvestiya*, March 13, 1977, 4.

62. Arbatov, "Razvitie Sotsialnykh i Politicheskikh Protsessov v SShA na Sovremennom Etape" (The Development of Social and Political Processes in the U.S. at the Present Stage), *Vestnik, AN, SSSR*, 1978, no. 2, 29–41. This was a speech delivered to the Presidium of the Academy of Sciences on May 26, 1977.

of 'restoration.'"[63] In other words, American *dispositions* to behave aggressively in the world had never changed; they had merely been constrained by "extraordinary" and temporary *situational* conditions.

While Arbatov's views on American credibility in the Third World remained unchanged, he did perceive a shift in American attitudes toward detente and arms control. Both views can be explained by his assessment of the same causal variables. Arbatov became convinced in the late 1980s that the American people favored an end to the expensive Reagan defense buildup. He argued that conciliatory Soviet policies could reinforce this domestic political trend in the United States.[64] He lamented the fact that the Soviets had wrongly "borrowed a number of alien approaches to 'nuclear deterrence' and nuclear war." This only helped the West kill detente.[65] Soviet conventional superiority had made Western peoples feel needlessly insecure.[66]

Arbatov identified yet another new cause of American attitudes toward detente and arms control: Soviet *domestic* policy. He argued that "under the influence of perestroika, the soil has been shaken under the entire structure of international relations based on cold war principles. The building whose foundation was the belief in an image of the Soviet Union as a terrible enemy." But the Moscow summit showed the world a "completely different Soviet Union: a dynamic, prosperous society averse to messianic self-satisfaction and occupied with deep domestic reforms." In fact, the "hope that perestroika will fail" is the "last refuge of proponents of the cold war." He concluded that "perestroika is a guarantee for peace and survival."[67]

Finally, Arbatov identified American economic problems as another cause for believing that the American public would press its government to give up on the arms race. Arbatov argued, for example, that "super-patriotic feelings" are effective "only under normal economic conditions, but when the middle class becomes convinced that it has to pay" higher taxes for increasing military budgets, "the situation can substantially change."[68] The Reagan administration's strategy of accelerating the arms race so that the "Soviet Union will capitulate due to its economic problems" is no longer supported by

---

63. Arbatov, "Sovetsko-Amerikanskie Otnosheniya Sevodnya" (Soviet-American Relations Today), *Pravda*, August 3, 1977, 4–5.

64. Arbatov, "Tma Pered Rassvetom?" (The Darkness Before the Dawn?), *Pravda*, September 10, 1987, 4.

65. Arbatov, "Pered Vyborom" (Before a Choice), *Kommunist*, 1988, no. 5, 118.

66. Arbatov, "Prodvizhenie k Realizmu" (Advancement Toward Realism), *Pravda*, June 10, 1988, 6. For Soviet "excesses" in both the nuclear and conventional realm, see his interview in *KZ*, December 31, 1988, 5.

67. Arbatov, "Prodvizhenie."

68. Arbatov, "Ekonomicheskoe i Politicheskoe Polozhenie i Vybory 1984 Goda v SShA" (The Economic and Political Situation in the U.S. and the 1984 Elections), *Vestnik, AN, SSSR*, May 1985, 74.

"informed Americans. If only because they see how attempts to economically bleed us with the assistance of the arms race can lead to the bankruptcy of the United States itself."[69] The United States "has become the biggest debtor in the world" and it has the biggest trade deficit. These problems are "caused by excessive military expenditures." Even in the areas of traditional American superiority, "high-technology products, computers, communication equipment, and aerospace," the United States has lost its edge due to the "militarization of its scientific-technological" capacities.[70]

Arbatov importantly argued that these popular concerns were affecting the attitudes of the American ruling elite.

> The interests of the greater part of the ruling class are not advanced by the arms race. It enriches only an insignificant, narrow grouping of monopoly capital; the overwhelming majority of corporations either get only crumbs from military profits or are not involved at all in the "military economy." At the same time, the negative consequences of the arms race—the growth of inflation and budget deficits, increased unemployment, sluggish economic growth, and an aggravation of social contradictions—are felt by the entire ruling class and society.
>
> Can capitalism renounce militarism? I think one must not hurry with a negative answer. Let's recall that 50 years ago the collapse of colonial empires also seemed highly improbable. Excessive economic costs and the threat of unimaginable bloodshed that is inseparable from military preparations unites the very widest political and social forces in a struggle against militarism.[71]

Arbatov brought all the strands of his analysis together after the Reagan visit to Moscow in June 1988. He noted that "changes have begun in the United States under the influence of economic difficulties at home and the changes in the Soviet Union tied to glasnost and perestroika." These changes in the Soviet Union "are being examined very closely. And notions of the public about priorities are changing—domestic problems are being advanced to the front burner, not the accumulation of military power."[72] By early 1988, Arbatov was able to cite concrete examples that confirmed his theory about

---

69. Arbatov, "Kto Komu Bolshe Nuzhen?" (Who Needs Whom More?), *Pravda*, September 13, 1986, 4.

70. Arbatov, "Ne Ot Khoroshei Zhizni."

71. Arbatov, "Militarizm i Sovremennoe," 107. He argued that the "military-industrial complex is not omnipotent" also in "Perestroika Shatters Stereotypes," *NT*, 1987, no. 47, 3. See also "SSSR-SShA: Potentsial Torgovli" (USSR-U.S.: Trade Potential), *Izvestiya*, April 10, 1988, 5.

72. Arbatov, "Prodvizhenie."

the relationship between American economic problems and reduced defense spending. He argued that "the erosion of support for high military spending caused by the budget deficit severely limits freedom of action in the military area," citing congressional reductions of spending on "many military programs" requested by the administration.[73]

In sum, Arbatov had a causal theory about American foreign policy. He inferred from Vietnam that perhaps public and congressional concern for American economic problems might override the ruling elite's desire to behave aggressively in the Third World. These hopes were shattered by Angola. Public and congressional opposition to adventurism proved transient, largely as a consequence of a new causal variable: Soviet foreign policy. The latter provoked a sea change in American domestic politics. Only some ten years later, and only on the issues of detente and arms control, would Arbatov see the American people and Congress, again concerned about the economic costs of military spending, as conciliatory forces. Moreover, Arbatov added Soviet foreign policy concessions and domestic liberalization as two more necessary causes of American foreign policy moderation.

## Soviet Images of Regional Balancing

Many Soviets explicitly cited discrete acts by regional actors aimed at blunting, or even reversing, the victories just achieved by local Soviet allies. For example, in the case of Angola, Brezhnev commented on the RSA's continual armed incursions and bombing raids against Angola, Mozambique, and Zimbabwe; its continued prosecution of a counterinsurgency campaign against SWAPO in Namibia; and its ongoing repression of the African National Congress (ANC) at home in South Africa.[74] On the Horn, Soviets wrote of the military, logistical, and financial power being arrayed against the Ethiopian revolution by Egypt, Saudi Arabia, the Sudan, and Iran, not to mention Somalia.[75]

In the case of Afghanistan, Gromyko and Belyaev, for example, analyzed the effects of Soviet actions on the domestic political climate in Iran.

---

73. Arbatov, "Pered Vyborom," 114.

74. See, for example, his message to the World Conference of Actions against Apartheid, meeting in Lagos, Nigeria, *Pravda*, August 22, 1977, 1, and his speeches at dinners for Ethiopian president Mengistu, *Pravda*, November 18, 1978, and October 13, 1982, 2. Other examples include Kim, "Sovetskii Soiuz i Natsionalno-Osvoboditelnoe Dvizhenie" (The Soviet Union and the National Liberation Movement), *MEIMO*, September 1982, 19–33; Iordansky, "Iuzhnaya Afrika: Potvorstvuiut Rasistam" (Southern Africa: They are Pandering to Racists), *Pravda*, January 31, 1979, 4; and Gromyko's speech at a dinner for Portuguese president Soares, *Pravda*, November 24, 1987, 4.

75. See citations in note 49.

They concluded that the events in Afghanistan had shifted Iran to an anti-Soviet position.[76] Gromyko interpreted the deliberations at the first meeting of the Islamic Conference after the invasion that the entire community of states with Moslem populations was shifting against the Soviet Union.[77] Belyaev cited his personal conversations with officials and scholars in Saudi Arabia and the UAE in support of his argument that Afghanistan was the main obstacle to better Soviet relations with gulf states.[78] Finally, Primakov identified the Sadat government's agreement to hold joint air force training exercises with the United States as demonstrating Egyptian opposition to Soviet actions in Afghanistan.[79]

*Universal Disconfirmation of Deterrence Theory*
Soviet lessons from their three victories in Angola, Ethiopia, and Afghanistan are prima facie disconfirmation of deterrence theory assumptions about Soviet perceptions of U.S. credibility and regional dynamics. The fact that these lessons are the products of rational information processing common to the universe of decision makers implies that the theory's assumptions about *all* challengers' perceptions of *any* defender's credibility and regional dynamics are invalid.

## General Explanations for Soviet Lessons from Angola, Ethiopia, and Afghanistan

Numerous Soviets inferred lessons from these three victories that can be explained by psychological models with general validity. These individuals, including Gorbachev, generated their lessons by analyzing a limited set of crucial values, consistent with the model of bounded rationality. They relied on this set of factors to predict future U.S. behavior and the prospects for revolutionary progress in the periphery. Just how *general* these general explanations are depends on *how* Soviets select their critical sets of variables. If they are the product of common decision-making heuristics, then this is evidence of a more general explanation than if these variables are selected on the basis of some underlying belief system. In the latter event, the explanations slide toward the category of "peculiar explanations" and so lose their more general validity as a test for deterrence theory.

---

76. Gromyko's speech at a breakfast for the Bulgarian foreign minister, *Pravda*, January 25, 1980, 4. Belyaev, "Islam i Politika."
77. His speech at a breakfast for the Indian foreign minister, *Pravda*, June 4, 1980, 4.
78. Belyaev, "Viza v Emiraty."
79. "Kogda Chernoe."

*Soviet Images of High U.S. Credibility in*
*Strategic Areas of the Globe*

As was the case after Vietnam, Soviet attention to absolute U.S. military capabilities ensured continuous Soviet assessments of a very powerful and resolute United States, committed to defending its interests in Europe, Northeast Asia, and the Middle East.

*Soviet Images of High U.S. Credibility in*
*Peripheral Areas of the Globe*

Gorbachev is the most important example of those Soviets who determined that U.S. credibility was high and did so with only a few critical variables. Gorbachev's list of causes of American foreign policy were divided into two parts: those which were arrived at through rational attribution processes, and those which were provided by adherence to an orthodox Marxist-Leninist belief system. Below I describe and analyze in detail Gorbachev's analysis of American foreign policy. There are obvious reasons for doing so. Gorbachev's fundamental reorientation of Soviet foreign policy largely rested on his ideas about the United States. It is important that we understand how Gorbachev understood American domestic politics and foreign policy. Gorbachev also provides a very rich exemplar of a more general class of Soviet observers who lie between universal rationality and peculiar beliefs.

Unlike previous general secretaries, such as Brezhnev, Gorbachev recognized the role of public opinion in the formulation of American foreign policy.[80] This permitted him to have confidence that Soviet behavior, operating through the American public and its representatives, could "cause" American foreign policy. Also unlike Brezhnev and his foreign policy elite, Gorbachev denied the existence of any world revolutionary alliance. This nonideological view of the Third World allowed him to design a moderate Soviet foreign policy that could reassure the American public about Soviet intentions.

Gorbachev's pattern of perceptions of American behavior in the Third World is consistent with the "naive scientist" using a crude model of Mills's method of difference that is posited by classical attribution theory. Gorbachev identified a number of causes for American behavior in the Third World based on both his prior beliefs about the nature of imperialism and his observations of American conduct abroad and domestic politics in the United States itself. He then developed various antidotes or responses to these causes that were designed to dampen American propensities for future adventurism in the

---

80. See chap. 2 for a short description of the Leninist belief system's assumptions about American foreign policy. A more detailed analysis follows in the section below on explanations for Soviet lessons.

periphery. He identified causes based on various sources of evidence and then developed a strategy to influence these causes. This empirical testing places Gorbachev in the universal-rational category. However, his continued use of Marxism-Leninism to select some of his critical variables implies a peculiar belief system as well.

Gorbachev's beliefs about the causes of American foreign policy provided him with a foundation on which to develop an effective Soviet response. He saw a number of factors driving American aggressiveness in the Third World. First and foremost, he believed that exploitation of the Third World provides substantial rewards for the American economy.[81] In addition, the military-industrial complex in the United States deliberately provokes tensions in the Third World in order to justify ever-rising defense budgets and directly finances that budget through the economic extortion of the periphery.[82] The American elite pursues a strategy of "social imperialism," heating up tensions abroad in order to divert the attention of the American public from its domestic problems.[83] Cold war stereotypes plague the American ruling elite, so it sees opposition to progressive regimes in the Third World as a form of struggle against Communism and the Soviet Union. Finally, the American elite's adherence to a strategy of deterrence compels it to demonstrate its resolve and capabilities by using force in various regions of the Third World.[84] The only brake on American elite propensities to use force is the opposition of the American people.

Gorbachev's commitment to changing and reinforcing the pressure of public opinion on Western governments, especially the United States, was reflected in his ever-broadening conception of the participants in the peace movement. He rejected the idea of Communist parties and the working class as vanguards in the struggle for peace before audiences who would rightly expect the opposite point of view. For example, when addressing a Portuguese Communist Party congress, he did not even mention Communists as part of the "tens of millions of honorable people who are coming out against the arms race."[85] The fact that Gorbachev saw Western governments directing a good

81. For one among numerous examples, see his speech at the Dnepropetrovsk metallurgical plant, *Pravda*, June 27, 1985, 1–2.

82. See, for example, his speech at a Central Committee Plenum, *Pravda*, October 16, 1985, 1–2.

83. Address to the Fifth Congress of the Vietnamese Communist Party, *Pravda*, March 29, 1982, 4.

84. For example, in a speech at a dinner for Britain's prime minister Thatcher, *Pravda*, March 31, 1987, 2.

85. *Pravda*, December 17, 1983, 4. Similarly, he expressed disappointment with the less than "harmonious" relationship of Communists to other members of the peace movement in a speech to the Italian Communist Party general secretary, *Pravda*, January 29, 1986, 2. For two other examples of Gorbachev telling an orthodox audience what they probably did not expect to

deal of their energies to deceiving public opinion is more proof that he believed that their own people are the weak link in imperialist foreign policy. For example, in his TV address to the Soviet people after the Reykjavik summit, he explained to his listeners that

> the forces resisting . . . disarmament . . . with all their might . . . aspire to lead people astray. They are trying to take under their control the feelings of wide circles of the world public, to extinguish their impulse toward peace and prevent governments from taking a clear position at this decisive historical moment. At the disposal of these circles are political power, economic levers, and powerful media outlets. I said in Reykjavik that we hope that the president will consult with Congress and the American people. Some thing completely different occurred. They distorted the whole picture of the talks in Reykjavik. They concealed the facts of Reykjavik from the American people. So much is said about the openness of American society, its freedom of information, about the pluralism of opinions, and one can hear and see whatever he wants.

He then argued that the American government, through the services of the United States Customs Service, was deliberately preventing the importation of the Novosti English translation of his press conference in Reykjavik. He declared:

> Here's the right to hear any point of view for you! It looks like the United States is becoming an increasingly closed society; they are cleverly and effectively isolating their own people from objective information. This is a dangerous process. *The American people must know the truth about what is happening in the Soviet Union and the true content of Soviet foreign policy.* I would say that this is acquiring extraordinary significance.[86]

---

hear, see his speech in Prague to the Czech-Soviet Friendship Society, *Pravda*, April 11, 1987, 1–2, and at a meeting with the leadership of the World Federation of Free Trade Unions, *Pravda*, October 10, 1987, 1. The only exception to this expansive view of Western public opinion is illustrative of the demands that a particular audience can place on a Soviet speaker. This was a speech before the East German leader, Erich Honecker, at a dedication of a monument to the German Communist, Ernst Thalmann. In that address Gorbachev said that "the working class, even to this day, occupies a special place" in the antiwar movement. This deviation can be explained by the fact that Honecker was one of the most orthodox leaders in Eastern Europe at the time, and Ernst Thalmann was the man who oversaw the destruction of the German Communist Party under Hitler—a consequence of its slavish devotion to the Stalinist line of nonalignment with "social fascists" in the Social Democratic Party. *Pravda*, October 4, 1986, 1.

86. Emphasis in the reproduced text in *Pravda*, October 23, 1986, 1–2. For two, among many, examples of Gorbachev arguing that the American ruling elite prevents its people from

Gorbachev only slowly and haltingly came to realize explicitly that concrete Soviet foreign policy actions had a significant effect on Western, including American, publics. Soviet foreign policy might empower the American people to resist its government's predisposition of hostility toward the Soviet Union. Earlier, and more often, he had argued that Soviet *domestic* reforms had this desirable consequence. Before a meeting of Soviet trade union officials, Gorbachev admitted that "today we well know and understand that the massive attack—economic, political, psychological, and militaristic—begun by reactionary forces at the end of the 1970s and beginning of the 1980s, was, along with other reasons, dictated by the state of our internal affairs."[87] Gorbachev later argued that "anti-Soviet forces are clearly worried about the interest of people and political circles in the West in what is happening now in the Soviet Union," worried that it will "erase the artificially created enemy image, an image that they have exploited for decades."[88]

Gorbachev first obliquely acknowledged the link between Soviet external behavior and American foreign policy in July 1987: "Conservative forces do not apprehend and reject new thinking. All kinds of dogmatists and skeptics have ended up in alliance with them. Words alone are not destined to overcome this view of foreign policy. The problems and barriers there are colossal."[89]

Gorbachev elaborated on this linkage in a speech in Murmansk in October of the same year.

---

learning the truth about Soviet foreign policy, see his report to the Twenty-seventh Party Congress, *Pravda*, February 26, 1986, 2–3, 7–9, and his speech to the Polish parliament, *Pravda*, July 12, 1988, 2. To demonstrate the crucial differences between those with Brezhnevite belief systems and someone like Gorbachev, it is very illuminating to remark on a selection from Ustinov. Whereas Gorbachev believed Soviet foreign policy suffered from presenting too aggressive a face to the American people, Ustinov argued that the American government was trying to conceal *coercive* Soviet behavior from the American people, namely, the redeployment of Soviet SSBNs along American shores after the first Pershing-IIs and Ground-Launched Cruise Missiles (GLCMs) reached Europe. Here is an excellent example of how different views of politics in the United States lead to completely different Soviet policy prescriptions. For Ustinov, see his answers to a TASS correspondent, *Pravda*, May 21, 1984, 4.

87. *Pravda*, February 26, 1987, 1–2. The high level of ideological orthodoxy of this audience gives added power to this admission by Gorbachev.

88. Speech in Murmansk, *Pravda*, October 2, 1987, 2–3. In a speech to the Australian prime minister Robert Hawke, Gorbachev argued that the erosion of the enemy image held by the American people made the INF treaty possible, *Pravda*, December 2, 1987, 2. See also his speech before Soviet leaders of media, ideological institutions, and creative unions, *Pravda*, May 11, 1988 p. 1; his address at the Nineteenth Party Conference, *Pravda*, June 29, 1988, 3–4; and before the Polish parliament, *Pravda*, July 12, 1988, 2. This is not to imply that Gorbachev pursued domestic reform in order to influence Western opinion, but only that he came to realize that such influence was a fortuitous by-product of those efforts.

89. Speech at a breakfast for Gandhi, *Pravda*, July 4, 1987, 2.

If one judges the situation only by the speeches of certain highly placed Western figures, then it would look as if everything is as it was before: the same anti-Soviet attacks, the same demands for us to prove our adherence to peace. However, with the passage of several days, no one remembers these speeches. It means something is changing. And one of the elements of the changes is that now it is hard to suggest to people that our foreign policy is only propaganda. New thinking's power is that it corresponds to popular common sense. That is why, despite all the efforts to belittle and slander our foreign initiatives, they are making their way.[90]

After returning from the summit in Washington, Gorbachev told the Soviet people he was encouraged by the fact that "the wave of goodwill on the part of average Americans has grown, to the degree that they, through television and the press, have found out what our real views are, what we want."[91]

In his speech on the seventieth anniversary of the Bolshevik revolution, Gorbachev admitted that those who had developed postwar Soviet foreign policy had made mistakes. They did not "take advantage of opportunities" or "reinforce the peace-loving, democratic forces and stop the organizers of the cold war." But new thinking has "begun to destroy the stereotypes of anti-Sovietism and the suspicion of [Soviet] initiatives and actions."[92] In the same vein, Gorbachev suggested at the Nineteenth Party Conference that only a foreign policy characterized by realism could expect a "realistic attitude by those to whom it is directed," implying a previous lack of such realism in Soviet foreign policy. He admitted that the Soviet Union "inadequately responded to international events and the policies of other states, and so erroneous decisions were made." In addition, alternative actions were not evaluated in terms "of how they would turn out or how much they would cost." Gorbachev also dwelt on the overemphasis on the military aspect of Soviet foreign policy.

Having concentrated enormous resources and attention on the military side of the competition with imperialism, we did not always use the political opportunities that opened up in the world for reducing tensions and increasing mutual understanding among peoples. Meanwhile, the arms race approached a critical point. On this background, our political

---

90. *Pravda*, October 2, 1987, 2–3. Gorbachev also expressed confidence that Soviet foreign policy initiatives were undermining the "enemy image" in his speech at a Central Committee Plenum, *Pravda*, February 19, 1988, 3.

91. Text reproduced in *Pravda*, December 15, 1987, 1. He expressed the same heightened confidence in the American people in a speech before the Soviet-American economic council, *Pravda*, April 14, 1988, 1.

92. *Pravda*, November 3, 1987, 5.

and public activity in favor of peace and disarmament began to lose its persuasiveness. And if one speaks more frankly—a failure to break the logic of such a development could have really ended up on the brink of military confrontation. That is why not merely a perfection, but rather the decisive renewal, of foreign policy is demanded. For this, new political thinking is needed.

He went on to argue that "precisely new thinking allows us to find new opportunities to resist a policy of force on a political basis," one that is far wider than before.[93]

In his speech before the Polish parliament, Gorbachev explained why detente failed in the 1970s and how a new Soviet approach to foreign policy was being designed to avert a premature passing of detente in the 1980s.

> Far from all opportunities were used either in the the West or the East to slow and stop the dangerous process of the arms race. The concept of new political thinking has allowed us to see things in their true measure. All members of the world community, including of course also us, need to learn the high political art of a balance of interests. Western society knows the realities of the socialist world poorly. From the cradle, they drum into the people that Communists are miscreants who have enslaved their own peoples and are sharpening their knives against the free nations of the West. Our foreign policy ideas and especially the processes of perestroika in the Soviet Union and other socialist countries, glasnost, openness, and democratization—all this undoubtedly will destroy the primitive myths about socialism. This is extraordinarily important. After all, false stereotypes prevent the realistic conduct of affairs. I will observe that we also must rid ourselves of the simplistic approaches we have taken to depicting Western realities.[94]

Gorbachev's redefinition of the causes of regional conflicts in the Third World also was aimed at American public opinion. By shifting the blame from imperialism to indigenous forces, he made the Soviet Union a less antagonistic negotiating partner in the eyes of Americans who were fed up with Soviet accusations of absolute responsibility for all third world ills. By shifting the blame off Soviet shoulders, he hoped to convince the American elite that their adherence to a deterrent strategy was misplaced. If changes in the status quo

---

93. *Pravda*, June 29, 1988, 3–4.

94. *Pravda*, July 12, 1988, 2. It is noteworthy that the word *free* in the phrase "free nations of the West" is not in quotation marks. This is the first speech by a Soviet leader I have seen in which this qualification was not added.

occur continually, almost randomly, but certainly inevitably, then Americans have no reason to make attributions about American credibilty based on these completely arbitrary and autonomous events.

Until October 1985, Gorbachev argued that imperialism was the root cause of conflicts in the Third World.[95] But some six weeks later, at his press conference in Geneva after the conclusion of the summit, he reversed course.

> Tension, conflict, and even wars between different states have their roots either in the past or present socieconomic conditions of these countries and regions. To depict things as if all these knots of contradictions are caused by the competition between East and West is not only wrong, but extremely dangerous. I said all this to the president. If today, for example, Mexico, Brazil, and a number of other states cannot pay not only their debts, but even interest on them, then one can imagine what kind of processes are occurring in these countries. This can heat up the situation and lead to an explosion. And what then, they will speak of the "hand of Moscow" again? These banalities still occur everywhere, but they are impermissible at meetings such as this.[96]

In sum, Gorbachev expected that a combination of Soviet domestic reforms and foreign policy initiatives would succeed in changing the attitude of the American people toward the Soviet Union. It, in turn, would influence its government to adopt a more cooperative foreign policy. These Soviet actions operate on two elements that Gorbachev saw driving American foreign policy —the cold war stereotypes held by the American public and the hostility toward the Soviet Union inherent to the American ruling elite. Gorbachev's recognition that "unrealistic" Soviet foreign policy actions caused unnecessary hostility in the relationship operates on American elite adherence to deterrent strategies. A search for a balance of interests was calculated to

---

95. In a speech at a dinner with Mitterand in Paris, *Pravda*, October 4, 1985, 4. This in itself is a sign of emphasis, as Soviet leaders generally went out of their way to avoid anti-imperialist statements before West European audiences.

96. *Pravda*, November 22, 1985, 3. Further examples include his speeches before the Supreme Soviet upon his return from Geneva, *Pravda*, November 28, 1985, 1, 2, at the party congress, *Pravda*, February 26, 1986, 2, 3, 7–9, at a dinner for Algeria's Chedli Benjedid, *Pravda*, March 27, 1986, 2, and on the seventieth anniversary of the revolution, *Pravda*, November 3, 1987, 4–5. I select these examples to again demonstrate that Gorbachev expressed ideas that are most probably not in accord with audience preferences. This is not to say that Gorbachev completely absolved imperialism of responsibility for conflicts in the Third World. He continued to blame the United States for instability in Afghanistan, for example, at a joint press conference with Gandhi in India, *Pravda*, November 29, 1986, 1–2, and in his interview with Tom Brokaw, *Pravda*, December 2, 1987, 1–2. The latter, however, was the last time he made such an attribution.

obviate the American need to establish its "reputation for resolve" in peripheral conflicts.[97]

But the two causal variables generated by the Marxist-Leninist in Gorbachev remained unaddressed by any Soviet foreign policy strategy. First, the military-industrial complex maintains an interest in pursuing the arms race and increasing tensions in the periphery. Second, interests in the exploitation of third world economies still drive American foreign policy toward adventurism in the Third World. Gorbachev's strategy dealt with the military-industrial complex in several ways. But he never came to grips with how to reduce American interests in economic plunder.

Gorbachev identified several factors that he believed would ultimately cause a diminution in the pernicious influence exercised by the miltary-industrial complex on the formulation of American foreign policy. First, he believed that this complex was an enormous drag on American economic growth and that the American people and elite were coming to share this view. For example, before a group of visiting American businessmen, he suggested that "business circles in the United States cannot help but be troubled by the economic and financial consequences of excessive military spending and the consequences caused by militarization of the economy, its lopsided development."[98]

In the same vein, Gorbachev tried to demonstrate to the American people and government that the military-industrial complex was indeed an obstacle to economic growth. Before an audience of American teachers of Russian, he said that one of the biggest obstacles to reduced military budgets is that people are concerned about the loss of jobs. He counterargued that "one can create three jobs in the civilian sector for the price of one job in the military-industrial complex. Second, there is surplus capacity in the military economy that can be used for peaceful aims. Third, we together can come up with big joint programs, combining our resources and scientific and intellectual potentials."[99]

He buttressed his case by citing the experiences of several capitalist

---

97. In Gorbachev's search for a "balance of interests," he is, most likely unknowingly, following the work of Glenn Snyder and Paul Diesing, who argued that concern for credibility is one of the most difficult obstacles to overcome in crisis management. Snyder and Diesing, *Conflict among Nations*, 183–89.

98. *Pravda*, December 11, 1985, 2. On the economic costs of pursuing the complex's agenda, see also his answers to questions of the editor of the Algerian publication *Revolution Africaine*, *Pravda*, April 3, 1986, 1–2.

99. *Pravda*, August 8, 1987, 2. See also his speech on the seventieth anniversary of the revolution in which he proposed that the United States and Soviet Union jointly prepare programs to convert their military industries to civilian uses, *Pravda*, November 3, 1987, 4–5. He repeated this offer in his speech before the UN, *Pravda*, December 8, 1988, 1–2.

countries: "Can a capitalist economy develop without militarization? The 'economic miracles' in Japan, the FRG, and Italy come to mind. A period of rapid development of modern capitalist economies in a number of countries has taken place with minimal military expenditures."[100] Seventeen months after assuming power, Gorbachev began to differentiate between those American business interests that were connected to the production of armaments and those "who really look at things as they are, who are not sick with the paranoia of anticommunism and who do not bind themselves to the profits from the arms race."[101] Gorbachev expected these latter interests to pose an obstacle to the continued dominance of American foreign policy by the complex. Gorbachev's constant refrain was that "the interests and goals of the military-industrial complex are not one and the same thing as the interests and goals of the American people."[102] He expected that eventually the American people would realize this and oppose its influence.

While Gorbachev saw an array of factors that might ultimately erode the negative influence exerted by the military-industrial complex in the United States, he offered no antidotes to American economic dependence on the exploitation of the Third World.

So far, I have described Gorbachev's beliefs about what drives an American foreign policy of adventurism and the factors he identified that can alter it. The second half of Gorbachev's foreign policy strategy rested on his views of the Third World. Gorbachev's commitment to changing and reinforcing the pressure of public opinion on Western governments, especially the United States, was reflected in a new approach to the Third World. It is very telling that before third world audiences, Gorbachev tried to argue that anti-imperialist concerns must be subordinated to the struggle against the nuclear threat. A most striking piece of evidence for this interpretation is how Gorbachev redefined the "world revolutionary alliance" at the Twenty-seventh Party Congress. Unlike Brezhnev, and indeed all previous general secretaries, who defined the alliance's constituent parts as the socialist community, international working class, and national liberation movement, Gorbachev couched it in terms of the antinuclear movement and in fact placed it in his report to the party congress in that section of his address. He said that

> the arms race continues and the threat of nuclear war remains. However, international reactionary forces are not omnipotent. The development of

---

100. *Pravda*, November 3, 1987, 4–5.

101. Speech awarding Vladivostok an Order of Lenin, *Pravda*, July 29, 1986, 3.

102. Report to the Twenty-seventh Party Congress, *Pravda*, February 26, 1986, 8. For Gorbachev's view of the potential power of the American people to restrain the influence of the complex, see also, for one among many examples, his press conference in Reykjavik, *Pravda*, October 14, 1986, 1–2.

the world revolutionary process, the rise of the mass democratic and antiwar movement has significantly expanded and increasingly strengthens the *enormous potential of peace, reason, and goodwill.* This is a powerful counterweight to the aggressive policy of imperialism.[103]

Later in his speech, Gorbachev lumped the commitment of the Communist Party of the Soviet Union (CPSU) to solidarity with "the forces of national and social liberation" together with a readiness to "develop close ties with noncommunist tendencies and organizations, including religious ones, who come out against war." This is very strange company indeed for third world revolutionaries to find themselves among. And the next paragraph contained an appeal to cooperate with social-democratic parties on the basis of antinuclear sentiments. Gorbachev stated that "in liberated states, they increasingly better understand that in order to achieve full independence, to increase economic growth and secure the democratic restructuring of international economic relations, they must be in close coordination with the struggle against the arms race and threat of war."[104]

Gorbachev explicitly told his audiences that third world objectives in the area of economic development and other problems must be subordinated to the issue of arms control. In India, for example, he told that country's parliament that only the "elimination of nuclear weapons will yield the resources necessary for an improvement in the lives of peoples. Ending the arms race will facilitate the realization of the idea of a new international economic order [NIEO]."[105] Later, in another forum, he said that all global problems—third world conflicts, economic development, food shortages, and nuclear arms control—are interdependent. But then he declared that their "dependence on each other is not equal: without curtailing the arms race, one cannot really solve any of the other problems."[106] Gorbachev's ideas about how the United States finances the arms race through the exploitation of third world economies provided a substantive basis for his appeals to his third world allies to help resist American military programs before turning to their agenda on the NIEO.

In sum, Gorbachev's set of beliefs about the role of domestic opinion in

---

103. *Pravda*, February 26, 1986, 7. His emphasis.

104. *Pravda*, February 26, 1986, 8. Gorbachev argues for the primacy of antinuclear activities over revolutionary aims before audiences that contextually demand precisely the opposite emphasis—for example, in a speech to Ethiopia's Mengistu, *Pravda*, November 2, 1985, 3, a speech before the Indian parliament, *Pravda*, November 28, 1986, 2, a message to meeting of the OAU, *Pravda*, May 25, 1988, 1, and a dinner for the Brazilian president, Jose Sarney, *Pravda*, October 19, 1988, 2.

105. *Pravda*, November 28, 1986, 2.

106. *Pravda*, February 17, 1987, 2.

the formulation of American foreign policy and the role of the Third World in international affairs allowed him to develop a strategy for detente with the United States far different from any that Brezhnev could have devised. Like a good attribution theorist, Gorbachev discovered one of the causes of the downfall of detente was American reactions to progressive change in the Third World. Consistent with bounded rationality, he generated a menu of independent variables that could account for this kind of reaction. It included economic motivations, the role of the military-industrial complex in American politics, the cold war stereotypes that gripped both the American people and ruling elite, the latter's adherence to deterrence theory, as well as Soviet behavior itself in various regional conflicts.

Gorbachev developed a policy that was consistent with his beliefs about both the American political scene and the place of the Third World on the international arena. Through a combination of Soviet domestic and foreign policy initiatives, he expected to erode the enemy images held by the American people and elite. Through a process of education, he expected to teach the American people that the military-industrial complex was inimical to American national interests and could be profitably reconverted to civilian production tasks. Finally, through constructive Soviet behavior in regional conflicts, Gorbachev expected to be able to remove one of the conditions that motivated American deterrent strategy. He hoped to convince American leaders that they no longer had to worry about demonstrating their resolve in regional conflicts, because the Soviet Union was more than willing to accept a mutually arrived at conception of a "balance of interests" in any given case. Moreover, Gorbachev's conception of third world actors as contributors to the process of arms control, rather than as revolutionary forces designed to shift the correlation of forces against imperialism, allowed him to abandon longtime Soviet commitments to the victories of national liberation movements around the globe.

Gorbachev learned from the Soviet victories in Angola, Ethiopia, and Afghanistan that revolutionary gains in the Third World came with a high price for Soviet foreign policy in general. He was able to calculate this price because he analyzed American foreign policy as a rational attribution theorist and because he had no psychological need to maintain a set of beliefs about a "world revolutionary alliance" in the Third World.

*Soviet Images of Falling Dominoes around Angola*
The lessons of some Soviets who were encouraged by the victory in Angola can be explained by the representative heuristic, a general cognitive psychological phenomenon. These Soviets, most notably Brezhnev and Podgorny, concluded that certain salient features of the Angola case were reason enough to be initially encouraged about revolutionary prospects elsewhere. The

heuristic invoked most often in this case, as in the case of Vietnam, was geographical proximity. Dominoes were expected to fall in the region of southern Africa: in Namibia, Zimbabwe, and the RSA. Another salient feature used as a representative heuristic was the "antiracist, anticolonialist" aspect of the the MPLA's struggle. This served to channel Soviet expectations of dominoes to other national liberation movements who were fighting against white domination and colonial relationships: the Zimbabwe African National Union (ZANU) in Zimbabwe; SWAPO in Namibia; and the ANC in South Africa.

Since these heuristics are produced by cognitive economizing, a characteristic of all individuals, and not demanded to maintain the consistency of some peculiar belief system, we reasonably can conclude that deterrence theory's assumption about regional dynamics receives general validation in this case.

### General Confirmation and Disconfirmation
### of Deterrence Theory

Deterrence theory's assumptions about a defender's credibility receive general disconfirmation from these three cases. On the other hand, the theory's predictions about a challenger's view—at least initially—of regional dynamics after a victory receive general validation.

## Peculiar Explanations for Soviet Lessons from Angola, Ethiopia, and Afghanistan

Many important Soviets, including Brezhnev and his politburo, and most of his foreign policy elite, maintained their images of high U.S. credibility and of falling dominoes because they adhered to orthodox Marxist-Leninist belief systems. I briefly described the role of these peculiar beliefs in chapter 2.[107] Below, I use Brezhnev's belief system as a representative example of other Soviets with very similar orthodox views of American foreign policy and the Third World.

### Soviet Images of High U.S. Credibility

Brezhnev's analysis of American credibility reflects a tightly structured belief system that barely responds to new information from the external environment. Three elements of this belief system combined both to make him undeterrable in the Third World and, ironically, to make him constantly perceive a highly credible United States. These elements included (1) an ultra-orthodox view of politics under imperialism that limited the relevant actors to

---

107. See the material under the heading "Peculiar Pscyhological Explanations."

a narrow ruling elite; (2) a commitment to the "world revolutionary process" of which the national liberation movement was an integral part; and (3) a policy of offensive detente that combined strategic detente with the West with a policy of supporting progressive change in the periphery. His ability to learn from Soviet behavior in the Third World was severely constrained by this set of beliefs.

At the core of Brezhnev's belief system was his view that American foreign policy is made by a narrow ruling elite. These ruling circles are rarely, if ever, subject to pressures from the legislative branch of government, let alone the popular masses. This view of how American foreign policy is caused is reflected in how Brezhnev responded to evidence that Soviet victories in Angola, Ethiopia, and Afghanistan were correlated with the erosion of American support for detente. He argued that certain members of the elite, usually identified as connected with the military-industrial complex or simply inveterate cold warriors, were seizing on events they did not like in Angola to propagate myths about a growing Soviet threat. This effort was intended to deceive public opinion in the United States so that Americans would reject detente. Brezhnev's orthodox view of American politics prevented him from adopting an effective foreign policy response to this eroding American public support for detente. If Brezhnev had been able to grant a role to the American public and its representative institutions, he might have fashioned a policy that would have reassured the American people that detente was not a "one-way street," as Reagan called it during the 1976 Republican presidential primaries.

One can imagine a Soviet effort to explain to the American side that Angola was simply an aberration, that the collapse of the Portuguese colonial empire was simply a fortuitous event, that if the South Africans had not intervened, the Soviets would not have provided such strong support to the MPLA, that the Soviet Union was willing to forswear all kinds of military activities in Angola, that they were willing to work with the administration on Zimbabwean and Namibian independence, and so on. Instead, Brezhnev simply attacked the United States for unjustifiably undermining detente[108] and placed Angola into the context of an inexorable course of history leading to future revolutions[109]—hardly a strategy calculated to cool the hotheaded militarists in Washington.

The three elements of Brezhnev's belief system combined to prevent him from making the appropriate policy adjustment. His commitment to the

---

108. For example, in his speech to a meeting of European Communists in East Berlin, *Pravda*, June 30, 1976, 1. Other examples from orthodox Soviets include Andropov's Supreme Soviet election speech, *Pravda*, February 23, 1979, 2; and Ponomarev's speech at a meeting of ideological workers in Moscow, *Pravda*, October 18, 1979, 2.

109. I discuss how this peculiar belief system implies images of falling dominoes below.

"world revolutionary process" as a central organizing principle of his world-view prevented him from ending support for national liberation movements; if he had, his entire view of how world history operated would have required fundamental rearrangement, which is the last psychological operation in which a person with a tightly organized belief system engages.[110] His ortho-dox view of American politics made a Soviet policy adjustment unnecessary, in that Brezhnev believed it was just a matter of the elites coming to grips with this Soviet behavior, but not a case where there was public support for a harder line against the Soviets due to their behavior in Angola and elsewhere. Finally, his commitment to offensive detente also hindered a rational re-sponse, as Brezhnev would have had to abandon a central element of his foreign policy program.

As detente came under increasing attack in the United States, Brezhnev had to protect his commitment to offensive detente by "bolstering" his ortho-dox beliefs about American foreign policymaking. By 1980 Brezhnev was compelled to adduce additional motives for the American elite's abandonment of detente. Still unable to make the connection between Soviet behavior and American attitude change, he invoked the orthodox Leninist argument about the imperialist need for raw materials in the Third World. In addition, the United States needed military bases around the globe to protect current clients and overthrow progressive governments.

In sum, Brezhnev's peculiar set of beliefs made him consistently see a highly credible American opponent, while simultaneously being undissuad-able from his commitment to support progressive change in the Third World. Brezhnev's beliefs about politics in America and the world revolutionary process, and the policy strategy of offensive detente derived therefrom, had a paradoxical effect on his perceptions of the cost of third world adventures.

On the one hand, Brezhnev did not learn from the Soviet gains in this chapter that the United States had lost its willingness or capacity to resist future progressive changes in the Third World. By focusing his attention on a narrow American elite, axiomatically hostile to such changes, Brezhnev ig-nored the fact that the American people and Congress were exerting a counter-vailing influence on the aggressive predispositions of the executive branch, at least in the case of Angola. In effect, Brezhnev was self-deterred by his own peculiar set of beliefs.

---

110. There is a subtantial body of experimental psychology literature that supports the idea that people with tightly organized belief systems will resort to all sorts of inconsistency-reducing mechanisms before they will make the psychologically very painful, and hence expensive, choice of reordering their central beliefs. See, for example, McGuire, "Current Status," 15; Aronson, "Dissonance Theory;" Robert P. Abelson, "Psychological Implications," in Abelson et. al., *Theories*, 116; Weick, "Processes of Ramification," 512–19; Kaplan and Crockett, "Develop-mental Analysis," 667–68; and Sweeney and Gruber, "Selective Exposure."

On the other hand, however, through the operation of this same set of beliefs, Brezhnev could not be deterred from future support of revolutionary forces by American efforts to increase the price of such support. His tightly constructed view of a world revolutionary alliance made the abandonment or even reduction of commitment to national liberation movements psychologically too costly. Such a revision of his beliefs would have compelled him to fundamentally alter his entire structure of beliefs about how the world operated. Moreover, since he saw no role for the American people and Congress in the foreign policy process, he could see no reason why any moderation in Soviet behavior in the periphery would have any effect on American aggressiveness. As a consequence, Brezhnev was unable to make any effective adjustments in his strategy of offensive detente, even as the presumed centerpiece of that strategy—arms control and economic cooperation with the West—was lost through Soviet actions in the Third World.

## Soviet Images of Falling Dominoes

Brezhnev and his orthodox colleagues on the politburo and in the foreign policy community saw falling dominoes after these three victories due to their belief in the "world revolutionary process" and the role of the Soviet Union as the leader of the alliance that would advance that process.[111] Brezhnev's words of encouragement to President Agostinho Neto of Angola are an example of this variety of lesson: "The events in Angola once again have confirmed the truth of our days: the resolve of a people defending freedom [the national liberation movement], multiplied by international solidarity [the international working class and socialist community, the latter led by the Soviet Union], is an invincible force."[112] I have added the explanatory language in the brackets to highlight how victories such as the MPLA in Angola cause orthodox Soviets to see prospective dominoes around the Third World because of their adherence to this view of how the world works.

## Deterrence Theory's Peculiar (Dis)Confirmation

The findings of this section cannot be assumed to travel too far. Only if others have belief systems that assume highly credible foes can we generalize from Soviet belief systems. However, deterrence theory's assumptions about victories giving rise to domino imagery are confirmed only under the same restrictive circumstances.

---

111. See my discussion in chapter 2 on the similar effects of this belief system on Soviet lessons from Vietnam.

112. *Pravda*, October 8, 1976, 2. For other examples, see Kosygin, *Pravda*, March 22, 1979, 4, and September 13, 1979, 4; Suslov, *Pravda*, September 19, 1979, 2; Ogarkov, *KZ*, June 5, 1980, 2; and Ulyanovsky, "Natsionalno-Osvoboditelnoe Dvizhenie v Borbe za Ekonomicheskiuiu Nezavisimost" (The National Liberation Movement in Struggle for Economic Independence), *Kommunist*, 1976, no. 14, 116.

## A Scorecard for Deterrence Theory: A Failing Grade

The findings that follow are self-explanatory.

1. Universal explanations that confirm deterrence theory: *None*
2. General explanations that confirm deterrence theory: Many Soviets felt that dominoes would fall in southern Africa, namely, Namibia, Zimbabwe, and the Republic of South Africa, based on their invocation of several "representativeness heuristics."
3. Peculiar explanations that confirm deterrence theory: Those Soviets with orthodox Marxist-Leninist belief systems, especially the party leadership, predicted future victories for national liberation movements around the world based on this set of beliefs.
4. Universal explanations that disconfirm deterrence theory:
   a. All Soviets continued to attribute high credibility to the United States in strategic areas of the globe because they saw no logical connection between U.S. behavior in areas of negligible interest and its future conduct in places with critical stakes.
   b. All Soviets derived their images of U.S. strategic credibility almost exclusively from its behavior on strategic issues because U.S. behavior in the Third World was of only peripheral salience to Soviet analysis of this question.
   c. The community of Americanists was convinced of U.S. capability and resolve in the Third World based on their analysis of the "causes" of American foreign policy, including, but not limited to, public opinion, congressional sentiments, and the state of the economy.
5. General explanations that disconfirm deterrence theory:
   a. Many Soviets, including virtually the entire party leadership and military and foreign policy elite, maintained images of a highly credible America because they operated with a very restricted menu of critical variables in their analyses, namely, military spending and deployments.
   b. An increasing number of Soviets, including, most importantly, General Secretary Gorbachev, maintained images of an extremely credible United States based on their understanding of the causal chain from Soviet foreign and domestic behavior to the American people and its representatives to U.S. foreign policy decision makers.
6. Peculiar explanations that disconfirm deterrence theory: Most members of the pre-Gorbachev party leadership and military and foreign policy elites considered high U.S. credibility to be axiomatic, given their adherence to orthodox Marxist-Leninist belief systems.

Confirmation for deterrence theory propositions in this set of crucially easy cases is limited only to general lessons of dominoes falling in southern Africa. Meanwhile, the theory is disconfirmed in the area of credibility and regional dynamics by explanations with universal and general validity.

## Considering Alternative Explanations for Soviet Lessons from Angola, Ethiopia, and Afghanistan

There are several strong objections that can be raised against my interpretation of the empirical evidence from these three Soviet victories. I discuss only briefly two of the alternatives that I dealt with in chapter 2.[113] I then consider at greater length two new competing explanations for Soviet lessons from these cases.

### A Soviet Bias to Perceive the United States as Inherently Aggressive

I argued against this alternative in chapter 2. Its major flaws are two: different Soviet observers saw different levels of U.S. credibility on different issues between the two countries, and many Soviets, especially Americanists, treated U.S. credibility as a variable, not a constant. My counterargument is only strengthened by the evidence in this chapter, in that Gorbachev and his foreign policy associates all considered American resolve and capabilities to be variables that are effected by various causes.

### A Soviet Lulling Strategy

This alternative, as in the case of Vietnam, suffers from a poor fit with the evidence. First, as noted above, not all Soviets reassured U.S. decision makers and the American public with consistently high evaluations of American credibility on all issues. More important, reassurance is not produced when Soviets assert that their victories in Vietnam, Angola, Ethiopia, and Afghanistan are portents of future revolutionary successes all over the Third World.

### A General Soviet Foreign Policy Line for Domestic and Foreign Consumption

It could be argued that the pattern of lessons I identify from these cases comprises examples of managed, strategic speech, not genuine responses to

---

113. The third one, "An insoluble foreign policy dilemma," does not arise in these cases, because Soviets did not argue that their victories in Angola, Ethiopia, and Afghanistan were the

these events. For this to be true, at the very minimum, there must be consistency in the stories being told to various audiences by different Soviet leaders and authors. There are two different ways this alternative explanation does not pass this initial validity test. First, there are differences *among* Soviet observers. Second, there are inconsistencies *within* the stories being told by individual Soviets.

On the first count, there are a number of very vivid examples that prove the point. For example, while Gorbachev and Primakov both were arguing that Soviet domestic liberalization would cause American foreign policy to moderate, Arbatov adhered to a quite different interpretation of how the internal characteristics of the Soviet Union had affected U.S. policy in the past.[114] Instead of arguing like his colleagues above that reforms were necessary to communicate a more benign image of a democratizing Soviet Union, Arbatov asserted they were required to ensure that the Americans did not see a weak and vulnerable Soviet Union. He wrote that the "phenomena of stagnation in the Soviet Union played their role in undermining detente in the late 1970s" as it evoked "among part of the American ruling class illusory hopes that socialism had entered an era of decline, that it was slipping on a slope and one had only to push it and the problem would be solved once and for all." He concluded that the early stages of Reagan's foreign policy can be "largely explained by precisely such hopes."[115] So, while Gorbachev and others understood Soviet domestic reforms as sending a message that the Soviet Union was not threatening to the West, Arbatov interpreted the same policies as a way to communicate to the West that the Soviet Union could no longer be pushed around. This kind of profound disagreement is not consistent with a general line in Soviet foreign policy.

Gromyko and Shevardnadze's rejection of Gorbachev's conviction that public opinion was a critical element in influencing American foreign policy also undermines the argument for a general line. Whereas Gorbachev pinned all his hopes on the American people, Gromyko, at as important an occasion as the Twenty-seventh Party Congress, explicitly ridiculed such hopes. He asserted that "any protests by working people against reductions in social spending are ignored. And if there are demonstrations, they are often severely suppressed, especially if they have an antiwar direction." At most, in the U.S. Congress, only "two to three speeches are delivered in favor of working people. But these speeches never change anything."[116]

---

fruits of detente. Quite the contrary, since they recognized detente was damaged by these revolutionary successes.

114. For specific examples of the views of these Soviets and other discussed below, please refer to the preceding empirical discussions of this chapter.

115. Arbatov, "Pered Vyborom," 112. His first discussion of this issue was in "Tma Pered."

116. *Izvestiya*, February 27, 1986, 5–6.

Shevardnadze's view of public opinion was initially much like Gromyko's orthodox approach. Before a meeting of Portuguese Communists, Shevardnadze told them that Communists were in the vanguard of the peace movement.[117] Gorbachev told this same audience only six months later that seemingly every group *but* the Communists were critical to the peace movement's success.[118] Shevardandze also continued to advance the "social imperialist" explanation for American foreign policy after Gorbachev had abandoned that theory. He accused Reagan, in his State of the Union address, of "clearly trying to divert attention from the urgent problems of his own country" by "convincing Congress to approve a record new military budget, SDI, aid the Afghani dushmans and Nicaraguan contras."[119] The implications of this are that the American people support third world adventurism; otherwise, why entertain them with it?

Finally, unlike Gorbachev, Shevardnadze did not argue that the American public was going to be a factor in reducing the influence of the military-industrial complex on foreign policy. Instead, Shevardnadze argued that the military-industrial complex was *good* for the American economy: "It is well known that the stimulation of the [American] economy is guaranteed by its militarization and the colossal resources used to finance military programs."[120]

Again, these differences between Gromyko and Shevardnadze with Gorbachev and Primakov are not consistent with the argument that Soviets were expressing some general foreign policy line, rather than genuinely held beliefs. The second way of demonstrating the invalidity of this alternative explanation is to show how no coherent foreign policy strategy could be constructed with the beliefs expressed by Soviet leaders. I show this with examples from Brezhnev and Gorbachev.

One could argue that Brezhnev's speeches are consistent with a foreign policy strategy of offensive detente. He made the claim, at least until after the fallout from Afghanistan, that his program simultaneously would gain the Soviet Union arms control and economic intercourse with the West, security in Europe, and national liberation movement victories in the Third World. Given this foreign policy program, Brezhnev should have described American foreign policy in a manner consistent with the attainment of the fruits of offensive detente. But I contend that Brezhnev's Marxist-Leninist belief system precluded him from interpreting reality in a way that would have most

---

117. *Pravda*, June 24, 1983, 4.

118. *Pravda*, December 17, 1983, 4.

119. Speech at dinner for Mongolian foreign minister Dugersuen, *Pravda*, January 31, 1987, 4. Gorbachev had dropped this line of argument almost four years before this speech by his foreign minister.

120. Speech on Lenin's birthday, *Pravda*, April 23, 1986, 1–2.

fruitfully advanced his agenda. His orthodox view of how American foreign policy is made, its rejection of genuine influence from Congress or the public, caused Brezhnev to exaggerate American credibility after Vietnam and Angola.

If Brezhnev had been able to understand that it was Congress and the American people that thwarted the Nixon-Ford administration in Vietnam, and the Ford administration in Angola, then he would have perceived greater revolutionary opportunities in the Third World. That he did not is very strong evidence for my argument that Brezhnev operated with a belief system, since it is both consistent with the evidence and explains an anomaly left unaccounted for by the alternative explanation of a general line.

Gorbachev's beliefs also got in the way of advancing his foreign policy strategy. If there were a general line, Gorbachev's analysis of American foreign policy should not imply the failure of his own foreign policy program. But Gorbachev's adherence to the Leninist position on imperialism's relationship to the periphery prevented him from declaring his foreign policy strategy a success. Again, the fact that my interpretation is rooted in a more general psychological theory of belief systems, and it explains a result that is anomalous for its competitor, imparts additional power to my explanation.

Gorbachev's overall foreign policy strategy contended that the United States would ultimately curb its adventurism in the Third World. But in continuing to adhere to the Leninist dogma of the need for imperialist states to exploit lesser-developed economies, Gorbachev predicted the failure of his own policy strategy. This interpretation is further supported by the fact that American dependence on exploiting the Third World is an easily testable proposition.[121] It is obvious to even the most casual observer that American economic interests in the Third World in general are far less than its interests in Western Europe, East Asia, and the oil-producing areas of the Middle East. Moreover, the share of the Third World in total American trade turnover, foreign investment, and repatriated profits has been in secular decline since the late 1960s. Gorbachev most certainly had been exposed to these facts.[122] Moreover, American economic interests in Angola, Ethiopia, and Afghanistan are trivial. The case of Gulf Oil's interests in Angola should have further disconfirmed Gorbachev's beliefs. There is no need for the United States to

---

121. It has been found that people tend to handle quantitative data, such as would be available in any assessment of American economic dependence on third world countries, in a far more rational and rigorous manner than qualitative information. See, for example, Paul Slovic and Douglas MacPhillamy, "Dimensional Commensurability and Cue Utilization in Comparative Judgment," *Organizational Behavior and Human Performance*, 11, no. 2 (February 1974): 172–94. This distinction between qualitative and quantitative evidence has special significance to the discussions about regional dynamics in chaps. 5 and 8.

122. Primakov, for example, provides the relevant figures in "Zakon Neravnomernosti."

overthrow a government in Luanda that allows its country to be exploited by American monopoly capital.

This discussion of Brezhnev and Gorbachev raises an important epistemological point. What I have done here is not only show that competing explanations cannot account for the pattern of lessons inferred by these two general secretaries. More important, I have, by the use of more general psychological theories, both explained that pattern of lessons *and* accounted for anomalies left by the alternatives. The principle demonstrated here is "less is more." Even if these alternatives had a good fit with the evidence, they still would be inferior to any explanation that was situated at a higher level of abstraction or generality, as are psychological theories. One wants to explain more with less; the alternative of some set of general lines in Soviet foreign policy smacks of *ad hocery* that changes with every shift in Soviet speeches. The theoretical foundations of my explanations, on the contrary, remain fixed, and hence more powerful than their more fluid competitors.

### Gorbachev's "New Thinking" is Just a Post Facto Rationalization

It has been argued that Gorbachev's new foreign policy program, and, by implication, the lessons of Gorbachev and his colleagues I have discussed here, were just the Soviets making the best of a bad situation. Having been compelled to renounce support for national liberation movmements in the Third World due to economic weakness and the high costs imposed by the "Reagan Doctrine" of arming anticommunist insurgencies, the Soviets developed a face-saving strategy in the form of "new thinking" in foreign policy. Despite the wide currency given this alternative explanation, it lacks empirical support.

The argument that the Soviets retreated from the Third World due to economic constraints does not hold up to even cursory scrutiny.[123] For this position to have credence, there should be a reduction in Soviet expenditures in the Third World after Gorbachev came to power. This did not happen, however, until the collapse of the Soviet Union itself after the abortive August 1991 coup. But this is seven years *after* the economic crisis presumedly caused the Soviet retreat. Second, this argument gains validity insofar as there is a positive correlation between Soviet economic decline and a more moderate foreign policy. In other words, Soviet economic decline should have

---

123. For a comprehensive refutation of the argument that economic constraints caused foreign policy moderation under Gorbachev, specifically, and of the argument that periods of economic difficulties are associated with Soviet foreign policy moderation, in general, see David R. Rivera, "Ronald Reagan, Economic Decline, and the Collapse of the Soviet Empire: Testing Prominent Explanations of the Wane of Soviet Expansionism" (1994, typescript).

started shortly before Gorbachev came to power in 1985. In fact, as Matthew Evangelista has shown, the greatest percentage falloff in Soviet GNP growth rates occurred in the early 1970s.[124] This time period is precisely when many argue Soviet foreign policy became far more adventuristic in the Third World. This negative correlation confounds any economic explanation for Soviet strategy in the Third World.

This does not mean, however, that an economic explanation cannot be fruitfully combined with my own. Essentially, one could argue that Brezhnev and Gorbachev were both faced with economic decline; under similar circumstances, one chose a strategy of offensive detente, the other a conciliatory foreign policy program. The critical variable here obviously is the two different leaders, more specifically, how they understood both the causes of American foreign policy and the role of the Soviet Union in the periphery. While economic decline was a necessary condition of Soviet foreign policy moderation, it was not at all sufficient. Gorbachev's beliefs, when combined with Soviet economic troubles, however, were both necessary and sufficient.

Others argue that the Reagan Doctrine raised the costs of Soviet policy in the Third World. Unfortunately, this particular argument in defense of the doctrine has no determinate predictions for Soviet behavior. Its claims are not falsifiable. On the one hand, for this argument to be true, we should see reductions in Soviet aid to, or complete abandonment of, those governments that were under attack by insurgencies supported by the United States. But instead Soviet aid *increased* precisely to those governments under attack: Angola from 1985 to 1991; Afghanistan from 1985 to 1991; and Nicaragua from 1985 to 1990. While advocates of the Reagan Doctrine could rightly point out that the policy increased the costs to Moscow, to wit, the increased expenditures on these three allies, it could not claim that the Soviets abandoned their allies in the face of these costs. Nor, given the relatively trivial sums of money involved in supporting these governments relative to total Soviet defense expenditures, could the doctrine's supporters claim that these costs tipped the balance in Gorbachev's foreign policy.

Moreover, and ironically, Soviet aid was reduced or even eliminated to those allies who were not faced by insurgencies backed by the United States: Mozambique and Ethiopia. And Soviet aid was cut to Luanda and Managua as soon as the Reagan Doctrine was no longer applied to UNITA and the contras. In other words, the doctrine has a perfect negative correlation with Soviet aid levels. Finally, perhaps the most peculiar implication of the doctrine's claim is

---

124. See Matthew Evangelista, "Economic Constraints on Soviet Grand Strategy: When Do they Constrain?" (1991, typescript), and "Transnational Alliances and Soviet Demilitarization" (paper prepared for the Council on Economic Priorities Project on Military Expenditure and Economic Priorities, October 1990).

that had the Soviets simply cut and run from Angola, Afghanistan, and Nicaragua, this would disprove the policy's effectiveness, because the Soviets reduced their costs in these cases, rather than allow the ante to be raised by Washington. In sum, the Reagan Doctrine simply was not a factor in causing the fundamental turn in Soviet foreign policy under Gorbachev.

Finally, the argument that the Soviet foreign policy program is merely propaganda cover for retreat is unconvincing because many of the concepts that constitute this program *preceded* any changes in Soviet behavior.[125] We could be far more persuaded if the change in Soviet foreign policy antedated or at least was contemporaneous with the propaganda that was purportedly advanced to rationalize that shift. Instead, elements of Gorbachev's understanding of American foreign policy are to be found years before any policy change.

Gorbachev himself, for example, advanced his more inclusive view of public opinion eighteen months *before* becoming general secretary after Chernenko's death. This was during the "era of stagnation" in Soviet foreign and domestic policy and before an audience, the delegates to a congress of the Portuguese Communist Party, that hardly could be considered enthusiastically awaiting such sentiments. Other examples include Primakov, who, three years prior to Gorbachev, suggested that it might be possible for the United States to develop economically without militarism.[126] Primakov also was ahead of other members of the party leadership and foreign policy elite in identifying the causal link between Soviet foreign policy, American public opinion, and U.S. foreign policy. A year before Gorbachev noted this role for Soviet foreign policy, Primakov explained Reagan's "peace-loving words before Congress after his return from Geneva" as the product of a "definite change in public opinion." This change occurred "especially after we escalated our peace proposals." He noted that the Soviet Union was now "effectively using reserves that previously had gone unemployed." One example was the Soviet approach to arms control verification. In the United States, "they tried to prove that their unreadiness for arms control was dictated by our 'closed

---

125. Our confidence should be further bolstered by the fact that other scholars have independently reached the same conclusion based on unrelated theoretical approaches and research techniques. See, for example, Jeff Checkel, "Ideas, Institutions, and the Gorbachev Foreign Policy Revolution," *World Politics* 45 (January 1993): 271–300; Sarah E. Mendelson, "Internal Battles and External Wars: Politics, Learning, and the Soviet Withdrawal from Afghanistan," *World Politics* 45 (April 1993): 327–60; and Douglas W. Blum, "The Soviet Foreign Policy Belief System: Beliefs, Politics, and Foreign Policy Outcomes," *International Studies Quarterly* 37 (December 1993): 373–94.

126. "'Imperiya Dollara' v Proshlom i Nastoyashchem" ("Empire of the Dollar" in the Past and the Present), *MEIMO*, May 1983, 134–36. Primakov elaborated on this argument in "U Poroga Tretevo Tysyacheletiya" (On the Threshold of the Third Millenium), *LG*, February 5, 1986, 14. Gorbachev's first recognition of this possibility was in a speech before U.S. commerce secretary Baldridge, *Pravda*, December 11, 1985, 2.

society' and our unwillingness to allow verification." He asked rhetorically whether the new Soviet approach to verification has influenced public opinion. He answered: "unconditionally yes."[127]

Primakov also identified the link between Soviet domestic reforms and American foreign policy before his senior colleagues. He wrote that "it is increasingly hard for anti-Soviets to maintain the image, artificially created by them, of the Soviet Union as a militaristic, undemocratic state looming over the world and thinking only about expansion. Public opinion polls in the United States and West European countries attest that this myth is not withstanding the encounter with perestroika and glasnost in the Soviet Union or its constructive foreign policy." Soviet foreign policy concessions "keep those militaristic forces that would feel far more comfortable with stagnation in constant tension and do not give them a breathing spell."[128]

Finally, several years before Gorbachev, Arbatov established the link between the state of the American economy, military spending, public opinion, and American foreign policy. Foreshadowing Gorbachev's rhetorical question on the seventieth anniversary of the Russian Revolution, Arbatov, ten months before, gave an affirmative answer to the question of whether American imperialism could economically survive without militarism. In so doing, he went beyond simply sensing public support for less military spending, asserting that the American ruling elite itself was adopting the sensible views of the American people.

The interests of the greater part of the ruling class are not advanced by the arms race. It enriches only an insignificant, narrow grouping of monopoly capital; the overwhelming majority of corporations either get only crumbs from military profits or are not involved at all in the "military economy." At the same time, the negative consequences of the arms race—the growth of inflation and budget deficits, increased unemployment, sluggish economic growth, and an aggravation of social contradictions—are felt by the entire ruling class and society.

Can capitalism renounce militarism? I think one must not hurry with a negative answer. Let's recall that fifty years ago the collapse of colonial

---

127. Primakov, "U Poroga." Gorbachev picked up this theme for the first time only in a speech before Soviet trade union officials in *Pravda*, February 26, 1987, 1–2.

128. "Novaya Filosofiya." On the effects on American behavior of both Soviet domestic and foreign policy, see also Primakov, "Novye Protivorechiya Kapitalisticheskoi Ekonomiki" (New Contradictions of the Capitalist Economics), *Pravda*, September 15, 1987, 4. Gorbachev made the Soviet domestic policy argument only three months later in a speech in Murmansk, *Pravda*, October 2, 1987, 2–3. Karen Brutents, a high-ranking member of the Central Committee's International Department, did not acknowledge this effect until July 1988 at a conference held in the Ministry of Foreign Affairs addressed by Shevardnaze. Reprinted as "Cooperation and Dialogue with Political Parties and Movements," *IA*, November 1988, 37–40.

empires also seemed highly improbable. Excessive economic costs and the threat of unimaginable bloodshed that is inseparable from military preparations unite the very widest political and social forces in a struggle against militarism.[129]

The point here is that if all these lessons are merely post facto rationalizations for a Soviet foreign policy retrenchment taken on other grounds, then we should expect to see Soviet policy retreats *followed* by the reformulations; instead we see most of the reformulations *preceding* Gorbachev's foreign policy innovations. Moreover, the alleged causes of this policy moderation, economic decline and the Reagan Doctrine, have poor empirical fits with the historical record.

## Soviet Behavior after the "Arc of Crisis"

Deterrence theory assumptions should predict a more activist Soviet foreign policy in the Third World after the invasion of Afghanistan. As I showed in the previous chapter, such activism did not manifest itself from the American withdrawal from Vietnam to the Soviet intervention on the Horn of Africa. Instead, one saw a random mixture of victories and defeats, with most of the former coming with no help from Moscow. The pattern, or, more precisely, nonpattern, continues in this period.

| | | |
|---|---|---|
| Afghanistan | 1979 | Gain |
| Iran | 1979 | Gain |
| Nicaragua | 1979 | Gain |
| Grenada | 1979 | Gain |
| Zimbabwe | 1980 | Loss |
| El Salvador | 1981 | Loss |
| Grenada | 1983 | Loss |
| Mozambique | 1984 | Loss |

As can be seen in the above chronology of Soviet gains and losses, 1979 was a very good year for deterrence theory. The shah was overthrown in Iran;

---

129. Arbatov, "Militarizm i Sovremennoe," 113. He argued that the "military-industrial complex is not omnipotent" also in "Perestroika Shatters Stereotypes," 3. See also "USSR-SShA." Three years before Arbatov and a year before Gorbachev became general secretary, one of Gorbachev's future advisers, Alcksandr Yakovlev, noted the link between lower defense spending in Germany and Japan and the consequent competitive edge this gave those two countries over the United States. See "Rakovaya Opukhol Imperskikh Ambitsii v yadernyi Vek [*sic*]" (Cancerous Tumor of Imperial Ambitions in the Nuclear Age), *MEIMO*, January 1984, 3–17, and "Imperializm: Sopernichestvo i Protivorechiya" (Imperialism: Competition and Contradictions), *Pravda*, March 23, 1984, 3–4.

the New Jewel Movement came to power in Grenada; Somoza was ousted in Nicaragua; and the Red Army invaded Afghanistan. But the next five years saw nothing but Soviet losses. A national liberation victory was denied them in Zimbabwe; a right-wing military coup deprived El Salvador of a government of progressive military officers; the Reagan administration invaded Grenada; and the National Front for the Liberation of Mozambique (FRELIMO) government in Maputo signed a humiliating peace treaty with Pretoria. While it is tempting to argue that there is a pattern of Soviet (non)behavior that *negatively* correlates with deterrence theory's predictions, I think, given the broader data set, it is safer to argue that Soviet behavior is simply *unrelated* to whether it has previously lost or won in the Third World. In other words, deterrence assumptions are irrelevant to Soviet foreign policy conduct in the periphery.

## Conclusion: Deterrence Theory Fails a Crucially Easy Test

The string of Soviet victories from 1975 to 1979 caused some to dub the region from the Indian subcontinent to Southwest Africa the "Arc of Crisis." Despite these consecutive American losses, deterrence theory's predictions about Soviet lessons from their good fortune are not empirically validated. Moreover, Soviet images of high U.S. credibility are the product of universally or generally rational treatments of the evidence. Hence, we can conclude that deterrence theory in general has been invalidated in these cases. Deterrence theory does receive empirical confirmation from the case of Angola. But this expectation of further revolutionary gains in southern Africa was soon replaced by pessimistic appraisals. Soviets also saw global dominoes set off by their victories. But these lessons were the products of peculiar belief systems having very limited validity beyond the Soviet case.

Finally, the cases of Brezhnev and Gorbachev are excellent illustrations of the futility of implementing prescriptive deterrence theory, at least as it is currently conceived. In the case of Brezhnev, U.S. deterrent tactics were largely irrelevant; he treated high American credibility as a constant and yet was unalterably committed to advancing the world revolutionary alliance with national liberation forces around the globe. Gorbachev was deterred from third world adventurism, but not by the costs imposed by U.S. deterrent strategy. Instead, he was dissuaded by the costs to detente that previous Soviet policy in the periphery had incurred. And his nonorthodox view of American domestic politics and foreign policymaking, combined with his non-Leninist view of the Third World, allowed him to make this cost-benefit calculation.

In sum, deterrence theory's assumptions are not validated even under the easiest of circumstances.

# CHAPTER 4

# Soviet Lessons from Iran and Nicaragua: Deterrence Theory Fails Another Easy Test

Using Nicaragua as a base, the Soviets and Cubans can become the dominant power in the crucial corridor between North and South America. Established there, they will be in a position to threaten the Panama Canal, interdict our vital Caribbean sea lanes and, ultimately, move against Mexico. Will we turn our backs and ignore the malignancy in Managua until it spreads and becomes a mortal threat to the entire New World?

—Ronald Reagan

If we don't want to see the map of Central America covered in a sea of red, eventually lapping at our own borders, we must act now.

—Ronald Reagan

Deterrence theory does not pass yet another set of crucial tests. The Soviet Union made gains in both Iran and Nicaragua in 1979, right on the heels of its victories in Vietnam, Angola, and Ethiopia. These are very easy conditions for the validation of deterrence theory's predictions. Moreover, the case of Iran is an easy test for the theory's assumptions about the interconnectedness of interests between the Third World and strategic areas. If the United States did not lose its reputation for defending Europe, Northeast Asia, and the Middle East after losing in a country of as much strategic importance as Iran, then where else in the Third World could such a loss of credibility occur? As in the two previous chapters, deterrence theory assumptions are prima facie empirically invalidated by the evidence of Soviet lessons from these two victories. However, this cannot be considered a failure of deterrence theory in general until we establish *how* these disconfirming lessons were generated.

The theory fails this crucially easy set of tests because Soviets continued to see the United States as highly credible, and they reached these conclusions through processes of universal and general relevance. The theory further fails

---

The epigraphs are taken from a national television address to the American people before a congressional vote on aid to the Contras, *New York Times*, March 17, 1986, and from an address to a meeting of Jewish organizations, *New York Times*, March 6, 1986.

because most Soviets expected regional balancing against their gains in the Gulf and Central America, and these lessons were also the product of rational or bounded rational analyses. Moreover, Soviet optimism about revolutionary prospects after these two victories was the product of *peculiar* belief systems, not common to the universe of deterrence cases.

## Soviet Lessons about U.S. Credibility

Each of these two Soviet victories is a crucially easy test for deterrence theory. If the theory passes, then Soviets should have inferred from American inaction in the face of the removal of its longtime allies in Teheran and Managua that the United States was neither willing nor able to prevent future revolutionary changes in the Third World.[1] Both Soviet victories occurred under easy conditions for deterrence theory to pass its test. The replacement of the shah in February 1979 and the removal of Somoza in July 1979 both occurred on the heels of a string of previous American defeats—in Vietnam, Angola, and Ethiopia. Surely the United States should have appeared weak and irresolute by late 1979. Moreover, given the strategic importance of Iran to the United States, the Khomeini revolution was the Soviet victory in the Third World most likely to evoke Soviet images of American weakness in other strategic areas of the world.

Finally, the case of Nicaragua provides a set of discrete subtests for deterrence theory. More specifically, the theory should make different predictions depending on whether or not the United States is arming the Contras. American credibility should be at a low point from July 1979 to November 1981, before Washington began to provide military aid to the Contras. When the United States was sending military aid to the Contras (from November 1981 to October 1984 and from June 1986 to February 1988), there should have been Soviet images of higher American credibility than when such

---

1. There is an interesting theoretical point here. Strictly speaking, American inaction logically should imply only that the United States lacks resolve, but not capability, since it did not demonstrate positively any inability to prevent these two revolutions. On the other hand, there is a feasible argument that by not even trying to prevent these gains, the defender reveals even less ability than had it made some effort. This, in fact, is the implication of Glenn Snyder's argument that even U.S. losses are better for American credibility than U.S. inaction, in Glenn H. Snyder, *Deterrence and Defense* (Princeton, N.J.: Princeton University Press). But at least one formal modeler of deterrence encounters assumes precisely the opposite, namely, that a state loses more reputation by trying to deter, and then capitulating, than by never trying in the first place. See James D. Fearon, "Deterrence and the Spiral Model: The Role of Costly Signals in Crisis Bargaining" (paper presented at the 1990 annual meeting of the American Political Science Association, San Francisco, August 30–September 2, 1990). The point here is that neither position has any greater logical validity. Once again, empirical validation is the only avenue for demonstrating the superior truth-value of an assumption of deterrence theory.

military aid was suspended (from October 1984 to June 1986 and from February 1988 to Violeta Chamorro's election as president in February 1990).

Deterrence theory does not pass any of these crucially easy tests. Soviet observers, instead of being absorbed by U.S. losses in Iran and Nicaragua, focused on subsequent actions taken by the United States to ameliorate the effects of these Soviet victories. They perceived the United States balancing the loss of Somoza by trying to economically subvert the Sandinista regime, arming other Central American countries, and providing military aid to the Salvadoran government against its guerilla opposition. They did not cite the overthrow of Somoza as evidence of reduced American credibility. Similarly, while ignoring the fall of the shah, Soviets saw the American response to the shah's ouster, namely, increased naval deployments, closer military relationships with Saudi Arabia and other Gulf states, and the development of new military bases, as evidence of enhanced American balancing efforts.

As in every other case, there were no Soviet inferences about U.S. credibility in strategic areas based on American behavior in Nicaragua and Iran. As usual, Soviet views of American credibility were generated primarily from assessments of U.S. attitudes toward detente, arms control, and military programs. For example, members of the Soviet party leadership, military and foreign policy elite, and community of Americanists discussed American credibility 274 times from 1977 to 1982. In over half of these instances (141), their assessments were based on strategic U.S. behavior. They cited Iran in a significant proportion of cases ($N=61$, or 22 percent)[2] but still did not learn from that strategic American loss that the United States would be less likely to protect its strategic interests in the future. Hence, deterrence theory does not pass a crucially easy test.

The data in table 15 show that Soviet lessons about American credibility in these two cases are contrary to deterrence theory predictions.

## Iran

The evidence in table 15 shows that of the 61 lessons about American credibility Soviets inferred from the overthrow of the shah, not a single one of those lessons confirmed deterrence theory's predictions. This is a very powerful invalidation of the theory under crucially easy conditions for that theory. The preponderance of Soviet lessons that fall in the "peripheral interest" category obscures the fact that Soviets saw the United States as credible in a wide variety of different contexts. At a minimum, Soviets inferred from the "open and provocative [American] military pressure against Iran" that the

---

2. Nicaragua was a source of credibility inferences in only fourteen instances, or in 5 percent of the cases.

**TABLE 15.   Deterrence Theory's Predictions and Soviet Lessons**

| Soviet Inferences from Iran and Nicaragua (N) | |
| --- | --- |
| Confirming | Disconfirming |
| The United States will not defend its strategic interests. | The United States will attack the Soviet Union (Iran: 1). |
| The United states will not defend its peripheral interests (Nicaragua: 1). | The United States will attack socialist Soviet allies. |
| The United States will negotiate on third world conflicts. | The United States will resist detente and arms control. |
| The United States will continue detente and arms control. | The United States will not negotiate on third world conflicts. |
| The United States will not attack socialist Soviet allies. | The United States will defend its peripheral interests (Iran: 29, Nicaragua: 50). |
| The United States will not attack the Soviet Union. | The United States will defend its strategic interests (Iran: 2). |

*Note*: Lessons are listed in order of decreasing strength as evidence.

United States was not going to let the Khomeini revolution succeed.[3] Soviets also noted that as a consequence of the loss of Iran, the United States was gaining compensation by expanding its military presence elsewhere in the region, such as in Somalia.[4] Some were convinced that U.S. actions were aimed at controlling the oil resources of the entire Middle East.[5]

Some Soviets inferred far stronger lessons about American credibility, learning from U.S. actions against Iran that the United States was now ready to use force "to stop the liberation process" in general in the Third World.[6] Latin Americanists inferred from Iran that Washington would not allow any

3. Gromyko's speech at a breakfast for the Polish minister of foreign affairs in Moscow, *Pravda*, January 16, 1980, 4. For similar views, see also Primakov, "Kogda Chernoe"; Chernenko's speech awarding Chelyabinsk an Order of Lenin, *Pravda*, May 30, 1980, 2; Ustinov, "Otvesti Ugrozu Yadernoi Voiny" (To Avert the Threat of Nuclear War), *Pravda*, July 12, 1982, 4.

4. For example, Gromyko, "Razoruzhenie—Nasushchnaya Problema Sovremennosti" (Disarmament—Vital Problem of our Time), *Kommunist*, 1980, no. 11, 6–23; Kislov, "Blizhnii Vostok"; Suslov's speech at the Eighth Party Congress of the Polish Communist Party, *Pravda*, February 23, 1980, 1–2; Ogarkov also identified Egypt, Kenya, Oman, and Saudi Arabia as new military outposts for the United States in "Zavetam Lenina Verny." For more malevolent American designs in the region, see also Kremeniuk, "Razvivaiushchiesya Strany"; Primakov, "Islam"; Falin, "Voennaya Razryadka Vozmozhna—Otvet za Zapadom" (Military Detente is Possible—The Ball is in the West's Court), *Pravda*, September 19, 1979, 4.

5. For example, Belyaev, "Operatsiya 'Neftepromysly'" (Operation "Oilfields"), *LG*, November 14, 1979, 14, and "Islam i Politika"; and Primakov, "Blizhnii Vostok."

6. Kosygin's Supreme Soviet election speech, *Pravda*, February 22, 1980, 1–2. See also Trofimenko, "Washington."

"future Nicaraguas" in Latin America[7] and that it would strengthen its commitment to control Mexican oil reserves.[8] Sergei Gorshkov inferred more threatening lessons, suggesting that the United States was getting ready to use force even in strategic areas of the world, such as Europe.[9] Valentin Falin attributed the most extreme intentions to Washington, citing President Reagan to the effect that the United States no longer lacked resolve, "right up to the use of nuclear weapons."[10]

In sum, deterrence theory does not pass its crucial test here. Not a single Soviet inferred a single lesson of American weakness from the fall of the shah in Iran. Moreover, Iran was a strategic loss for the United States, and still Soviets inferred no lessons about reduced American credibility to defend its interests in other strategic areas of the globe, not even in the Middle East or Gulf.

## Nicaragua

The evidence in table 15 clearly shows that the overwhelming preponderance of Soviet inferences about American credibility was contrary to the predictions of deterrence theory. With the exception of one observation by Iordansky, Soviets learned from the American reaction to the ouster of Somoza that the United States would not allow any "new Nicaraguas" elsewhere in Latin America and the rest of the world. As in the case of Iran, Soviet observers tended to ignore the American failure to prevent a Soviet gain; instead, they commented on those measures being taken by the American government to redress its losses. Most striking, of course, is the fact that these images of high U.S. credibility occurred *before* Washington began arming the Contras. Moreover, Soviets did not devalue American credibility during the periods in which Congress ended aid to the Contras.[11]

Soviets interpreted American policy toward Nicaragua as evidence of hostile designs ranging from Nicaragua and Central and Latin America to the rest of the Third World. The most narrow interpretation Soviet observers gave

---

7. Glinkin, "Administratsiya Cartera i Latinskaya Amerika" (The Carter Administration and Latin America), *LA*, 1979, no. 4, 101–6.

8. Petr Yakovlev, "Administratsiya Cartera i Latinskaya Amerika" (The Carter Administration and Latin America), *LA*, 1979, no. 4, 136–37.

9. Gorshkov, "Slavnoe Detishche Sovetskovo Naroda" (Glorious Offspring of the Soviet People), *Kommunist*, 1980, no. 3, 43–56. See also his interview on Navy Day, *Pravda*, July 26, 1981, 2.

10. "Politicheskoe Bezdorozhe" (Political Impasse), *Pravda*, January 20, 1982, 4.

11. Of course, now we know, from the testimony of Oliver North, John Poindexter, and others, that American funding of the Contras was not limited to congressionally authorized sources. The Soviets were more accurate in their assessment of American actions on behalf of the Contras than the American people could be.

to American actions against Nicaragua was that the United States was committed either to the overthrow of the Sandinistas or to coercing them into changing their foreign and domestic policies in such a manner as to make them indistinguishable from other pro-American clients in Central America.[12] Others linked U.S. policy against the Sandinistas to a renewed commitment to maintain the status quo in Central America.[13] Somewhat more broadly, the American efforts against Nicaragua demonstrated an American commitment to "unleash a campaign of threats and pressure against the states and national liberation movements of Central America and the Caribbean," and in Latin America in general.[14] American actions in Nicaragua also demonstrated American intentions toward third world countries writ large. Ustinov, for example, argued that American support for the Contras showed that the United States "will not tolerate changes that contradict American interests in developing countries that are rich with raw materials or occupy important strategic positions. They will not allow any more new Nicaraguas."[15]

---

12. See, from among numerous examples, Gromyko's speech at a dinner with Yugoslavian foreign minister Vrkhovets, *Pravda*, April 5, 1982, 4; Shevardnadze's speech at a reception for Argentine foreign minister Caputo, *Pravda*, January 30, 1986, 4; Glinkin, "Gegemonizm SShA v Zapadnom Polulsharii: Istoriya i Sovremennost" (U.S. Hegemony in the Western Hemisphere: History and Modern Times), *LA*, May 1982, 37–47; and Mikoyan, "Latin America: New Upsurge," *NT*, 1985, no. 16, 18–21.

13. For example, Petr Yakovlev, "Rabochii Klass i Vneshnyaya Politika" (The Working Class and Foreign Policy), *LA*, February 1982, 17–19.

14. Gromyko's speech in the Supreme Soviet, *Pravda*, June 17, 1983, 2. For other examples, from among many, see Ponomarev's speech before French MPs, *Pravda*, October 26, 1984, 4; Petr Yakovlev, "Dva Kursa v Mirovoi Politike i Latinskaya Amerika" (Two Courses in World Politics and Latin America), *LA*, March 1984, 6–16; Korolev, "Revoliutsionnyi Protsess v Stranakh Tsentralnoi Ameriki: Istoricheskaya Preemstvennost i Osobennosti" (The Revolutionary Process in Central American Countries: Historical Continuity and Peculiarities), *LA*, April 1984, 5–19; Glinkin, "Latinskaya Amerika v Globalnoi Strategii Imperializma" (Latin America in the Global Strategy of Imperialism), *MEIMO*, October 1982, 65–82; and Mikoyan, "Politika Bezrassudstva" (Policy of Recklessness), *Pravda*, June 9, 1984, 4.

15. Ustinov, "Otvesti Ugrozu Yadernoi Voiny," 4. Other examples include Ogarkov, "Na Strazhe Mirnovo Truda"; Kremeniuk, "Po Staromu Stsenariiu Interventsionizma" (According to the Old Scenario of Interventionism), *SShA*, May 1981, 52–7; Kim, "The National Liberation Movement Today," *IA*, April 1981, 27–37; Gromyko's speech at a breakfast for Kampuchean foreign minister Hun Sen, *Pravda*, September 21, 1983, 4; Chernenko's Supreme Soviet election speech, *Pravda*, March 3, 1984, 1–2; Shevardnadze's speech on Lenin's birthday, *Pravda*, April 23, 1986, 1–2; Gorbachev's speech at the Fifth Party Congress of the Vietnamese Communist Party, *Pravda*, March 29, 1982, 4; Gorshkov interview, *Pravda*, July 31, 1983, 2; Sokolov, "Pobeda"; Primakov, "Breeding Local Conflicts"; Ulyanovsky, "K Kharakteristike"; Ponomarev, "Sovremennaya Obstanovka i Rol Demokraticheskoi Pechati" (The Contemporary Situation and the Role of the Democratic Press), *Kommunist*, 1983, no. 17, 3–19; Brutents, "Mezhdunarodnaya Napryazhennost"; Falin, "Imperskaya Spes"; Arbatov, "Chto, Esli ne Mir?" (What, if not Peace?), *Pravda*, August 13, 1984, 6; and Dobrynin's speech in Moscow, *Pravda*, May 15, 1986, 4.

Only Iordansky was unreservedly optimistic that, despite its intentions, the United States was incapable of preventing "any more new Nicaraguas."[16]

## Deterrence Theory Fails an Easy Credibility Test

As is manifest from table 15, Soviet views of American credibility after the overthrow of the shah and Somoza were precisely the opposite of those predicted by deterrence theory. Since these Soviet victories came on the heels of other American defeats, these Soviet gains were a crucially easy test for the theory. It does not pass this test. Moreover, since Iran was a strategic loss for the United States, if Soviets ever were to infer lessons about American credibility in strategic areas of the globe based on American behavior in the periphery, this was the case. They did not. Deterrence theory fails the easiest possible third world test for that proposition.

## Soviet Lessons about Regional Dynamics

If deterrence theory assumptions are correct, then Soviets should have predicted that dominoes would fall after their gains in Iran and Nicaragua. After the overthrow of the shah, they should have expected, at a minimum, that the UAE, Qatar, Oman, Kuwait, Bahrain, and/or Saudi Arabia would be threatened by revolutionary upheaval. After Somoza's departure, Soviets should have written and spoken about imminent revolutions in El Salvador, Honduras, and Guatemala. Moreover, Soviets should have become less optimistic about revolutionary influence emanating from Nicaragua after the United States began to arm the Contras. And the level of Soviet optimism should correlate negatively with the level of American aid to the Contras from 1981 to 1990.

Again, as in the cases of Vietnam and Angola, deterrence theory receives its strongest confirmation in the area of regional dynamics. Similar to the case of Angola, however, Soviet optimism was either short-lived or replaced by pessimism. It bears repeating that for a theory to be confirmed in a crucially easy test, it must generate more than ambiguous supporting evidence. The latter appears in table 16.

## Iran

Similar to the aftermath of the MPLA's victory in Angola,[17] many Soviet observers initially were encouraged about the prospects for progressive

---

16. Iordansky, "Policy."
17. See chap. 3 under "Angola."

**TABLE 16.    Soviet Inferences and Deterrence Theory's Assumptions about Regional Dynamics**

| Soviet Lessons (N) | |
|---|---|
| Confirming | Disconfirming |
| Dominoes will fall in areas of strategic interest to the United States. | Countries contiguous to Iran or Nicaragua will effectively resist any further revolutionary change in the region (Iran: 9, Nicaragua: 7). |
| Dominoes will fall in other peripheral areas of the globe (Iran: 7, Nicaragua: 5). | Other third world countries around the globe will balance effectively against any regional revolutionary threats (Iran: 3). |
| Dominoes will fall in countries contiguous to Iran or Nicaragua (Iran: 7, Nicaragua: 9). | U.S. strategic allies will balance effectively against any threats of revolution in their area. |

*Note*: Lessons are listed in order of decreasing strength as evidence.

change in the world by the overthrow of the shah. But only one of these Soviets continued making such unreserved inferences after October 1980. All the rest either stopped inferring encouraging lessons about regional dynamics, shifted explicitly from optimism to pessimism, or consistently saw only regional balancing.

Suslov was one of those who was initially moved to see the overthrow of the shah as a sign that the prospects for revolution had improved throughout the Third World.[18] Brutents argued Iran demonstrated that the model of neo-capitalist development preferred by Washington in the Third World was doomed. He suggested that Iran had been a crucial case for this model; since it failed there, it was bound to fail many other places where conditions were not so conducive to capitalism. He concluded that "the lessons of Iran foretell gloomy prospects for contemporary neocolonialism."[19] Arbatov inferred from Iran that other dictatorial regimes were like "delayed-action mines," waiting to explode in Washington's face.[20] Other Soviets limited their optimistic inferences to the region.[21] The Soviets in this group were alike in that they stopped making optimistic assessments about the effects of Iran by October 1980.

18. In a Supreme Soviet election speech, *Pravda*, March 1, 1979, 2. Other expressions of global optimism included Kosygin's speech at a dinner for Thailand's prime minister in Moscow, *Pravda*, March 22, 1979, 4; and Ogarkov's speech to military commanders, *KZ*, June 5, 1980, 2.

19. Brutents, "Neokolonializm," 81–94.

20. Arbatov, "Na Poroge Novovo Desyatiletiya" (On the Threshold of a New Decade), *Pravda*, March 3, 1980, 6.

21. For example, Kim, "Sovetskii Soiuz."

Another group of Soviets was intitially encouraged by events in Iran, but then changed in light of subsequent events. Kremeniuk, for example, at first wrote that the fall of the shah was evidence of a continued change in the correlation of forces against the United States in the Third World.[22] A scant four months later, however, he remarked that other states in the region, namely, Oman, Kenya, and Somalia, had agreed to provide military bases for the United States.[23]

Some Soviets, however, never expressed any unreserved optimism based on events in Iran. Primakov, for example, expressed anxiety about the possibility of an "anticommunist direction being attached to the Islamic movement, which, as a result of Iranian events, had acquired a significant anti-imperialist impulse." Evidence for this fear was the outcome of the Islamic Conference meeting in Pakistan in 1980.[24] Primakov also lamented the fact that the Iran-Iraq war had made the Gulf states, in particular Kuwait, receptive to the idea of an "American military presence in the Gulf."[25]

Mirsky also never felt Iran portended future revolutionary gains. He rejected the arguments of Brutents, asserting instead that "the collapse of the Iranian variant of the development of a backward country according to the Western model is not at all the same as the bankruptcy of capitalist orientation in Africa and Asia in general. Such countries as India, Malaysia, Saudi Arabia, and many African states where capitalism is developing relatively rapidly can serve as examples."[26]

In sum, there is only ambiguous support for deterrence theory predictions here. One group of Soviet observers was initially encouraged and then either reverted to pessimism, or simply stopped making inferences about Iran. Another set of Soviets was always pessimistic about the revolution's regional

---

22. Kremeniuk, "Razvivaiushchiesya Strany."

23. Kremeniuk, "Po Staromu." Similar reversals are made by Simoniya in "Dvizhenie Neprisoedineniya Nabiraet Silu" (The Non-Aligned Movement Gathers Strength), *AIAS*, August 1979, 3–6, and then, "Newly-Free Countries: Problems of Development," *IA*, May 1982, 83–91; and Belyaev in "Iran: 'Da!' Respublike" (Iran: "Yes!" to the Republic), *LG*, April 18, 1979, 14, and then, "Islam i Politika," *LG*, January 16, 1980, 14.

24. Primakov, "Blizhnii Vostok," 110.

25. Primakov, "Kogda Voinu Nazyvaiut Mirom" (When They Call War Peace), *LG*, July 7, 1982, 14.

26. Mirsky, report at an Institute of World Economics and International Relations (IMEMO) conference on the scientific-technological revolution and the deepening of economic and sociopolitical contradictions, *MEIMO*, August 1979, 58. See also "Natsionalno-Osvoboditelnaya Borba: Sovremennyi Etap" (National Liberation Struggle: Modern Stage), *MEIMO*, June 1981, 17–30. See Sheinis for an economic argument on why the Iranian development model under the shah still had future prospects for success in "Ekonomicheskie i Sotsialnye Problemy Razvivaiushchikhsya Stran Vostoka" (Economic and Social Problems of Developing Countries of the East), *MEIMO*, December 1982, 115–23.

effects. This kind of evidence is neither strong invalidation nor powerful confirmation of deterrence theory.

## Nicaragua

Soviet lessons from Nicaragua had much in common with their inferences from Iran. Some Soviets at first were encouraged by the Sandinista victory, but then never spoke or wrote about it again. Others evolved from optimistic appraisals in the first several years to pessimistic analyses thereafter. This would appear consistent with deterrence theory, in that Soviet pessimism should rise with U.S. support for the Contras. But, instead, there is no correlation between these two phenomena. Finally, there are several Soviets who saw nothing but regional balancing against the Sandinistas from the first day of the revolution. In sum, there is only the weakest validation of the theory, but also only the weakest disconfirmation.

At the optimistic extreme are those Soviets who cited the Sandinista victory as evidence that the prospects for success of national liberation movements all over the world had been greatly improved by events in Nicaragua.[27] These Soviets neither repeated nor recanted their initially encouraging assessments. Other Soviets were only optimistic about the Nicaraguan revolution's effects on the region of Central or Latin America. Shulgovsky, for example, suggested that other Latin American militaries might become more progressive as a consequence of witnessing the lack of support the Nicaraguan army offered Somoza.[28] Glinkin cited Latin American "diplomatic and political support for the struggle of Nicaragua" as a sign that America's southern neighbors would no longer support American military intervention in Latin America along the lines of "Operation Guatemala."[29] He also identified the "invigoration of the struggle against the dictatorial regimes in El Salvador, Guatemala, and Honduras," as well as the 1979 coup in Grenada, as conse-

27. Examples include Suslov's speech giving Bryansk an Order of the October Revolution, *Pravda*, September 19, 1979, 2; and Chernenko's speech at the Second Party Congress of the Cuban Communist Party in Havana, *Pravda*, December 20, 1980, 4. This statement should be interpreted in light of the contextual demands created by Chernenko's audience. It would be quite disappointing to his Cuban friends had he not touted the revolutionizing effects of the Sandinista revolution, especially given long-standing Cuban support for the Sandinista National Liberation Front (FSLN).

28. Shulgovsky, "Eksperiment Bolshoi Istoricheskoi Vazhnosti" (An Experiment of Great Historical Importance), *LA*, March 1980, 6–12. For the regional influence of Nicaragua, also see Glinkin, "Administratsiya Cartera" and "Latinskaya Amerika."

29. Glinkin, "Sistemnyi Podkhod—Osnova Uglublennovo Analiza Vneshnepoliticheskoi Deyatelnosti Latinoamerikanskikh Gosudarstv" (Systems Approach—Basis of a Deepened Analysis of the Foreign Policy Activities of Latin American States), *LA*, August 1981, 50.

quences of the Sandinista victory.[30] It should be noted that, contrary to deterrence theory assumptions, Glinkin maintained his optimism about the regional effects of the Nicaraguan gain *after* the United States began arming the Contras.[31]

Finally, there was a group of Soviet observers who saw only balancing efforts by Nicaragua's neighbors. Korolev, for example, while recognizing the revolutionizing effect of Nicaragua on El Salvador, Honduras, and Guatemala, lamented that each of these regimes would come to the assistance of each other if one "finds itself driven into a corner" by any revolutionary threat.[32] Korolev also noted that whereas Latin American Christian Democrats had positively welcomed and supported Sandinista efforts to overthrow Somoza, they have "responded differently to events in El Salvador."[33]

## A Mixed Report on Deterrence Theory

In the case of Iran, a comparatively large group of Soviets concluded that the overthrow of the shah augured more American foreign policy defeats in the Third World. None of these observers—Suslov, Kosygin, Ogarkov, Ponomarev, Brutents, and Arbatov—continued expressing such optimism after October 1980, however. Others, such as Kremeniuk, Simoniya, and Belyaev, replaced their optimism with views of regional balancing.[34] Primakov, Landa, Sheinis, and Mirsky inferred only regional resistance as a consequence of the Iranian revolution. Only Kim, who saw progressive gains cumulating in the region at least until September 1982, inferred lessons consistent with deterrence theory.

In the case of Nicaragua, which, at least in raw numbers, lends the greatest support to traditional deterrence theory hypotheses, Suslov, Ogarkov, and Kremeniuk remained optimistic about the case as evidence of global progress; Ponomarev, Shulgovsky, and Glinkin remained optimistic about the regional dynamics set off by the Sandinista victory; and Korolev and Mikoyan

---

30. Glinkin, "Gegemonizm SShA," 38.

31. Glinkin, for example, "Gegemonizm SShA," and "Latinskaya Amerika."

32. Korolev, "El Salvador: The 'Hot Spot' in Latin America," *IA*, June 1981, 65. Shulgovsky identified the "repressive methods" of regimes in El Salvador and Guatemala, in particular, in "Social and Political Development in Latin America," *IA*, November 1979, 58.

33. Korolev, "Revoliutsionnye Protsessy i Voprosy Sotsialno-Politicheskovo Razvitiya v Latinskoi Amerike" (Revolutionary Processes and Questions of Sociopolitical Development in Latin America), *LA*, April 1981, 61. See also Mikoyan, "Venezuela: Vneshnyaya Politika, Nekotorye Predposylki i Osobennosti Formirovaniya" (Venezuela: Foreign Policy, Some Preconditions and Peculiarities of its Formulation), *LA*, December 1980, 8–11 and "Storm and Stress," *NT*, 1981, no. 13, 18–20.

34. Kislov changed his views from ongoing struggle to balancing by January 1981.

remained convinced that a battle between the two tendencies was underway in the region.

The unreservedly optimistic Soviet observers, however, did not make any optimistic appraisals after February 1981, that is, almost ten months prior to the American decision to become indirectly involved in resisting the San dinista regime.[35] This fact implies that whatever encouragement the Sandinista revolution offered Soviet observers, it was fleeting.

## Explaining Soviet Lessons from Iran and Nicaragua

Deterrence theory, for the most part, fails another crucially easy test in this chapter. Soviets continued to ascribe high credibility to the United States, despite a strategic loss in Iran, and two more losses in the "arc of crisis" of the 1970s. Most Soviets also described regional actors in the Gulf and Central America as primed to balance against the effects of Soviet gains in Iran and Nicaragua. Those who were encouraged by these victories maintained such outlooks only temporarily. But the results of these two tests, as important an indictment of deterrence theory as they are, can claim only that the theory fails in these cases. A test of the theory in general requires investigating *how* Soviets generated these disconfirming and validating lessons. The data in table 17 show the results of this step.

The strongest possible validation of deterrence theory would be if all Soviet lessons fell into the upper left box, or universal confirmation. The most telling refutation of the theory would be if all these lessons were located in the lower left box, or universal disconfirmation. The general theory is not validated, and it is disconfirmed in a more profound way than the data in the box imply. Though universal confirmation of the theory does occur, the discussion below will show the weakness of this evidence. Moreover, the theory's predictions about U.S. credibility and regional dynamics are both universally disconfirmed. Deterrence assumptions about U.S. credibility receive no confirmation of any variety. Finally, we must remember that this theory is being considered under crucially easy circumstances. Consequently, we should expect a far more convincing performance than the results in table 17.

### Universal Explanations for Soviet Lessons from Iran and Nicaragua

Explanations with universal validity beyond the particular Soviet case come in three varieties. They can be the empirical resolution of some logically indeterminate or logically inconsistent proposition of the theory. They can be the

---

35. With the exception of Glinkin, whose last optimistic inference was in October 1982.

**TABLE 17.  The Power of Different Explanations for Soviet Lessons**

| | Types of Explanations | | |
| --- | --- | --- | --- |
| | Universal | General | Peculiar |
| Lessons confirming deterrence theory | Global and regional dominoes | Global and regional dominoes | Global and regional dominoes |
| Lessons disconfirming deterrence theory | High overall U.S. credibility | High overall U.S. credibility | High overall U.S. credibility |
| | Regional and global balancing | | Regional balancing |

product of a rational attribution process, or they can be more simple empirical conclusions that are not the obvious product of any kind of cognitive economizing or heuristic devices. Each of these three types of universal explanations are applicable to Soviet lessons from Iran and Nicaragua.

Deterrence theory's logically weak assumption of a tight interconnectedness between peripheral and strategic reputation is invalidated empirically in these cases. Soviet images of a highly credible America, of balancing regional actors, and of dominoes set off by Iran are the products of rational attribution processes. Regional balancing is a simple empirical conclusion.

*Soviet Images of High U.S. Credibility in Strategic Areas*
*of the Globe*
Continued Soviet confidence that the United States would defend its strategic interests effectively despite its setbacks in Iran and Nicaragua reinforces identical findings after Vietnam, Angola, Ethiopia, and Afghanistan. Since Iran itself is a strategic interest to the United States, deterrence theory fails in a crucially easy case here. The implication is that this logically weak assumption of the theory is universally invalid.

*Soviet Images of High U.S. Credibility in the Periphery*
In the previous two chapters, I described Soviets, primarily Americanists, who constructed rational attribution models that treated American credibility as a variable after Vietnam. However, within a year after the fall of Saigon, each of them had concluded that his hopes for less adventuristic American behavior in the Third World were misplaced. Hence, these Soviets' interpretations of American policy toward Iran and Nicaragua only reinforced prior convictions that the United States was committed and able to counter future revolutionary eruptions in the Third World. Given the redundant character of these Soviet lessons, I will only briefly describe how events in Iran and Nicaragua affected the causal attributions of these Soviet observers.

Soviet Americanists continued to see American public opinion as a most critical cause of U.S. foreign policy after the fall of the shah and, more particularly, after the seizure of the hostages in November 1979. Trofimenko, for example, argued that the "indignation of Americans at the holding of the hostages" explained the "shift to the right" in the United States and the election of Ronald Reagan as president in November 1980. The voters had given Reagan a "mandate to pursue a hard-line policy, right up to the use of force," if it was directed at "raising American prestige abroad."[36]

One would think that obvious American interests in Iranian oil would result in Soviet Americanists simply explaining American resolve as a function of its imperialist economic interests. That this did not happen is strong evidence that these Soviets did not construct their causal models of American foreign policy on an ideological basis. Kokoshin's discussion is an apt illustration of this studious avoidance of Marxist-Leninist particularism. He identified three main groups of American business. Those in the "military-industrial complex" are most interested in adventurism in the Third World and preventing detente with the Soviet Union. Multinational corporations (MNCs)dependent on returns from foreign investments generally support detente, but also selectively support interventions when their profits are threatened. The third group comprises many small and medium businesses focused on the domestic market: their political views are basically indeterminate.

Kokoshin suggested that the overthrow of the shah caused MNCs to support adventurism in the Third World, while the opening of the Chinese market made them less and less interested in detente. Increased oil prices following the Iranian revolution evoked "nationalistic feelings" among the third group of small entrepreneurs, tipping the overall balance in favor of adventurism.[37] The accuracy of Kokoshin's analysis is irrelevant for our purposes. What matters is that his analysis is consistent with a rational attribution model, and so his lessons have evidentiary value for the universe of deterrence cases.

## Soviet Images of Regional and Global Balancing
These universal disconfirming lessons come in two varieties. There are the simple statements of empirical fact and there are analyses based on rational

36. Trofimenko, "Osnovnye Postulaty Vneshnei Politiki SShA i Sudby Razryadki" (The Main Postulates of American Foreign Policy and the Fate of Detente), *SShA*, June 1980, 6; See also Arbatov, "Vneshnyaya Politika SShA na Poroge 80-x Godov" (U.S. Foreign Policy on the Eve of the 1980s), *SShA*, April 1980, 43–54; Kokoshin, "Vnutrennie Prichiny Peremen vo Vneshnei Politike" (Domestic Causes of Changes in Foreign Policy), *SShA*, July 1980, 3–13; and Kremeniuk, "Po Staromu."

37. Kokoshin, "Gruppirovki Amerikanskoi Burzhuazii i Vneshnepoliticheskii Kurs SShA" (Groupings of the American Bourgeoisie and the Course of American Foreign Policy), *SShA*, October 1981, 3–14. Kremeniuk also rejects crude Leninist interpretations of American economic interests, "Sovetsko-Amerikanskie."

attribution processes. The first involves Soviets observing that states in the Gulf and Central America responded to the revolutions in Teheran and Managua by adopting policies designed to counter any possible revolutionary processes provoked by these two events.[38]

Another group of Soviets who denied that the revolutions in Iran or Nicaragua portended future revolutions in the Third World did so because their theories of national liberation revolution and socialist construction in the Third World were not confirmed by these two events. Broadly speaking, Soviets used two general categories of analysis when pondering the causes of revolution in the Third World. The first category comprises political issues: the relationship among various classes and groups including the bourgeoisie, working class, and peasantry; the role of the military and the bureaucracy in domestic affairs; and the nature of the ruling party, its ideology, and its attitudes toward the local Communist party and toward building a vanguard organization. The second category comprises economic matters: the attitude of the government toward foreign investment, aid, and trade; toward private agriculture, industry, and commerce; and toward the possibility of adapting the Soviet economic development model to conditions in the Third World.

Soviet observers fall into two general categories: those whose analyses are driven by Marxism-Leninism and those who assess revolutionary prospects by analyzing a more catholic set of variables. In shorthand, I refer to the former as orthodox, and the latter as liberal. While I present ideal types of both views below, it must be kept in mind that the views of orthodox Soviets are the product of *peculiar* belief systems. Only the liberals are reasonably categorized as making rational attributions. I present the two opposing views together only because the juxtaposition is the best way to explain both.[39]

An orthodox Soviet observer's ideal situation is one in which he sees a conscious and organized working class leading an alliance with the peasantry whose ultimate aim is the construction of socialism. The bourgeoisie, if it exists, is an important anti-imperialist force, but can never even approach the task of building socialism. The local Communist party should ideally run the government, but since this is never the case, a revolutionary democratic party, imbued with the ideas of scientific socialism, should head a government in which the local Communist party plays a substantial role. This party should rely on the working class and peasantry and pursue policies that address their interests. The military and bureaucracy are to be completely subordinated to the party, and all officers, soldiers, and civil servants should be committed to socialism.

---

38. For examples of such commentary, see above, "Soviet Lessons about Regional Dynamics.

39. I discuss the Marxist-Leninists in detail in the section on peculiar explanations below. In chap. 7, I show the critical effects that adherence to orthodoxy or liberalism have on Soviet lessons from the fall of Nkrumah in Ghana.

On the economic front, foreign investment, trade, and aid associated with imperialist powers should be eliminated or at least put under the strictest state control. Private agriculture, industry, and commerce should be treated similarly. The experience of noncapitalist development in the Soviet Central Asian republics and in the People's Republic of Mongolia (PRM) is directly relevant to the tasks faced by Soviet allies in the Third World.

Liberal observers, at their most extreme, do not care which class heads the ruling alliance in a "country of socialist orientation" (CSO), so long as it is implementing a program leading to socialism. The working class, peasantry, bourgeoisie, and intelligentsia, in some combination, are capable of effecting progressive reforms. The Communist Party is not necessarily a desirable coalition partner; a vanguard party is not critical to the success of the regime; and ideologies alien to Marxism-Leninism can still serve progressive ends. The military has a considerable degree of autonomy from any class and so is an independent actor on the political arena. The bureaucracy should be purged of corruption and staffed with competent people who stress professionalism over ideology.

Trade with capitalist countries and receipt of their aid and investments are unavoidable and generally desirable. Private agriculture, industry, and commerce are necessary for economic development and should be left free of strict state controls. The objective of these regimes is to manage their economies efficiently to spur high economic growth rates. The experiences of "noncapitalist development" in Soviet Central Asia and the People's Republic of Mongolia are largely irrelevant to the Third World.

There are two broad effects that the revolutions in Iran or Nicaragua could have had on Soviet beliefs about the prospects for progressive change in the Third World. They could be encouraged or discouraged about socialist construction in current Soviet allies in the Third World, or countries of socialist orientation. They could also be more or less optimistic about the prospects for revolutionary upheavals in erstwhile American allies, or countries on the capitalist development path, as they were called. Liberal attribution theorists, after analyzing events in Iran, were encouraged neither about the future fate of Soviet allies nor about future developments in American allies in the Third World. The four possible ideal types are presented in table 18.

The arguments of Viktor Sheinis, though at the extreme liberal fringe of Soviet academia, show why pessimism prevailed among this group of Soviet observers, despite Soviet victories in Iran and Nicaragua. Sheinis not only incorporated all the liberal variables of other Soviets, but developed new liberal arguments on the basis of his observations. He was explicitly committed to strict positivism when assessing "hard" economic variables.[40] He was

---

40. My discussion of the very significant difference between "hard" and "soft" variables is in the section on peculiar lessons below.

**TABLE 18.   Soviet Observers: From Liberal
Pessimists to Orthodox Optimists**

|          | Optimistic | Pessimistic |
| -------- | ---------- | ----------- |
| Liberal  |            |             |
| Orthodox |            |             |

very pessimstic about revolutionary developments occurring in countries on the capitalist path due to his liberal optimism about their ability to successfully develop their economies. He combined this with great pessimism about the ability of CSOs to do the same.

In his analysis of capitalist countries, he rejected the most long-standing arguments of other Soviets. He asserted that there was no such phenomenon as "unequal exchange" between an exploited periphery and manipulative capitalist centers. These "unfavorable prices on third world products simply reflect the movement of international values."[41] He also argued that the market mechanism was superior to pure planning.[42] He warned his colleagues against seeing imperialist aid as an instrument of domination, accusing them of confusing imperialist intentions, which were indeed evil, with the aid's actual effects, which depended on how a government chose to use it.[43] He saw the economic development of newly industrializing countries (NICs) and members of the Organization of Petroleum Exporting Countries (OPEC) as a form of immunization against revolution. He argued that in such countries "capitalism is not in balance with other sectors; it is far stronger than they are combined; it is not simply system forming but is the sector *that has formed the system*, which is affirmed in the means of production." He rejected the "simple dichotomy" of dependent and independent economies, suggesting there should be a sliding scale of dependence: "One and the same state is both dependent and keeps others dependent on it." He concluded with respect to Latin American NICs that even "definite social progress" is possible under capitalism. This last point is striking because even the most liberal Soviets were willing to concede only that capitalism could yield economic growth,

41. Sheinis, "Izmeneniya v Ekonomike Kapitalizma i Nekotorye Osobennosti Neo-kolonializma 70-x Godov" (Changes in the Economy of Capitalism and Certain Peculiarities of Neocolonialism in the 1970s), *Ekonomicheskie Nauki*, January 1974, 66.

42. Sheinis, "Aktualnye Problemy Stran Azii i Afriki" (Actual Problems of Asian and African Countries), *NAIA*, 1975, no. 3, 37–52.

43. Ibid.

while simultaneously denying it could bring any social benefits. Sheinis rejected that view here.[44]

At the same conference, he defended himself against charges made by his orthodox colleagues by questioning their methodology. This position bears repeating in full, for it demonstrates the clear differences between Soviets characterized by rational attribution processes and those driven by Marxist-Leninist belief systems.

> Some have argued that the theory of dependent capitalism responds to the anti-imperialist struggle, while the concept of middle-developed capitalism allegedly is oriented toward reconciliation with imperialism. I decisively reject the transferral of a scientific discussion to such a plane. Both revolutionary and antirevolutionary conclusions can be drawn from either theory. All of us are interested not in resonant names, but in formulating ideas that most adequately reflect real processes, whether we like them or not. For Gramsci was totally right, saying that a revolution requires truth.[45]

In a later article, Sheinis put his finger precisely on the problem that affected those with rigid belief systems. He accused them of not using available statistical data to validate their general theoretical claims.[46] Sheinis expressed further optimism about capitalist countries in subsequent articles. He argued that some of them were on their way to leaving the developing world altogether and would soon join the ranks of the developed.[47] The only time he

44. "Srednerazvityi Kapitalizm: Realnost Latinskoi Ameriki" (Middle-Developed Capitalism: A Reality of Latin America), *LA*, 1979, no. 1, 65–73. This is a report he gave to a conference at the Latin American Institute in Moscow. Indeed, in a subsequent article, Sheinis told his colleagues that "one important task for Marxist analysis is to discover elements of social progess in developing countries on the capitalist path." "O Kriteriyakh Sotsialnovo Progressa v Razvivaiushchikhsya Stranakh" (On Criteria of Social Progress in Developing Countries), *NAIA*, 1981, no. 5, 66. Acknowledging the controversial nature of Sheinis's ideas, the editors of this issue cautioned its readers that the article was published "for discussion purposes" only.

45. Sheinis, "Srednerazvityi Kapitalizm: Realnost Latinskoi Ameriki," *LA*, 1979, no. 2, 130. This is a continuation of the proceedings published in *LA*, 1979, no. 1.

46. Of course, many of these Soviets did not have to meet this challenge, for they relied on orthodox "soft" variables unsusceptible to valid or reliable measurement. See Sheinis's book review in *NAIA*, 1981, no. 4, 194–201.

47. Sheinis, "Sotsialno-Ekonomicheskaya Differentsiatsiya i Problemy Tipologii Razvivaiushchikhsya Stran" (Socioeconomic Differentiation and Problems of Typologizing Developing Countries), *MEIMO*, August 1978, 94–107. More orthodox Soviets attributed whatever economic independence is attainable while being in the world capitalist system to Soviet foreign policy. For more optimistic appraisals, see Sheinis, "Razvivaiushchiesya Strany v 80-e Gody: Itogi i Perspektivy Sotsialno-Ekonomicheskoi Perestroiki" (Developing Countries in the 1980s: Results and Prospects of Socioeconomic Restructuring), *AIAS*, September 1982, 28–32, and

discussed an orthodox class variable, Sheinis treated it with liberal categories, turning it into an argument for why revolutionary prospects in capitalist countries in the Third World were virtually excluded. Drawing on ongoing events in Iran, he argued that class formation is seriously hindered even where capitalism is highly developed, since

> communities of a socioclass type coexist with ethnic, religious, and geographic communities that evolve according to their own laws and not rarely cut across classes. Noneconomic social phenomena and social processes have acquired a certain autonomy. Along with economic interests, and sometimes even stronger than them, operate other kinds of interests. Great masses of people sense their ties with caste, tribal, and other associations more acutely and directly than with class. The growth of the potential labor force beyond the number of jobs in the modern sector supports traditionalism in the society in general. It is hard to say how long the transition will take to a modern bipolar structure of bourgeoisie-proletariat. Its length will probably extend for the lifetimes of many generations.[48]

Sheinis combined his optimism about the prospects for economic development in the capitalist Third World (and, hence, pessimism about revolutionary prospects) with pessimism about economic prospects in CSOs. In fact, he recommended that Soviet allies adopt the same strategies that had brought success to their capitalist counterparts. He argued that these states should use market mechanisms and adopt policies implied by Lenin's post-Civil War New Economic Policy (NEP), rather than the model of socialist construction in Soviet Central Asia or the PRM suggested by his orthodox colleagues.[49] Sheinis criticized those who assessed the progress of CSOs by their superstructural arrangements, rather than by economic achievement.[50] The logical

---

"Ekonomicheskie i Sotsialnye Problemy." In another article, he unreservedly endorsed the "Green Revolution" in India for its effects on food production and reducing the bill for imported food. Orthodox Soviets who rarely spoke positively of its economic effects also argued it led to deleterious social phenomena, such as the kulakization of the peasantry. "Razvivaiushchiesya Strany: Osobennosti Poslevoennovo Ekonomicheskovo Rosta" (Developing Countries: Peculiarities of Postwar Economic Growth), *MEIMO*, December 1981, 57–69.

48. Sheinis, "O Spetsifike Sotsialnykh Protsessov v Razvivaiushchikhsya Stranakh" (On the Specifics of Social Processes in Developing Countries), part 1, *AIAS*, October 1981, 28.

49. Sheinis, "Aktualnye Problemy." NEP was the economic strategy adopted by the Bolshevik Party at their Tenth Party Congress in March 1921 after almost four years of "War Communism" during the civil war and foreign intervention from 1917 to 1921. It implied a mixed economy, rather than a socialized one, with elements of capitalism in the retail and agricultural sectors combined with state control of the "commanding heights."

50. "Sotsialno-Ekonomicheskaya," *MEIMO*, August 1978, 94–107.

conclusion of Sheinis's focus on economic variables to categorize less developed countries was his placement of CSOs into the fourth rank of middle-developed capitalism. He argued that Nicaragua, Syria, Algeria, Angola, and the Congo all had "capitalist-forming capitalist sectors, though they are not as secure as the first echelon."[51]

Pursuant to the Iranian revolution, and no doubt greatly influenced by it, Sheinis added new liberal elements to his list of critical variables. He saw these new factors as yet another brake on progressive developments in the Third World. Not so implicit in Sheinis's argument was the fact that a whole array of noneconomic factors made relying on Marxist-Leninist analysis only obscure the real moving forces of developing societies.

> The most important social institutions, such as the family, caste system, schools, churches, etc., and value orientations that rely on age-old traditions, only indirectly, through a number of intermediate links, and with a lag, perceive the impulses from the socioeconomic sphere: the influence of industrialization, urbanization, and sociopolitical reforms. Not rarely, the effect of social reforms is diluted and traditional structures reestablish themselves in new forms, becoming obstacles on the path of social development that are difficult to overcome. So, socioeconomic reforms are not criteria in themselves of social progress. Their role in social development can only be evaluated by the results they produce.

He concluded this article with a quote from Lenin: "To imagine world history going forward easily without gigantic leaps backward is undialectic, unscientific, and theoretically incorrect."[52]

In sum, Sheinis was quite pessimistic about revolutionary prospects in capitalist countries in the Third World due to their increasing economic development. Events in Iran did not reverse this pessimism, for he, and other

---

51. "Differentsiatsiya Razvivaiushchikhsya Stran: Ochertaniya i Masshtaby" (Differentiation of Developing Countries: Outline and Scales), *AIAS*, January 1980, 33. No other Soviet ever committed the heresy of putting radical Soviet allies into the same category as states on the capitalist path, but Sheinis's adherence to measurable economic variables made this analysis natural.

52. Sheinis, "O Kriteriyakh," 79. Remember this was published "for discussion purposes" only. This passage was a veiled swipe at orthodox Soviets who often used the declaratory programs of revolutionary democrats as evidence of social progress. Consistent with his positivistic bent, Sheinis even offered a way to indirectly measure the strength of traditional values, suggesting that Soviet scholars use statistics available on the accessibility of culture, education, and media to the peoples of these countries. See also his "O Spetsifike Sotsialnykh Problem v Razvivaiushchikhsya Stran" (On the Specifics of Social Problems in Developing Countries), part 2, *AIAS*, November 1981, 26–30; "Razvivaiushchiesya Strany v 80-e Gody"; and "Ekonomicheskie i Sotsialnye Problemy."

Soviets with similar views,[53] had access to data on many, many other cases of successful capitalist development in the Third World that allowed him to treat Iran as just one data point among many others pointing in the opposite direction. He was equally pessimistic about socialist construction in Soviet allies due to their abysmal economic records. The revolution in impoverished Nicaragua did nothing to reverse those views. Events in Iran only reinforced his sober assessment of CSOs by introducing a host of noneconomic factors that made orthodox class formation, party construction, and ideological annealing even less likely outcomes.

### Soviet Images of Falling Dominoes

There were two instances of universal explanations for Soviet lessons from Iran and Nicaragua that confirm deterrence theory. In one case, however, domino imagery was not repeated. Karen Brutents, for example, explicitly termed Iran a crucial case for the capitalist development model in the Third World. The overthrow of the shah, he argued, demonstrated that such reversals were inevitable elsewhere around the globe. But he never repeated this argument after initially stating it.[54]

On the other hand, Anatolii Glinkin, a Latin Americanist, remained optimistic throughout the 1980s. He explicitly identified behavior by other Latin American countries after the Sandinista victory that implied that progressive change was on its way in these countries, too. He noted, for example, that the national liberation movements in Central America showed new signs of life[55] and the Sandinista revolution itself had been supported by many moderate Latin American governments.[56] And once the Contra war was under way in earnest, Glinkin was encouraged by the fact that Nicaragua's neighbors, instead of joining in Washington's policies, created the Contadora process aimed at bringing the war to an end.[57]

### Mostly Universal Disconfirmation of Deterrence Theory

With the limited exception of the short-lived lessons of Brutents and the real exception of Glinkin, all Soviet lessons from Iran and Nicaragua with univer-

---

53. For example, see Mirsky's arguments that Iran was an aberration, not a representative case of capitalism's demise in the Third World: report at an IMEMO conference on the scientific-technological revolution and the deepening of economic and sociopolitcal contradictions, *MEIMO*, August 1979, 58, and "Natsionalno-Osvoboditelnaya."

54. In Brutents, "Neokolonializm."

55. Glinkin, "Gegemonizm SShA," and "Latinskaya Amerika."

56. Glinkin, "Sistemnyi Podkhod," *LA*, August 1981, 47–53.

57. For example, Glinkin, "Sovremennaya Strategiya Imperializma SShA v Latinskoi Amerika i Karibskom Basseini" (Contemporary Strategy of U.S. Imperialism in Latin American and the Caribbean Basin), *SShA*, June 1984, 16–28.

sal explanations disconfirm deterrence theory. Soviets unanimously ignored any reputational linkage between Iran and strategic areas, despite Iran's strategic value to the United States. Those Soviets who assessed American credibility and the prospects for further revolutionary developments in the Third World consistent with rational attribution models concluded that U.S. resolve and capabilities were both unchanged and that victories in Iran and Nicaragua did not presage future revolutionary upheavals elsewhere.

## General Explanations for Soviet Lessons from Iran and Nicaragua

General explanations for Soviet perceptions come in several varieties. The focus on the American military budget, procurement, and deployments continued to cause Soviets to see a highly credible America despite these defeats for the United States. Other Soviet observers relied on a more developed, though still bounded, menu of variables to explain American foreign policy. Finally, several Soviets used a kind of representative heuristic to conclude that Iran and Nicaragua meant further victories in the Third World in general.

### Soviet Images of High Overall U.S. Credibility

As was the case after Vietnam, and after the string of Soviet victories from Angola to Afghanistan, virtually all Soviets zeroed in on absolute American military capabilities when assessing U.S. credibility. This reliance on a single indicator guaranteed no reputational losses for Washington after these Soviet gains.

Many other Soviets had more elaborate, though still truncated or bounded, menus of variables they assessed in order to gauge American credibility. Evgenii Primakov's analyses provide an excellent example of someone who combined variables selected on the basis of the demands of a rigid belief system with variables selected on a more rational, and so general, basis.

On the general side of the menu, Primakov perceived the United States as credible because American leaders erroneously believed the Soviet Union was responsible for all American defeats in the Third World and also because the Washington leadership adhered to the tenets of the domino theory. The American government misconstrued the deal struck with the Soviet Union on mutual restraint in the periphery to mean that the Soviet Union would cooperate in protecting the "social status quo." The American leadership consequently interpreted events in Ethiopia, Afghanistan, and Iran as Soviet malfeasance and betrayal of these principles. He also acknowledged that the United States had "strategic interests" in the Gulf, namely, protecting oil transportation routes. The overthrow of the shah removed an ally who could protect these sea-lanes.[58] The American response was especially forceful, for the shah's Iran was one of the "subimperialist centers" increasingly relied upon by the United States after its defeat in Vietnam.[59] Since "strategic interests" are a variable, Primakov allowed that American behavior could be different according to the level of American interests in any given region.

Primakov, however, also adhered to Leninist beliefs about American motives, singling out economic motives for American behavior after the fall of the shah.[60] He argued that U.S. actions were aimed at regaining control over oil supplies in the region. Belief systems, by definition, require maintenance and protection from disconfirming evidence. Primakov defended his Leninist beliefs by ignoring arguments he himself had advanced elsewhere. Not more than four months prior to the Iranian revolution, Primakov had argued that the United States and other imperialist states had compensated for OPEC price increases through increasing the prices of their manufactured exports, developing a system of petrodollar recycling, investing in OPEC countries themselves, and selling them military hardware.[61] In the same article, in adjoining paragraphs, he argued both that the "growth of the militaristic accent in American foreign policy in the region of the Gulf is caused mainly by its loss of unhindered access and uncontrolled exploitation of the oil" and that increased oil prices "do not really threaten the American economy, since it has adapted itself to higher prices."[62] With respect to the periphery in general, Primakov acknowledged that "developed capitalist countries are the main sphere of activity of international monopolies." But he saved his belief system by arguing that "in absolute terms, their operations in developing states are growing."[63] If Primakov were to believe his own prior assertions, it would have threatened his Leninist explanation of how American foreign policy operated.

In sum, Primakov's views can be explained by a general model of bounded rationality supplemented by peculiar elements that are the fruit of a Leninist belief system.

### Soviet Images of Falling Dominoes around Nicaragua and Iran

There were two instances of what might be called the "dictatorship representativeness heuristic" invoked by Georgii Arbatov and Boris Ponomarev in

---

58. Primakov's positions are advanced in "Blizhnii Vostok."
59. Primakov, "Zakon Neravnomernosti."
60. See, for example, Primakov, "Kogda Chernoe," "Blizhnii Vostok," and "Islam."
61. Primakov, "Neocolonialism: Essence, Forms, Limits," *IA*, November 1978, 66–71.
62. Primakov, "Blizhnii Vostok," 109.
63. Primakov, "Zakon Neravnomernosti," 30.

their evaluations of the meaning of the overthrow of the shah and Somoza. Both Arbatov, with respect to the Iranian revolution, and Ponomarev, with regard to Nicaragua, concluded that other capitalist dictatorships around the world would meet the same fate as those in Teheran and Managua.[64] We should, however, probably evaluate differently the level of generality of the two usages. Whereas Arbatov has demonstrated all the characteristics of rational attribution in his evaluations of American foreign policy, Ponomarev has shown himself to be a rigid Marxist-Leninist. Therefore, it is reasonable to imagine Arbatov using his dictatorship heuristic as a purely cognitive shortcut, while it is equally reasonable to believe that Ponomarev's heuristic is derived from his belief system, which demands that capitalism be equated with dictatorial repression of the working masses and that national liberation movements be destined to replace this repression with socialism. Hence, Arbatov's use of the heuristic is more generally relevant to the universe of deterrence cases than Ponomarev's.

*General (Dis)Confirmation of Deterrence Theory*
Deterrence theory's assumptions about credibility are invalidated empirically by Soviet lessons that can be explained using a general model of bounded rationality. This implies a general disconfirmation of this proposition of the theory. However, Arbatov's use, if not Ponomarev's, of a representative heuristic to infer lessons from the ouster of the shah in Iran is a general confirmation of the theory's assumption about regional effects. Again, there is a clear difference between Arbatov and Ponomarev in that the former's writings manifested clear rational-attribution processes, whereas Ponomarev's writings and speeches displayed the clear imprint of Marxist-Leninist beliefs.

## Peculiar Explanations for Soviet Lessons from Iran and Nicaragua

Marxist-Leninist belief systems make demands upon their adherents. There are two values that might be maximized: revolutionary commitment or ideological orthodoxy. Revolutionary commitment stresses the Leninist side of the set of beliefs. A premium is placed on making one's perceptions of reality consistent with continual advances of the world revolutionary alliance. The result is inexorable confidence that the Third World is a place where successful national liberation revolutions that lead to socialism are inevitable. Hence, Soviet gains in Iran and Nicaragua simply vindicated these beliefs. In terms of

---

64. Arbatov, "Na Poroge"; and Ponomarev's speech at a *Problems of Peace and Socialism* editorial board conference in East Berlin, *Pravda*, October 21, 1980, 4.

the boxes in table 18, those Soviets committed to revolutionary progess are the orthodox optimists at the lower left.

*Soviet Images of High Overall U.S. Credibility*
The Soviet party and military leadership and many members of the foreign policy elite remained convinced of high American resolve and capabilities because of their adherence to Marxism-Leninism. Consequently, Soviet lessons from Iran and Nicaragua were formally identical to those that I have described in the previous two chapters on Vietnam, Angola, Ethiopia, and Afghanistan.

*Soviet Images of Falling Dominoes*
The vast preponderance of Soviets who expected future gains in the Third World on the basis of their victories in Iran and Nicaragua did so because of their orthodox Marxist-Leninist view of the world revolutionary process, and developments within third world countries. As I have noted with regard to lessons from Vietnam to Afghanistan, Soviets with a commitment to the world revolutionary alliance headed by the Soviet Union invariably cited their victories as evidence that, first, Soviet leadership of this alliance was effective and, second, future victories were on the way. Lessons from Iran and Nicaragua continued this pattern.[65]

More specifically, there was a group of Soviets who maintained optimism about revolutionary prospects in the Third World because of their manipulation of orthodox variables. The critical variables orthodox Soviets monitored are largely unfalsifiable. Such notions as the level of consciousness of the working class or ideological rectitude of party cadres are inherently hard to measure, let alone verify. This allows those orthodox Soviets who have belief systems committed to revolutionary change to easily maintain high confidence in their rosy outlooks. This is in contrast to liberal Soviets who monitored more concrete and even quantifiable critical variables, such as food production or particular policy actions by revolutionary democrats. Measures of these variables are harder to distort or ignore than the "softer" units of analysis used by orthodox observers.[66]

---

65. See, for example, Suslov's speech giving Bryansk an Order of the October Revolution, *Pravda*, September 19, 1979, 2; Chernenko's speech at the Second Party Congress of the Cuban Communist Party in Havana, *Pravda*, December 20, 1980, 4; Ponomarev's speech at a *Problems of Peace and Socialism* conference in East Berlin, *Pravda*, October 21, 1980, 4; and Brutents, "A Great Force of Modern Times," *IA*, March 1981, 74–85.

66. Experimental psychologists have found that subjects resort to a variety of cognitive shortcuts when faced with values they cannot combine easily, that is, qualitative rather than quantitative attributes about some person or event. See Slovic and MacPhillamy, "Dimensional

The orthodox Soviet's concentration on the political superstructure of these allied regimes, rather than on the economic base, allowed him to ignore the material constraints that impede any movement forward on a progressive development path. By selectively avoiding evidence of economic failures and seizing on the fact that local Communists are allowed to operate legally, orthodox observers were able to maintain high levels of commitment to a regime that was on the brink of collapse. Liberals, as noted above, derived their levels of confidence much more directly from evidence of economic performance.

When an orthodox observer did remark on the economic travails of a Soviet ally, his explanation centered on the colonialist legacy of that country or the current neocolonialist plundering by imperialist states. This has two mutually reinforcing effects. First, by never coming to grips with indigenous obstacles to economic development, he overestimated this potential. By identifying such difficulties with imperialism, he directly invoked the internationalist responsibilities of the Soviet Union to support such countries in their battles with the West. Both of these cause the orthodox Soviet to believe in both the desirability and the need to support such regimes.

The orthodox Soviet observer's concentration on class analysis and party development also directly translates into greater confidence that the Soviet Union could provide crucial aid to these regimes. Given the inability of the Soviet economy to provide even a minimal counterweight to the resources controlled by Western multinational corporations, markets, multilateral aid consortia, and bilateral aid arrangements, orthodox observers, by emphasizing the critical significance of party construction and the social aspects of economic development, diverted their attention from those needs of their allies that the Soviet Union could not even hope to meet. Instead, the Soviet Union could train ideological cadres, build party schools, and help develop the state sector to train a working class. Liberals, conversely, saw the lack of an international socialist division of labor as a major obstacle to progressive developments in these regimes.

Orthodox Soviets employed class analysis to gauge the prospects for progressive development in a given country. This tends to obscure such geopolitical factors as that country's importance to the United States as either a supplier of some critical imported products or simply its geographical proximity to the United States. This factor is most marked in orthodox analyses of Latin American countries with their relatively developed, by third world standards, working classes. This led orthodox observers to underestimate the

Commensurability," 172. Slovic and MacPhillamy cite additional work that shows that even people with expertise in a particular area, such as internists diagnosing illnesses, manifest these subrational decision-making processes when faced with qualitative data.

credibility of an American response to progressive change in these countries, so undermining deterrence.

Finally, orthodox observers would overestimate the prospects of socialist development in Soviet allies by invoking the analogy with the historical experience of Soviet Central Asian republics and the PRM. Having an available success story of noncapitalist development allowed these Soviets to exaggerate the ease with which their third world allies would be able to traverse the same path to socialism.[67] Taken together, orthodox beliefs are very powerful generators of optimistic predictions about revolutionary prospects in the Third World after Soviet victories there.

Georgii Kim displayed a number of devices common to individuals trying to maintain the pscyhological integrity of their belief systems. For example, he engaged in selective attention; that is, he seized on the victories in Iran and Nicaragua in order to validate his revolutionary optimism, while paying far less attention to Soviet defeats in Somalia, Zaire, Zimbabwe, and Grenada. As noted, orthodox Soviets believe that socialist construction in their allied CSOs was possible only if there is a close alliance between the ruling "revolutionary democrats" and local representatives of the working class, namely, the local Communist party. In other words there needs to be a "united front" between the radical bourgeois leadership and local Communists. Kim recognized that this alliance rarely, if ever, occurred in reality. To square these dissonant perceptions, Kim came up with the argument that even though revolutionary democrats had no intention of giving way to working-class influence, their own radical reforms, "independent of their subjective aspirations," would result in the necessary Communist participation in the revolution.[68] In this way, Kim was able to be encouraged by the Sandinista revolution, despite the absence of the critical orthodox ingredient of a united front in that revolution.

Kim was also representative of the orthodox school in that he had to believe that economic progress was less important than superstructural phenomena in CSOs if he was going to maintain revolutionary optimism in the face of evidence that CSOs were economically backward. Kim had to argue that strict adherence to Marxism-Leninism, construction of a vanguard party imbued with scientific socialism and allied with local Communists, could overcome these economic barriers to a socialist future.[69] Much as the success of the Sandinistas in Nicaragua validated Kim's optimism about developments

---

67. It seems that some kind of "availability heuristic" may be operating here.

68. Kim's conversion of necessity into virtue first occurred in "Natsionalizm, Proletarskii Internatsionalizm i Revoliutsionnyi Protsess na Vostoke" (Nationalism, Proletarian Internationalism, and the Revolutionary Process in the East), *PDV*, 1973, no. 1, 74–83.

69. And he did so. See Kim, "World Socialism and Present-Day National Liberation Revolutions," *IA*, August 1977, 67–76.

in CSOs in general, the Iranian revolution reinforced his confidence that countries on the capitalist path in the Third World were fated to have revolutionary explosions. The basis for this optimism was his belief that none of these states could successfully develop economically following the capitalist model. In order to make this argument, in the face of clear evidence of economic growth in a host of NICs and OPEC countries, Kim countered by arguing these states' inattention to social inequality portended eventual revolution regardless of economic progress.[70] Kim showed the inherent unfalsifiability of the orthodox belief system by arguing that even rich oil producers who spend money on social problems only "make these conflicts more acute."[71] Essentially, if capitalist countries are poor, then a revolutionary situation is unavoidable due to the poverty of its masses; if it is rich, this only increases "social contradictions."

The Iranian revolution challenged Kim's orthodoxy because of the revolution's obvious religious content. But Kim protected his revolutionary optimism by recasting Khomeini's revolution in terms of traditional class analysis. The revolution was not "simply trying to revive traditional religious institutions"[72] but rather was a reaction against "bourgeois-capitalist means and methods."[73]

In sum, Soviets with orthodox Leninist beliefs were guaranteed encouragement from victories like Iran and Nicaragua. They were used as evidence to validate revolutionary optimism about the Third World in general.

## Soviet Images of Balancing around Iran

As I noted above, orthodox Soviet belief systems can have either of two central values that are most highly protected by their adherents: ideological orthodoxy or revolutionary optimism. Those who saw global dominoes in the victories in Iran and Nicaragua seized on those two events to protect their revolutionary optimism. Another set of orthodox Soviets, however, were not

---

70. This was a constant refrain. See, for example, Kim, "Nekotorye Problemy Sovremennykh Natsionalno-Osvoboditelnykh Revoliutsii v Azii i Afrike" (Certain Problems of National Liberation Revolutions in Asia and Africa), *VI*, August 1973, 73–85, "Natsionalno-Osvoboditelnoe Dvizhenie"; "XXV Syezd KPSS i Problemy Natsionalno-Osvoboditelnykh Revoliutsii" (The Twenty-fifth Congress of the CPSU and Problems of National-Liberation Revolutions), *NAIA*, 1976, no. 3, 3–15, "World Socialism," "Razryadka i Razvivaiushchiesya Strany" (Detente and Developing Countries), *Pravda*, August 9, 1977, 4, and "Usilenie Sotsialno-Klassovoi Differentsiatsii" (The Strengthening of Socio-class Differentiation), *AIAS*, November 1981, 4–9.

71. "The National Liberation Movement Today," *IA*, April 1981, 33.

72. Kim, "Social Development and Ideological Struggle in Developing Countries," *IA*, April 1980, 68.

73. "Usilenie Sotsialno-Klassovoi," 6.

at all encouraged by the revolution in Iran, at least, because its content was at dramatic variance with their orthodox Marxist categories of analysis. Those Soviets committed to maintaining their ideological orthodoxy fall into the orthodox pessimist box at the lower left in table 18.

Rostislav Ulyanovsky's analysis of the Iranian revolution is an excellent example of "orthodox pessimism," the product of a commitment to ideological orthodoxy over revolutionary progress. The religious hue of Khomeini's revolution caused Ulyanovsky to identify "traditionalism" as yet another obstacle to socialist construction in the Third World.

He argued that traditions are a "wall against progress," in that they prevent people from seeing scientific socialism as the only appropriate ideology. Progressive social and economic reforms are resisted by an "excessive fixation of public attention on the past." He concluded in dismay that "it is not at all accidental that the Christian countries of the West, and not the Islamic-Buddhist countries of the East, became the birthplace of capitalism."[74] Ulyanovksy recognized that Islam was hardly conducive to developing a united front between Iranian Communists and members of Khoemini's movement. He warned that "left-democratic organizations [in Iran] have no basis to breathe easily."[75] Ulyanovsky also condemned the Iranian search for a "third way between socialism and capitalism" that can only end up as a "camouflage for the capitalist development path."[76]

*Peculiar (Dis)Confirmation of Deterrence Theory*

Two sets of Soviet lessons that disconfirm deterrence theory are the product of peculiar belief systems. Many Soviet images of high American credibility after the removals of the shah and Somoza are the product of adherence to a Marxist-Leninist understanding of imperialism. A few Soviets were positively discouraged by the Iranian revolution because their orthodox prescriptions for progress in the Third World were violated by Khomeini's program in Iran. Deterrence theory is also confirmed by peculiar lessons. Many Soviets predicted, on the basis of these two Soviet victories, that revolutions elsewhere in the periphery were inevitable. These predictions were based on adherence to Leninist views of the world revolutionary process and the role of the national liberation movement in that process.

---

74. Ulyanovsky, "K Voprosu o Spetsifike Razvitiya Stran Vostoka" (On the Question of the Specifics of the Development of Eastern Countries), *NAIA*, 1979, no. 5, 58–74.

75. Ulyanovsky, "O Natsionalnom Osvobozhdenii i Natsionalizme" (On National Liberation and Nationalism), *AIAS*, October 1980, 4.

76. Ulyanovsky, "Iranskaya Revoliutsiya i ee Osobennosti" (The Iranian Revolution and its Peculiarities), *Kommunist*, 1982, no. 10, 111.

A Scorecard for Deterrence Theory:
Another Failing Grade

The information in the following scorecard for deterrence theory is self-explanatory.

1. Universal explanations that confirm deterrence theory: One Soviet, Anatolii Glinkin, saw Latin American support for the Sandinista revolution and heightened revolutionary prospects in Central America.
2. General explanations that confirm deterrence theory: One Soviet, Arbatov, invoked a "representativeness heuristic" on dictatorships that convinced him that American allies throughout the Third World were facing revolutionary upheavals, as the shah had in Iran.
3. Peculiar explanations that confirm deterrence theory: Those Soviets with orthodox Marxist-Leninist belief systems, especially the party leadership, predicted future victories for national liberation movements around the world based on this set of beliefs.
4. Universal explanations that disconfirm deterrence theory:
   a. All Soviets continued to attribute high credibility to the United States in strategic areas of the globe because they saw no logical connection between U.S. behavior in areas of negligible interest and its future conduct in places with critical stakes. Moreover, Iran is a crucially easy case for deterrence theory to pass, given that country's strategic value to the United States.
   b. All Soviets derived their images of U.S. strategic credibility almost exclusively from its behavior on strategic issues because U.S. behavior in the Third World was of only peripheral salience to Soviet analysis of this question.
   c. The community of Americanists was convinced of U.S. capability and resolve in the Third World based on their analysis of the "causes" of American foreign policy, including, but not limited to, public opinion, congressional sentiments, and the state of the economy.
   d. Many Soviets identified acts of balancing by regional actors in the Gulf and Central and Latin America that discouraged them from expecting any revolutionizing effects from these two victories.
   e. Soviets who were "liberal pessimists" had their theories of socialist development in the Third World confirmed by revolutionary developments in Iran. They concluded both that Soviet allies in the Third World were in trouble and that American allies were getting stronger.

5. General explanations that disconfirm deterrence theory:
   a. Many Soviets, including virtually the entire party leadership and military and foreign policy elite, maintained images of a highly credible America because they operated with a very restricted menu of critical variables in their analyses, namely, military spending and deployments.
   b. Several Soviets, including Evgenii Primakov, believed the United States to be highly credible because they assessed American foreign policy with the aid of a limited menu of variables, some rationally selected, the others chosen by adherence to a Marxist-Leninist belief system about imperialism.
6. Peculiar explanations that disconfirm deterrence theory:
   a. Most members of the party leadership and military and foreign policy elites considered high U.S. credibility to be axiomatic, given their adherence to orthodox Marxist-Leninist belief systems.
   b. A few Soviets, including Rostislav Ulyanovsky, gained no optimism from the revolution in Iran because of a commitment to ideological orthodoxy. The religious underpinnings of that revolution only served to underline the enormous distance between orthodox Marxist prescriptions and actual revolutionary practice.

Under crucially easy circumstances, deterrence theory fails to generate more than a modicum of evidence that can be considered applicable beyond the Soviet case itself. Its strongest confirming evidence is peculiar to belief systems that fall into the same conceptual box as Marxism-Leninism. Meanwhile, the theory was disconfirmed by a wide variety of evidence.

## Considering Alternative Explanations for Soviet Lessons from Iran and Nicaragua

The discussion of these two cases does not offer many obvious alternative interpretations of my own analysis of Soviet lessons—at least beyond those already dealt with in chapters 2 and 3. The only objection might be that I have mischaracterized the debate between orthodox and liberal Soviet analysts of the Third World. The argument would be that liberals also have a belief system. It just has different components. So, my argument that liberal lessons are universal, but orthodox inferences are peculiar, is not fair. I think, however, that there are clear differences between the two ideal types that demonstrate that my labels are justified.

Belief systems have two obvious features that allow easy identification. First, the people who adhere to them treat evidence in predictable ways.

Second, there is a set of underlying motives that drives their view of the world. On both counts, orthodox Soviets had belief systems, and liberals did not.

For example, Kim's analysis of developments in the Third World revealed patterns that are typical of efforts at belief system maintenance: selective attention and inattention; unfalsifiable propositions; and theory-driven, rather than data-driven, inferences. Compare this to Sheinis, who explicitly advanced arguments whose validity could be tested by anyone with access to data about third world countries. His hard, quantifiable, variables of economic growth rates, per capita income, level of industrial employment, and so on, stand in sharp contrast to orthodox variables of class consciousness, ideological commitment, and party unity. Moreover, whereas Sheinis added additional variables to his causal model when his own categories proved insufficiently diagnostic—as happened in his lessons from Iran—Kim predictably, given his need to see revolutionary advances, tried to cram the incongruent information, such as the role of religion, into his previous categories of class analysis.

This segues into the other critical distinction: Kim, and other orthodox analysts, have a *need* to see what they see. If they do not manipulate reality to make it consonant with their prior set of beliefs, they will be forced to sacrifice some very central values. In the case of Kim, and many other Soviets with this belief system, a need to see revolutionary progress drove them. This need derived, as I have disucssed elsewhere in this book, from their worldview of the "world revolutionary alliance" and the Soviet role in it. If Kim were not encouraged by events in Iran and Nicaragua, he would have to wonder why this alliance was not working under Soviet leadership. Just as important is the connection between Soviet history and socialist construction in Soviet third world allies.

It was no accident that the model prescribed by orthodox analysts for socialist construction in the Third World bore a close resemblance to an idealized or mythologized version of how the Bolshevik revolution played itself out in the Soviet Union. There is a working-class vanguard party, annealed by Marxist-Leninist ideology, introducing socialized means of production, collectivizing the backward peasantry, eliminating dependence on the world capitalist economy, and uprooting all archaic obstacles to progress, such as religious and ethnic differences. Orthodox Soviets would be denying their beliefs in their own country's history if they were to make different recommendations to their third world allies. What would it say to Soviet citizens or Soviet allies in Eastern Europe if Kim were to argue that the Soviet development experience was only optional, and that different conditions in the Third World permitted, if not demanded, deviations from the Soviet model that had been replicated in Central Asia and the PRM. It is easy to see both the political and psychological imperatives that prevented Kim and many other Soviets from abandoning their own experience.

Finally, acknowledging alternative routes to social and economic development, let alone socialism, would undermine the Marxist-Leninist canon. Since this canon was the intellectual foundation for Kim and others, violating it would be extremely painful. Therefore, the distortions of reality made by orthodox analysts to maintain their confidence in revolutionary progress are perfectly understandable. The absence of any such motives for liberal analysts allows them to be driven by their data, rather than by their needs.

## Conclusion: Deterrence Theory Fails a Crucially Easy Test

In 1979, the shah was forced to relinquish power to a virulently anti-American regime in a country with vast oil reserves situated in an area whose resources were deemed vital to the United States and its West European and Japanese allies. The ouster of the shah was followed months later by the Sandinista victory in Nicaragua. Both of these victories came on the heels of a string of Soviet gains in Vietnam, Angola, Ethiopia, and Afghanistan. If deterrence theory cannot make accurate predictions about Soviet perceptions after these events, it fails in a set of crucially easy cases.

Soviet views of consistently high American credibility invalidate the theory. This constancy gives the lie to the view that arming the Contras was necessary to teach the Soviets the right lessons about American credibility. Instead, aid for the Contras was both irrelevant and unnecessary. Temporary Soviet encouragement from these victories about the future prospects for revolutionary change in the Third World initially confirms the theory. The prompt reversal to pessimism or failure to remain optimistic for more than a year or so disconfirms the theory, especially given the favorable conditions for the theory's success. Not a single Soviet inference of any connection between Iran and American credibility in other strategic areas of the world invalidates the theory—again, under the easiest possible circumstances in any third world case.

As for deterrence theory in general, its overall validity is also undermined by the evidence and analysis of this chapter. On the one hand, the preponderance of Soviet lessons that confirmed the theory—inferences of falling dominoes around the world—were the products of a belief system with very restricted applicability to the universe of deterrence cases. On the other hand, Soviet lessons that disconfirm the theory run the gamut from universal to general to peculiar.

# Soviet Losses

# CHAPTER 5

# Grenada 1983: Sufficient, but Unnecessary and Inferior

As the title of this chapter implies, the American removal of the Bernard Coard government in Grenada in October 1983 succeeded in teaching the Soviet Union that the United States was resolute and capable of protecting American interests in the Third World. But this American action was both unnecessary and inferior for this purpose. It was unnecessary because Soviets believed the United States highly credible in the absence of the American intervention in Grenada. It was deficient because it caused Soviets to ignore other deterrent lessons that would otherwise have been learned had the United States not invaded.[1]

## Soviet Lessons about U.S. Credibility

There is no doubt whatever that the American military intervention in Grenada caused Soviets to infer the lessons about American credibility predicted by deterrence theory. There were no Soviets who inferred lessons from Grenada that disconfirmed the predictions of the theory. Soviets saw American actions against Grenada as evidence of aggressive intentions against a wide variety of other targets. For instance, Konstantin Chernenko, soon to become general secretary, asserted that the intervention was a sign of Washington's "open militarism, pretension to global dominance, resistance to progress, and infringement on the rights and freedoms of peoples."[2] Some Soviets went much farther, arguing that the intervention in Grenada meant that the United

---

1. The case of the American intervention in the Dominican Republic in 1965 also qualifies as a case of direct American military involvement causing a Soviet defeat. I do not discuss it here because it only reinforces the evidence from Grenada, without adding any new insights. For those interested in a more thorough analysis of the Dominican case, see Hopf, "Deterrence Theory," chapter 3.

2. Supreme Soviet election speech, *Pravda*, March 3, 1984, 1. Other representative examples include Gorbachev's speech at the Tenth Congress of the Portuguese Communist Party, *Pravda*, December 17, 1983, 4; Aleksandr Yakovlev, "Rakovaya Opukhol"; Falin, "Podvodya Itogi . . ." (Summing Up . . . ), *MEIMO*, December 1983, 3–15; and Arbatov, "Chto, Esli ne Mir?"

States was an increasing threat not just to liberation movements in the Third World, but also to socialist countries, including the Soviet Union.[3]

At a minimum, Soviets learned that the United States was likely to intervene in Latin America in the future. For example, General Secretary Andropov spoke of El Salvador and Nicaragua as potential targets of U.S. aggression.[4] Primakov concluded from Grenada that the United States was more likely to intervene in the Middle East and Persian Gulf.[5] Many other Soviets inferred the more general lesson that Soviet allies in the Third World overall were at risk.[6]

Soviet lessons from Grenada are summarized in table 19.

The data in the table clearly show that deterrence theory predictions are completely confirmed by the lessons Soviets inferred from Grenada. But these results are evidence only that successful American military interventions are *sufficient* to teach the Soviets that American credibility is high. However, we know that such American actions are not at all *necessary*, because even American defeats, as shown in the previous three chapters, did not reduce Soviet expectations of a vigorous American defense of its interests in the world. And, as the next two chapters will show, American credibility was strengthened by *nonmilitary* American actions that led to Soviet defeats.

## Soviet Lessons about Regional Dynamics

If the predictions of deterrence theory were accurate, then Soviet observers should have seen American allies in the Caribbean and Central and Latin America as supporting the American intervention and exhibiting a renewed commitment to resist local progressive states and movements. In fact, Soviet perceptions were, by and large, precisely the opposite. Moreover, very few

---

3. See, for example, Ustinov, "Borotsya za Mir, Ukreplyat Oboronosposobnost" (Fight for Peace and Increase Defense Capabilities), *Pravda*, November 19, 1983, 4; Ponomarev, "Sovremennaya Obstanovka"; and Falin, "Vashington Topchet Pravo i Moral" (Washington Tramples on Right and Morality), *Izvestiya*, October 28, 1983, 5. This is similar to the arguments made by Sergei Gorshkov and Valentin Falin about American intentions after the fall of the shah. See chap. 4.

4. In answers to a *Pravda* correspondent, *Pravda*, January 25, 1984, 1. Petr Yakovlev also made inferences limited only to Central America in "Dva Kursa."

5. Primakov, "Kursom Diktata i Agressii" (On a Course of Diktat and Aggression), *Izvestiya*, July 20, 1984, 5.

6. For example, Gromyko's speech at a breakfast for the GDR's foreign minister, Oscar Fischer, *Pravda*, January 5, 1984, 4; Simoniya, "Struggle"; Mikoyan, "Politika Bezrassudstva"; Korolev, "Reckless Policy: How the United States Is 'Saving' Central America," *IA*, December 1984, 94–102; Brutents, "Osvobodivshiesya Strany v Nachale 80-x Godov" (Liberated Countries at the Beginning of the 1980s), *Kommunist*, 1984, no. 3, 103–13; and Kremeniuk, "Imperializm i Razvivaiushchiesya Strany: Evoliutsiya Vzaimootnoshenii" (Imperialism and Developing Countries: The Evolution of Relations), *AIAS*, December 1983, 4–7.

**TABLE 19.   Deterrence Theory's Predictions and Soviet Lessons**

| Soviet Inferences from Grenada (N) | |
| --- | --- |
| Confirming | Disconfirming |
| The United States will attack the Soviet Union (3). | The United States will not defend its peripheral interests. |
| The United States will attack other members of the socialist community. | The United States will continue detente and arms control. |
| The United States will defend its strategic interests. | The United States will not defend its strategic interests. |
| The United States will not continue detente and arms control (5). | The United States will not attack Soviet socialist allies. |
| The United States will defend its peripheral interests (12). | The United States will not attack the Soviet Union. |
| The United States will protect its allies in the Third World. | |
| The United States will not attack the Soviet Union. | |

*Note*: Lessons are listed in order of decreasing strength as evidence.

Soviets drew any inferences at all about future prospects for revolutionary change in the region from Grenada. Only four Soviets inferred such lessons and each of them was a Latin Americanist, implying that such analyses were demanded by their regional specialization.

In general, these four scholars saw the American invasion of Grenada as causing increased regional resistance to, not support for, American adventurism. Korolev, for example, wrote that the invasion had "caused growing outrage in Latin America" and indeed had given new impetus to the Contadora group to reach a political settlement, so as to avoid a repetition of Grenada in Nicaragua.[7] Glinkin wrote of a broader Latin American reaction:

> In its aggression against Grenada, Washington expected to intimidate the peoples of the Caribbean; however, Washington itself ended up in the pillory. One hundred eight states, including many American allies, voted for the UN resolution that qualified the invasion as a gross violation of international law. They demanded that the United States immediately end

---

7. "Reckless Policy," 97.

the intervention and withdraw its forces. The reaction in Latin America was especially stormy. The occupation of Grenada showed that any Latin American country can become a victim of the armed intervention of American imperialism if the White House does not like the policies of its government.[8]

Moreover, Soviets discounted the participation of various Caribbean states in the invasion. Instead of seeing this as evidence of support for American policy in the region, they accused the United States of coercing these weaker states into providing "a cloak" for the American invasion.[9] Soviet lessons from Grenada are categorized in table 20.

Deterrence theory's predictions are disconfirmed both by the lack of attention received by an American action intended to focus Soviet attention and by the fact that what lessons Soviets did learn from the American invasion were precisely the opposite of those assumed by the theory.

## Explaining Soviet Lessons from Grenada

Prima facie, Soviet lessons from Grenada confirm deterrence theory's assumptions about credibility and invalidate its predictions about regional dynamics. However, for these lessons to qualify as evidence for or against deterrence theory in general, they must have been generated by a process with universal, or at least very general, applicability.

### Soviet Images of High Overall U.S. Credibility

As was true in the previous three chapters, Soviet views on American credibility are explained by each of the three categories of information processing in table 21. The critical difference, of course, is that here this provides very powerful *confirmation* of deterrence theory. In the previous three chapters, this broad set of explanations implied strong invalidation of the theory.

*Universal*. The invasion of Grenada simply validated the rational causal attribution models long employed by the community of Americanists. They

8. Glinkin, "Sovremennaya Strategiya," 16–28. In another article, Glinkin argued that the Grenada invasion had shown Latin Americans how recklessly the United States behaves on the international arena and therefore had convinced them of the need to fight against American nuclear weapons programs. "Latinskaya Amerika." Mikoyan also wrote of increased resistance in Latin America to American adventurism as a consequence of Grenada in "Politika Bezrassudstva."

9. Petr Yakovlev, "American Neocolonialism's Testing Range in the Caribbean," *IA*, February 1985, 70–76. Glinkin, when speaking of the request Washington received from these states to intervene in Grenada, qualified it as "clearly inspired by the United States," in "Sovremennaya Strategiya," 18.

**TABLE 20.   Soviet Inferences and Deterrence Theory's Assumptions about Regional Dynamics**

| Soviet Lessons from Grenada (N) | |
| --- | --- |
| Confirming | Disconfirming |
| Strategic American allies will increase their balancing efforts against the Soviet Union and its allies. | Countries around Grenada will oppose American policy in the region (4). |
| Other countries around the Third World will intensify their opposition to local Soviet allies. | Countries elsewhere in the Third World will oppose American policy in their respective regions, and in the Third World overall. |
| Countries around Grenada will support American policy in the region. | Strategic American allies will oppose American policy in the Third World overall (1). |

*Note*: Lessons are listed in order of decreasing strength as evidence.

explained the invasion as a function of public and congressional support for the aggressive line adopted by the Reagan administration in the Third World.[10] Sergo Mikoyan, a Latin Americanist, also inferred rational attributions from Grenada, assigning causality to the state of domestic politics in the United States at the time.[11]

*General.* Several Soviets, such as Primakov and Gorbachev, used their bounded rational models to explain the American invasion of Grenada. A number of other Soviets also evaluated American credibility by utilizing a limited menu of variables combined with elements of a Marxist-Leninist belief system. These Soviets can be arrayed on a continuum from most general to most peculiar, depending on how much of their analysis relied on variables generated by psychological need. At the peculiar end of this continuum is General Secretary Andropov, who relied mainly on orthodox Leninist economic imperatives to explain American foreign policy. In addition, however, he recognized a struggle between "hawks and doves" within the American elite. He also suggested that American leaders might be suffering from misperceptions, erroneously believing that the Soviet Union was behind all revolutionary developments in the world.

---

10. See, for example, their explanations of the American invasion of Grenada and the evolution of their views on American foreign policy in general, Arbatov, "Chto, Esli ne Mir?" "Ekonomicheskoe i Politicheskoe Polozhenie," "Ne Ot Khoroshei Zhizni," "Militarizm i Sovremennoe," and "Prodvizhenie"; Kremeniuk, "Imperializm i Razvivaiushchiesya," "Doktrina Reagana," and "SShA v Regionalnykh Konfliktakh"; and Aleksandr Kislov, "Blizhnii Vostok i Pentagon" (The Middle East and the Pentagon), *SShA*, April 1987, 13–24.

11. Mikoyan, "Politika Bezrassudstva" and "Latin America."

**TABLE 21. The Power of Different Explanations for Soviet Lessons**

| | Types of Explanations | | |
| --- | --- | --- | --- |
| | Universal | General | Peculiar |
| Lessons confirming deterrence theory | High overall U.S. credibility | High overall U.S. credibility | High overall U.S. credibility |
| Lessons disconfirming deterrence theory | | Regional anti-Americanism | |
| | | Lack of deterrent lessons | |

Aleksandr Yakovlev was much farther away from the peculiar end of the continuum, akin to Primakov or Gorbachev, rather than Andropov. Leninism was the source of Yakovlev's belief that narrow economic motives drive American aggressiveness. However, he also allowed that both Congress and the American public are autonomous factors in American politics.[12] Iurii Korolev, a Latin Americanist, went much farther than Yakovlev in developing a relatively diverse menu of critical variables to explain American foreign policy. Beyond the Leninist economic motives, he argued that American elite adherence to deterrence theory and American public support for adventurism explained American interventionism in the Third World, and the invasion of Grenada, in particular.[13]

*Peculiar*. Finally, at the peculiar extreme, along with Chernenko, Ogarkov, Gorshkov, Ponomarev, and Ulyanovksy, was Valentin Falin, then an *Izvestiya* correspondent, but soon to become an adviser to Gorbachev.[14] These Soviets applied their Marxist-Leninist interpretations of imperialism to the Grenada

---

12. See Yakovlev, "Protiv Militarizma i Revanshizma" (Against Militarism and Revanchism), *MEIMO*, December 1984, 106–10, and his interview in *KP*, December 25, 1983, 1, 3.

13. See Korolev, "Revoliutsionnyi Protsess," and "Reckless Policy." For similar combinations of bounded rationality with Leninism, see Anatoly Glinkin, "Latinskaya Amerika," and "Sovremennaya Strategiya." See also Petr Yakovlev, another Latin Americanist, "American Neocolonialism's Testing Range."

14. Given the fact that Falin sometimes wrote as many as two articles a week for *Izvestiya*, the evidence for his beliefs is simply too voluminous to cite in detail. But his future influence within the official foreign policy elite of Gorbachev requires that I cite some of the more illuminating pieces: "Imperskaya Spes," "Dvulichie v Politike" (Hypocrisy in Politics), *Izvestiya*, September 11, 1983, 4–5, "Gde Koren Zla" (Where the Root of Evil Is), *Izvestiya*, October 21, 1983, 5, "Vashington Topchet," "Podvodya Itogi," "SShA v God Vyborov" (The U.S. in an Election Year), *Izvestiya*, January 8, 1984, 4–5, "Raschety i Proschety" (Calculations and Miscalculations), *Izvestiya*, March 14, 1984, 5, and "Vcherashnii Den v Sevodnyashnem Vashingtone" (Yesterday in Today's Washington), *Kommunist*, 1984, no. 8, 120–25.

case, concluding that the "monopolists" who direct American foreign policy were intent on returning Grenada to the ranks of the exploited periphery.

### Regional Dynamics: The Dearth of Deterrent Lessons

*Universal/General.* More important than the fact that all the lessons inferred disconfirmed deterrence theory's predictions is that so few lessons about regional dynamics were inferred at all. The lack of such lessons was caused by the overwhelming salience of the American invasion in causing the ouster of the Coard government in Grenada. The American intervention provided a single and sufficient explanation for the Soviet defeat. Consequently, any deterrent lessons Soviets might have learned by investigating the behavior of the Maurice Bishop and Bernard Coard regimes in Grenada were impeded.

This lack of attention can be explained by a combination of rational attribution processes and heuristics. It is an application of attribution theory in that Soviets concluded that the removal of their ally in Grenada was caused by American actions. But it cannot be considered wholly rational in that Soviets did not bother to investigate alternative or other contributing explanations for the political turmoil in Grenada that preceded the American invasion. A reasonable interpretation of this failure to assess other possible causes is Soviet employment of a kind of "availability" heuristic. The explanation of the American invasion was much more vivid and salient than any possible competing cause, and so was far more "available" to Soviet analysts when they considered the Grenada case.

This explanation is much more convincing when evaluated in conjunction with the findings of the next two chapters. In both cases of indirect American involvement in Soviet defeats and even more so in cases where there was no American action at all, Soviets learned far more, and far more powerful, deterrent lessons than they did in the cases of Grenada or the Dominican Republic.[15] Essentially, American military action prevented Soviets from learning the kinds of deterrent lessons the theory predicts they should have learned about regional dynamics.

### A Scorecard for Deterrence Theory: A Mixed Report

Soviet images of high American credibility based on the successful American military intervention in Grenada provide the strongest possible confirmation of deterrence theory. However, as we know from the cases of Soviet victories, this Soviet defeat was not necessary to evoke those kinds of images. And, as we'll see in the next chapter, nonmilitary instruments are just as effective in

---

15. For the Dominican case, see Hopf, "Deterrence Theory," chap. 3.

teaching the Soviets these deterrent lessons. Moreover, the lack of deterrent lessons at the regional level is very strong disconfirming evidence for the theory.

### Considering Alternative Explanations for Soviet Lessons from Grenada

One possible alternative interpretation of Soviet assertions that regional actors in the Caribbean and Latin America opposed the American intervention is that there was a general Soviet foreign policy propaganda line that was designed to minimize the damage the loss in Grenada did to Soviet prestige in the area, and in the Third World overall. Soviets had to write about the unanimous condemnation reaped by the United States in order to demonstrate that American actions were not winning Washington any allies in the region but rather had deleterious effects on American interests in the area. This explanation would account for the lack of any dissenting voices among Soviet observers on this question.

Though perhaps initially convincing, this alternative explanation is flawed. First, if the Soviet leadership were trying to put the best possible gloss on an embarassing defeat, they would hardly assign this task only to four academic Latin Americanists who wrote only in scholarly journals. We should expect members of the Soviet party and foreign policy elite to be propagating this line before all available, especially third world, audiences. They did not. In addition, there was not unalloyed optimism, as Soviet inferences about high American credibility suggest. Nor was there consistent optimism about trends in the region, as we know from the discussion of Nicaragua in the last chapter. If there was a Panglossian line being pursued, then Soviets would not be identifying El Salvadoran and Honduran aid to the Contras and the withdrawal of Christian Democratic support for the Sandinista government.

### Conclusion: Deterrence Theory—Both Too Sufficient and Unnecessary

Though short, the evidence in this chapter supports a very important argument. As the subtitle of this section implies, the military interventions prescribed by deterrence theory are sufficient. But they are equally sufficient to both *cause and prevent* deterrent lessons from being learned. Moreover, the prescriptions are unnecessary to achieve the posited tasks. Soviets rationally learned from the American invasion of Grenada that the United States was credible. However, we know, both from the chapters on Soviet gains and the next two chapters on Soviet defeats, that they equally rationally believed the United States was credible in the absence of that intervention. Soviets also rationally did not learn that their other allies in the region were in domestic trouble. They did not learn that Cuba, Nicaragua, Guyana, and other radical Soviet allies were pursuing policies likely to lead to the domestic political turmoil that had occurred in Grenada. This lack of learning reduced the deterrent power of the operation in Grenada. The American intervention provided a single sufficient explanation for the fall of the Coard government that allowed Soviets to avoid considering the domestic roots of the reversal of the Grenadian revolution. In sum, the direct military interventions prescribed by deterrence theory are not the most effective instructional tools.

# CHAPTER 6

# The Middle East, 1967–80: A Boon for Deterrence, but Proof of the Need for an Expansion of the Theory

From 1967 to 1980, the Soviet Union experienced a series of setbacks in the Middle East. In June 1967, Israel soundly defeated the armed forces of Egypt, Syria, and Jordan in the Six Day War. Israel consequently occupied Egyptian territory in the Sinai desert and Gaza, Syrian land on the Golan Heights, and Jordanian territory along the West Bank and in East Jerusalem. In October 1973, after suffering heavy initial setbacks in both the Sinai and on the Golan from Egyptian and Syrian forces, Israeli forces regained the initiative, containing the Arab offensive and ultimately assuming the offensive themselves. By the end of the war, though Egyptian forces were still on the eastern bank of the Suez Canal, Israeli forces were within seventy-five miles of Cairo and twenty-five miles of Damascus.

Soon after the conclusion of the October War, three successive American administrations, those of Nixon, Ford, and Carter, reversed Egypt's nearly twenty-year alliance with the Soviet Union, dealing the Soviet Union its greatest setback in the Middle East in the postwar period. This American effort was punctuated by a number of critical turning points. In January 1974, Secretary of State Kissinger negotiated the first Sinai disengagement agreement between Israel and Egypt. In February, Cairo and Washington resumed diplomatic relations. A month later, Arab oil-producing countries lifted the oil embargo they had imposed on Western countries after the start of the war. In April 1974, Sadat announced Egypt's decision to diversify its sources of military aid. In June 1974, Nixon visited Sadat in Cairo. A year later, Ford met Sadat in Geneva. In September 1975, Kissinger achieved the second Sinai disengagement between Egypt and Israel. A month later, Sadat visited Washington, the first trip by an Egyptian president to the United States, and received a positive response from the Ford administration to his requests for military aid. In March 1976, Sadat abrogated the Treaty of Friendship and Cooperation with the Soviet Union. In November 1977, Sadat made his historic trip to Jerusalem, which was followed by the Camp David talks in September 1978 and the Egyptian-Israeli peace treaty of March 1979.

There are two crucial aspects to these events that have fundamental importance for an assessment of deterrence theory. First, these defeats for the Soviet Union were *not* the product of American military actions. They were the result of both *allied* military actions and American diplomatic, political, and economic power in the region. Second, and related, these defeats are *not* within the domain of traditional deterrence theory. The latter, as conceived by Thomas Schelling, Glenn Snyder, and others, is a theory about raising the expected *military* costs to a challenger considering upsetting the status quo in the world.[1] Moreover, policymakers who have applied deterrence theory's prescriptions have assumed that only military means could possibly teach the Soviets the right lessons about American credibility.

This is not to say that the theory cannot capture the costs imposed by nonmilitary instruments. Indeed, it can and should. The purpose here is simply to demonstrate that deterrent rewards were reaped by the United States when it adopted policies that were *not* prescribed by the traditional theory. Any improved version of deterrence theory will have to expand its domain to include these kinds of nonmilitary costs for potential challengers. It should be noted that this addition to the theory does not in any way violate its fundamental assumption that increasing costs for a challenger is necessary for deterrence success.

This omission by the theory is still more problematic if we consider the findings of the previous chapter on Grenada. In that case, American military actions were sufficient to *prevent* Soviets from learning deterrent lessons about regional dynamics. In the cases of indirect American involvement in the Middle East discussed here, Soviets learned very powerful deterrent lessons about the regional dynamics of that part of the world. And they learned lessons about American credibility that were at least as powerful as those imparted by the United States in Grenada. In sum, it is precisely the kinds of

1. A close reading of the classics of traditional deterrence theory shows the virtually complete omission of nonmilitary methods of raising the costs of expansionism to a challenger of the status quo. See, for example, Schelling's definition of deterrence as the "diplomacy of violence" in the preface of *Arms and Influence*. See also his earlier work, *The Strategy of Conflict* (Cambridge: Harvard University Press, 1960), 6–7. One sees the same exclusive focus on military force in Herman Kahn's description of "Type II Deterrence" in *On Thermonuclear War* (Princeton: Princeton University Press, 1960). In the introduction to this book, I noted the arguments of Glenn Snyder in *Deterrence and Defense* about the need to mount military interventions in unimportant areas of the globe. Arnold Wolfers explicitly distinguished between the credibility produced by "power" and the "influence" among allies begat by diplomacy. See *Discord and Collaboration*, esp. chap. 7, but see also 130 and 138–40. The argument that traditional deterrence theory is based virtually exclusively on military measures is further strengthened by an examination of the literature that has tested this theory. It is very hard to find a single case whose selection was not based on the use, or threat of the use, of military force. See, for example, Huth, *Extended Deterrence*; George and Smoke, *Deterrence*; Snyder and Diesing, *Conflict among Nations*; and any random sampling of articles appearing in the last twenty years in *Journal of Conflict Resolution*.

**TABLE 22.   Soviet Lessons about American Credibility:
The Middle East, 1967–80**

| Lesson | N |
|---|---|
| The United States intends to reverse the Soviet alliance with Egypt. | 10 |
| The United States intends to overthrow Soviet allies in the Middle East. | 41 |
| The United States intends to mount an assault on the global liberation movement. | 6 |
| The United States opposes detente with the Soviet Union. | 6 |
| The United States is planning to attack members of the socialist community. | 1 |
| The United States is planning to attack the Soviet Union. | 3 |

*Note*: Lessons are listed in order from least aggressive to most aggressive.

American actions that are outside the domain of deterrence theory that send the most powerful deterrent messages of all.

### Soviet Lessons about U.S. Credibility

American credibility reaped very significant rewards from American policy in the Middle East after the Six Day War in June 1967. Soviets were convinced that the United States was resolved and able not only to dominate the Middle East peace process, but also to reverse Soviet alliance relationships with its most progressive partners in the region. Moreover, the United States demonstrated its ability to turn such previous Soviet allies as Egypt into important military assets in the region. These lessons are presented in table 22. For the sake of clarity, I divide the period into three parts.

### Middle East, 1967–73

One can divide Soviet perceptions of American credibility after the Six Day War into two categories. The first deals with Soviet views of American credibility as a consequence of the Israeli military victory; the second concerns Soviet lessons inferred from American diplomatic behavior in the six years leading up to the October War in 1973.

At the most general level, Soviets saw the June war as simply another example of the lengths to which the United States was prepared to go to resist the global national liberation movement. Brezhnev, for example, connected American support for Israel to American actions in Vietnam and U.S. connivance in overthrowing progressive governments in Ghana and Indonesia.[2]

2. Brezhnev, "Pyatdesyat Let Velikikh Pobed Sotsializma" (Fifty Years of the Great Victories of Socialism), *Kommunist*, 1967, no. 16, 3–47. See also Podgorny's speech in Ulan Bator, Mongolia, *Pravda*, May 24, 1969, 4; Ulyanovsky, "O Edinstve Sil Sotsializma i Natsionalno-Osvoboditelnovo Dvizheniya" (On the Unity of the Forces of Socialism and the National Libera-

More specifically, Soviets saw Israeli aggression as evidence that the United States was trying to overthrow by force all progressive Arab governments, in particular Nasser's in Egypt. Primakov, for example, reporting from Cairo only days after the war ended, asserted that "there is no doubt that one of the main political objectives of the imperialist club that supports Israeli aggression was the overthrow of progressive regimes in Arab countries."[3]

Belyaev, like Primakov, also reporting from Cairo in the aftermath of the war, identified another American goal, one that would achieve ever greater salience in subsequent years. He wrote that this aim was to "drive a wedge between Arab states and the Soviet Union, to disorient millions of Egyptians, Syrians, Algerians, Iraqis, and all Arabs and to deprive them of their faith in their best friends."[4] Belyaev was also prescient about another aspect of American policy in the region. He noted that American promises of economic aid threatened the Soviet position in Egypt. The consequence of this promised largesse was that an "American lobby" had sprung up in Egypt that argued against maintaining Egypt's alliance relationship with the Soviet Union.[5]

During the years leading up to the October War, Soviets were divided in their evaluations of American diplomatic conduct in the Middle East. Some argued American policy was aimed at the same goals pursued during the Six Day War. The United States, by strongly supporting Israel, was preventing any acceptable peace settlement. The United States used the absence of a settlement to destabilize progressive Arab governments. When the United States did undertake diplomatic initiatives, such as the Rogers plan in early

---

tion Movement), *Pravda*, October 14, 1968, 4–5; and Brutents, "Epokha Sotsializma i Natsionalnoe Osvobozhdenie Narodov" (The Epoch of Socialism and the National Liberation of Peoples), *Kommunist*, 1967, no. 18, 91–102.

3. Primakov, "Narod na Zashchite Svoikh Zavoevanii" (People in Defense of their Triumphs), *Pravda*, June 13, 1967, 3. Primakov was the first Soviet to argue that this was the primary war aim of Washington. However, many other Soviets soon began to repeat it very frequently. See, for example, Brezhnev's speech before graduating military academy cadets, *Pravda*, July 6, 1967, 1–2; Belyaev, "Tuchi Sgushchaiutsya" (Clouds Are Gathering), *Pravda*, July 29, 1967, 4; Mirsky, "Israel: Illusions and Miscalculations," *NT*, 1968, no. 39, 6–8; Grechko's order of the day on Soviet Armed Forces Day, *Pravda*, February 23, 1970, 1; Butlitsky, "Afrikanskie Mirazhi Vashingtona" (African Mirages of Washington), *Gudok*, March 25, 1970, 3; Ulyanovsky, "Lenin and the National Liberation Movement," *NT*, 1970, no. 16, 8–11; Kislov, "Blizhnevostochnoi Konflikt i Manevry Vashingtona" (The Middle East Conflict and Washington's Maneuvers), *SShA*, April 1971, 74–76; Ponomarev's speech at the Arab Socialist Union's party congress in Cairo, *Pravda*, July 25, 1971, 4; and Kremeniuk, "Prezidentskie Vybory i Blizhnii Vostok" (Presidential Elections and the Middle East), *SShA*, January 1973, 71 77.

4. Belyaev, "'Nash Drug—Sovetskii Soiuz!'" ("Our Friend—the Soviet Union!"), *Pravda*, August 9, 1967, 4.

5. Belyaev, "Snova Samoobman—Na Sbito Rasschityvaet Izrail" (Again Self-Deception—Israel Miscalculates), *Pravda*, March 8, 1968, 4. Mirsky also warned of this danger in "The Rebirth of the Arab World," *NT*, 1968, no. 25, 10–12.

1969, its only goal was to lure Soviet allies away from the Soviet Union and into the American-Israeli camp. Other Soviets, if even only fleetingly, expected the United States to make good-faith efforts in cooperation with the Soviet government to reach a peace settlement that would not be at the expense of Soviet Arab allies.

Brezhnev was among those Soviets who only saw the United States as "encouraging the policy of the Israeli aggressors to undermine the negotiations."[6] Brezhnev was joined in this consistently negative assessment of American intentions by Podgorny, Grechko, Ulyanovsky, Primakov, and Kokoshin.[7]

Once again, Belyaev led the way in voicing guarded optimism about American sincerity in searching for a balanced agreement in the Middle East. Soon after Rogers launched his peace initiative in March 1969, Belyaev wrote that it was his impression, "inferred from Nixon's statements, that many in the United States are really prepared to work for a peace settlement." While remarking that Israel was still erecting obstacles on this path, he argued that "this has done nothing to dampen the desire for a settlement displayed in Moscow, Washington, Paris, and London." He concluded that it "is correct to believe that Americans have been focusing their attention on a search for new approaches in the Middle East."[8] But seven months later Belyaev reversed course, arguing that the peace pursued by Israel, the United States, and Britain showed that the "aims of imperialism in the Middle East remain unchanged—to liquidate progressive regimes at any price, undermine national liberation movements, and reestablish its former dominance in the region."[9] Moreover, Belyaev later identified yet another American objective that would loom far larger in Soviet perceptions after the October War, namely, that the United States wanted to become "the sole arbiter in the Middle East," to control the peace process there at the expense of Soviet participation.[10]

Arbatov also changed his originally negative assessment of American

---

6. Speech in Baku on the fiftieth anniversary of the Azerbaijan Communist Party, *Pravda*, October 3, 1970, 1–2. See also his speech at the Fifteenth Congress of Soviet Trade Unions, *Pravda*, March 21, 1972, 1–3.

7. For Podgorny, see his speech in Bulgaria, *Pravda*, July 8, 1973, 4. For Grechko, see, among other examples, his order of the day on Soviet Armed Forces Day, *Pravda*, February 23, 1969, 1. For Ulyanovsky, see "Lenin." For Primakov, see, among many other examples, "Peace Prospects in the Middle East," *IA*, February 1969, 49–50. For Kokoshin, see "US Foreign Policy Strategy for the 1970s," *IA*, October 1973, 67–73, which was written prior to the October War.

8. Belyaev, "Washington's Asian Boomerang," *IA*, May 1969, 65–70. He continued to express cautious optimism in "Neodolimaya Sila" (Invincible Force), *Pravda*, May 25, 1969, 4, and "Arabskii Yashchik Pandory" (Arab Pandora's Box), *AIAS*, July 1969, 31–33.

9. Belyaev, "Velenie Vremeni" (Wave of the Times), *Pravda*, November 23, 1969, 4. He expressed an even harsher evaluation in "Middle East Crisis and Washington's Maneuvers," *IA*, April 1970, 30–35.

10. Belyaev, "Who is Obstructing a Middle East Settlement?" *IA*, November 1970, 87.

diplomatic efforts in the region, though, unlike Belyaev, he did not revert to a more pessimistic interpretation prior to the October War. In November 1970, Arbatov argued that "talks in themselves do not guarantee a solution of problems," especially if there "is no aspiration for a settlement," but rather, they are only "used to reassure the public and as a screen for an aggressive policy."[11] After Brezhnev's summit with Nixon in the United States in June 1972, Arbatov expressed grounds for optimism about American intentions, citing the fact that the American administration had agreed that UN Resolution 242 was the only basis for a settlement and had expressed support for the Jarring mediation efforts.[12]

Some Soviets identified particular objectives the United States was trying to achieve by preventing a Middle East settlement. Belyaev argued that by dragging out the crisis, the United States hoped that "this will lead to the overthrow of progressive regimes in Egypt, Syria, Algeria, and Iraq" and also to conflicts among Arab countries themselves about how best to proceed on the diplomatic front, thereby destroying the Arab unity necessary to confront Israel.[13] Kislov argued that American diplomatic efforts in part were designed to "undermine Arab friendship with the Soviet Union." In fact, he quoted an October 4, 1970, *Washington Post* editorial to make his case: "'Nixon has spoken a lot about a transition from an era of confrontation to one of negotiations. However, he has tried to press solutions that would preserve American superiority around the globe, including in the Middle East.'" Kislov further singled out the danger of American subornation of Soviet allies in the region, arguing that "to make the American plan more acceptable to Arab countries and, first of all, Egypt, Washington has offered a number of alluring economic proposals."[14] Some members of the party leadership also recognized that Washington was using diplomacy to detach Arab countries from the Soviet Union.[15]

---

11. Arbatov, "'Doctrina Nixona': Deklaratsii i Realnost" (The "Nixon Doctrine": Declaration and Reality), *SShA*, February 1971, 23.

12. See Arbatov, "Sila Politika Realizma" (The Power of a Policy of Realism), *Izvestiya*, June 22, 1972, 3–4, and "Sobytie Vazhnovo Mezhdunarodnovo Znacheniya" (An Event of Important International Significance), *SShA*, August 1972, 3–12.

13. Belyaev, "Kto Torpediruet Missiu Jarringa?" (Who is Torpedoing the Jarring Mission?), *Pravda*, June 3, 1968, 4. See also Primakov, "Blizhnemu Vostoku—Spravdelivyi i Prochnyi Mir" (A Just and Lasting Peace for the Middle East), *Pravda*, January 5, 1972, 4.

14. "Blizhnevostochnyi Konflikt," *SShA*, April 1971, 74–76. Primakov also believed that American diplomacy was launched simply to "weaken ties between Arab countries and its friends." See "Manevry SShA na Blizhnem Vostoke" (U.S. Maneuvers in the Middle East), *Pravda*, June 5, 1971, 4. On American economic enticements, also see Belyaev, "Uverennaya Postup Svobodu" (A Resolute Step toward Freedom), *KZ*, May 25, 1971, 3.

15. For example, Podgorny's Supreme Soviet election speech, *Izvestiya*, June 11, 1971, 1–2; and Kosygin's speech in Algiers, *Pravda*, October 7, 1971, 5.

In sum, the results of the 1967 war showed the Soviets that the United States was willing and able to use Israel as a military instrument to overthrow or seriously destabilize Soviet allies in Egypt and Syria. Worse yet, however, from the point of view of Soviet observers, the postwar diplomatic competition also revealed significant American capacity to endanger Soviet positions in the region. If the United States took a rigid position in support of Israeli demands, then progressive Arab states could suffer domestic instability, as their governments had proved unable to "liquidate the consequences of Arab aggression." If, however, the United States took a more flexible diplomatic approach and combined this with economic inducements, then the Soviets faced a possible loss of allies.

## Middle East, 1973–76

Whereas virtually all Soviets saw the 1967 war as evidence that the United States was intent on overthrowing progressive Arab regimes, no Soviets made such arguments about American intentions as a result of the October 1973 war.[16] Indeed, in the aftermath of the war, several Soviets saw American behavior during the war and in the immediate postwar period as evidence that the American leadership both subscribed to the tenets of detente with the Soviet Union and was prepared to cooperate constructively with the Soviets in reaching a fair settlement in the Middle East. Soviet Americanists, in particular, adhered to both views.[17]

Those Soviets who felt that American behavior during the war meant the United States government had accepted detente also expressed at least short-term optimism about future American willingness to sincerely seek a settlement of the Arab-Israeli conflict. Brezhnev, for example, in a speech before the Indian parliament shortly after the war, told his audience that "events of recent weeks have given us still more evidence of how the last few years' work on detente is useful for overall peace. I think you will agree that without detente, things would have looked completely different. The Middle East conflict could have become far more dangerous." Moreover, the United States

---

16. The closest any Soviets came to making such a case was Brezhnev immediately after the war when he suggested that "some forces of the capitalist world aspire to prevent the free and independent development of progressive Arab states." Speech to a Congress of Peaceloving Forces in Moscow, *Pravda*, October 27, 1973, 2. See also Kosygin's speech to Iraq's Saddam Hussein in Moscow, *Pravda*, April 15, 1975, 4; and Kremeniuk, "Conflicts in Developing Countries and Imperialist Policy," *IA*, January 1974, 61–65.

17. See, for example, Arbatov, "Sovetsko-Amerikanskie Otnosheniya v 70-e Gody"; and Trofimenko, "Voprosy Ukrepleniya Mira i Bezopasnosti v Sovetsko-Amerikanskikh Otnosheniyakh" (Questions of Consolidating Peace and Security in Soviet-American Relations), *SShA*, September 1974, 8–18, and "From Confrontation to Coexistence," *IA*, October 1975, 35–41.

and Soviet Union never would have been able to agree on a UN resolution or cease-fire.[18]

Brezhnev, however, only six months after the war, voiced his doubts, identifying the "danger that the aggressor and its patrons can once again try to avoid a comprehensive solution."[19] Podgorny also declaimed American intransigence and went even further to charge that American behavior showed that at least part of its ruling elite was rejecting detente.[20] Kislov also argued initially that American-Soviet cooperation in reaching a cease-fire demonstrated both sides' adherence to the Basic Principals Agreement signed by both parties at the May 1972 summit in Moscow.[21] However, less than nine months later, that is, after Nixon's trip to Cairo, Kislov expressed anxiety about the fact that the United States was beginning to control the peace process.[22] By April 1975, Kislov concluded that American intentions were not so benign. The United States was out to "weaken the unity of Arab countries, to invigorate reactionary elements in the Arab world, and to consolidate American positions there."[23] Unlike Kislov or Brezhnev, neither Arbatov nor Trofimenko evolved in the same skeptical direction. Instead, they continued to stress that detente had saved the world from a major confrontation, ignoring the deleterious consequences of American diplomacy for Soviet interests in the region.[24]

---

18. *Pravda*, November 30, 1973, 2. Even before an audience that most probably was not that keen on hearing about the successes of detente, Fidel Castro, Brezhnev reiterated this argument. See *Pravda*, January 31, 1974, 2.

19. Speech to Syria's Hafez Assad in Moscow, *Pravda*, April 12, 1974, 2. As late as June 1974, however, Brezhnev was still arguing that detente had both prevented a military conflagration and established the necessary, if not sufficient, conditions for a just settlement. See his Supreme Soviet election speech, *Pravda*, June 15, 1974, 1–3. For his expressions of frustration with American diplomatic unilateralism, see also his speech in Kishinev on the fiftieth anniversary of the Moldavian Soviet Socialist Republic (SSR), *Pravda*, October 12, 1974, 2, and his speech in Ulan Bator, Mongolia, *Pravda*, November 27, 1974, 3.

20. Speech in Dushanbe on the fiftieth anniversary of the Tadzhik SSR, *Pravda*, November 30, 1974, 1–3. Suslov made the same charges on detente in his Supreme Soviet election speech in *Pravda*, June 10, 1975, 2.

21. Kislov, "Vokrug Blizhnevostochnovo Krizisa" (About the Middle East Crisis), *SShA*, January 1974, 20–27.

22. "Sovetsko-Amerikanskie Otnosheniya i Blizhnii Vostok" (Soviet-American Relations and the Middle East), *SShA*, September 1974, 63–68.

23. Kislov, "Diplomatiya SShA i Blizhnevostochnoe Uregulirovanie" (U.S. Diplomacy and a Middle East Settlement), *SShA*, May 1975, 79. For another example of an evolution similar to Kislov's, see Belyaev's initially hopeful views in "Prochnyi Mir Blizhnemu Vostoku" (A Stable Peace for the Middle East), *Izvestiya*, July 9, 1974, 4, and his subsequent disappointment in "SShA i Blizhnevostochnyi Krizis" (The U.S. and the Middle East Crisis), *SShA*, March 1976, 17–27.

24. See, for example, Arbatov, "O Sovetsko-Amerikanskikh Otnosheniyakh" (On Soviet-American Relations), *Pravda*, April 2, 1976, 4–5. It is remarkable that Arbatov maintained this

Kosygin never expressed unreserved confidence either in American adherence to detente or in its good-faith diplomatic efforts. He ultimately concluded that the United States was picking off "Arab countries one by one," getting them to "make concessions that in fact would legalize Israeli occupation of significant Arab territories." Meanwhile, these Arab countries "would have to make significant political concessions that strike at their fundamental interests" for the sake of only partial agreements.[25]

Soviets saw their own fears about American intentions after both Middle East wars become a reality in 1975–76. Belyaev enumerated each of these concerns. First, the United States was "deepening the split among Arab countries and hence weakening their unity." By pursuing its policy of "separate deals," the American role in the Middle East peace process had "gone far beyond the role of a mediator who maintains relations with both sides." Belyaev, who was the first Soviet to identify the American threat to Soviet relations with Egypt, now acknowledged that the United States had "changed the political and social situation in Egypt and other Arab countries in its favor." Through economic and military aid, the United States wanted to "reestablish its positions" there and go beyond "simply returning to the Middle East." Instead, "we are speaking of American diplomatic efforts to create in the region a new system of interstate relations and interdependence that will allow the biggest U.S. oil and other monopolies not only to feel secure, but to dominate." He concluded that "for the sake of these goals in the Middle East, Washington is prepared to pay enormous costs. Aid only to Israel and Egypt in the next five years will be more than $15 billion."[26]

In sum, all the elements of American credibility that Soviet observers had indicated were threats to progressive Arab countries and their relationships with the Soviet Union were seen after the October War as finally bearing fruit for American foreign policy. Through a combination of diplomatic domination of the peace process and economic and military enticements, the United States had succeeded in reversing the allegiance of the Soviet Union's most powerful ally in the Middle East.

---

optimism about American behavior after the October War even after it had become clear that the United States had no intentions of reviving the Geneva Conference and after Sadat had abrogated the Treaty of Friendship and Cooperation with the Soviet Union.

25. Speech to Iraq's Hussein, *Pravda*, April 15, 1975, 4. See also his speech at a dinner with Turkey's prime minister, Demirel, in Ankara, *Pravda*, December 28, 1975, 4.

26. Belyaev, "SShA i Blizhnevostochnyi Krizis." On American bribery of the Egyptian leadership, including the use of Saudi Arabian petrodollars, see Brutents, "V. I. Lenin i Natsionalno-Osvoboditelnoe Dvizhenie" (V.I. Lenin and the National Liberation Movement), part 1, *AIAS*, April 1975, 4–5. On American penetration of Egyptian society and its consequences for Egyptian relations with the Soviet Union, see Mirsky, "Menyaiushchiisya Oblik 'Tretevo Mira' " (The Changing Cast of the Third World), *Kommunist*, 1976, no. 2, 107–15.

## Egypt, 1976–80

If in the period after the October War, Soviet observers argued that American efforts were aimed at driving a wedge between the government of Anwar Sadat and the Soviet Union as an end in itself, then subsequently they saw Egypt as simply a means by which the United States was trying to achieve more far-reaching goals. At first, they saw Egypt's abrogation of its Treaty of Friendship and Cooperation with the Soviet Union, Sadat's subsequent trip to Jerusalem, American unilateral renunciation of the Joint Soviet-U.S. Statement on the Middle East of October 1, 1977, and the Camp David peace process and treaty as evidence that the United States was out to dominate Middle East negotiations and prevent Soviet participation, altogether.

After the fall of the shah, they recognized the American military relationship with Egypt as a significant counterweight to the loss the United States had experienced in Iran. Moreover, they saw the United States as gaining a constant military presence in the Middle East both as a consequence of Camp David and of Egyptian willingness to allow the United States to use Egyptian military facilities. Some Soviets even went so far as to credit Egypt's provision of these bases with extending the American military reach to the point of threatening the Soviet homeland itself.

The evolving American relationship with Egypt also reinforced previous Soviet concerns that the American instruments of economic and military aid were effective tools against Soviet allies, not only in the Middle East, but throughout the world. Finally, American behavior in the Middle East also strengthened some Soviets' convictions that detente had powerful enemies among the American ruling elite.

Primakov expressed the unanimous Soviet frustration at how the United States had managed to manipulate the diplomatic game to its advantage over the previous three years. "After October 1973, many thought that there was more basis for hoping that a political solution was possible." Instead, "a number of opportunities have been squandered as a result of the unilateral 'mediation mission' of the United States." This happened because the United States looked at the Middle East only in "the plane of U.S.-Soviet relations" and in how to "undermine the national liberation anti-imperialist struggle." To buttress his case, Primakov cited the March 24, 1975, *U.S. News and World Report*: "'The Kissinger mission was perhaps the decisive step in deciding the outcome of the competition of the superpowers in the region. Kissinger sees the new Egyptian-Israeli agreement [Sinai II] as significantly enhancing American influence in Cairo. If it succeeds, the United States will become the dominant foreign power in the Middle East.'" Primakov remarked that the United States had "pushed Sadat to annul the Treaty of Friendship and Cooperation with the Soviet Union." Primakov concluded that "even in conditions of detente, the Middle East is seen by the United States as a most important link in the global competition with the Soviet Union, one of the aims of which is the isolation of national liberation forces from Soviet support."[27]

Brutents was the first Soviet observer to remark on the fact that Egypt was slated to replace Iran as a "subimperialist center," identifying it as a "country whose policies develop in favor of imperialist policy and whose pretensions to dominance in its region are supported by imperialism. These countries are assigned the role of a substantial counterweight to the forces of anti-imperialism and socialist orientation in different regions of the world." He wrote that the Camp David "deal had created the necessary preconditions" for Egypt becoming such a counterweight. Egypt's "military dependence on the United States is increasing, as is the American military presence." He lamented the fact that Egypt, "which for decades had been in the vanguard of the national liberation struggle of Arabs, now under Sadat wants to become a pawn in the American game in the Middle East, Arab world, and Africa. After the collapse of the shah's regime in Iran, plans are being openly discussed for turning Egypt into the gendarme of the region. For his part, Sadat zealously displays his readiness to assume this role." Finally, he concluded that the Camp David agreement was a "neocolonialist plot having far-reaching goals: to prepare a 'reconquista' by American imperialism and to reestablish the positions it lost during recent decades."[28]

Kislov first touched on the American view of the Middle East as an "important military-strategic springboard" that "directly abuts on the borders of the socialist community."[29] Marshal Ogarkov went farther, however, in arguing that the "enormous" amounts of money being spent on "guaranteeing

27. Primakov, "Pruzhiny Blizhnevostochnoi Politiki SShA" (Mainsprings of U.S. Middle East Policy), *SShA*, November 1976, 3–15. On American diplomatic unilateralism, see also Trofimenko, "Vneshnyaya Politika"; and Kremeniuk, "Washington."

28. Brutents, "Neokolonializm," 81–94. The enhanced American military presence in the region was the single most frequently cited consequence of Egypt's alliance switch and Camp David. I cite only a representative sample. Gromyko's speech before the UN General Assembly, *Pravda*, September 24, 1980, 4; Brezhnev, *Documents and Resolutions: The Twenty-sixth Congress of the Communist Party of the Soviet Union* (Moscow: Novosti, 1981), 28; Ogarkov, "Zavetam Lenina Verny"; Ustinov, "Voennaya Razryadka—Velenie Vremeni" (Military Detente—Wave of the Times), Pravda, October 25, 1979, 4–5; Gorshkov, "Bazy Agressii" (Bases of Aggression), *Pravda*, April 15, 1983, 4–5; Ulyanovsky, "Pod Pritselom Washingtona" (In the Gun Sights of Washington), *Pravda* September 27, 1983, 4; Arbatov, "Vneshnyaya Politika"; and Simoniya, "Gonka Vooruzhenii i Razvivaiushchiesya Strany" (The Arms Race and Developing Countries), *AIAS*, January 1984, 2–5. Many Soviets also cited this enhanced American military presence as being an effective counterweight to its loss in Iran. See, for a representative sample, Primakov, "Islam"; Falin, "Voennaya Razryadka Vozmozhna"; Trofimenko, "Washington"; Kislov, "Pentagon Adventurism in the Middle East," *IA*, April 1983, 100–107; and Belyaev, "Operatsiya 'Neftepromysly.' "

29. "Blizhnevostochnaya Politika SShA," 12.

an American military presence in different regions of the world," including Egypt, are aimed, in part at least, at gaining "military superiority over the Soviet Union."[30]

Prior to Egypt's abrogation of its treaty with the Soviet Union, only a few Soviet scholars and journalists had identified American economic and military aid as an effective instrument for influencing events in Arab countries. After this Egyptian reversal, however, Brezhnev himself told Syria's Hafez Assad that "all of us see that the stronger states that have gained independence become, the more insistently imperialism tries to turn them back and reestablish its lost influence there. Imperialists strive to split the national liberation movement, find conciliators in its ranks, and promise them economic and financial aid."[31]

Brutents generalized the experience of Egypt to all progressive Soviet allies in the Third World. He argued that the United States was increasingly "considering long-term tendencies and the power of economic factors. This is obvious in the example of CSOs." The United States was increasingly abandoning "open hostility toward them." Instead, it has been replaced by "outward friendliness and the development of economic and cultural ties with them. But the goal remains the same: patiently waiting for 'the hour,' preventing the further radicalization of progressive regimes and ultimately destabilizing them." The United States "plays on their economic needs, their dependence on the world capitalist economy that is hard or impossible to do away with." This American policy has been "reinforced by the experience of Egypt and other countries that showed that the final resolution of the direction of social development can be a prolonged affair and the choice of socialist orientation still does not guarantee the victory of socialism, nor exclude moving backward, returning to capitalist development."[32]

Finally, Soviet observers saw the American achievement of Egypt's alliance switch, its unilateral abandonment of the October 1977 pledge to work with the Soviet Union to achieve a Middle East settlement, and the Camp

---

30. Ogarkov, "Na Strazhe Mirnovo Truda," 89. Ogarkov explicitly separated the various missions of different American military activities and identified the American presence in Egypt and elsewhere in the Middle East as having a strategic purpose. See also Kremeniuk, "Strategiya Ugroz i Agressii" (Strategy of Threats and Aggression), *KZ*, March 26, 1983, 5; and Brutents, "Kto Prepyatstvuet Miru v Livane" (Who Is Preventing Peace in Lebanon), *Pravda*, February 4, 1984, 4.

31. *Pravda*, February 22, 1978, 2. On the effects of American military aid to Egypt, see Kislov, "The Arms Race in the Middle East," *IA*, July 1978, 88-93. On American economic instruments in Egypt, see Primakov, "Nekotorye Problemy." On how the United States "bribed" Egypt for military bases, see Ustinov, "Protiv Gonki Vooruzhenii i Ugrozy Voiny" (Against the Arms Race and the Threat of War), *Pravda*, July 25, 1981, 4; and Ulyanovsky, "Pod Pritselom."

32. Brutents, "Neokolonializm," 81–94.

David negotiations and resultant treaty as evidence that the United States was trying to undermine detente with the Soviet Union. As Ponomarev put it, the "intrigues of imperialism in the Middle East are an integral part of a policy aimed at undermining detente and returning to the times of the cold war."[33]

## Summary

Clearly, the two Middle East wars and subsequent American diplomacy made a great impression on Soviet perceptions of American credibility. In the aftermath of the June 1967 war, Soviet observers felt that the United States was intent on overthrowing the progressive governments of Egypt, Syria, Algeria, and Iraq. As the postwar diplomatic picture unfolded in subsequent years, however, Soviets became increasingly concerned with another threat. The United States threatened Soviet positions in the Middle East, particularly in Egypt, by either blocking a settlement or by manipulating the negotiations and making promises of economic aid.

After the October 1973 war, Soviet fears were realized. They watched the United States pursue a policy of "separate deals" and "bribe" the Egyptian leadership to forsake its alliance with the Soviet Union. By 1979–80, Soviets commented on the effectiveness of the American instrument of economic and military aid to undermine Soviet relationships with its progressive allies in the Third World, in general. Moreover, the United States had turned Egypt into a military ally, able to replace Iran as a "subimperialist" center in the region.

### Soviet Lessons about Regional Dynamics

It is impossible to overstate just how pessimistically Soviets evaluated the prospects for future progressive change in the Middle East in light of Israeli military victories in the two wars and American diplomatic successes. Soviets paid attention to at least six discrete elements in developing their predictions about future trends in the region:

a. They evaluated the stability of Soviet alliance relationships with its progressive Arab allies, in particular, with Egypt.

---

33. Speech at a joint meeting of the foreign affairs committees of the Supreme Soviet, *Pravda*, November 4, 1980, 2. On Camp David in particular, see Ustinov, "Delu Partii Verny." On American renunciation of the October 1977 agreement, see Trofimenko, "Politika bez Perspektivy" (Policy without a Future), *MEIMO*, March 1980, 17–27. On just how high Soviet expectations were of fruitful U.S.-Soviet cooperation in the Middle East immediately after the statement, see Kislov, "Posle Sovetsko-Amerikanskovo Zayavleniya po Blizhnemu Vostoku" (After the Soviet-American Statement on the Middle East), *SShA*, December 1977, 43–48.

    b. They assessed the relative levels of Arab unity in resisting Israel, and supporting Egypt, Syria, Jordan, and the Palestinian Resistance Movement, and in resisting Egypt and Israel after 1976.

    c. They paid close attention to the military balance between Israel and its Arab foes. This consideration often was reflected both in Soviet expressions of support for a political or military solution to the Arab-Israeli conflict and in the nature of the demands on Israel supported by the Soviets.

    d. They closely followed domestic political developments in Arab countries, especially Egypt, to gauge the viability of continued progressive tendencies in these countries.

    e. They assessed the contributions made to the general struggle against Israel by various Palestinian guerilla groups.

    f. Soviets evaluated the broad demographic, geographical, and economic balance between Israel and its Arab opponents.

Variations in these six indicators accounted for the ebbs and flows of pessimism expressed by Soviet observers. One constant, however, accounted for the complete absence of any statements of unalloyed optimism by any Soviets at any time. This constant was Israel. Every Soviet observer agreed that Israel was both resolved and capable of defending its own pre-1967 borders and maintaining control over the occupied territories. The only differences among observers were just how much damage Israel was deemed able to impose on the Arab allies of the Soviet Union.

    In table 23, I show Soviet lessons about the region from the end of the Six Day War in June 1967 until the onset of the October War of 1973.

**TABLE 23.  Soviet Lessons about Regional Dynamics: The Middle East, 1967–73**

| Lesson | $N^a$ |
| --- | --- |
| National liberation movements around the world are at risk. | 5 |
| Soviet influence is at risk throughout the Middle East. | 6 |
| Soviet influence is at risk in Egypt. | 5 |
| Socialist orientation is in trouble in Egypt. | 3 (13) |
| Arab unity against Israel is unlikely. | 9 |
| Israel possesses sufficient military power to deter any Arab military attack. | 20 (7) |
| Israel is a credible opponent. | 7 |
| Long-term trends favor Israel. | 0 (4) |

*Note*: Lessons are listed in order from strongest deterrent to weakest deterrent.

aNumbers in parentheses represent lessons that disconfirm that particular hypothesis, e.g., where Soviets thrice mentioned that Socialist orientation was in trouble in Egypt, they denied the same in 13 instances.

Middle East, 1967

As the figures in table 23 show, Soviets learned mostly deterrent lessons about the Middle East after the 1967 war. The only unequivocal exceptions concern the stability of socialist orientation in Egypt and long-term demographic trends in the area against Israel. Otherwise, Soviets recognized a highly capable and resolute foe in Israel, helped both by Arab disunity and by reactionary tendencies in the region. Moreover, Soviets feared anti-Soviet dominoes both in the region and elsewhere in the world. I treat each of the six elements in turn below.

*Soviet Influence under Threat*
Soviet observers acknowledged that one of the most troubling consequences in the Middle East of the Arab military defeat was that Soviet influence in the region, especially in Egypt, was at risk of being supplanted by that of the United States. Only days after the cease-fire, Primakov noted that reactionary forces in Egypt had begun a campaign of "sowing seeds of defeatist feelings and disbelief in the government and [were] arousing doubts in the minds of Egyptians with respect to the support given to Arab countries by socialist countries."[34] Belyaev identified the Egyptian economy as a possible weak link in Cairo's ties with Moscow, writing that "now the pro-American lobby is trying to scare people with the argument that, without the United States, Egypt will not be able to overcome the economic difficulties caused by the closure of the canal."[35] Soviets also feared that Arab countries in general would conclude that the United States held the key to the peace process, and so would accommodate themselves to the imperialists.[36]

Soviets identified increased Soviet military aid as a critical weapon against Egypt abandoning its alliance with Moscow.[37] The Rogers initiatives again raised serious Soviet concerns about Egypt's stability as an ally. Soviets dampened these fears by citing the signing of the Treaty of Friendship and Cooperation between Egypt and the Soviet Union in May 1971. Primakov described the importance of this document in precisely these terms. "The

---

34. Primakov, "Narod," 3. See also Brezhnev's speech to a graduating class at the military academy, *Pravda*, July 6, 1967, 1–2.

35. Belyaev, "'Nash Drug,'" 4. See also Mirsky, "Rebirth."

36. For example, Belyaev, "V Plenu Samoobmana—Kto Zatyagivaet Blizhnevostochnoi Krizis?" (A Prisoner of Self-Deception—Who is Prolonging the Middle East Crisis?), *Pravda*, February 2, 1968, 4. See also Mirsky, "Israel."

37. For example, Primakov, "Pochti Dva Goda Spustya" (Almost Two Years Later), *Pravda*, May 13, 1969, 4. See also Belyaev, "Torzhestvo Revoliutsii" (Triumph of the Revolution), *Pravda*, July 23, 1970, 4.

Rogers trip [spring 1971] was mainly aimed at invigorating pro-American feelings that still have a definite presence in a number of Arab countries. Isolated Arab journalists wrote that the 'key' to the Middle East problem lies in American hands." Primakov concluded that these plans were "dealt a crushing blow by the treaty."[38]

In sum, Soviets feared that the United States could undermine Soviet relationships with their allies in the Middle East through the deft manipulation of the peace process and economic largesse.

### Arab Dominoes and Dissensus

Soviet observers saw a variety of events in the region that militated against the establishment of Arab unity to balance against Israel.[39] First, several Soviets, invoking the lessons of Munich, predicted that if Israel was not forced to evacuate the occupied territories, no other progressive Arab country could be secure from Israeli attack, and other progressive countries around the world should also be concerned. Soviets also discovered that some of the richest Arab countries saw the United States as their ally, regardless of American support for Israel. Moreover, some of the Soviet Union's progressive Arab allies refused to cooperate with each other against Israel, instead pursuing their own individual agendas. The only relief from these pessimistic assessments came in the wake of the coups in the Sudan and Libya.

Kosygin was the first Soviet to warn that appeasing the aggressor would make all liberated states insecure. "To leave Israeli actions unpunished would mean opposing the cause of national liberation and the interests of many African, Asian, and Latin American states. If the pretensions of Israel are not given a rebuff, then tomorrow both big and small aggressors can try to seize territory from other peace-loving countries."[40]

---

38. Primakov, "Manevry SShA," 4. See also Belyaev, "Nasledie Prezidenta Nasera" (The Legacy of President Nasser), *AIAS*, November 1971, 8-11; Mirsky, "The Path of the Egyptian Revolution," *NT*, 1972, no. 30, 21–24; and Brutents, "Pravyashchaya Revoliutsionnaya Demokratiya: Nekotorye Cherty Prakticheskoi Deyatelnosti" (Ruling Revolutionary Democracy: Some Features of Practical Activities), part 1, *MEIMO*, November 1972, 104–17.

39. That Arab unity was an important causal variable for Soviet observers was demonstrated by the fact that many Soviets, such as Belyaev, argued that Israel "risked aggression only because Arab countries were not united in the face of danger." "Politika Mira i Politika Agresii" (Policy of Peace and Policy of Aggression), *Pravda*, December 4, 1967, 1.

40. *Pravda*, June 20, 1967, 3. "Big aggressor" here most probably refers to the United States. This, of course, is precisely the argument made by deterrence theorists in the United States about the inevitable consequences of encouraging Soviet adventurism by not punishing them in peripheral areas. Primakov also highlighted the dangers to the global national liberation movement of not punishing Israel, in "Politika, Vedushchaya v Tupik" (Policy Leading to a Dead End), *Pravda*, June 21, 1968, 4. Gromyko also invoked the lessons of Munich, reaching the same conclusion: see, for example, his speech at the special UN General Assembly session on the Middle East, *Pravda*, July 5, 1967, 4. He repeated this warning at the end of this session in

Immediately after the war, Soviet observers argued that Israeli aggression had caused all Arabs to unite against their common foe. They cited a variety of evidence. Primakov noted that Egypt and Tunisia had resumed diplomatic relations;[41] there were anti-British demonstrations in Aden; strikes in Libya had "paralyzed oil drilling at concerns belonging to American capital"; the movement of Kuwaiti and Iraqi oil had stopped; Sudanese workers had demanded the "nationalization of British and American banks and enterprises"; and Saudi Arabia's King Faisal had agreed to participate in the upcoming Arab summit.[42] Libya had demanded "the early evacuation of Wheelus [an American air force base] and Saudi Arabia had embargoed oil supplies to the United States and Britain."[43]

While these signs of Arab unity were positive in themselves, Belyaev reported that there was a price to be paid for this unity in terms of a hardening of Israel's position. Israeli politicians, fearing a closing window of opportunity, had annexed East Jerusalem and stated unequivocally that they would never relinquish the occupied territories. Israel took these actions because they feared that the increased Arab resistance to the West was making "American and British politicians increasingly fear for their positions in Arab countries. In these conditions, Israeli politicians are clearly hurrying."[44]

By August 1967, however, these signs of Arab unity had begun to fade. One cost of creating a "united anti-imperialist front" was that Egypt had to withdraw all its troops from South Yemen at the request of Saudi Arabia.[45] Moreover, "Libya has renewed oil exports to a number of NATO countries," and "Saudi Arabia plans to resume exports even to the United States and Britain." Worse, from the viewpoint of the Soviet Union, was the question of "how to explain these phenomena. You cannot escape the fact that in certain Arab countries, influential groups, who even sometimes make policy, have fused with imperialism. Each of the partners in this alliance pursues its own goals. There was a time when one could consider such people to be agents of foreign states." But now, "these ties between Arab reaction and imperialism

---

*Pravda*, July 23, 1967, 4, and yet again before the UN General Assembly more than three years later, *Pravda*, October 23, 1970, 4.

41. "Narod."

42. Primakov, "Vragi Arabskikh Narodov Proschitalis" (The Enemies of Arabs Have Miscalculated), *Pravda*, June 14, 1967, 5. On the Arab summit as evidence of Arab unity, also see Belyaev, "Otpor Avantiuristam" (A Rebuff to Adventurists), *Pravda*, June 19, 1967, 1.

43. Primakov, "Hour of Ordeal," *NT*, 1967, no. 26, 8. Also see "Kair v Eti Dni" (Cairo in These Days), *Ogonek*, 1967, no. 26, 4–5.

44. Belyaev, "Politicheskie Diversii Izrailya" (Political Diversions of Israel), *Pravda*, June 30, 1967, 5.

45. On the costs to progressive Arab goals of this concession to Saudi Arabia, see Primakov, "Yemen: Reaction on the Offensive," *NT*, 1968, no. 3, 18–20. Belyaev also assailed Saudi activities in Yemen in "V Plenu." See also Mirsky, "Israel."

can be mostly explained by the mutual aspiration to create 'normal' conditions for the exploitation of Arab oil. The maintenance of regular production in a number of countries is far more important than common Arab interests."[46] Belyaev singled out Saudi Arabia as a particularly implacable balancer against progressive change in the region, arguing that "those who reduce Faisal's role to that of a lackey of the Americans are wrong, for he has his own policy for the [Arabian] peninsula. He savors the idea of replacing the British in Bahrein, Muscat and Oman. Faisal plans, with British aid, to oppose both national liberation revolutions and the spread of socialist ideas in the Arab world."[47]

There was also dissension in the ranks of progressive Soviet allies in the Middle East. For example, the Syrian delegation "left for home before the [Khartoum] summit."[48] And at the summit itself, Algeria and Syria "insisted on continuing the armed struggle and declaring a people's war against Israel. Many Arab leaders thought this was unrealistic, to say the least. The defeat in the Six Day War bears out this view." The common Arab cause was also harmed by "extremist forces in the Arab world" whose "speeches have already done a great deal of damage to the positions of Arabs. Their adventurism plays into the hands of imperialist and Zionist circles."[49] These "extremist forces" were Palestinian guerillas.

The coups in the Sudan and Libya in 1969 provided some relief to Soviet observers. Libya and the Sudan were strategic assets in the struggle against Israel. "Libyan leaders recently announced they are ready to impose an oil embargo against the West if Egypt so requests. The Sudan now ensures that the rear of the Egyptian revolution is secure."[50] Moreover, as a consequence of the new front of Egypt, Sudan, Iraq, and Syria, "instead of the disorder among Arab countries that Washington and Tel Aviv had hoped to cause by

---

46. Belyaev, "Ot Tripoli do Khartouma" (From Tripoli to Khartoum), *Pravda*, August 6, 1967, 4. See also Belyaev, "Posle Khartouma" (After Khartoum), *Pravda*, September 5, 1967, 4; and Belyaev, "Middle East Powder Keg," *NT*, 1969, no. 11, 5–7.

47. Belyaev, "Lessons of the 1967 Middle East Crisis," *IA*, March 1968, 42. See also "Dragged-Out Middle East Conflict: Who Stands to Gain?" *IA*, September 1969, 67–70, and "Sily Soprotivoleniya Agressoru Rastut" (Forces of Resistance to the Aggressor are Growing), *MEIMO*, May 1970, 73–78.

48. Belyaev, "Ot Tripoli."

49. Primakov, "Vopreki Proiskam" (Despite Intrigues), *Pravda*, January 19, 1968, 4. For more criticism of Palestinian extremism, see Primakov, "Politika, Vedushchaya"; and Mirsky, "Israel."

50. Belyaev, "Sily Soprotivoleniya," 77. On the loss of Wheelus in Libya, see Kislov, "SShA v Sredizemnomorye: Novye Realnosti" (The U.S. in the Mediterranean: New Realities), *SShA*, April 1972, 32–39; and Kokoshin, "Naval Power in U.S. Strategic Plans," *IA*, April 1973, 56–62.

the Six Day War, there has been political consolidation."[51] However, this "new front" was ridden with disunity almost as soon as it was identified. Belyaev, for example, remarked that Nasser's 23 July acceptance of a cease-fire with Israel had been met with "Libya saying it would define its position somewhat later and Iraq, Algeria, and Syria adopting negative positions." Belyaev characterized the "sharply negative attitudes of the leaders of Palestinian organizations as puzzling, to say the least." Belyaev argued that the only ones who will "benefit by torpedoing the Egyptian peace initiative are those who want Israeli aggression and occupation of Arab lands to continue" because then Israel "will have an excuse to complain that Arab countries are opposed to a political settlement." He warned that "those who cherish Arab interests, including Palestinian, should not forget that there can be no other solution than a political one."[52]

In sum, Soviets recognized that enmity toward Israel was insufficient to unify the ranks of Arabs. Not only were there rifts between conservative and radical Arab regimes, but even the latter were not able to cooperate among themselves against Israel.

## The Arab-Israeli Military Balance

Soviet observers were unanimous in their initial appraisal of obvious Arab military inferiority with respect to Israel after the war. By 1970, however, these Soviets were equally unanimous in arguing that their Arab allies, Egypt in particular, had built up their military capabilities to the point that they were stronger than before the Six Day War. But these capabilities were seen only as an effective deterrent against Israeli attacks on Arab homelands, not as forces sufficient to recover the territories occupied by Israel by force. This ceiling on Soviet optimism was consistently reflected in their continual expressions of support for a peaceful settlement and equally constant criticisms of those Arabs who irresponsibly, in their view, argued for a military solution.

A month after the war, Mirsky acknowledged that "Israel had succeeded in changing the military balance for a time."[53] Recognition of Israeli military advantage was reflected in Soviet analyses of Arab attitudes toward a political settlement. After the Khartoum summit, for example, Belyaev approvingly reported that "a change has occurred from the position of war with Israel. And

---

51. Belyaev, "Middle East Crisis," 31. See also Belyaev, "Sily Soprotivoleniya."

52. Belyaev, "Downed Phantoms and Peace Prospects," *NT*, 1970, no. 32, 4–5.

53. Mirsky, "Israeli Aggression and Arab Unity," *NT*, 1967, no. 28, 4. Note Mirsky's disclaimer "for a time." Soviets often added such phrases to dilute their own arguments. The most common one of these was "the Arab territories *temporarily* occupied by Israel." On Israeli military superiority, also see Belyaev, "Raschety na Peske" (Calculations on Sand), *Pravda*, November 19, 1967, 4.

this is natural, a more sensible position. The conference stresses the need to apply all methods, including political and economic."[54] Soviets thought the military balance so unfavorable that they argued that those Arabs who argued for military operations against Israel were actually playing into Israeli hands.[55]

In January 1969, Mirsky led the way in optimism about the military balance.[56] He argued that Israeli "hopes that the defeat would set Arabs back for years in military terms have proven quite false. With Soviet aid, Egypt has re-equipped its forces and they are stronger now than in June 1967."[57] Consistent with this belief, he argued that though the "Egyptian leadership is for a peaceful settlement, it is compelled also to prepare for the possibility of a military resolution of the conflict."[58] Primakov, while acknowledging the restoration of Egyptian defensive capabilities, approvingly reported that "one of Egypt's leaders told me that Egypt will not let itself be provoked and will not give up on efforts for a political settlement."[59]

Belyaev, however, remained skeptical about Egypt's military capabilities long after his colleagues had become more sanguine. In June 1969, Belyaev explained that "as a result of almost a century of imperialist domination, Egypt, Syria, and Jordan are *now* greatly inferior to Israel militarily." He went

---

54. Belyaev, "Posle Khartouma," 4. See also Belyaev's criticism of those Palestinian leaders who called for war with Israel in "Kogda Osela Pyl" (When the Dust Has Settled), *Pravda*, August 3, 1967, 4. Also see his criticism of Syria and Algeria above, in "Situation in the Arab World," *NT*, 1967, no. 39, 8–11. Belyaev also expressed impatience at the procedural objections raised by Arabs against direct talks with Israel: "Ways of Ending the Middle East Crisis," *IA*, October 1968, 25–28, 34, and "Washington's Asian Boomerang." See also Primakov, "Vopreki Proiskam." Mirsky also criticized Arabs who would not unequivocally accept UN Resolution 242, in "Israeli Aggression: One Year Later," *NT*, 1968, no. 22, 12–14.

55. For example, Mirsky, "Arabskie Narody Prodolzhaiut Borbu" (Arabs Continue the Struggle), *MEIMO*, March 1968, 120–25. That Israel would love to provoke Egypt and other Arab countries into premature military operations was a constant refrain of Soviet observers, reflecting their lack of confidence in Arab military capabilities. See, for example, Belyaev, "I Golova Uvyazla, I Khvost Uvyaz" (If You Grab the Head, the Tail Will Follow), *Pravda*, March 24, 1968, 1, 4; Primakov, "UAR: Put k Budushchemu" (UAR: Path to the Future), *Pravda*, April 28, 1968, 4; Mirsky, "Rebirth," and "UAR: Home Front," *NT*, 1968, no. 50, 8–10.

56. This isn't quite true: he expressed hope earlier but did not repeat it, and his views were shared by no one. See Mirsky, "Arab East: Moment of Truth," *NT*, 1967, nos. 46–47, 27–29.

57. Mirsky, "The Third World: Illusions and Realities," *NT*, 1969, no. 1, 10. Primakov agreed with Mirsky's assessment in "Peace Prospects." See also "Suez: Na Perednem Krae" (Suez: On the Front Line), *Kazakhstanskaya Pravda*, June 5, 1969, 4.

58. Mirsky, "'Novaya Revoliutsiya' v Egipte" ("New Revolution" in Egypt), *MEIMO*, January 1969, 41. See also Primakov, "Podderzhka Spravdelivoi Borby" (Support of a Just Struggle), *Pravda*, January 31, 1969, 5.

59. "Two Years After," *NT*, 1969, no. 24, 10.

on to say that this advantage cannot "last forever."[60] Even those Soviets who had been most optimistic about Egyptian military capabilities, Mirsky and Kislov, fell silent after June 1969. Perhaps Belyaev expressed why. He wrote that the "Arabs really lost the Six Day War. Now Israeli Phantoms are bombing Egypt in depth. The Israeli army still maintains an advantage, firstly in the air and especially in air force personnel."[61] Soviet supplies of surface-to-air missiles (SAMs), however, effectively deterred any further deep-penetration raids by the Israeli air force.[62] Belyaev attributed responsibility to the SAMs for getting Israel to agree to a resumption of the Jarring peace mission.[63] Soviets continued, however, to reassure their readers that Egypt was primarily interested in a political, not a military, settlement.[64]

Mirsky, however, remained an outlier among his colleagues, convinced of the viability of a military option. He argued that people in the West are "profoundly deluded" if they think that there is no reason to take seriously "talk about coming battles for liberation." In fact, "Egyptian honor and national dignity are at stake. Should they have no alternative to a political settlement based on Resolution 242, they will take up arms."[65]

In sum, Soviet observers, with the exception of Mirsky, only cautiously appraised the military balance between their Arab allies and Israel. It was seen as sufficiently strong to deter Israeli attacks on Arab countries, but not so strong as to allow for Arab military efforts to retake the lands lost in June 1967.

## The Stability of Egypt's Socialist Orientation

Immediately after the 1967 war, Soviets expressed some concern about Egypt's ability to maintain itself on the progressive noncapitalist path of development. Very shortly thereafter, however, Soviet observers were unanimous in believing that Egypt had overcome these temporary difficulties. Nevertheless, throughout the period, most Soviets continued to see a struggle being waged between the forces of progress and reaction within Egypt, though all were optimistic that ultimately revolutionary elements would prevail.

---

60. Belyaev, "Arabskii Yashchik Pandory," 4 (emphasis added).

61. Belyaev, "Sily Soprotivoleniya," 74.

62. Primakov, "Po Puti Avantiurizma" (On the Path of Adventurism), *Selskaya Zhizn*, June 7, 1970, 3. Belyaev concurred in this assessment in "Who Is Encouraging Whom?" *NT*, 1970, no. 29, 11, and "Iz-za Chuzhoi Spiny" (Behind Someone Else's Back), *Pravda*, July 21, 1970, 5.

63. "Downed Phantoms." See also his "Who is Obstructing"; and Primakov, "Manevry SShA."

64. For example, Kislov, "Blizhnevostochnoi Konflikt."

65. Mirsky, "The Path," 24.

Just days after the war ended, Primakov expressed confidence in Nasser's staying power, citing the fact that people took to the streets in support of Nasser after the latter offered his resignation as president on June 9.[66] But Soviet observers also acknowledged that the "Sinai defeat created a complicated situation. Local reaction immediately tried to take advantage of the feelings of pessimism and dejection. They argued that the cause of everything was the socialist choice of Egypt and its progressive domestic policies. Egyptian reaction is not surrendering."[67]

Belyaev and others gained confidence from the fact that Marshal Amir "and his entourage have been arrested." But this "marks only the beginning of the struggle between the proponents and enemies of progressive development that is far from over."[68] The loss of revenues from the closure of the Suez Canal and the dramatic drop in tourism created "rich soil for the revival of domestic reaction. Twice last year [1968], Egyptian cities became arenas for demonstrations that led to clashes with the police with resultant injuries." But Nasser's response to this unrest, in particular the proclamation of the more radical March 30th Program, inspired Soviet confidence in Egypt.[69]

Mirsky, however, consistent with his early optimistic appraisal of the Arab-Israeli military balance, argued that progressive tendencies in Egypt had actually gotten stronger as a result of the war. He was alone in this assessment.[70] Soviets were also favorably impressed by the response of the Egyptian people to the deep-penetration bombing raids of Israel. Instead of the "demoralization, on which the aggressors calculated, the bombing caused still closer unity among the people in the face of the danger."[71] The 1971 Treaty of Friendship and Cooperation between Egypt and the Soviet Union was also seen as "creating a most important condition for the consolidation of Egypt as the bastion of progressive forces in the Arab world."[72] Summarizing for his colleagues, Belyaev wrote shortly before the October War that "the progres-

---

66. Primakov, "Narod." Soviet observers often cited these demonstrations as evidence of the stability of the progressive path in Egypt. See, for example, Mirsky, "Israeli Aggression and Arab Unity"; and Belyaev, "UAR: Narod i Revoliutsiya" (UAR: People and Revolution), *Pravda*, July 23, 1967, 5.

67. Belyaev, "'Nash Drug,'" 4.

68. Belyaev, "Atmosfera Ochishchaetsya" (The Atmosphere is Clearing), *Pravda*, September 6, 1967, 4. On the positive effects of removing Amir, also see Mirsky, "Arab East."

69. Kislov, "Ded Moroz v Armeiskikh Botinkakh" (Father Christmas in Army Boots), *Pravda*, January 3, 1969, 4. See also Belyaev, "Torzhestvo Revoliutsii" (Triumph of the Revolution), *Pravda*, July 23, 1970, 4.

70. Mirsky, "Arabskie Narody."

71. Belyaev, "Sily Soprotivoleniya," 75. See also Primakov, "Blizhnevostochnaya Politika SShA: Istoki, Perspektivy" (U.S. Middle East Policy: Sources and Prospects), *SShA*, September 1970, 3–13.

72. Primakov, "Manevry SShA."

sive regime endured in Egypt despite the calculations of its enemies. Egyptians have successfully overcome not insignificant economic difficulties tied to the war and have parried the attacks of the 'neocapitalists.'"[73]

*The Palestinian Factor*

Soviet observers treated the emergence of Palestinian guerillas as a mixed blessing. On the one hand, they saw them as an additional increment to the power of the Arab national liberation movement. On the other hand, as noted in the section on Arab unity above, they regarded their extremism as both an unfortunate boon to Israel and as a threat to productive Arab unity. These ambivalent attitudes were reflected in Soviet comments in the period.

Mirsky offered the first guardedly positive appraisal of the Palestinians, writing that the "resistance movement is getting stronger in the occupied territories." But, "needless to say, the guerilla struggle cannot redeem the territories." For that, Arab unity and stable progressive regimes are required.[74] Gromyko remarked on one of the major drawbacks of the Palestinians as progressive allies. "One cannot of course approve of the terrorist actions of some elements of the Palestinian movement that led, in particular, to the tragic events in Munich. Their criminal actions deal a blow to the national interests and desires of Palestinians and are used by Israeli criminals to cover their own plundering policy against the Arabs."[75]

*Long-Term Trends in the Middle East and Israel*

Several Soviet observers, as if as a last resort, expressed confidence that ultimately demographic and economic trends would catch up with the Israelis and convince their leadership to renounce its control over the occupied territories. Once again, Mirsky was first in drawing encouragement from the fact that "demographic trends" would have to eventually compel "Israeli leaders to reexamine old concepts and see the need to seek understanding with Arabs."[76] Essentially, "Time does not work for Israel. The transient factors that gave Israel victory will be reduced to nought by another permanent factor: the vast superiority of the Arab world in people, territory and resources."[77]

Until these long-term factors made themselves felt, however, Soviets

---

73. Belyaev, "Slavnaya Godovshchina" (Glorious Anniversary), *Pravda*, July 23, 1973, 3.

74. Mirsky, "Israel," 6–8. See also Primakov, "Tel Aviv: Na Stsene i za Kulisami" (Tel Aviv: On Stage and Behind the Scenes), *Pravda*, February 5, 1970, 5. It is notable, however, that neither Primakov nor Mirsky wrote again about the Palestinians in this period. See also Ulyanovsky, "Lenin"; and Belyaev, "Sily Soprotivoleniya."

75. Gromyko, Speech at the UN General Assembly, *Pravda*, September 27, 1972, 4.

76. Mirsky, "Israeli Aggression: One Year Later," *NT*, 1968, no. 22, 14.

77. Mirsky, "Israel," 8. On the three latter factors, see also Belyaev, "Sily Soprotivoleniya"; and Primakov, "Blizhnemu Vostoku."

agreed that Israel was a remarkably capable and resolute opponent. Belyaev presented a variety of evidence to explain why Israel was so bellicose and politically intransigent. First, he noted that "Jews have been enormously victimized. Six million were destroyed by Hitlerites in World War II alone."[78] As evidence of Israeli autonomy from Washington, Belyaev reported that "Meir demonstratively rejected even the new American plan for a Middle East settlement."[79] In fact, "Meir hastened to say no even before Rogers had made public the details of his plan."[80] Finally, in a retrospective analysis of the origins of the Six Day War, Belyaev described how Foreign Minister Eban had desperately tried to elicit American military and political support for the war in late May, but returned home empty-handed. After returning to Israel from Washington, "in a May 27 cabinet meeting, Eban exaggerated American and French support for Israel" in order to get the cabinet to vote for war.[81]

## Middle East, 1973–76

From the end of the October War until Sadat's abrogation of Egypt's Treaty of Friendship and Cooperation with the Soviet Union in March 1976, Soviet perceptions of regional dynamics in the Middle East went from initial optimism immediately after the war to growing pessimism. They expressed confidence in Soviet relations with its Arab allies, especially Egypt, believing that Arabs both supported Soviet efforts to comanage the search for peace with the United States and that Egypt and Syria appreciated Soviet military aid. But, as Kissinger unilaterally commandeered the peace process, Soviet confidence waned.

Soviet confidence also dissipated regarding the Arab-Israeli military balance and Arab unity. At first impressed by the initial Arab advances in the

---

78. Belyaev, "Arabskii Yashchik Pandory," 32. It was rare indeed for any Soviet to ever acknowledge that the people of Israel had experienced a peculiarly terrible past that could explain their present security concerns. Moreover, it was equally as rare for any Soviet to bother even to analyze the domestic political roots of a regional actor's foreign policy. In another article explaining the causes of the Six Day War, Belyaev again cited "Hitler's final solution" as a major contributor to Israel's decision making. "S Chernovo Khoda, Dokumentalnaya Povest" (Through the Back Door, Documentary Story), part 3, *Znamya*, November 1971, 91–123.

79. Belyaev, "Zharkoe Leto 70-vo" (The Hot Summer of 1970), *Pravda*, July 5, 1970, 5. If Israel were not considered an actor independent of the United States, Belyaev and other Soviets would have argued that Meir's actions were simply staged by Washington to curry favor with Arabs. For similar evaluations of Israel, see Arbatov, " 'Doktrina Nixona' "; and, despite the title, Kislov, "Zionisty na Sluzhbe Amerikanskovo Imperializma" (Zionists in the Service of American Imperialism), *Izvestiya*, January 20, 1972, 4.

80. Belyaev, "Who Is Encouraging Whom?" 11.

81. Belyaev, "S Chernovo," part 2, *Znamya*, October 1971, 202.

October War, Soviet observers ultimately became more depressed by the fact that Egypt had removed itself from the order of battle against Israel. Likewise, initially encouraged by Arab cooperation in imposing an oil embargo, its cancellation only four months after the war reversed this Soviet optimism. Finally, domestic developments in Egypt also contributed to Soviet pessimism.

A little over a month after the war had ended, Brezhnev asserted that the war had "proven, in practice, the effectiveness of the friendly aid and solidarity of the Soviet Union with the Arabs."[82] Mirsky focused on Arab appreciation for Soviet military assistance, arguing that

> one myth that has been blasted is that Arab weaponry is inferior to that of Israel. It has become clear that Egyptian and Syrian troops have types of weapons that Israel does not. The foreign press has reported that most of the planes lost by Israel were downed by new missiles against which Phantoms and Skyhawks proved defenseless and that in the Sinai and on the Golan, hundreds of tanks were destroyed by new guided anti-tank missiles.[83]

Kislov wrote that Arabs supported Soviet cooperation with the United States in the search for a political settlement.[84]

However, by the time Kissinger was in the midsts of negotiating Sinai II, Belyaev acknowledged that "in some Arab capitals, they continue to argue that the 'key to peace' in the Middle East is in the hands of the United States, which supposedly is in a position to exert pressure on Israel."[85] Soviets also initially were impressed by the degree of Arab unity manifested both during and in the immediate aftermath of the war. As Brezhnev put it, "The world has seen the effective solidarity of Arab states, both in the military area and in political and economic measures."[86] Mirsky was impressed that "even such countries as Kuwait and Saudi Arabia have announced an oil boycott of countries supporting Israel and decided to reduce the production and export of oil until Israel withdraws from the occupied territories."[87] All Soviets stopped mentioning the oil weapon as a sign of Arab solidarity even before that

---

82. Brezhnev, *Pravda*, November 30, 1973, 3.

83. Mirsky, "Middle East: New Factors," *NT*, 1973, no. 48, 18. See also, on this point, Belyaev, "Krax 'Filosofii Sily'—Izrail: Chto zhe Dalshe" (The Collapse of the "Philosophy of Force"—Israel: What Next), *LG*, December 12, 1973, 14.

84. Kislov, "Vokrug Blizhnevostochnovo Krizisa."

85. Belyaev, "Put k Spravedlivomu Miru" (Path to a Just Peace), *Izvestiya*, May 28, 1975, 4.

86. *Pravda*, November 30, 1973, 2.

87. Mirsky, "Middle East," 18. See also Belyaev, "Krax 'Filosofii.'"

embargo was lifted in March 1974. The only exception was Mirsky, who remained true to his uniquely optimistic beliefs.[88]

Even Mirsky, however, had to admit that Arab solidarity had been fatally breached by Egypt. He cited, in particular, the fact that Egypt had roundly condemned "Syria's aspiration to establish its dominance in Lebanon" during the Lebanese civil war.[89] Belyaev noted that Sinai II had removed Egypt from the Arab front against Israel as well as provoking disagreement among Arab countries about what attitudes to take toward the disengagement accord.[90]

Soviet observers were also initially encouraged by Arab military performance in the October War. Mirsky argued that yet another "myth destroyed was the assumption that Israel would always enjoy military superiority, that in any war with the Arabs, the Israeli army was bound to win. Arabs fought courageously and skillfully, as even Israeli military experts have to admit. Arab soldiers and Arabs in general have regained faith in their own power."[91] Again, however, the perceived consequences of Sinai II reversed Soviet optimism. Belyaev outlined how the "'neutralizaton' of Egypt and the transfer of Israeli military pressure onto Syria and Jordan has substantially changed the situation in the Middle East. The fact is that Egypt has the biggest army. Now this army will not be able to participate in military operations against Israel unless Israel attacks Egypt. The Jordanian-Israeli border is the longest and to defend it under these conditions will undoubtedly be difficult."[92]

There was initial optimism that the war had left the progressive domestic structures of the Soviet Union's Arab allies intact. Mirsky argued that "the policy of discrediting the 'Nasser line' collapsed. The prestige of the Egyptian and Syrian leadership has been markedly enhanced."[93] However, shortly after Nixon's trip to Egypt, Belyaev lamented that "right-wing forces in Egypt and other Arab countries have tried to use the results of the war in their own interests to impede the national liberation revolution in the Arab world." In particular, these forces explained "the success of the Arabs not by the deepened social revolutions, but by the 'contribution of all elements of the nation,' including the bourgeoisie. So, it was stressed that the struggle against Israel demands class peace, not social revolution." As a consequence, Egypt wel-

---

88. Mirsky, "Menyaiushchiisya Oblik." In this article, he cited the oil embargo as evidence of the anti-imperialism of even reactionary Arab regimes.

89. Mirsky, "Chto Proiskhodit v Livane" (What Is Happening in Lebanon), *LG*, March 24, 1976, 15.

90. Belyaev, "SShA i Blizhnevostochnoi Krizis," 17–27.

91. Mirsky, "Middle East," 18. See also Brezhnev, *Pravda*, November 30, 1973, 3; Belyaev, "Krax 'Filosofii'"; and Kim, "Solidarnost: Novyi Podem" (A New Rise in Solidarity), *AIAS*, June 1974, 2–4.

92. Belyaev, "SShA i Blizhnevostochnyi Krizis," 24.

93. Mirsky, "Middle East," 18.

comes "Arab oil and foreign capital." This shift toward a reactionary domestic agenda was accelerated by the "growing economic difficulties caused by the war and by the fact that the United States, certain West European countries, Iran, and Japan have promised $3 billion in loans."[94]

Finally, two elements that helped maintain a modicum of optimism among Soviet observers after the Six Day War were absent in this period. First, no Soviet ever mentioned that the Palestinian guerillas were contributing to the Arab struggle against Israel. Second, there was no longer any discussion of how "long-term trends" favored the Arabs over Israel. One possible explanation for this could be Egypt's removal from the Arab front.

### Egypt, 1976–80

After Sadat's turn to the United States and pursuit of a bilateral peace with Israel, Soviet views of the Middle East were predictably discouraged, though there were some glimmers of hopefulness. On the one hand, Soviets acknowledged that Egypt had completely forsworn its alliance with the Soviet Union. On the other hand, as a consequence of this shift by Egypt, other radical Arab states and the Palestine Liberation Organization (PLO) developed far closer relations with the Soviet Union. Moreover, there were isolated and muted expectations after Sadat's death that Egypt might reassess its relations with the Soviet Union. Likewise, though Egypt's exit from the struggle against Israel had severely weakened the Arab front of resistance, all the other Arab countries, even the conservative monarchies, balanced among themselves in opposing the Camp David deal. This anti-Egyptian unity, however, was shattered by the Iran-Iraq war.[95]

The one area in which there was not a scintilla of Soviet optimism was their evaluation of the Arab-Israeli military balance. Not only did Egypt's defection remove the most powerful Arab military force from the order of battle against Israel, but this defection allowed Israel to behave more aggressively against other Arab states, especially in Lebanon. Moreover, Soviets felt that the military balance had been shifted against progressive forces beyond the Middle East itself, in particular, in southern Africa and the Horn of Africa.

### *Soviet Influence Undermined*
Primakov described the reversal in Egyptian foreign policy as the product of the "development of anti-Soviet tendencies in Egypt" during Kissinger's

---

94. Belyaev, "Egipet: Etapy Revoliutsii" (Egypt: Stages of the Revolution), *AIAS*, July 1975, 3, 4. See also Mirsky, "Menyaiushchiisya Oblik."

95. For equally frustrated Soviet perceptions of this war's consequences on regional dynamics after the overthrow of the shah, see chap. 4.

shuttle diplomacy. These shifts in foreign policy were "mainly expressed in the departure from close relations with the Soviet Union and their replacement by a pro-Western orientation, by the aspiration, at any price, to buy an improvement in relations with the United States. The culmination of anti-Soviet actions was Sadat's decision on March 15, 1976, to unilaterally annul the Treaty of Friendship and Cooperation."[96] However, Sadat's participation in the Camp David peace negotiations gave Primakov cause to believe that at least the other Arab states and the PLO were still interested in close relations with the Soviet Union.[97] Belyaev later identified these "progressive countries" as Syria, Algeria, Libya, and the People's Democratic Republic of Yemen (PDRY).[98]

Belyaev also found encouragement in Egypt itself after Sadat's death. During a visit there, his first since the abrogation of the treaty, he reported that "in Egypt, they have not forgotten what was done for them while in friendship with the Soviet Union. Today, everyone gave me to understand that the black page in the relations between our two countries is closed."[99] He further reported Egyptian disappointment with the United States. "Egyptians remark on how costly are American military aid and equipment and loans. Also, the quantities are so small and with so much red tape that many Egyptians say the United States is disarming us. In any event, the biggest army in the Arab world is weaker than in 1973." Belyaev was also encouraged about future Soviet-Egyptian relations from the "statements of Mubarak and his ministers" that make apparent Cairo's "aspiration to continue a dialogue with Moscow. The Soviet Union has met Egypt halfway, having renewed economic cooperation and trade."[100] Belyaev, however, was the only Soviet observer to make such encouraging predictions about the possible future of this relationship.

## Arab Disunity

Soviets also saw Egypt's defection as a severe blow to Arab unity. Primakov argued, for example, that not only had Egypt "been removed from the

---

96. Primakov, "'Sbalansirovannyi Kurs' na Blizhnem Vostoke ili Staraya Politika Inymi Sredstvami?" ("Balanced Course" in the Middle East or Old Policy by Other Means?), part 2, *MEIMO*, January 1977, 53. See also Podgorny's speech at a dinner for King Hussein of Jordan, *Pravda*, June 19, 1976, 4.

97. Primakov, "A Dead-End. See also Brutents, "The Soviet Union and Newly-Independent Countries," *IA*, April 1979, 3–14; and Gromyko's speech before the Syrian foreign minister, *Pravda*, January 28, 1980, 4. One probably should discount this speech as evidence, given the demands of the audience.

98. Belyaev, "Kto Seet Kamni" (Who Is Sowing Stones), *LG*, February 4, 1981, 9.

99. Belyaev, "Egipet—Strana Chudes" (Egypt—Country of Wonders), part 1, *LG*, January 12, 1983, 10. It should be noted that Belyaev's "everyone" consisted of primarily radical friends from his days as a correspondent in Egypt whom he interviewed for this article.

100. Belyaev, "Egipet '83: Inye Vremena?" (Egypt 1983: Different Times?), *AIAS*, July 1983, 20–23.

struggle against Israel, which has undermined the unity of the countries and forces participating in the confrontation with Israel," but the consequences of this disunity have "vividly manifested themselves in the tragic events in Lebanon."[101] Other Soviets also remarked on the appearance of a new disunifying phenomenon. Conservative Arab regimes, like Saudi Arabia, through their amassed petrodollars, were financing Egypt's treachery.[102]

After the meeting between Sadat and Begin hosted by Carter at Camp David in September 1978, Soviet observers were encouraged by the fact that "Egypt has found itself isolated in the Arab world."[103] Primakov approvingly reported that the participants in the November 1978 Baghdad summit of Arab leaders, "even Saudi Arabia, condemned the treaty." Moreover, Arab OPEC members agreed to provide financial aid to Syria, Jordan, and the PLO. "The closer relationship between Syria and Iraq that has now come about is of immense value in the context of Egypt's capitulationist policy. The Soviet Union has always looked forward to Syria and Iraq drawing closer together on an anti-imperialist basis."[104]

But conservative Arab regimes like Saudi Arabia still prevented the creation of the kind of united front for which Soviets hoped. Belyaev wrote that "despite [Saudi] participation in the [Baghdad] conference, Prince Fahd did not renounce the 'special relationship' with the United States. Despite Camp David, the prince thought it possible to state in Baghdad that 'the American umbrella solves all Saudi Arabia's security problems.'" Moreover,

---

101. Primakov, "'Sbalansirovannyi Kurs," part 1, *MEIMO*, December 1976, 40. Primakov was referring to the Lebanese civil war in which Israel was supporting Christian forces against both Lebanese Moslems and Palestinian guerillas, while Syria was both supporting the Moslems and simultaneously settling scores with factions of the PLO that it did not support. On Egypt's defection being responsible for events in Lebanon, see also, Kislov, "Nasushchnye Problemy Blizhnevostochnovo Uregulirovaniya" (Vital Problems of a Middle East Settlement), *SShA*, July 1977, 22–33; and Primakov, "Blizhnevostochnyi Tupik: V Chem Prichina?" (Middle East Dead End: Who's to Blame?), *Pravda*, July 26, 1978, 4. On the removal of Egypt from the "confrontation with Israel," see Belyaev, "V Spiske 'Zapreshchennykh'" (On the "Banned" List), *LG*, August 30, 1978, 14; and Gromyko's speech before the UN General Assembly, *Pravda*, September 27, 1978, 4.

102. For example, see Kislov, "Blizhnevostochnaya Stavka Vashingtona" (Washington's Middle East Headquarters), *Pravda*, September 21, 1977, 4. See also Simoniya, "Osvobodivshiesya Strany i Mirovoe Razvitie" (Liberated Countries and World Development), *AIAS*, January 1978, 4–8.

103. Kislov, "Sdelka v Kemp-Devide—'Illiuziya Uregulirovaniya'" (The Deal at Camp David—"The Illusion of a Settlement"), *SShA*, November 1978, 60. See also Primakov, "Blizhnii Vostok."

104. Primakov, "A Dead-End," 40. On Arab unity against Camp David, see also Belyaev, "Izrail: Upovaya na Voinu Protiv Sovetskovo Soiuza" (Israel: Setting Hopes on War against the Soviet Union), *LG*, December 16, 1981, 9, 14, 15; Iordansky, "Policy"; Kislov, "Blizhnii Vostok i Kemp-Devidskii Tupik" (The Middle East and the Camp David Dead End), *SShA*, March 1982, 36–41; and Zorina, "Razvivaiushchiesya Strany."

in Baghdad, the Saudis "made it known that they do not consider the Soviet Union to be a proponent of the Arabs in their struggle for a just Middle East settlement." And instead of condemning the United States, as "the entire Arab world expected, the Saudis limited themselves to condemning only Israel!"[105] Moreover, Soviets blamed Camp David for the lack of Arab unity shown in Lebanon after Israel's invasion in 1982. Brutents argued that this Israeli action was facilitated by "the extremely weak resistance given them by the Arab world, the definite passivity of many Arab states in such dramatic days, and the absence of unity among them that made even convening an Arab summit impossible. There is no doubt that, along with other factors, this is the result of Camp David, which removed Egypt from the Arab ranks."[106]

Finally, the Iran-Iraq war had begun to restore Egypt to the Arab fold, but on Egypt's and Camp David's terms. Kislov complained that before, "despite all the social, political, economic, ideological, and even religious differences between Arab countries, they overcame them during the most acute military confrontations with Israel in a more or less united front." But now, the Iran-Iraq war has "injected such a split into the Arab world that it was not overcome even" by the Israeli invasion of Lebanon. Worst of all, if before the war, the Arab world,

> at least verbally, almost unanimously condemned the Camp David deal and Egypt was in isolation, then now the door to the possible rapprochement between Egypt and conservative Arab countries has been virtually thrown open. And Iraq has become a propagandist for such a merger, and on the conditions of Cairo, that is, the maintenance of the existing level of relations of Egypt with the United States and Israel, and on a platform of the virtual renunciation by a number of Arab countries of real opposition to Camp David.[107]

## The Arab-Israeli Military Balance

Soviet observers were virtually unanimous in their gloomy assessments of the Arab-Israeli military balance after Egypt's defection. This shift in the military balance was held responsible for, among other things, allowing Israel to intervene in the Lebanese civil war in 1975–76.[108] Moreover, "Sinai II has

---

105. Belyaev, "Saudovskaya Arabiya: Chto zhe Dalshe?" (Saudi Arabia: What Next?), *LG*, January 31, 1979, 14.

106. Brutents, "Livanskaya Tragediya" (Lebanese Tragedy), *SShA*, September 1982, 6. See also Gromyko's critical comments at a breakfast for the Syrian foreign minister, *Pravda*, November 12, 1983, 4.

107. Kislov, "SShA i Blizhnii Vostok, God 1982" (The U.S. and the Middle East, 1982), *SShA*, January 1983, 18–28.

108. For example, see Primakov, "Pruzhiny Blizhnevostochnoi"; and Kosygin's speech in the PDRY, *Pravda*, September 17, 1979, 4.

had an extremely unfavorable result for Arabs. Israel has received extremely favorable conditions from the military viewpoint. Israel has guaranteed itself, with the aid of American early warning systems, against any 'surprises' in a confrontation with the militarily strongest Arab country—Egypt, the latter being virtually neutralized for a long time."[109]

The Camp David treaty in itself was seen as a severe blow to Arab military power. Primakov, for example, wrote that the "treaty virtually neutralizes Egypt even in the event of a new war of Israel against its Arab neighbors. This means that Egypt must remain on the sidelines if Israel should unleash armed operations against Syria, Jordan, or Lebanon." Moreover, "the treaty excludes the presence of Palestinian patriots on Egyptian soil."[110] There was only one optimistic appraisal of the military balance after Sadat's defection. But Belyaev could argue only that "Syria has sufficient forces to defend its borders."[111]

The Camp David accords were also seen as responsible for both Israel's bombing of the Iraqi nuclear reactor in 1981 and its subsequent invasion of Lebanon in 1982.[112] Gromyko told his UN audience that the "roots of the Lebanese tragedy are in Camp David. What this did for peace is especially clear from the fact that more blood has been spilled since Camp David than during Israel's aggression in June 1967."[113] Egypt's defection also affected the military balance beyond the Middle East itself. "Evidence of this is the participation of Egyptian detachments in support of the Mobutu regime in Zaire and actions heating up the conflict on the Horn of Africa. This position of Sadat has unequivocally shown that he is more concerned about 'containing communism' in Africa than resisting Israeli aggression and that he is ready to turn Egypt into the nucleus of anticommunist forces both in the Arab world and in Africa in general."[114] Another region in which Egypt was prepared to play the role of "regional gendarme" was Afghanistan.[115]

---

109. Primakov, "'Sbalansirovannyi Kurs," part 2, 57. See also Kislov, "Sdelka."

110. Primakov, "Tsena Separatnoi Sdelki" (The Price of a Separate Deal), *Pravda*, December 15, 1978, 4. See also Primakov, "Dead-End," where he argued part of the Camp David deal was for Sadat to redirect his armed forces against Libya; and Belyaev, "Operatsiya 'Neftepromysly.'"

111. Belyaev, "Kto Seet Kamni," 14.

112. On the reactor, see Kislov, "Kemp-Davidskii Tupik."

113. *Pravda*, October 2, 1982, 5. See also Primakov, "Kogda Voinu"; Brutents, "Livanskaya Tragediya"; and Kislov, "SShA i Blizhnii Vostok."

114. Kislov, "Blizhnevostochnaya Politika SShA," 12. On Egypt's activities directed against Mengistu in Ethiopia, see Khazanov, "Problema Mezhgosudarstvennykh"; and Primakov, "Dead-End." On Egypt's military participation in support of Mobutu in Shaba II, see Kislov, "Nyneshnii Etap"; Primakov, "Neocolonialism"; and Brutents, "A Great Force."

115. Kislov, "Blizhnii Vostok i SShA: 'Novyi Kurs' v Prezhnem Napravlenii" (The Middle East and the U.S.: "New Course" in the Previous Direction), *AIAS*, June 1980, 8–11. See also Primakov, "Zakon Neravnomernosti."

In sum, Egypt's abrogation of its treaty with the Soviet Union, alliance shift toward the United States, and signing of the Camp David treaty made Soviet observers extremely pessimistic about prospects for any positive, let alone progressive, change in the Middle East. Egypt's reversal of alliances was a powerful blow to Soviet positions in the region, hardly compensated for by closer relations with "progressive Arab countries and the PLO." Egypt's exit from the common Arab struggle against Israel was a severe loss for Arab unity, despite the creation of a "Steadfastness and Resistance Front" of Syria, Iraq, Libya, and the PDRY. Finally, the military balance not only dramatically tilted against progressive forces in the Middle East, but also was influenced in Zaire, the Horn of Africa, and Afghanistan.

## Summary

American diplomatic and political maneuvers, along with support for Israel and the latter's military prowess, combined to teach the Soviets a host of deterrent lessons about the Middle East. They learned that Soviet influence with its allies was friable, and that the United States, in cooperation with local, conservative regimes, was able to suborn even the most important Soviet friend, Egypt. Soviets discovered that Israel would always maintain a military advantage against any combination of possible Arab opponents. Moreover, with the loss of Egypt, Soviets discovered that the military balance could be adversely affected as far away as the Horn of Africa, Zaire, and Afghanistan. Soviets were reminded frequently that Arab unity against Israel, and later, Egypt, was an unusual occurrence. There were simply too many other sources of differences among Arab states, differences upon which the United States masterfully played. Finally, Soviets discovered that "socialist orientation" was reversible, even in the closest of allies.

The mere fact that deterrent lessons were learned at all is important. As we saw in the previous chapter on Grenada, there were virtually no Soviet lessons about regional dynamics—except ones that disconfirmed deterrence theory. I argued there that this was because the direct American military intervention served to block out any possible lessons by providing a very salient, single sufficient cause for the Soviet loss. The evidence in this section provides additional confirmation for that line of argument. In the absence of direct military involvement, indirect and nonmilitary American intervention succeeded in generating a vast array of regional deterrent lessons for Soviet observers.

## Explaining Soviet Lessons from the Middle East

There is a far stronger case for adding this class of "indirect" cases to the domain of deterrence theory if Soviet lessons were produced by universal-rational or general-cognitive processes. This is so because both rationality and cognitive economy capture far more of the universe of decision makers in the world than do any models of decision making that rely on belief systems or motivated biases. As one can see from table 24, there is a very strong need to supplement the theory with losses caused by nonmilitary instruments.

Soviets inferred deterrent lessons about American credibility and regional dynamics that are both universally and generally applicable to the entire set of deterrence cases. This concentration of lessons in the most generally applicable categories implies the need to expand deterrence theory to include this type of defeat for a challenger. Moreover, the only disconfirming evidence is provided by "orthodox optimists," who, while not inferring encouraging lessons from the defeats in the Middle East, protected their belief systems about revolutionary change in the Third World. Below I provide examples of each of the categories of Soviet lessons.

## Universal Explanations for Soviet Lessons from the Middle East

Soviets learned from the Middle East about U.S. credibility and regional dynamics by applying rational attribution models. They developed a set of causal variables for American behavior and for the political and military situation in the Middle East. They then assessed the values of these variables when reaching conclusions about probable American policy and prospects for Soviet policy in the region.

### Soviet Images of High Overall U.S. Credibility
A number of Soviets developed and employed causal attribution models when learning from American behavior in the Middle East that the United States was going to defend its interests effectively both in that strategic area of the

**TABLE 24.  The Power of Different Explanations for Soviet Lessons**

|  | Types of Explanations | | |
|---|---|---|---|
|  | Universal | General | Peculiar |
| Lessons confirming expanded deterrence theory | High overall U.S. credibility | High overall U.S. credibility | High overall U.S. credibility |
|  | Regional and global balancing | Regional balancing |  |
| Lessons disconfirming expanded deterrence theory | None | None | No global effects |

globe and in the Third World more generally. Such a pattern of rationality went beyond the community of Americanists to include Middle East experts such as Igor Belyaev, and Gorbachev adviser and aide Evgenii Primakov.

These Soviets attributed various causes to American behavior in the Middle East. They treated some of these causes as variables, holding out the hope that perhaps American policy there could change in a more moderate direction. Other causes were constants, undergirding bedrock American support for Israel and conservative Arab regimes, and ensuring continued opposition to any Soviet gains in the region.

The most important variable identified by Soviet observers was American public opinion. Some Soviets thought that eventually the American people would come to understand that their economic and strategic interests in Arab countries were threatened by continued support for Israel.[116] They hoped that Israeli intransigence in the peace process would lead Americans to press their representatives and president to lean on Israel to moderate its negotiating position on the occupied territories.[117] Soviets hoped that Americans would realize that not only was Israel unreasonable, but that its obstinacy might lead the United States into war in the Middle East.[118] Some suggested that this Israeli extremism, if combined with Arab moderation, would incline Americans to take a more balanced view of the elements necessary for a just and lasting peace in the Middle East.[119] Kislov suggested that the American people ultimately would attack the "Zionist lobby" in the United States, due not to its support for Israel directly, but rather to its efforts to undermine American-Soviet detente with such obstacles as the Jackson-Vanik Amendment. Hence, American public support for Israel would wane, but only as a by-product of popular irritation at the intransigent enemies of detente.[120]

But after the October War, Soviets stopped treating the American public as a variable. They were forced to recognize that the administration had developed a policy that satisfied the public on all counts. It combined the very strongest economic and military support for Israel with movement on a peace settlement with Egypt. This diplomatic opening to Egypt achieved the Arab cancellation of the oil embargo, the key economic instrument on which Soviet commentators had placed great hopes to change American public attitudes

---

116. For example, Belyaev, "V Plenu"; and Kislov, "Arabskaya Neft."

117. For example, Mirsky, "Third World"; and Belyaev, "Conference in Bologna," *NT*, 1973, no. 21, 16–17.

118. For example, Primakov, "Kto Meshaet Uregulirovaniiu" (Who Is Preventing a Settlement), *Pravda*, January 14, 1970, 4.

119. Primakov, "Vopreki Proiskam." This analysis of American policy helps explain Soviet frustration at Arab radicalism and Palestinian terrorism in the period.

120. Kislov, "Antisovetskie Proiski Amerikanskikh Sionistov" (Anti-Soviet Intrigues of American Zionists), *SShA*, March 1973, 46–55.

toward Israel. Moreover, economic and military aid to Egypt achieved a host of objectives: it enhanced Israel's security; it gained the "overthrow of a progressive Arab regime"; it fulfilled the anti-Soviet mission of American foreign policy; and finally, it satisfied the demands of both Congress and the public on the ruling elite.

The most important constant Soviets identified as underlying American policy in the Middle East was virtually unanimous congressional backing for Tel Aviv[121] and for the American bribery of Sadat.[122] Indeed, Congress very often went beyond the demands of the administration to increase military and economic aid to Israel and also to insist on harder "anti-Arab" and "anti-Soviet" elements in administration negotiating positions in the Middle East.[123] Another constant identified by Soviet observers were the attitudes of the American ruling elite. They suggested that the latter's adherence to deterrence theory, manifested in a fear of dominoes in the region, accounted for its hard line there. Therefore, the United States supported Israeli efforts to overthrow Nasser in Cairo and the Baath government in Damascus.[124] In general, the American government believed that it had to "give battle to the Communists on distant frontiers where they engage in threatening activities. In dealing them defeats there, one can hope that the 'Red menace' will not penetrate the line drawn by American politicians."[125] Belyaev argued that elite support for Israel also was in part motivated by an American desire to compensate for its loss in Vietnam by recapturing any lost credibility.[126]

*Soviet Images of Regional and Global Balancing*
Several Soviets, but especially Belyaev and Primakov, developed elaborate causal models for analyzing the prospects for Soviet foreign policy in the Middle East. As is reflected in the discussion above, Soviets generated a rather lengthy list of variables to monitor when assessing the dynamics of the region. To recapitulate, they evaluated the stability of alliance ties between Moscow and Arab countries, the level of Arab unity, the military balance between Israel and its Arab opponents, domestic political developments in

---

121. See Mirsky, "Arab East"; Primakov, "Pruzhiny Blizhnevostochnoi"; Kremeniuk, "Prezidentskie Vybory"; and Kislov "Antisovetskie Proiski."

122. Belyaev, "SShA i Blizhnevostochnyi Krizis."

123. Kislov, "Obsuzhdenie Sinaiskovo Soglasheniya" (Discussion of the Sinai Agreement), *SShA*, December 1975, 71–77, and "Posle Sovetsko-Amerikanskovo Zayavleniya."

124. This argument was first developed by Primakov during the course of the Six Day War, in "Behind the Scenes of the Israeli Gamble," *IA*, July 1967, 58–61. Primakov gave a similar "deterrent" explanation for American reactions to the fall of the shah in Iran in 1979. See chap. 5. Belyaev seconded Primakov's explanation in "UAR"; as did Brutents in "O Revoliutsionnoi Demokratii" (On Revolutionary Democracy), part 2, *MEIMO*, April 1968, 24–35.

125. Belyaev, "S Chernovo," 117.

126. Belyaev, "Put k Spravedlivomu Miru."

both Soviet allies and conservative Arab states, the behavior of the Palestinians, and long-term demographic trends. Soviets very explicitly treated these factors as variables that determined the range of possibilities for Soviet policy in the region.

This vast array of lessons about the region stands in stark contrast to the absence of such lessons from the American invasion of Grenada discussed in chapter 5. Direct American military actions provide an easy explanation for Soviet observers. American diplomacy, and economic and military aid, on the contrary, compelled Soviets to grapple with an array of factors that stood in the way of future Soviet victories in the region.

In sum, the rational attribution model can explain how many Soviets developed views of both high American credibility and regional balancing from the Middle East cases. This implies that the kinds of defeats dealt the Soviets in this region are very likely to teach strong deterrent lessons in the universe of cases.

## General Explanations for Soviet Lessons from the Middle East

General Soviet lessons come in three varieties, familiar from previous discussions. The first is the focus on absolute American military capabilities. The second is a combination of Leninist beliefs with rational attributions. The third is a very truncated menu of variables chosen on a nonbiased basis to analyze the regional dynamics of the Middle East. These variables are not selected as a consequence of any adherence to a belief system or due to a bias motivated by some political, bureaucratic, or psychological need. A new factor described below is the recognition, by otherwise entirely orthodox Soviets, of the diplomatic and economic instruments employed by the United States in the region.

### Soviet Images of High Overall U.S. Credibility
As has been true for every case in this book, American credibility receives a boost from the fact that virtually all Soviets use absolute American military capabilities as an indicator of U.S. strength and resolve. In the case of the Middle East, Soviets assessed both the level of American defense expenditures and the access the United States was receiving to military bases in the region, especially after the Egyptian alliance switch.[127]

---

127. A representative sample of numerous examples includes Gromyko's speech before the UN General Assembly, *Pravda*, September 24, 1980, 4; Brezhnev, *Documents and Resolutions;* Ogarkov, "Zavetam Lenina Veryny"; Ustinov, "Voennaya Razryadka"; Gorshkov, "Bazu Agressii"; Ulyanovsky, "Pod Pritselom"; Arbatov, "Vneshnyaya Politika," April 1980 *SShA*, 43-54; Simoniya, "Gonka Vooruzhenii"; Primakov, "Islam"; Falin, "Voennaya Razryadka Vozmozhna";

Special mention should be made here of those Soviets with orthodox Leninist belief systems who nonetheless learned from American policy in the Middle East that the array of policy levers available to the United States ranged far beyond military interventions. As I noted in chapter 4, orthodox Soviets had strong incentives not to recognize economic obstacles to revolutionary victories, not least because of Soviet incapacity to compete effectively with the West in that area. Given the psychological costs of such lessons, therefore, it is important to recognize that orthodox Soviets nonetheless added American economic and military aid to their list of American capabilities, largely as a consequence of the loss of Egypt. This deterrent lesson can be considered "general" in that the choice of these two variables to monitor is not at all obviously motivated by any psychological or political need. On the contrary, its selection had to overcome costs imparted by precisely such needs.[128]

The last group of general inferences of high U.S. credibility comprise those Soviets who combined orthodox Leninist belief systems with rational attribution processes. Primakov is a good example of this blend of the peculiar and the universal. Since I have discussed him at some length in chapter 4, here I only show how adherence to a Leninist analysis of American motives in foreign policy leads to predictable distortions of the evidence.

Primakov argued that American oil monopolies, interested in maintaining control over Arab oil supplies, encouraged Israel in 1967 to overthrow the governments in Cairo and Damascus. Apparently realizing that since neither Egypt nor Syria had any appreciable oil reserves, let alone ones in which American multinationals had any investments, he then asserted that the overthrow of these regimes would serve to eliminate "their revolutionizing influence" on conservative Arab regimes who did possess vast quantities of oil. The fact that Primakov never mentioned any Saudi or Kuwaiti vulnerability to Nasser's influence prior to the Six Day War implies that this argument was simply an ad hoc attempt by Primakov to cover over the manifest logical inconsistency in his reasoning.[129]

If American oil companies drove American foreign policy in the Middle East, then why did the U.S. government shift its strategy from the overthrow of progressive regimes to launching peace initiatives in 1969 and 1970? Primakov's response was that actually there are two discrete groups of oil monopolies in the United States. There is a Texas group that wants high oil

Trofimenko, "Washington"; Kislov, "Pentagon Adventurism"; Belyaev, "Operatsiya 'Neftepromysly'"; Kremeniuk, "Strategiya Ugroz i Agressii"; and Brutents, "Kto Prepyatstvuet Miru."

128. I am referring to Brezhnev, Ustinov, Ulyanovsky, and Brutents as the otherwise orthodox Soviets.

129. See Primakov, "Blizhnevostochnaya Politika SShA." For similar protective *ad hocery*, see Kremeniuk, "Prezidentskie Vybory."

prices so that it can reap monopoly profits from its domestic sources of production. Its close links to the Johnson administration explain why the United States was against any settlement during that administration. Continued closure of the Suez Canal raised world oil prices. The second, Rockefeller oil group, however, has direct foreign investment in oil recovery in the Middle East and consequently wants low oil prices. The Nixon administration, being a captive of these interests, searched for a peace settlement, though of course on American terms. The illogic here, of course, is that this "Rockefeller oil group" would equally profit from high oil prices, since it controls all downstream oil refining, wholesaling, and retailing—a fact that Primakov himself acknowledged in another context.[130] Primakov used a common method of belief system maintenance here. When faced by discrepant evidence, in this case American oil interests predicting an aggressive American policy, Primakov had to divide the intolerable piece of data in two. Hence, he split American oil interests conveniently into two camps. He also developed a useful tautology: when the United States is aggressive, Texas rules. When the United States pursues diplomacy, the Rockefeller brothers are in control of the White House.

Finally, in the aftermath of the oil embargo and OPEC price increases, Primakov admitted that the United States was not greatly harmed by these economic costs. He cited increased domestic coal, natural gas, and oil production, research on alternative energy supplies, and conservation as effective American responses to higher oil prices.[131] Moreover, in recognizing a dissonant fact he had ignored in the past, he argued that in fact American oil and nonoil monopolies, as well as the American economy in general, were doing quite well as a *consequence* of increased oil prices. He remarked, in particular, on the downstream profits of American oil companies, the value of petrodollar recycling for the American economy, the increased foreign investment opportunities opening up in the Arab world for American companies, and Arab investment in the United States itself.[132] Of course all of this contradicts the other arguments he made about the effects of oil interests on American foreign policy, but recognizing these positions would threaten his adherence to a Leninist interpretation of imperialism.

## Soviet Images of Regional Balancing

Several Soviets inferred deterrent lessons about the Middle East because they identified one or two factors they believed to be diagnostic about the dynamics of the region. This group is different from those using rational attribution

---

130. Primakov, "Blizhnevostochnaya Politika SShA" and "Manevry SShA."

131. Primakov, "Nekotorye Voprosy Energeticheskovo Krizisa i evo Vliyaniya na Sovremennyi Mir" (Certain Questions of the Energy Crisis and Its Influence on the Contemporary World), *MEIMO*, February 1974, 66–72.

132. Primakov, "Pruzhiny Blizhnevostochnoi."

theory described above in that their list of critical variables is very truncated. These lessons are general because the variables chosen by the Soviets are not selected for any obvious motivated reason. Examples include Mirsky, who writes about the consequences of Israeli intransigence on a peace settlement and the Israeli-Arab military balance; Brutents, who describes the unfortunate effects of rich, conservative Arab regimes allying with the United States; Gromyko, who bemoans the consequences of Palestinian terrorism; and Kislov, who criticizes the inability of progressive Arab governments to cooperate against Israel and reactionary Arabs.[133]

In sum, many of the deterrent lessons Soviets inferred from their losses in the Middle East were the products of general models of information processing. Consequently, they imply the need to incorporate this class of Soviet defeats with only indirect American involvement into a more comprehensive theory of deterrence.

## Peculiar Explanations for Soviet Lessons from the Middle East

The Leninist belief system once again contributed to Soviet views of a highly credible United States. It also, however, limited the level of discouragement felt by Soviets after their losses in the Middle East, especially Egypt's alliance switch. The Leninist need to see revolutionary progress led many Soviets to treat Egypt as an aberration, rather than as the start of a trend.

### Soviet Images of High U.S. Credibility
Many Soviets, but especially members of the party leadership and military elite, learned from American policy in the Middle East that the United States was a resolute and capable opponent because of their adherence to Leninist belief systems.[134] This finding is of course consistent with the evidence in each of the other chapters in this book.

### Soviet Global Optimism Unaffected by the Loss of Egypt
Whereas Soviet observers were unanimous in learning powerful deterrent lessons about the Middle East itself, their optimism about future revolutionary change in the Third World in general was not fundamentally shaken. This

---

133. All these positions are taken from the discussion of regional dynamics above.

134. For a representative sample, see Brezhnev, *Pravda*, July 6, 1967, 1–2; Kosygin's speech in Algeria, *Pravda*, October 7, 1971, 5; Podgorny (on Chile), *Pravda*, October 16, 1974, 4; Suslov's speech at meeting of representatives of Communist and workers' parties in Budapest, *Pravda*, February 29, 1968, 4; Chernenko's speech awarding an Order of Lenin to Chelyabinsk, *Pravda*, May 30, 1980, 2; Grechko's speech on the twenty-third anniversary of V-Day, *Pravda*, May 9, 1968, 2; and Ogarkov, "Stoim na Strazhe" (We Stand in Defense), *Izvestiya*, July 20, 1967, 3.

apparent paradox is explained by the fact that these Soviet analysts used orthodox Leninist categories when explaining events in Egypt. As I showed in chapter 4, orthodox Soviets who operate with a set of soft, and hence unfalsifiable, indicators of revolutionary progress are largely immunized against pessimistic conclusions from failures of allies in the Third World. Of course, there are differences between those committed to ideological orthodoxy, who are more pessimistic, and those who are committed to Leninist revolutionary progress, who are more optimistic.

While Egypt's fall from the progressive ranks was clearly distressing to Soviet observers, the general recommendation of those committed to Leninism was for other revolutionary democrats to adhere more closely to the orthodox line. For example, the Egyptian experience compelled Primakov to recognize a nasty dilemma for all countries of socialist orientation (CSOs). The latter were faced with severe economic difficulties, and yet the Soviet Union had only a limited capacity to provide the resources needed to address their critical problems. Meanwhile, the United States, Western Europe, Japan, and oil-rich conservative Arab regimes could offer a very attractive way out for Soviet allies in the Third World. Primakov, constrained by his own orthodoxy and Soviet economic weakness, could recommend only that other revolutionary democrats take *political* measures to overcome this temptation— purging their militaries and bureaucracies of nonrevolutionary elements and creating mass parties so that the whims of a single individual like Sadat could be counteracted by a strong institution imbued with progressive ideals.[135]

Belyaev also attributed the failure of the Egyptian revolution to inadequate fidelity to Leninist policy prescriptions. He charged, post facto of course, that Nasser himself was never a Marxist; he had never really cooperated with local Communists and never established a mass base for the revolution, let alone one that would yield its hegemony to the working class.[136] Belyaev also was critical of the fact that private capitalism in agriculture, services, and commerce had been allowed to run rampant. He argued this had

---

135. Primakov's diagnosis of Egypt's ills and his orthodox recommendations are drawn from the sources already cited and the following: "Cairo-Conspiracy Trial," *NT*, 1968, no. 7, 15– 16; "Dlya Razvitiya Revoliutsii" (For the Development of the Revolution), *Pravda*, March 1, 1968, 5; "The March 30 Programme," *NT*, 1968, no. 17, 15–16; "Borba v Puti" (Struggle Under Way), *Pravda*, May 7, 1969, 4; and "Strany Sotsialisticheskoi Orientatsii: Trudny, no Realnyi Perekhod k Sotsializmu" (Countries of Socialist Orientation: Difficult, but Real, Transition to Socialism), *MEIMO*, July 1981, 3–16.

136. Belyaev, "Gamal Abdel Naser—Nekotorye Cherty Ideinoi Evoliutsii" (Gamal Abdel Naser—Certain Features of his Ideological Evolution), *NAIA*, 1972, no. 2, 73–89. Mirsky also concluded that the Egyptian revolution had suffered from the lack of an ideologically orthodox vanguard party. See, for example, "Path," and "Natsionalizm i Nekapitalisticheskii Put Razvitiya" (Nationalism and the Noncapitalist Path of Development), *MEIMO*, October 1972, 121–23.

spawned an alliance between the bureaucratic and the petite bourgeoisie that had derailed the revolution.[137]

Ulyanovsky, by the late 1970s, had become increasingly convinced that revolutionary democrats were simply incapable of implementing consistent socialist reforms. His frustration with the Egyptian leadership's inability to cooperate with local Marxists, adopt scientific socialism as its ideology, and build a genuine vanguard party played no small part in contributing to this heightened pessimism.[138] The Egyptian experience also compelled Ulyanovsky to recognize one insuperable dilemma: revolutionary democrats could not survive with capitalism, and they could not survive without it. Some capitalist development was necessary for purely economic reasons. However, this very development also caused the emergence of new bourgeois strata who hastened the degeneration of the regime.[139] Like Primakov, he also acknowledged that Egypt, like all CSOs, was dependent on the world capitalist economy, with all its powerful instruments of influence on these countries' domestic life. Unlike Primakov and Belyaev, however, Ulyanovsky did not see the implementation of more orthodox policies as a panacea to the ills that beset Egypt. While he made such recommendations, he simultaneously recognized that their previous record of consistent fulfillment had been very spotty.

In sum, Egypt's fall from progressive grace simultaneously compelled Soviet analysts to recognize some very thorny dilemmas for their third world allies and led them to recommend even more orthodox policy prescriptions for these regimes. Their orthodoxy saved them from reaching more pessimistic conclusions about revolutionary prospects in the Third World in general, though Ulyanovsky's commitment to orthodoxy over revolution made him far less sanguine than his colleagues.

---

137. Belyaev, "Egipet: Etapy Revoliutsii," and "Egipet '83." Mirsky also lamented the Egyptian government's lax attitude toward private enterprise in agriculture and other sectors and its benign neglect of an emerging bureaucratic bourgeoisie feasting off the state sector. See, for example, "Rol Armii v Obshchestvennom Razvitii" (Role of the Army in Social Development), *AIAS*, January 1976, 16–17; "Menyaiushchiesya Oblik"; and "Razvivaiushchiesya Strany v Sovremennom Mire" (Developing Countries in the Contemporary World), *MEIMO*, January 1977, 140–41.

138. See, for example, Ulyanovsky, "Nekotorye Voprosy Nekapitalisticheskovo Razvitiya" (Certain Questions of Noncapitalist Development), *Kommunist*, 1971, no. 4, 103–12, hereafter cited as "Nekotorye Voprosy," 1971; "'The Third World'—Problems of Socialist Orientation," *IA*, September 1971, 26–35; "Idei Velikovo Oktyabrya i Sovremennye Problemy Natsionalno-Osvoboditelnovo Dvizheniya" (Ideas of Great October and Contemporary Problems of the National Liberation Movement) *NINI*, 1977, no. 3, 3–25; "O Stranakh Sotsialisticheskoi Orientatsii" (On Countries of Socialist Orientation), *Kommunist*, 1979, no. 11, 115–23; "O Natsionalnom Osvobozhdenii"; and "O Natsionalnoi i Revoliutsionoi [*sic*] Demokratii: Puti Evoliutsii" (On National and Revolutionary Democracy: Paths of Evolution), *NAIA*, 1984, no. 2, 9–18.

139. See, for example, beyond the sources cited in the preceding note, Ulyanovsky, "Paths and Prospects."

A Scorecard for an Expanded Theory of Deterrence

The overwhelming concentration of Soviet lessons from the Middle East in the universal/general confirmation of deterrence assumptions category implies the need to expand traditional deterrence theory to capture these indirect deterrent actions of the defender. Very powerful sources of deterrent lessons are neglected by the prevailing version of the theory. A comprehensive version requires expansion to include nonmilitary actions by the defender and the policies of its allies in the region and beyond. It is also evident that indirect American behavior is a better source of deterrent lessons than direct American military involvement. The United States retains its reputation for high credibility while simultaneously allowing Soviets to learn about sources of regional resistance to revolutionary change. The latter lesson, as the evidence in chapter 5 demonstrates, is blocked out by American military intervention.

## Considering Alternative Explanations for Soviet Lessons from the Middle East

Perhaps the most compelling counterargument to my conclusions in this chapter is that the Middle East is a special case that predictably caused Soviet observers to infer very powerful deterrent lessons from American policy there. Given that region's strategic importance to both the United States and the Soviet Union, it is only natural that the Soviets would see a highly credible United States committed to defending its interests in the region. In fact, the Middle East is a crucially easy case for assuming that Soviets will learn very powerful deterrent lessons. Hence, any attempt to generalize to some class of cases of "indirect American involvement" is simply spurious. My call for expanding deterrence theory to encompass these cases is, therefore, supported only by this nonrepresentative sample.

### The Middle East as Anomaly

There is no denying that the Middle East is a special case. As the data in appendix A show, it and the Vietnam War are easily the two most salient regions of the Third World to the Soviets. But the importance of a region to the Soviet Union does not yield logically determinate predictions about Soviet lessons from its losses in that area. While it makes sense that Soviets would recognize the American commitment to defend its vital interests in the Middle East, why should it be more likely for Soviets to see regional actors balancing against revolutionary change there, rather than progressive dominoes? Moreover, the point of my argument is not so much that Soviets would infer particular *kinds* of lessons in the region when the United States did not intervene directly, but rather simply that Soviets would get the chance to infer lessons about the region, period. That these lessons are deterrent ones in the cases of this chapter is no surprise, given Soviet losses in the Middle East from 1967 to 1980. The argument is that American military intervention prevented Soviets from inferring regional deterrent lessons that were available to be learned. The latter would have been inferred, if only the United States had not provided a single sufficient explanation through its military actions. The lessons Soviets learned here about regional dynamics validate that argument.

Finally, the Middle East is not the only case of indirect American involvement leading to Soviet losses. From 1965 to 1990, Soviets experienced eleven losses that were the product of either American nonmilitary actions or non-American actions. These included the overthrow of Allende in Chile in 1973; the two Western suppressions of unrest in Shaba Province in Zaire in 1977 and 1978; the alliance switch of the Barre government in Somalia in 1977–78; the peaceful transition to black majority rule in Zimbabwe in 1980; the successful defense of the Salvadoran government from the Faribundo Marti National Liberation Front from 1980 to 1990; and the capitulation of Mozambique to South Africa, as codified in the 1984 Nkomati Accords.

None of these cases can obviously be construed as affecting the strategic interests of either the Soviet Union or the United States. They, therefore, cannot evoke the same objections as the Middle East case. In fact, however, consistent with my interpretation of the evidence from the Middle East, these Soviet defeats had the effect of compelling Soviets to learn deterrent lessons about the regional actors in the particular areas of the defeat. For example, the ouster of Allende caused Soviets to become less optimistic about the prospects for revolutionary change in Latin America.[140] The two interventions in support of the Mobutu government in Zaire taught Soviets that American allies in both Western Europe and Africa would cooperate to oppose any threats to conservative African regimes.[141] The successful reversal of the Soviet alliance with Somalia not only reinforced the lessons taught by Sadat, but also demonstrated to the Soviets the power of the Saudi purse. The Lancaster House agreement on Zimbabwean independence also reinforced a lesson learned in the Middle East, namely, that the West was capable of using diplomacy effectively to preempt any revolutionary opportunities.

In sum, the evidence from both the Middle East case and a sample of other similar cases strongly suggests that the strategic importance of the Middle East does not account for the power of deterrent lessons inferred by Soviets. Rather, the lack of direct American involvement explains the strength of these inferences.

---

140. See Hopf, "Deterrence Theory," chap. 5.
141. Ibid., chap. 6.

Considering Soviet Behavior

Given the string of setbacks suffered by the Soviet Union in the Middle East from 1967 to 1980, one would sensibly expect reduced Soviet activism, both in the Middle East and in the Third World in general. This expectation would be justified if one believed that deterrent lessons are *sufficient* to deter a potential challenger from attempting to change the status quo. But deterrence theory wisely makes no such claims, realizing that there are many factors exogenous to a challenger's view of a defender's credibility and a region's balancing dynamics that cause a challenger to mount an attack on the status quo.

Soviet behavior from 1967 to 1980 looks much like a challenger who, after every defeat, adopts a posture of "never again," as hypothesized in the introductory chapter of this book. After the June 1967 war, Moscow responded by rearming its Arab allies, sending air-defense forces to Egypt, and pressing for a diplomatic settlement. After the October 1973 war, Moscow tried to become a player in the Geneva talks on the Middle East and rearmed Syria. After Sadat's turn to the West, the Soviets sold record amounts of weaponry to Iraq, Libya, and Iraq.

In sum, the pattern is clear. While deterrent lessons may be necessary to teach a challenger it does not pay to violate the status quo, they are certainly not sufficient. While deterrence theory makes concrete predictions about the consequences of allowing a challenger to win—it will be encouraged to challenge the status quo again—the theory wisely remains indeterminate about what a challenger will do after it loses. In this sense, Soviet behavior neither confirms nor disconfirms the theory's assumptions here.

## Conclusion: Deterrence Theory in Need of Expansion

The Soviets learned very powerful deterrent lessons from the Middle East. They learned that the United States was a very able defender of its interests there, and they learned that the local actors in that region posed extraordinary obstacles to Soviet foreign policy gains. The problem is that these powerful deterrent lessons lie outside the domain of traditional deterrence theory. But this defect is easily remedied. We need only add this class of *indirect, nonmilitary* defeats to the scope of the theory. Such an addition violates neither the logical integrity nor the basic assumptions of the theory. In exchange, it greatly enhances the theory's validity.

In fact, indirect defeats are the most effective teachers of deterrent lessons. Direct military interventions, as in Grenada, ably communicate resolve and capabilities, but prevent the communication of deterrent lessons from the region itself. This is so because the fact of American military involvement provides a very powerful and sufficient cause for the Soviet defeat. Consequently, Soviets looked no further for more complicated explanations for their losses. This effectively puts a ceiling on just how pessimistic Soviets could become as a result of their losses. As we will see in chapter 7, no involvement is an effective way of ensuring inferences from the region of the defeat but is a very weak communicator of credibility. But indirect involvement, where the defender uses nonmilitary instruments or allows regional actors to do the work, maximizes *both* sets of deterrent lessons. The Soviets learned both that the United States was highly credible and that the local environment was not one likely to yield foreign policy gains.

Non-military instruments provide the added deterrent bonus, at least in the case of an opponent long on military power and short on economic wherewithal, of compelling the defender to contemplate terms of competition that are not to its advantage. Even the most orthodox Soviets, who had a single-minded focus on American military capabilities, were forced to pay attention to the economic and diplomatic power displayed by Washington in the Middle East. This recognition reinforced deterrent lessons about American credibility, for these Soviet leaders had to acknowledge that the Soviet Union simply could not hope to outbid the West for Sadat's allegiance.

Finally, the use of indirect means to impart deterrent lessons creates the opportunity for the challenger to learn that its objectives are being countered, not only by its major opponent, but also by an array of *autonomous* actors, whose self-defined interests are also counter to the challenger's. For instance, Soviets discovered that in the Middle East at least, Israeli and Saudi interests diverge on virtually all issues, save one: opposition to Soviet encroachments in the region, whether directly or through radical allies.

In sum, deterrence theory's domain has been mistakenly underspecified. Its expansion will capture an arsenal of deterrent instruments heretofore wrongly ignored.

# CHAPTER 7

# Ghana 1966: The Deterrent Case That Didn't Bark

In February 1966 the Kwame Nkrumah government of Ghana was overthrown in a military coup while the president was out of the country. At the time, Ghana was one of only several countries in the Third World Soviets considered to be progressive, since their ruling regimes were on the path of "noncapitalist development" and had anti-imperialist foreign policy positions.

Deterrence theory has nothing at all to say about this kind of case, since the United States was not in any way involved in dealing the Soviet Union this defeat. This is a major deficiency in the theory. As in the case of indirect American efforts in the Middle East, no American involvement at all still produces deterrent lessons for Soviet policymakers. The theory's scope must be expanded to capture this class of cases.[1] Despite the fact that the United States had no role in removing Nkrumah, some Soviets still attributed high credibility to the United States. Many more Soviets concluded from events in Ghana that revolutionary prospects elsewhere in the Third World were dimmer than before Nkrumah's removal. However, unlike these liberal analysts, orthodox Soviets committed to Leninist revolutionary progress did not become more pessimistic.

### Soviet Lessons about U.S. Credibility

The Soviets who used events in Ghana as evidence of American credibility all concluded that U.S. resolve and capabilities were high, but they held different views about what kinds of behavior could be expected from the United States in the future. Brezhnev, for example, identified "progressive states" as the most probable next victims of imperialism.[2] Soviets saw the coup as yet

---

1. The other instances of Soviet losses with no American involvement include the overthrow of Sukarno in Indonesia in 1965, the ouster of Keita in Mali in 1968, Nimieri's suppression of a Communist coup attempt in the Sudan in 1971, the overthrow of the Suarez government in Bolivia the same year, and the military coup against the Velasco government in Peru in 1975. For discussions of each of these cases, save the last, see Hopf, "Deterrence Theory," chap. 1.

2. Speech at the international conference of Communist and workers' parties in Moscow, *Pravda*, June 8, 1969, 1, 4. Similar views were expressed by Kim, "Nekotorye Problemy";

another example of the American neocolonialist strategy of "promoting the development of captalism in former colonies, so as to more easily plunder them."[3] Brutents outlined some of the tactics the United States had developed to attain this goal, namely, using the local bourgeoisie, educating the African intelligentsia, and providing military training. He expected that the United States would try to infiltrate African militaries in general.[4] Some argued the United States merely was adding another tactic to its arsenal—the use of reactionary military coups.[5]

Brutents further claimed that it was the American ruling elite's fear of progressive dominoes that caused it to mount a "successful counterattack" against a state like Ghana on the "noncapitalist path of development."[6] Moreover, American imperialists "calculate that the failure of the noncapitalist development path in these countries will weaken the attraction of the socialist system in the entire Third World." That is why American "efforts at changing the direction of development are becoming increasingly persistent."[7]

Simoniya, "Za Aktivizatsiiu Antiimperialisticheskoi Borby" (For the Invigoration of the Antiimperialist Struggle), *AIAS* October 1971, 13–15; Ulyanovsky, "O Nekotorykh Chertakh Sovremennovo Etapa Natsionalno-Osvobitelnovo Dvizheniya" (On Certain Features of the Contemporary Stage of the National-Liberation Movement), *NAIA*, 1967, no. 5, 21–36; and Brutents "Voprosy Ideologii v Natsionalno-Osvoboditelnom Dvizhenii" (Questions of Ideology in the National Liberation Movement), *Kommunist*, 1966, no. 18, 37–50.

3. Brezhnev in a speech before a joint session of the Central Committee, Supreme Soviet, and Supreme Soviet of the Russian Soviet Federated Socialist Republic (RSFSR) on Lenin's one hundredth birthday, *Pravda*, April 22, 1970, 4; more or less identical views were expressed by Podgorny in a speech in Ulan Bator, in *Pravda*, May 24, 1969, 4; Suslov in a speech on the fifty-third anniversary of the Bolshevik Revolution, *Pravda*, November 7, 1970, 1, 2; and Ulyanovsky, "Pod Devizom Solidarnosti—Posle Vstrech v Nicosia i Beirut" (Under the Motto of Solidarity—After Meetings in Nicosia and Beirut), *Pravda*, May 22, 1967, 4.

4. Brutents, "The African Revolution: Gains and Problems," *IA*, January 1967, 20–28. See also Simoniya, "O Kharaktere Natsionalno-Osvoboditelnykh Revoliutsii" (On the Character of National Liberation Revolutions), *NAIA*, 1966, no. 6, 3–21.

5. For example, Kim, "Dorogoi Internatsionalizma" (On the Road of Internationalism), *AIAS*, November 1967, 32–35; Ponomarev, Supreme Soviet election speech, *Pravda*, June 3, 1966, 4.; and Suslov, speech at consultative meeting of representatives of Communist and workers' parties in Budapest, *Pravda*, February 29, 1968, 4.

6. Brutents, "African Revolution," 21.

7. Brutents, "O Revoliutsionnoi Demokratii," 29. Ulyanovsky also argued that the United States hoped that the fall of Nkrumah would teach other third world leaders that the noncapitalist development path was hopeless. "Dekolonizatsiya: Itogi i Perspektivy" (Decolonization: Results and Prospects), *Pravda*, November 12, 1970, 4. He also asserted that the "reactionary coups in several African and Asian countries" (most probably Ghana, Mali, and Indonesia) led bourgeois propaganda to assert that socialism was now on the defensive. Though he of course rejected this analysis as untrue, he still recognized that American leaders were encouraged by the turn of events. "Krepit Edinstvo Natsionalno-Osvoboditelnykh Sil" (Strengthen the Unity of National

Ulyanovsky argued that the "defeat of anti-imperialist and democratic forces in Indonesia, Ghana, and certain other countries [probably including Mali] attest" that the imperialist tactics of using "reactionary nationalism to inject discord among them" and "anticommunism" to isolate these states from socialist countries "can bring some success."[8]

In sum, even when the United States engaged in absolutely no behavior designed to bolster its deterrent credibility, it still gained a reputation for resolve and capability when the Soviet Union experienced a loss in the Third World. Of course, this finding is only as robust as the explanations for the Soviet lessons. I discuss these in the third section.

**Soviet Lessons about Regional Dynamics**

The loss in Ghana resulted in two kinds of lessons for Soviet observers. A small number of Soviets linked the coup in Ghana explicitly to revolutionary prospects elsewhere in the region. A far larger number of Soviets used their analysis of the failure of the progressive path in Accra, along with the experiences of other revolutionary democrats, to reach more general conclusions about the possibility of constructing socialism in "newly liberated countries." I analyze the latter set of lessons in the next section.

Mirsky connected the overthrow of the Nkrumah regime to reduced opportunities for national liberation in southern Africa. As he put it, "Africa is beginning to look at things more soberly and realistically."[9] But a mere eight months later, Mirsky's pessimism was tempered, and he advised third world revolutionaries that they need not be so glum.

> Events in Ghana have generated pessimism in some African circles about the prospects of noncapitalist development in general. Actually, however, there are no grounds for pessimism. On the whole, however, it is necessary to view things soberly and realistically. Nevertheless, [events in Guinea, Congo-Brazzaville, Tanzania, and Zambia] indicate that Tropical African anti-imperialist forces are gaining in size and strength. Pro-Western regimes have been unsaddled swiftly and with amazing ease in the Sudan and Libya; India is nationalizing private banks; in Zambia,

Liberation Forces), *Pravda*, March 20, 1969, 4–5. Belyaev argued that through subversion, the American leadership's "goal is to prove that socialism is alien to 'African nature,'" in "Slovo Revoliutsionnoi Afriki" (The Word of Revolutionary Africa), *Pravda*, November 4, 1966, 5.

8. Ulyanovsky, "Aktualnye Problemy Natsionalno-Osvoboditelnovo Dvizheniya" (Real Problems of the National Liberation Movement), *NAIA*, 1969, no. 4, 9.

9. Mirsky, "The Third World"; 12.

copper mines are being put under state control and positive changes are occurring in Peru.[10]

As there are seemingly always "anti-imperialist" measures being taken by third world governments somewhere in the world, there is a vast store of events to maintain Soviet optimism. For example, Iordansky argued that "few in Ghana believe the present regime will last," citing a recent coup attempt and political differences between the military and civilian leadership.[11]

In sum, Soviets largely did not infer from the loss in Ghana that other African revolutionary democrats were at risk of being overthrown. But as we will see in the next section, Soviets split in their evalutions of the meaning of the coup: those Soviets who used orthodox Leninist variables to assess the event remained optimistic; those who used rational attribution models with hard variables were discouraged by Nkrumah's ouster.

## Explaining Soviet Lessons from Ghana

The more universal the explanation for Soviet lessons, the stronger the need to expand deterrence theory to capture this set of cases of Soviet losses with no American involvement. In fact, there is a powerful case for expanding the domain of the theory. While Soviet lessons about American credibility under these circumstances were mostly the product of idiosyncratic Leninist belief systems, their pessimistic lessons about the viability of "revolutionary democracy" in the Third World were generated by universal rational attribution processes. Moreover, Soviet lessons that disconfirm an expanded deterrence theory are the peculiar outcome of Leninist beliefs.

### Soviet Images of High U.S. Credibility

Not unexpectedly, given the fact that the United States was not even involved in Nkrumah's overthrow, Soviets who attributed responsibility to the United States did so on the basis of their Leninist interpretation of American foreign policy motives. Since imperialism relies on economic exploitation of the Third World for its survival, Washington must have inspired the coup for this

---

10. Mirsky, "Changes in the Third World," *NT*, 1969, no. 39, 4. Belyaev similiarly argued that the negative consequences of the Ghanaian coup were countered by the nationalization of foreign mining companies in Zaire, "Kinshasskii Kaleidoskop" (Kinshasa Kaleidoscope), *Pravda*, January 30, 1967, 4.

11. Iordansky, "Ghana: The Power Crisis," *NT*, 1967, no. 25, 12. See also, Iordansky, "O Kharaktere Voennykh Diktatur v Tropicheskoi Afrike" (On the Character of Military Dictatorships in Tropical Africa), *NAIA*, 1967, no. 4, 22–37.

reason and would continue to behave in like manner toward other progressive governments.

## Soviet Images of a Third World Resistant to Revolution

Soviet "liberal pessimists"[12] learned from Ghana that the progressive path of development in the Third World was very long, rocky, and reversible. The beliefs of Nodari Simoniya illustrate this pattern of learning.[13]

Simoniya gave credence neither to class analysis nor to the issue of party development. He was very skeptical about the ability of progressive regimes to overcome economic obstacles with purely political instruments. He allowed for all kinds of deviations from purely socialist approaches to solving economic problems. His emphasis on economic issues logically led him to downplay the ability of Soviet policy to play much of a role in compensating for the indigenous weaknesses of its progressive allies. His liberal pessimistic beliefs were reinforced by the ouster of Nkrumah, though he had to add new elements to his causal attribution model of revolutionary development. His menu of variables turned out to be somewhat insufficient to explain the outcome in Ghana, so he added new ones that could capture the previously unexplained variance.

Simoniya consistently argued for the primacy of the economic base over the political superstructure in determining the future of progressive regimes. He argued for the "sober evaluation of the complexity and difficulty of the problems on the noncapitalist path," noting that the prerequisites for advancing on this route included eliminating the dominance of foreign capital, bringing the level of economic development up to a certain necessary threshold, and ending economic dependence on the West.[14] Writing in the aftermath of the coup, he asserted that "subjective factors cannot replace objective tasks or change their character. You cannot impose new social tasks on revolutions if these tasks have not matured economically."[15] Simoniya also took to task those

---

12. For a comprehensive definition, see chap. 4.

13. For a more comprehensive and nuanced discussion of several Soviets, including Karen Brutents and Georgi Mirsky, who fall between Simoniya and more orthodox colleagues, see Hopf, "Deterrence Theory," chap. 1, 141–57.

14. Simoniya, "Nekapitalisticheskii Put Razvitiya—Put Progressa" (Noncapitalist Path of Development—Path of Progress), *Kommunist*, 1965, no. 9, 121–24. It is perhaps not accidental that Simoniya did not publish any more articles in this official organ of the Central Committee of the Communist Party of the Soviet Union ever again.

15. Simoniya, "O Kharaktere," 8. As evidence of the controversial status of Simoniya's arguments, the editors of this journal felt it necessary to add a note to its readers saying that "a number of Simoniya's propositions bear a debatable character." They went on to invite its readers to respond to his arguments. It should be further remarked that in this article Simoniya explicitly attacked the work of another Soviet analyst, Tyagunenko. See also his attack on the authors of

Soviet analysts who asserted that national liberation movements automatically evolve into socialist revolutions. "Even in those cases where there is a new revolutionary eruption, its result is not necessarily a bourgeois-democratic revolution growing over into a general-democratic one. As the coups in Africa showed in the beginning of 1966, preventive explosions can occur from circles interested in maintaining the extant order."[16]

Simoniya also found fault with the orthodox treatment of class relations in the Third World. He questioned the notion that the "motive force of ruling groups in Tropical African countries is nationalism and the desire to improve the lives of the people" and that an alliance with the peasantry naturally leads "the ruling circles to greater democratization and a wave of progressive reforms. The coups in Ghana and Mali say that actually everything is not so simple and logical." He went on to attack Iordansky and the other authors of the book he was reviewing for grossly overestimating the peasantry's "objective interest in the noncapitalist development path," as if it was the "natural ally of the proletariat." He argued that the authors had underestimated the degree of capitalist penetration in the countryside, and, what is more, he accused them of a dearth of evidence and of ignoring their own evidence that they had presented elsewhere in the book.[17] He criticized some for believing that national, ethnic, religious, and tribal differences could be resolved on a class basis or that such problems were inherent only to countries on the capitalist path in the Third World. Instead of assuming proletarian power could solve these problems, Simoniya called for "full democracy in all areas right up to complete freedom of secession."[18]

Simoniya introduced a new element into his thinking as a consequence of events in Ghana and Indonesia—the burden of bureaucratism on progressive development. In his evaluation of Ghana three years after the coup, Simoniya quoted the authors of the book he was reviewing approvingly.

> Even revolutionary democrats do not always succeed in immunizing themselves against the evils of corruption and bureaucratization. Proof is

---

another book for arguing that socialist economic reforms could be implemented prior to a socialist revolution, in "Po Povodu Monografii *Klassy i Klassovaya Borba v Razvivaiushchikhsya Stranakh*" (On the Monograph *Classes and Class Struggle in Developing Countries*), *NAIA*, 1969, no. 3, 49–54. On the need for material preconditions, see also "O Roli 'Natsionalnykh Sotsializmov' v Revoliutsiyakh Vostoka" (On the Role of "National Socialisms" in Revolutions of the East), *VI*), 1967, no. 4, 47–58.

16. Simoniya, "O Kharaktere," 11.

17. Simoniya, "Po Povodu," 49–54. Note the methodological critique that is common to liberal pessimists such as Sheinis (see chap. 5.)

18. Simoniya, "Natsionalizm i Politicheskaya Borba v Osvobodivshikhsya Stranakh" (Nationalism and Political Struggle in Liberated Countries), *MEIMO*, January 1972, 98. It is of note that he quoted Lenin himself when making his right-to-secession argument.

the February 1966 military coup in Ghana, which occurred in a situation of mass political apathy. It is necessary to emphasize that bureaucratism is an objectively inevitable evil in every backward country. Lenin said that "one can drive out the czar, landlords, and capitalists, but one cannot get rid of bureaucratism in a peasant country. One can only reduce it with slow and persistent work."[19]

Simoniya manifested both liberal and orthodox qualities when he discussed the role of parties in progressive countries. Like his orthodox colleagues, he would have preferred to have local Communist parties actively participate in national fronts, but he was quite pessimistic about such cooperation actually being pursued by revolutionary democratic leaders. He likewise preferred that these petit bourgeois leaders adopt the tenets of scientific socialism, but recognized that this too was extremely difficult. Unlike his orthodox and most of his liberal colleagues, Simoniya never expressed the need for a Marxist-Leninist vanguard party in these countries. Simoniya sharply criticized the Maoist approach of denying any possibility of cooperation with petit bourgeois revolutionaries, but also cautioned revolutionary democrats against allying too closely with the bourgeoisie. Simoniya was not hopeful about the ability of revolutionary democrats to master scientific socialist ideology. Reflecting his conviction that the economic base dominated the political superstructure, he argued that a genuine apprehension of Marxism-Leninism is possible only "once the material conditions are created for it." Given the low level of economic development, one must expect "an inevitably prolonged period of backward kinds of socialism" in developing countries. Moreover, "one should not think that petit bourgeois socialist teachings can evolve only in one direction—that of scientific socialism."[20]

Only once did Simoniya express optimism about the ideological prospects of revolutionary democrats, and he did this only to make a liberal argument about the need for local Communist parties to restrain themselves. He asked his readers the rhetorical question:

Is it true that after revolutionary democracy fulfills its historical mission, the problem of a new revolution will arise? Absolutely not. The progressive part of revolutionary democracy can evolve. It can gradually move

---

19. Simoniya, "Po Povodu," 52. On the evils of bureaucratism, see also Brutents, "African Revolution." See also Mirsky, "Changes."

20. All quotes from "O Roli." He repeated his arguments about the economic prerequisites for ideological change in "Leninskaya Ideya Revoliutsionno-Demokraticheskoi Diktatury i Nekapitalisticheskii Put Razvitiya" (The Leninist Idea of the Revolutionary-Democratic Dictator and the Noncapitalist Development Path), *NAIA*, 1968, no. 2, 3–14. For the negative effects of non-Marxist ideologies on domestic programs, see "Za Aktivizatsiiu."

in the direction of scientific socialism. This opens the prospects for a peaceful transition to socialism, without the violent destruction of the state machinery.[21]

Besides trying to counter the Maoist argument for the military path to socialism, Simoniya was also reassuring local revolutionary democrats that Soviet relationships with local Communist parties were not a threat to the political longevity of their regimes. As will become clear in the discussion of orthodox believers such as Ulyanovsky, the latter made no such efforts at reassurance.

The fact that Simoniya did not learn from the coup that revolutionary democrats should set to work building vanguard parties is further evidence of the weight he gave economic variables over the political superstructure. What kind of party a progressive leader chose to build was a superfluous concern to Simoniya, as long as both the state and party machinery were purged of corrupt and reactionary bureaucrats. Again, this distinguished Simoniya from his orthodox counterparts, who argued for ideologically pure bureaucrats.

On virtually every economic issue, Simoniya's views were heretical. At least some of these views were the product of the economic failures he observed in Ghana. Simoniya was able to view separately the economic, class, domestic political, and foreign policy aspects of a third world country. He was not driven to maintain cognitive consistency among these variables, as someone with a tightly constructed belief system would be. A typical consistent belief system would see all bourgeois governments as incapable of effecting economic development, reactionary at home and proimperialist abroad. Simoniya, on the contrary, was able to see bourgeois reactionaries who nonetheless developed their countries economically. In this regard Simoniya manifested a rare ability to explicitly recognize value trade-offs, a characteristic uncommon to those with tight belief systems. He criticized the authors of a book for asserting that developing countries have absolutely no possibility of achieving economic development while dependent on the world capitalist economy.

> It is indisputable that in social relations, the noncapitalist path is more progressive. But this obvious truth in no way contradicts the fact that also many other countries on the capitalist development path are achieving serious successes in the economic area and, in their way, are solving the problem of economic independence. Is not India trying to achieve economic independence?[22]

---

21. Simoniya, "Revoliutsionnaya Demokratiya i Nekapitalisticheskii Put" (Revolutionary Democracy and the Noncapitalist Path), *AIAS*, September 1967, 4.

22. Simoniya, "Po Povodu," 52. He argued the bourgeoisie has been able to achieve relatively high levels of economic growth in "O Kharaktere." Remember that this article was identified by the editors for its "sporny" (arguable) character. Brutents also showed the ability to

Notice how Simoniya was able to separate two issues—income generation and income distribution—that other Soviet observers consistently conflated. He distinguished himself from his orthodox colleagues on a great number of economic issues. He attacked those who advocated unrestrained nationalizations of foreign and local private property, noting that

> even now, some aspire to see the degree and scale of nationalization as the most important criterion of the level of development of socialist relations. But socialism is not reduced to the public ownership of the means of production. One should add that Marxism-Leninism never rejected the idea of using the bourgeoisie in the name of creating a socialist base or the idea of buying the means of production from them.[23]

No Soviet analyst other than Simoniya ever suggested anything but expropriating the means of production from the bourgeoisie. Simoniya continually argued that revolutionary democracies had to use the private sector to develop their economies and at one point asserted that it was inappropriate to even speak of skipping capitalism, as it emerges spontaneously everywhere.[24]

He criticized those Soviet academics who argued that Western aid and investment necessarily lead to the dependence of the recipient. He told them they should not confuse the subjective goal of imperialism, which is of course precisely such dependence, with the objective result of such foreign capital, which can obtain "independent of the will of imperialism."[25] He criticized these same authors for arguing that bourgeois agrarian policies only contradict the interests of the peasantry, exacerbate the agricultural situation, and make the peasantry landless. As he put it: "It is wrong to adopt such purely negative attitudes."[26] Finally, in another article that his editors felt necessary to qualify as "published for discussion," he suggested that Soviet scholarship was wrong on the question of foreign trade relations with imperialist countries.

> Tiulpanov is right when he argues there is not unequal exchange, but simply differences in relative productivity, which is just. The relative enrichment of developed countries can be realized fully on the basis of equal exchange. L.V. Stepanov underestimates the difference between

---

differentiate between the social and economic aspects of capitalism, in "Natsionalno-Osvoboditelnoe Dvizhenie Sevodnya" (The National Liberation Movement Today), *Pravda*, February 1, 1967, 4–5. For a glowing account of capitalism's possibilities, see his "O Revoliutsionnoi Demokratii."

23. Simoniya, "Revoliutsionnaya Demokratiya," 3.

24. Ibid., 2–4. Also see "Leninskaya Ideya." Brutents also argued, albeit far more moderately, for the need to "use private enterprise within reasonable limits" in "African Revolution." See also his "Natsionalno-Osvoboditelnoe."

25. Simoniya, "Po Povodu," 53. Brutents also advocated the cautious use of foreign capital in "Epokha Sotsializma."

26. Ibid., 51.

relative enrichment and robbery. Neither Marx nor Engels ever mentioned unequal exchange. Is this an accident? Lenin also did not use the term.[27]

The coup in Ghana influenced Simoniya's views on economic development in revolutionary democracies. Prior to Nkrumah's fall he argued that Soviet Central Asian republics and the People's Republic of Mongolia (PRM) were appropriate models of noncapitalist development for progressive Soviet allies with all the orthodox lessons this implied for local revolutionary democrats.[28] After the coup, Simoniya softened the analogy somewhat, suggesting that only the PRM was an appropriate model and not an economic model, but an example of a revolutionary democratic party implementing progressive reforms without a Marxist-Leninist vanguard party.[29] Six months later, Simoniya explicitly denied the applicability of any Russian or Mongolian models for the Third World.[30] Simoniya's liberalism and relative pessimism combined to produce a very restrained evaluation of Soviet foreign policy capabilities with respect to its third world allies. Prior to the ouster of Nkrumah, Simoniya was in the orthodox camp on this score, asserting, "As Lenin said, with the aid of the proletariat of leading countries, the noncapitalist development path is possible." This has been proven by, among other countries, Ghana and Mali.[31]

After the coup, Simoniya's attitude changed drastically. He stated that the existence of the socialist system is only "a necessary condition" for noncapitalist development, not a sufficient one. He cautioned his colleagues that just because the capitalist path is not necessary does not "make the noncapitalist path obligatory." He criticized Mirsky for "significantly exaggerating the external factor." Then, in an explicit attack on those afflicted with cognitively consistent belief systems, he asserted that the "anti-imperialist direction of a revolution says nothing about the social content of this revolution. The aspiration to ascribe new class content deriving from the anti-imperialist direction of

27. Simoniya, "Ob Ekonomicheskom Soderzhanii 'Neekvivalentogogo Obmena'" (On the Economic Content of "Nonequivalent Exchange"), *NAIA*, 1972, no. 1, 33.

28. "Nekapitalisticheskii Put."

29. Simoniya, "Revoliutsionnaya Demokratiya." This is further evidence for Simoniya's low regard for vanguard parties; they are not necessary. Brutents was also very guarded about the relevance of the PRM's experience in "Epokha Sotsializma."

30. Simoniya, "Leniniskaya Ideya." See also Mirsky, "Aktualnye Problemy Natsionalno-Osvoboditelnovo Dvizheniya" (Actual Problems of the National Liberation Movement), *MEIMO*, November 1972, 155–57.

31. Simoniya, "Nekapitalisticheskii Put," 122. It should be noted that even here Simoniya was somewhat more moderate than his orthodox colleagues, as he only admitted to the "possibility" of noncapitalist development with Soviet aid. As will be seen below, orthodox analysts spoke of a guarantee.

national liberation revolutions sometimes leads to an inaccurate evaluation of their role and place in the world revolutionary process." He went on to state that Tyagunenko argued that the national liberation revolution is a constituent part of the world socialist revolution. He cited Lenin to demonstrate his point that such revolutions are only part of the world revolutionary process.[32]

Simoniya's selection of hard, quantifiable variables impelled him to derive lessons from Ghana that reinforced his already healthy pessimism about the prospects for revolutionary change in the Third World and about Soviet capabilities to accelerate or even maintain such progress. By focusing on economic variables, he was faced with irrefutable evidence of the difficulties faced by progressive regimes. His liberal beliefs about the need for private enterprise and foreign capital forced him to recognize that Soviet options were very limited in helping these countries. His focus on economic, rather than political, constraints on these regimes is critical to understanding why he was pessimistic about Soviet capabilities. If instead he felt that vanguard parties were the key to revolutionary change, Soviet aid in their construction would be a relatively easy and unfalsifiable way to square the circle of continued progressive development and Soviet foreign policy influence. In effect, as a consequence of his beliefs about the causes of socialist development, he ceded the economic field to the imperialist powers and local capitalists.

## Soviet Images of a Third World Still Ripe for Revolution

Ulyanovsky's tightly organized belief system stands in sharp contrast to Simoniya's rational attribution model. At this time, in the late 1960s and early 1970s, the need to see continual revolutionary progress in the Third World drove Ulyanovsky's beliefs.[33] When faced with evidence of failures such as the overthrow of Nkrumah, he first responded with a host of devices designed

---

32. Simoniya, "O Kharaktere," 3–21. In a similar indictment of those who overestimated the importance of national liberation revolutions to the socialist system as a whole, Simoniya accused the authors of the book he was reviewing of inaccurately saying that Marx and Engels wrote about national liberation movements. To paraphrase Simoniya: They did not, and the authors should say so. See "Po Povodu." For an equally restrained view of the possible effectiveness of Soviet aid, see Brutents, "Pravyashchaya Revoliutsionnaya Demokratiya: Nekotorye Cherty Prakticheskoi Deyatelnosti" (Ruling Revolutionary Democracy: Certain Features of Practical Activity), part 2, *MEIMO*, December 1972, 115–29. See also Mirksy, "O Kharaktere Sotsialnykh Sil v Azii i Afrike" (On the Character of Social Forces in Asia and Africa), *Kommunist*, 1968, no. 17, 89–102.

33. As we know from Ulyanovsky's reactions to the revolution in Iran, by the early 1980s he had become quite sober in his analysis of revolutionary prospects in the Third World. Since even revolutionary leaders were not adhering to Leninist orthodoxy, Ulyanovsky was unable to maintain the optimism of previous years, when it seemed that these revolutionary democrats only needed more years of experience, and then they would adopt the right policies.

to distort these realities, so they would remain consonant with his prior beliefs. Only when this was insufficient did he resort to checking reality against the limited Leninist selection of critical variables he monitored to gauge the performance of revolutionary democratic regimes. The elements of this menu are precisely the opposite of those found in Simoniya's model.

The central value in Ulyanovsky's belief system was socialist development in Soviet allies in the Third World. He protected this value by emphasizing the predominance of the political superstructure over the economic base. He continued to believe, despite the coup, that revolutionary democrats could direct their societies toward socialism so long as they were good Marxist-Leninists and cooperated with local Communist parties. They could overcome economic obstacles through political instruments. And if all else fails, Soviet aid could guarantee their success. In sum, the need to see revolutionary change in Soviet allies led him to rely on the political determinants of such progress, as emphasis on economic factors would have undermined his confidence in the prospect of socialist construction in these countries. His need further drove him to hold quite expansive views about Soviet capabilities to assist in the revolutionary restructuring of these societies. When domestic political factors appeared inadequate to the task of socialist reform, Ulyanovksy invoked Soviet capabilities to overcome the lack of domestic prerequisites.

There is a great deal of evidence that a need to see socialist development in the Third World lay at the heart of Ulyanovsky's belief system and drove his other beliefs about and perceptions of reality. For example, in discussing the economic problems encountered by progressive third world countries, he enunciated the orthodox belief that imperialism is their source. But instead of concluding that its strategy of neocolonialism was a hindrance to progressive change, Ulyanovsky argued that it was a positive factor, for it revolutionizes the class attitudes of various otherwise inert strata of society.[34] Unlike Simoniya, who saw capitalism spontaneously erupting even in countries on the noncapitalist path, Ulyanovsky believed that this path "deprives capitalism of its natural inevitability."[35]

He attacked those, like Simoniya, who argued that economic development was the key to socialist construction.

Leninism is categorically against the absolutization of economic prerequisites and against a strict definition of the economic and cultural level at

---

34. Ulyanovsky, "Aktualnye Problemy Natsionalno-Osvoboditelnovo Dvizheniya" (Actual Problems of the National Liberation Movement), *NAIA*, 1969, no. 4, 3–14.

35. Ulyanovsky, "Leninskaya Kontseptsiya Nekapitalisticheskogo Razvitiya i Sovremennost" (The Leninist Conception of Noncapitalist Development and Modern Times), *VI*, April 1970, 119. Reflecting his general optimism in the same article, he argued that national liberation revolutions themselves inevitably lead to noncapitalist development.

which the construction of socialism is possible. [It] is also against vulgar deterministic ideas about the political prerequisites of revolution emerging as a result of economic growth. Lenin wrote that insufficient economic preconditions can be compensated for by political ones, that political preconditions can and should become the foundation for the creation of economic ones.

The link between his beliefs about the primacy of politics and his need for revolutionary change is clear from his own statement that followed from the above quote: "Lenin rejected ideas that fetter the revolutionary energy of millions of people in the colonial world."[36] Ideas such as Simoniya's, according to Ulyanovsky, had precisely such a "fettering" effect.

Several years after the coup, Ulyanovsky tried to limit the damage caused to his confidence in revolutionary advances. In an article written in early 1971, he denied that countries such as Ghana and Mali had been lost to capitalism, describing them instead as countries "where coups interrupted their noncapitalist development but have not led to a significant growth in capitalism." He suggested that they still might return to the "progressive path." This was so, he argued, because the peasantry does not aspire to private landownership and consequently can play a "revolutionary role restructuring the countryside."[37] This argument would not be evidence of a motivated bias but for the fact that in the very same article Ulyanovsky asserted that the peasantry "in Tropical African countries [such as Ghana and Mali] is backward and often politically indifferent."[38] In order to save his revolutionary optimism, Ulyanovsky distorted the evidence to support the return of Ghana and Mali to the progressive path in the future.

As compared to Simoniya, Ulyanovsky exaggerated the power of the working class in the Third World.[39] But even when he recognized that the

---

36. Ibid., 122.

37. Ulyanovsky, "Sovremennyi Etap Natsionalno-Osvoboditelnogo Dvizeniya i Krestianstvo" (Contemporary Stage of the National Liberation Movement and the Peasantry), *MEIMO*, June 1971, 75–88.

38. Ibid., 79. In the first part of this article he also contradicted his predictions about Ghana and Mali. In that article he at first saw "traditional social relations predominating" in the countryside, but then concluded that religion, customs, and traditions were "increasingly losing their effectiveness and previous significance," which created better conditions for revolutionary activities. He further contradicted himself several months later. At that time he criticized revolutionary democrats for believing that there was an "anticapitalist potential" in the traditions of the peasantry. Instead, they were "the mainstays of ignorance and political backwardness." See "Third World," 26–35.

39. See, for example, Ulyanovsky "O Nekotorykh Chertakh," "Aktualnye Problemy," and "Natsionalno-Osvoboditelnoe Dvizhenie—Primety XX Stoletiya" (The National Liberation Movement—Signs of the Twentieth Century), *Izvestiya*, February 12, 1970, 2–3.

working class was weak and incapable of leading any kind of revolution, he was not dissuaded from arguing that revolutionary change was imminent. His arguments on this point were quite similar to those he made when criticizing those who believed in "economic determinants" of socialist development. "The proletariat is extremely small, weakly organized and not a class that determines social development. If an economically undeveloped country were to wait for the formation of a national dictatorship of the proletariat to begin the transition to socialist development, it would mean accelerating capitalism to form a working class on the basis of capitalist industrialization."[40] "Some recommend waiting until the proletariat and industry is born and until it comes to the leadership of the movement and to power. From the viewpoint of the doctrinaires who do not accept the theory of noncapitalist development, one must wait until hell freezes over [*do pribytiya grecheskovo kalendarya*].[41] For Ulyanovsky, the need for revolutionary development overrode the obstacles posed by the objective weakness of the working class, which is destined to lead the movement toward socialism in these countries.

Ulyanovsky, like his liberal pessimist counterparts, did not conclude from the loss in Ghana that progressive regimes should build vanguard parties. But he differed dramatically as to why he did not learn such lessons. Simoniya saw instability as caused by economic factors and sought the solution in more effective economic policies. Ulyanovsky, on the contrary, looked for a solution in greater ideological rectitude and greater involvement of *Communist*, not vanguard, parties in the government. Prior to Nkrumah's overthrow, Ulyanovsky credited the Ghanaian leader with building a vanguard party.[42] But Ulyanovsky did not even mention vanguard parties again until four years later, when he recommended that they be built.[43] If he indeed felt that the ouster of Nkrumah represented a case where vanguard party control had failed to ensure revolutionary gains, then his lack of regard for them after 1966 is understandable. Ulyanovsky instead inferred from these losses that adherence to scientific socialism and greater participation for local Communist parties were the antidotes to political instability.

In general, Ulyanovsky assumed an extremely orthodox position on ideol-

---

40. Ulyanovsky, "Nekotorye Voprosy Nekapitalisticheskovo Razvitiya Osvobodivshchikhsya Stran" (Certain Questions of the Noncapitalist Development of Liberated Countries), *Kommunist*, 1966, no. 1, 113. Hereafter cited as "Nekotorye Voprosy," 1966.

41. Ulyanovsky, "Sotsializm i Natsionalno-Osvoboditelnaya Borba—O Nekapitalisticheskom Puti Razvitiya" (Socialism and the National Liberation Struggle—On the Noncapitalist Development Path), *Pravda*, April 15, 1966, 4.

42. Ulyanvosky,"Nekotorye Voprosy," 1966.

43. Ulyanovsky, "Leninskaya Kontseptsiya." The only other article in which he remarked on such a party is "Nekotorye Voprosy," 1971. In this piece, he emphasized the role of the state over that of the vanguard party.

ogy, criticizing all revolutionary democrats who were not strict adherents to scientific socialism.[44] He adopted such an unyielding stand because he believed that if progressive third world leaders would master Marxism-Leninism, they would be more likely to pursue foreign and domestic policies aimed at the construction of socialism. Not only would ideological purity compensate for economic disadvantages, but it would also allow these leaders to recognize that their true allies local Communists at home and the Soviet Union abroad.[45] When faced with contrary evidence that revolutionary democrats were not very readily grasping the concepts of scientific socialism, a fact that threatened Ulyanovsky's need to see progressive change, he responded by creating a new category of revolutionary. He argued that while it is true that "national democrats" inadequately understood Marxism-Leninism, it is fine now since "revolutionary democracy is closer to Marxism-Leninism than national democracy."[46] Of course, after they were ousted, Ulyanovsky identified Sukarno, Nkrumah, and Keita as such national democrats, though he spoke of them as revolutionary democrats while they were in power—yet another example of cognitive distortions aimed at preserving the central value of his belief system.

Ulyanovsky saw cooperation with local Communists as the single most important tactic that revolutionary democrats should adopt if they were going to succeed in their efforts at building socialism. Drawing on the lessons of Indonesia, Ghana, and Mali, he commented that

> aspirations to monopolize state power and to ignore other anti-imperialist, progressive forces not rarely leads to political instability and to even a loss of power. Where a struggle for unity is replaced by declarations, and masses are on the sidelines in the management of the state, and progressive organizations and parties are ignored or suppressed, weak and isolated sections of the anti-imperialist front are formed, against which imperialism tries to mount a counteroffensive. So it was in a number of Afro-Asian countries in the last decade. Historical experience proves that the central task for the successful development of national liberation

44. For representative examples, see Ulyanovsky, "Nekotorye Voprosy," 1966, and "Aktualnye Problemy." He did, however, evince an understanding of revolutionary democrats' accommodating attitudes toward religion and did not argue for the propagation of atheism in the Third World. See, for example, "Nauchnyi Sotsializm i Osvobodivshiesya Strany" (Scientific Socialism and Liberated Countries), *Kommunist*, 1968, no. 4, 92–106, and "The Third World."

45. For evidence that a correct ideology is a necessary condition for correct policies toward local Communists and the Soviet Union, see Ulyanovsky, "Sotsializm," "Nauchnyi Sotsializm," "Leninskaya Kontseptsiya," and "Nekotorye Voprosy," 1971.

46. Ulyanovsky, "O Edinom Antiimperialisticheskom Fronte Progressivnykh Sil v Osvobodivshiksya Stranakh" (On a Single Anti-imperialist Front of Progressive Forces in Liberated Countries), *MEIMO*, September 1972, 80.

revolutions is the cooperation and close relations between the parties of the proletariat and revolutionary democracy. Its absence only plays into the hands of imperialism and domestic reaction.[47]

While Simoniya learned from Nkrumah's ouster that economic mismanagement leads to political instability and coups, Ulyanovsky argued that insufficient involvement of Communists in the political and governmental life of the country leads to the same and also encourages imperialists and local reactionaries to try to undermine these regimes. The notion that imperialists more strongly resist states without Communists in their governments than those with them contradicted what Ulyanovsky had argued about American foreign policy motives. He asserted that the United States aims its attacks precisely against those regimes that adopt the most progressive domestic and foreign policies;[48] presumably regimes with Communists in the government would be more progressive than those without them. This contradiction shows that Ulyanovsky was willing to ignore his own arguments about American foreign policy motives in order to assert the need for Communist political participation in revolutionary democracies.

Ulyanovksy's focus on the centrality of Communist participation impelled him to advance Lenin's crabbed view of democracy. The only opposition organizations to receive democratic rights are Communist parties. As Ulyanovsky put it: "National democrats cannot allow an opposition. This would sacrifice revolutionary prospects to fetishized concepts of bourgeois democracy. The need to limit democracy should be applied strictly against the class enemy."[49] This understanding of democracy in turn led to orthodox solutions to reactionary coups such as the one in Ghana. Ulyanovsky called for increasing mass participation in trade unions and peasant and other organizations, strengthening the ideological and organizational aspects of the ruling party and, of course, reinforcing "its alliance with Marxist-Leninists."[50]

His commitment to Communist participation also implicitly threatened the political longevity of ongoing revolutionary democratic regimes. This ran counter to Simoniya's efforts to reassure the latter about their ability to remain on the political stage for an extended period of time. Ulyanovsky accused "anti-Marxists" of trying to "prove that the task of Communists in all circumstances is to struggle for power." This means that revolutionary democrats should not cooperate with them nor believe in their good intentions. But in his response to these charges, Ulyanovsky did not deny that local Communists

47. Ulyanovsky, "Aktualnye Problemy," 9.

48. A representative sample of many examples includes Ulyanovsky, "Pod Devizom," "O Nekotorykh Chertakh," and "Dekolonizatsiya."

49. Ulyanovsky, "Leninskaya Kontseptsiya," 121. Mirsky shared this orthodox view of democracy: "Tendencies in the National Liberation Movement Today," *IA*, August 1971 , 18–20.

50. Ibid., 124.

were working for the ultimate replacement of revolutionary democrats by themselves.[51] In fact, in subsequent articles, he consistently argued that "the basic task of noncapitalist development is to create the conditions that will let the working class come to power."[52] Such formulations were hardly likely to inspire revolutionary democrats to share power with local Communist parties. But it appears that Ulyanovsky's commitment to an orthodox view of revolutionary change—with Communist participation—was more important to him than establishing long-term relationships with revolutionary democrats.

Ulyanovsky's treatment of the role of the bureaucracy in these countries also reveals the high value he placed on Communist participation. Unlike Simoniya, who suggested the removal of corrupt officials was the most critical task for revolutionary democrats to perform to combat bureaucratism, Ulyanovsky's solution was to involve local Communists in the government and the state and military apparat.[53] Ulyanovsky quite frequently cited economic variables to explain the overthrow of Nkrumah in Ghana. This is not unlike Simoniya. But Simoniya offered economic solutions to these problems; Ulyanovsky, given his system of beliefs, suggested that ideological perfection and an appropriate attitude toward Communist participation could overcome these obstacles. Soon after the fall of Nkrumah, Ulyanovsky argued that if a revolutionary democrat ignores the task of creating a strong economy and satisfying the growing demands of working people for increased standards of living, "contradictions" will arise. "Hasty decrees from above of insufficiently prepared reforms combined with masses who are not ready to support the reforms negatively affect noncapitalist development." But worst of all, according to Ulyanovsky, "imperialists aspire to discredit the idea and practice of noncapitalist development and use its difficulties for their aims. Recent events in Ghana especially showed this."[54]

In the same vein, attempts to "artificially accelerate noncapitalist development are dangerous" and can inflict "irreparable damage to its cause." This is so because the bourgeoisie's tendency to ally with imperialism is strengthened by "hasty nationalizations of enterprises" and other "economically foolhardy" measures.[55] It is interesting to note that Ulyanovsky was motivated to look at economic factors here not primarily due to their direct effects on the

---

51. Ulyanovsky, "Leninizm—Znamya Svobody i Progressa" (Leninism—Banner of Freedom and Progress), *Pravda*, October 25, 1969, 4.

52. Ulyanovsky, "Leninskaya Kontseptsiya," 120. See also "Sovremennyi Etap" and "Third World." In the latter article, he criticized the Sudanese government for its recent "difficulties" with regard to the Sudanese Communist Party. He did not criticize the Sudanese Communists for supporting a coup attempt in the first place.

53. Ulyanovsky, "O Nekotorykh Chertakh," in which he argued that coups such as the one in Ghana are caused in part by bribery and corruption characteristic of bureaucracies. See also "Nekotorye Voprosy," 1971, and "O Edinom Fronte."

54. Ulyanovsky, "Sotsializm."

55. Ulyanovsky, "Nekotorye Voprosy," 1971, 109.

success or failure of noncapitalist development, but rather because American foreign policy derived advantages from the economic failures of Soviet allies in the Third World.

The economic experience of Ghana appears to have pushed Ulyanovsky in a more liberal direction on economic issues. He ascribed the frequent regime changes in the Third World to the fact that "the masses and working people have not been saved from exploitation and poverty."[56] He also criticized revolutionary democrats for undertaking "hasty measures, e.g., unjustified nationalizations in retail trade, services, small and medium industry." But his solution combined economic elements with political ones. The reforms needed to be economically prepared and implemented without errors, but "not from above, bureaucratically, without relying on mass public participation."[57] "Mass public participation" in the orthodox Soviet lexicon meant involvement of party cadres in organizing workers, peasants, students, youth, women, and so on, in support of the government's goals. For Ulyanovsky, this kind of work was best performed by local Communists. He also chided those revolutionary democrats who had a "fascination for building expensive projects that are often useless economically—all kinds of monuments, huge stadiums, palaces, etc."[58] The more liberally Ulyanovsky evaluated the economic policies necessary for growth in Soviet allies, the more orthodox he became in selecting political instruments to prevent such policies from leading to the growth of capitalism.

> The coexistence of the state and private sectors is necessary. The financial possibilities for economic development are extremely limited and do not allow for the neglect of the potential and experience of the private sector. The use of the private sector is an economic necessity and for an extremely long time. And this cannot help but cause even the expansion and consolidation of some positions of private capital. Maximum economic growth demands this.
>
> This poses special demands for the political superstructure, primarily the state, army, and ruling party—the only levers in the hands of revolu-

---

56. Ulyanovsky, "Na Novykh Rubezhakh—O Nekotorykh Chertakh Sovremennogo Etapa Natsionalno-Osvoboditelnovo Dvizheniya" (On New Frontiers—On Certain Features of the Contemporary Stage of the National Liberation Movement), *Pravda*, January 3, 1968, 4.

57. Ulyanovsky, "Nauchnyi Sotsializm," 100. See also "Osvoboditelnaya Borba Narodov Afriki" (Liberation Struggle of Peoples of Africa), *Kommunist*, 1969, no. 11, 39–42, and "Leninskaya Kontseptsiya," in which he, for the first time, attacked the construction of unprofitable state enterprises and argued for the use of efficiency criteria to evaluate nationalized factories.

58. Ulyanovsky, "Osvoboditelnaya Borba," 41. It is not unlikely that Ulyanovsky had in mind Nkrumah's construction of a $30 million airport in the northern city of Tamale, two hundred miles from the populated areas along Ghana's coast and served by only the poorest of roads and "Job 600," the construction of a huge statehouse and conference facilities for the 1965 OAU conference held in Accra.

tionary forces able to guarantee development from a noncapitalist perspective. As Lenin said, the political organization of society is the main prerequisite for revolutionary changes. The most important guarantees are adherence to socialism, the growing organization of the working people and their influence on state affairs, the unity of all progressive forces, and their close alliance with the world socialist system.[59]

While Simoniya found economic obstacles to progressive development to be virtually insurmountable, except through painstaking labor and the passage of time, Ulyanovsky protected his need to see revolutionary change by believing that ideology, unity between revolutionary democrats and Communists, and a foreign policy oriented toward the Soviet Union could overcome any economic problems.

Ulyanovsky also protected his central value by differentiating among those interested in capitalism in third world countries. If allowing capitalist development led to a united bourgeoisie opposed to state intervention in the economy, then the political superstructure, on which Ulyanovsky placed most of his faith, would be severely strained. Ulyanovsky solved this problem by arguing that "far from being a hindrance to medium and small national capital, the state sector protects it from being absorbed by big capital and helps it compete with foreign commodities."[60] By creating distinctions between different capitalist groups, Ulyanovsky was able to mitigate the tension created by recognizing the necessity of capitalist economic development and the equal necessity of a political superstructure to prevent its development into a political force.[61]

Ulyanovsky did have a solid core of orthodox beliefs, as well. He argued for radical agrarian reforms aimed against feudal and big capitalist landlords, for a growing state industrial sector, centralized planning, and the nationalization of the banking system, natural resources, transportation, and communications.[62] The state should also control foreign and wholesale trade.[63] He was also anxious about the consequences of dependence on Western capital and

---

59. Ulyanovsky, "Leninskaya Kontscptsiya," 129. Onc year later, in an article marked by even greater liberalism with respect to economic matters, he said that "the success of economic policy is not determined by the scale of nationalized foreign or local private capital, but by the ability, relying on the state sector, to direct and effectively use the private capitalist and small commodity sector in the interests of the economy. "Nekotorye Voprosy," 1971.

60. Ulyanovsky, "Third World," 30.

61. This device is similar to his division of radical allies into "national" and "revolutionary" democrats to save his view of an ever-increasing mastery of the tenets of Marxism-Leninism, at least by the latter.

62. Ulyanovsky, "Nekotorye Voprosy," 1971, and "Sotsialno-Ekonomicheskie Problemy Osvobodivshikhsya Stran" (Socio-Economic Problems of Liberated Countries), *Kommunist*, 1972, no. 8, 87–98.

63. Ulyanovsky, "Third World."

trading links.[64] Ulyanovsky protected these more orthodox beliefs about the noncapitalist development path by choosing to weight the social aspects of development more heavily than the economic ones when evaluating the economic progress of third world countries and by arguing that only noncapitalist development could yield both benefits. Remember how Simoniya separated these two variables, admitting that the capitalist path had its economic advantages. Ulyanovsky argued that "the experience of twenty years of the development of a number of countries on the capitalist path has shown that, though the development of productive forces has advanced, the social, political, legal, and material situation of the working people remains extremely hard. Rapid *economic and social* progress can be achieved only on the noncapitalist path."[65]

Ulyanovsky's treatment of the applicability of the Soviet or Mongolian experiences to Soviet allies in the Third World shows the primacy he gave to Communist participation and foreshadows the role he saw for Soviet foreign policy in promoting revolutionary change. Ulyanovsky was rather early in conditioning the relevance of Soviet lessons for revolutionary democrats. He warned the latter that they were still dependent on the world capitalist economic system, whereas Soviet Eastern republics and the PRM had not been so burdened.[66] Subsequently, Ulyanovsky asserted that the main distinction between "contemporary" revolutionary democracies and their predecessors was that the latter's revolutions were led by Marxist-Leninist parties. In the following passage, written in 1970, he linked Soviet support to their willingness to cooperate with local Communist organizations.

> Economic, political, and military aid is a most important and necessary condition for noncapitalist development. But it is substantially different in character and volume from the relations between the RSFSR [Russian Soviet Federated Socialist Republic] and the Central Asian Republics and between the USSR and the PRM. In the latter, contacts were and remain incomparably closer. In them, Marxist parties led the changes, by dint of which there was unity on all questions of political and social development between them and the center of the proletarian revolution in Russia. One cannot say this of relations between socialist countries and the countries, leaders, and ideologues of contemporary noncapitalist development.[67]

---

64. For example, Ulyanovsky, "O Nekotorykh Chertakh," "Na Novykh," "Leninizm," and "Dekolonizatsiya."

65. Ulyanovsky, "Leninizm—Znamya," 4 (emphasis added).

66. Ulyanovsky, "O Nekotorykh Chertakh," and "Na Novykh."

67. Ulyanovsky, "Leninskaya Kontseptsiya," 132. On the need for a Marxist-Leninist party as the distinguishing characteristic, also see "Leninizm," "Nekotorye Voprosy," 1971, and "Third World."

In this selection, Ulyanovsky shows the great importance he placed on the role of local Communist parties in effecting revolutionary change. He implied that continued Soviet support was contingent on a revolutionary democrat's willingness to cooperate with local Communists in a united front. He put it perhaps most starkly in the following selection: "Soviet Communists will never refuse, while maintaining the most friendly ties with national democrats, to proceed from the fact that the chief goal of fraternal Communist parties and national democrats is unity. Recognition of the legal rights of Communists creates a favorable political climate for friendly relations with national democrats."[68]

Ulyanovsky's need to perceive revolutionary change demands the primacy of politics over economics. Herein lies the critical difference between the beliefs of Ulyanovsky and those of Simoniya. The latter, lacking a need to see revolutionary change in the Third World, when faced with economic obstacles and Soviet inability to surmount them, simply acknowledged that any socialist development in the Third World would take an incredibly long time, as the economic prerequisites had to be built first. Ulyanovsky, on the contrary, squares the circle by shifting causal primacy from economic preconditions to political ones. This manifests itself in his discussion of class relations, party building, and economic development. Moreover, by shifting to these noneconomic variables, he, in turn, made Soviet foreign policy relevant to progressive development in these countries. First, despite the absence of a working class in these countries, the Soviet Union itself could fulfill the role of international revolutionary vanguard. "Revolutionary forces in liberated countries cannot wait until all the necessary preconditions for socialism are formed through capitalist development and the creation of a powerful working class. Is this possible? The experience of Great October is evidence of the possibility."[69] According to Ulyanovsky, Soviet foreign policy could overcome the lack of class, party, and economic development in these countries.

> Private enterprise has already become a fairly strong element eroding the foundations of patriarchal life and feudal relations—isn't this rich soil for neo-capitalism? Economically and socially underdeveloped societies with a small and poorly-organized proletariat and in some cases without any, societies that still lack conditions for the creation of a Marxist-Leninist party as the vanguard of the working class—isn't this a guarantee of stable capitalist trends? [No, since] . . . the growing influence of world socialism has unbalanced the conventional course of the historical

---

68. Ulyanovsky, "Third World," 28. See also "O Edinstve Sil Sotsializma."

69. Ulyanovsky, "Sovremennyi Etap," 77. For other examples of overcoming domestic class obstacles to change through use of the "Soviet vanguard," see "Nekotorye Voprosy," 1966, "Sotsializm," and "Nauchnyi Sotsializm."

process and opened up new possibilities for a revolutionary departure from capitalism.[70]

In sum, Ulyanovksy's need to see revolutionary change in the Third World drove his beliefs about the appropriate domestic and foreign policies of Soviet revolutionary democratic allies. This need led to his belief in the primacy of political superstructure over economic factors. This belief allowed him to ignore the hard, measurable data that economic failures presented. It had the crucial added benefit of making Soviet foreign policy relevant to the process of progressive development. Given the lack of Soviet economic wherewithal to help its allies surmount economic impediments, Ulyanovsky's focus on political prerequisites for radical change allowed the Soviet Union to fulfill its role as "international proletarian vanguard" without having to invest many rubles in the endeavor.

When he did recognize economic factors as operative in determining the loss of power of an ally, his solutions remained largely political. Such solutions are advantageous to Ulyanovsky as they are largely unfalsifiable; hence, they helped protect his central value. It is very hard to measure ideological rectitude; it is almost as hard to measure "progressive unity," except in those cases where Communists are overtly repressed by revolutionary democrats. In fact, Ulyanovsky revealed much more pessimism with respect to the latter, for he could observe precisely such "hard" bits of evidence in Indonesia and the Sudan.

## Summary

Soviet lessons of high American credibility, since they were the product of peculiar Leninist beliefs, do not argue for an expansion of deterrence theory. However, the "liberal pessimistic" lessons from Ghana are strong evidence for the need to increase the domain of the theory to capture cases of Soviet losses with no U.S. involvement. Moreover, the only disconfirming lessons are those of the "orthodox optimists," whose belief systems are peculiar to Leninists.

### Considering Soviet Behavior

As discussed at the end of the last chapter, deterrence theory makes no determinate predictions about a challenger's reaction to defeat. The pattern of Soviet gains and losses in the Third World subsequent to the overthrow of Nkrumah is testimony to the wisdom of that indeterminancy.

---

70. Ulyanovsky, "Third World," 28.

If one takes a look at the following chronology of Soviet gains and losses in the Third World from 1966 to 1970, it is clear that no pattern emerges.

| Ghana | 1966 | Loss |
|---|---|---|
| Middle East | 1967 | Loss |
| Mali | 1968 | Loss |
| Peru | 1968 | Gain |
| Sudan | 1969 | Gain |
| Libya | 1969 | Gain |
| Somalia | 1969 | Gain |
| Bolivia | 1969 | Gain |
| Chile | 1970 | Gain |
| Jordan | 1970 | Loss |

On the one hand, the Soviets lose in the Middle East and Keita is overthrown in Mali, but then they experience six consecutive gains, though not a single one is even remotely caused by *Soviet* behavior. Military coups of varying degrees of anti-Americanism occur in rapid succession in Peru, the Sudan, Libya, Somalia, and Bolivia, and Allende is elected in Chile. Shortly after Allende's election, the Palestinian uprising in Jordan is quashed by King Hussein, with the deterrent help of Israel vis-à-vis Syria.

In sum, the behavioral record neither supports nor undermines deterrence theory assumptions and once again shows that deterrent lessons are not sufficient to cause deterrence.

### Conclusions: Expanding Deterrence Theory Still More

Deterrence theory has nothing to say about cases where the defender does nothing to cause the challenger a defeat. On the one hand, there is no reason for the theory to have such broad scope, for it is a theory intended to describe what kinds of behavior the defender must adopt if it is to dissuade a potential challenger from attacking the status quo. But deterrence theory must concern itself with the views of the challenger. If the latter learns deterrent lessons from events that are outside the scope of the theory, then such events should be brought within the domain of the theory. Otherwise, the theorist is left with an incomplete model of the challenger's decision-making calculus. The defender should have as complete a picture of the challenger's view of the costs and benefits facing it as possible.

The case in this chapter shows that even when the United States did nothing to cause the Soviet Union a loss, Soviets still inferred deterrent lessons from that experience. The lessons of theoretical interest here are those that are generated by rational attribution processes: the liberal pessimist conclusions from the coup in Ghana. Deterrence theory should be expanded to capture these kinds of deterrent lessons about the prospects of future revolutionary progress in the Third World based on losses there. The lessons of high American credibility are less significant theoretically, since they were the product of far less general Leninist beliefs.

The findings of this chapter reinforce those of the previous two. Direct American military intervention in Grenada prevented Soviets from learning deterrent lessons about the Third World in general but was sufficient to teach them that the United States was highly credible. Indirect American actions in the Middle East caused strong deterrent lessons at both levels. No American involvement in this chapter caused weak lessons about U.S. credibility, but significant deterrent lessons about revolutionary prospects in the Third World. There is one interesting difference, however, between the Middle East and Ghana. In the case of indirect American involvement, Soviets learned very powerful deterrent lessons about the dynamics in the Middle East itself but applied orthodox optimism to the rest of the Third World. In the case of Ghana, there were very few, if any, deterrent lessons about the region around Ghana, but liberal pessimist lessons about the Third World in general. It might be the case that indirect American action is *necessary* for deterrent regional dynamics, and *no* American involvement at all is necessary for deterrent lessons about the Third World writ large. In other words, any American participation at all is sufficient to prevent global deterrent lessons but is simultaneously necessary to teach Soviets that the region in which they are operating is not a hospitable environment for foreign policy adventures.

CHAPTER 8

# Conclusion: Deterrence Theory Revised

The evidence in the previous seven chapters has demonstrated the need to revise the assumptions of traditional deterrence theory and the theory's prescriptions in a fundamental fashion. Not only did deterrence theory empirically perform very poorly, but much of the disconfirming evidence was not the product of irrational information processing. This point is critical, for many of the most powerful arguments against traditional deterrence theory have asserted that the theory is invalid because it assumes rationality. I find, on the contrary, that even rational decision makers generate perceptions of credibility and regional dynamics that invalidate the theory. Moreover, and just as damning, much of the confirming evidence was generated through irrational processes.

But this empirical disconfirmation of the theory does not imply the need to discard deterrence principles in general. The basic core of the theory remains sound: if a defender wants to dissuade a potential challenger from grabbing some piece of territory, it is necessary, though not sufficient, to convince the challenger that the defender is both capable and resolved to defend that piece of territory or to impose unacceptable costs on the challenger if it tries to achieve that objective. Where deterrence theory fundamentally fails is in its assumptions about what kinds of steps are necessary by the defender to communicate credibility to the potential challenger. In a nutshell, convincing a challenger that a defender is credible and that regional actors are going to resist is a far easier task than the theory assumes. However, deterrence theory must expand its scope to capture an array of deterrent instruments that the theory's focus on military tools omits.

Below, I recapitulate the lessons Soviets learned from their victories and defeats in the Third World from 1965 to 1990 and show how they either confirm or disconfirm deterrence theory. I then show how Soviet *behavior* correlates neither with deterrence theory's assumptions nor with the empirical record of Soviet lessons. I then discuss what these findings imply about deterrence theory more generally. Finally, I conclude with a revised version of deterrence theory that incorporates the main findings of this study.

## Soviet Lessons from Their Victories

Two points need to be made immediately about all Soviet lessons from the Third World. First, with the exception of Vietnam and the Middle East, Soviets used events in the periphery to generate images of American credibility only rarely. Second, and directly related, not a single Soviet in twenty-five years inferred anything about American credibility in Europe or Northeast Asia based on any one of the thirty-eight cases in this book. Two assumptions of deterrence theory are therefore essentially falsified.

Soviet victories in the Third World came in three varieties: despite direct American military intervention; despite indirect American resistance; and with no American effort at all to impede the Soviet victory. Regardless of how the gains were achieved by the Soviets, they did not infer lessons supportive of deterrence theory, especially as each of these wins were crucially easy tests for the theory to pass. Since Soviet lessons do not provide unequivocal confirmation for the theory under these most comfortable of circumstances, the theory's validity is put into serious question. The theory's standing is further weakened by the fact that most of the lessons that confirmed the theory were the product of peculiar belief systems, whereas disconfirming inferences ran the entire gamut of explanations: from universal to peculiar.

The American debacle in Vietnam should be a very easy test for deterrence theory to pass, but the results are hardly unambiguous confirmation. The United States expended enormous resources and yet still lost, a situation that, according to deterrence theory, should lead to a severe loss of credibility and a cascade of falling dominoes. But American credibility did not suffer. Soviets with Marxist-Leninist belief systems attributed high capability and resolve to the United States axiomatically. Soviets who used rational-causal attribution models concluded that the United States would most probably continue to resist progressive change in the Third World. Regional dominoes were limited to Kampuchea and Laos; Soviets did not even see Thailand as threatened. And the only global domino imagery was the product of peculiar Leninist views of the world revolutionary alliance.

Deterrence theory failed still more clearly in another set of crucially easy cases, namely, the "arc of crisis" comprising Angola, Ethiopia, and Afghanistan. Despite the fact that the Soviets experienced a string of victories, they did not conclude that the United States was weak and bereft of will, or that regional dynamics were going to work in their favor. In each of the three cases, Soviets saw a highly credible United States either because of adherence to Marxism-Leninism or because they assessed American credibility in a universally rational manner. In each of the three cases, Soviets saw regional actors balancing against these gains. And these Soviet analyses provide disconfirmation of a universal or general scope. The only validating lessons, global dominoes set off by these victories, were the product of Leninist beliefs with very limited generalizability.

Deterrence theory did not pass a crucial test in the cases of Iran and Nicaragua. Both of these victories came right on the heels of the victory on the Horn of Africa and shortly before the invasion of Afghanistan. Once again, U.S. credibility remained intact, and its maintenance was due to both peculiar and universal Soviet lessons. Soviets saw regional actors resisting Iran, not falling like dominoes, and these lessons were a combination of belief systems and rational attribution processes. Soviets rationally inferred from Nicaragua that dominoes would fall in Central America, but these lessons were limited in geographic scope and were soon replaced by pessimistic assessments.

In sum, deterrence theory failed to pass a series of crucially easy tests. Moreover, many of these invalidating lessons were the product of decision-making processes applicable to the universe of deterrence cases. And all of the most serious confirmatory lessons, namely, global dominoes, were the product of peculiar Leninist beliefs, which are applicable only to a limited subset of deterrence cases.

## Lessons from Soviet Defeats

Soviet defeats in the Third World also came in three varieties: those that were caused by direct American military intervention; those that occurred through the use of American nonmilitary instruments or the actions of American allies; and those that happened with no U.S. involvement. Deterrence theory only speaks to the first type of Soviet defeat and predicts that such defeats will enhance deterrence. But the theory ignores the deterrent lessons that are taught by the other two kinds of losses, a very costly omission, since the most powerful deterrent lessons occur in precisely the cases that are left out.

Deterrence theory predictions about American credibility were borne out completely by Soviet lessons from the U.S. military intervention in Grenada. But while this intervention was sufficient to impart such lessons, it was both unnecessary and inadequate. It was not necessary because we know that Soviets viewed the United States as highly credible even after Soviet victories. It was inadequate because, while it generated Soviet images of a highly resolute and capable America, it simultaneously blocked out all Soviet lessons from the region itself. Consequently, there were no Soviet images of regional actors balancing against radical change in the Caribbean or Latin America. Direct military interventions, therefore, are sufficient to cause both the presence and absence of deterrent lessons.

The counterproductive nature of direct military actions is further amplified by considering the kinds of deterrent lessons produced in the cases of

Soviet defeats in the Middle East that were the products of indirect American efforts. U.S. diplomatic efforts, combined with economic and military assistance to its allies, taught the Soviets both that the United States was credible *and* that regional actors would resist Soviet encroachments in the region. This is precisely the combination of lessons deterrence theory predicts will be produced by the challenger experiencing *military* defeats. But they are not. Instead, these optimal lessons are taught by actions *not* captured by the theory. This fact underlines the importance of expanding the scope of the theory to encompass these kinds of losses for the challenger.

It should be stressed that such an expansion of the theory does not at all violate the basic logic of deterrence, namely, to increase the perceived costs of adventurism to a potential challenger. Instead, this addition to the theory merely expands the range of potential costs to better identify the set of likely utility calculations to be made by any potential challenger. Certainly it is not at all counterintuitive to suggest that a defender's credibility to protect some interest may be a function of how well it protected that interest in the past, even though it did not use military power to do so. Likewise, it is not odd to assume that a challenger's assessment of the likelihood of successful expansionism in some region is partly dependent on how those actors in the region have behaved toward threats in the past, independent of the defender's past behavior. These types of calculations are what we witnessed in the Middle East cases.

American use of diplomatic and economic instruments was especially effective in teaching the Soviets deterrent lessons because it compelled Soviet decision makers to contemplate competing with the United States in an arena where the Soviets were hopelessly outclassed. While the Soviet Union was able to hold its own as a supplier of military hardware, it could promise its allies neither the level of diplomatic leverage on Israel nor the amount of economic largesse that the United States and the rest of the West could. This inferiority played an enormous role in convincing the Soviets of very high U.S. credibility in the region.

It could be argued that the Soviets were uniquely vulnerable to such deterrent instruments, as the Soviet Union was a unidimensional superpower —long on military might, short on economic wherewithal. But even so, it underlines the need for any defender to try to shift the competition with a challenger to areas in which the defender has unique advantages, rather than adopting strategies independent of the features of the opponent being faced.[1]

---

1. In fact, it could be strongly argued that deterrence theory, at some point, became precisely the wrong theory to guide American policy toward the Soviet Union. The theory's exclusive emphasis on military force simply prolonged the life expectancy of Soviet foreign policy successes. Had the United States adopted policies of economic bribery and diplomatic problem solving, it is very likely that the Soviets would have learned far sooner that their economic

One can imagine a number of possible dimensions of power on which a future challenger may be vulnerable. For example, it may advance some kind of expansionist, racialist, or chauvinistic ideology that can be effectively countered with a more pluralist set of ideals. The result would be to minimize the probability that the challenger will gain allies around the world. Or perhaps the challenger is not self-sufficient in some set of critical raw materials for which there is no ready substitute. It then would make sense to underscore that vulnerability.

In sum, the most powerful deterrent lessons are those taught by nonmilitary instruments. They are lessons that are the result of the autonomous actions of regional actors, rather than the military intervention of the defender. They are lessons that play on the inherent weaknesses of the challenger rather than ignore the features of the challenger. And they are lessons that deterrence theory omits from its domain, but that must be captured if the theory is to be made productive.

Finally, there is another category of losses that deterrence theory wrongly elides, defeats that occur completely independent of any actions by the United States or its allies. While these kinds of defeats do not enhance the defender's credibility, they do impart deterrent lessons about the prospects for future gains in the world. In the case of Ghana, for example, the lack of any cause for the overthrow of Nkrumah, other than events that had been occurring in Ghana itself over the previous decade, compelled Soviet analysts to consider a wide array of obstacles to future revolutionary developments in the Third World. Considering the evidence from Grenada, this sober reconsideration would not have happened had the United States overthrown Nkrumah by military force.

In conclusion, deterrence theory requires fundamental reconstruction in light of the findings here. The only category of losses it encompasses, direct military defeats, is neither necessary nor adequate to the task of teaching deterrent lessons. And the best teacher of deterrent lessons, indirect efforts by the defender, are not captured by the theory. It is clear that deterrence theory must be expanded to include the two varieties of losses it ignores.

## Soviet Foreign Policy Behavior and Soviet Lessons

Perhaps the single most potent criticism that could be leveled against this work would be that all these arguments about beliefs is just phenomenological

---

failings were a source of insurmountable weakness in the global competition with the West. In turn, this would have required a turn toward domestic economic reform earlier than 1985.

In some respects, I am following up on the suggestions made by Alexander George and Richard Smoke over fifteen years ago who pointed out the need for deterrence theory to define its scope more rigorously. See George and Smoke, *Deterrence*, 77–78.

nonsense. They are irrelevant unless it can be shown that Soviet behavior did not correlate with the predictions of deterrence theory. The latter would predict that after victories, the Soviets were encouraged to try for another victory; after defeats, they were less likely to challenge the status quo. If Soviet challenges to the status quo are not related to past outcomes, then we should expect a random distribution of Soviet behavior from 1965 to 1990. And a nearly random distribution is what the empirical record shows. That record is in the following chronology of Soviet gains and losses in the Third World, 1965–90.

| | | | |
|---|---|---|---|
| Dominican Republic | 1965 | Loss | |
| Indonesia | 1965 | Loss | + |
| Ghana | 1966 | Loss | + |
| Middle East | 1967 | Loss | + |
| Mali | 1968 | Loss | + |
| Peru | 1968 | Gain | 0 |
| Sudan | 1969 | Gain | 0 |
| Libya | 1969 | Gain | 0 |
| Somalia | 1969 | Gain | 0 |
| Bolivia | 1969 | Gain | 0 |
| Chile | 1970 | Gain | 0 |
| Jordan | 1970 | Loss | − |
| Sudan | 1971 | Loss | + |
| Bolivia | 1971 | Loss | + |
| Vietnam | 1973 | Gain | − |
| Chile | 1973 | Loss | − |
| Middle East | 1973 | Loss | + |
| Afghanistan | 1973 | Gain | 0 |
| Ethiopia | 1974 | Gain | 0 |
| Vietnam | 1975 | Gain | + |
| Angola | 1975 | Gain | + |
| Mozambique | 1975 | Gain | 0 |
| Peru | 1975 | Loss | − |
| Egypt | 1976 | Loss | + |
| Zaire | 1977 | Loss | + |
| Ethiopia | 1977 | Gain | − |
| Somalia | 1978 | Loss | − |
| Zaire | 1978 | Loss | + |
| Afghanistan | 1978 | Gain | 0 |
| Afghanistan | 1979 | Gain | + |
| Iran | 1979 | Gain | 0 |
| Nicaragua | 1979 | Gain | 0 |

| Grenada | 1979 | Gain | 0 |
| Zimbabwe | 1980 | Loss | − |
| El Salvador | 1981 | Loss | + |
| Grenada | 1983 | Loss | + |
| Mozambique | 1984 | Loss | + |
| Nicaragua | 1990 | Loss | + |

The plus signs (+) indicate cases that are consistent with the predictions of deterrence theory. For example, the failure of the Soviet Union to prevent the removal of Sukarno in Indonesia is consistent with deterrence theory's prediction that after a defeat, in this case the U.S. intervention in the Dominican Republic, a challenger will be less likely to try to score a victory against the defender. Hence, the overthrow of Nkrumah in Ghana in 1966, the military debacle for Soviet Arab allies in the June War of 1967, and the removal of Keita in Mali in 1968 are each consistent with the predictions of the theory.

The zeroes (0) identify cases that neither confirm nor disconfirm deterrence theory. For example, the gains from Peru in 1968 to Chile in 1970 were not the product of any Soviet actions. Therefore, they cannot be considered confirmation of deterrence theory's prediction that victories for a challenger beget more such victories. Had the Soviets actually been a party to one of these victories, as they were, for example, in Vietnam in 1973, then deterrence theory would receive confirmation.

The minus signs (−) denote cases that are inconsistent with the predictions of deterrence theory. For example, the Soviet loss in Jordan in 1970 is inconsistent with the theory's prediction that after a victory, a challenger will be emboldened to seek future victories, so the Soviet Union should not have sat by while its allies—Syria and the PLO—were humiliated in the Middle East.

In raw numbers, deterrence theory's predictions are confirmed in seventeen cases, disconfirmed in seven, and moot in thirteen. It is very interesting to note that over half of the confirmations are accounted for by the string of losses from 1965 to 1968 and from 1981 to 1990. But over two-thirds of the Soviet victories are stochastic, unrelated to either previous defeats or victories. These findings imply that deterrence theory is much more accurate about losses begetting losses than it is about victories leading to more gains.

In sum, deterrence theory does not receive strong confirmation from the empirical record of the last twenty-five years. If we remove from consideration Soviet gains that were achieved without any Soviet effort, we get an ambiguous evidentiary record. Deterrence theory is validated by the string of losses from 1965 to 1973, because presumably the Soviets could have prevented them, but did not because of lessons learned from prior defeats. But the victory in Vietnam in 1973 disconfirms the theory, as does the Soviet failure, only seven months later, to prevent the ouster of Allende in Chile. The Soviet failure in the Middle East in 1973 either validates the theory, because it follows on the heels of its loss in Chile, or is inconsistent, because of the presumed effects of its victory in Southeast Asia earlier in the year. It is impossible to know a priori which outcome deterrence theory would assume governs here.

Similarly, is the fall of Saigon in 1975 inconsistent with the lessons the Soviets should have learned from their defeat in the Middle East eighteen months prior? Or, instead, should the theory be considered validated because the Paris peace accord is the salient benchmark for Soviet perceptions? I think it is safe to say that the theory itself cannot tell us which event is determinative. If the theory is confirmed by the Soviet success in Angola barely a year after the fall of Saigon, then it is certainly disconfirmed by the failure of the Soviets to prevent the loss of Egypt only months later.

As in the case of Vietnam and the Middle East, should the Soviet intervention on the Horn in 1977–78 be considered a disconfirmation of the theory, since it occurred on the heels of its loss in Egypt, or a confirmation, because of the MPLA victory in Angola? If it is considered a confirmation of the theory, then Soviet losses in Somalia and Zaire in quick succession invalidate the theory. Likewise, the Soviet invasion of Afghanistan in 1979 can be thought of as vindicating deterrence theory because it occurred after events in Ethiopia and Iran, or as an invalidation, if we assume the Soviets were focused on their losses in Somalia and Zaire.

The bottom line is that Soviet gains are neither necessary nor sufficient for Soviets to mount additional challenges in the Third World. Soviet losses are neither necessary nor sufficient to result in Soviet tolerance of more losses. Finally, Soviet views of a highly credible United States, willing and able to resist revolutionary progress in the Third World, are neither necessary nor sufficient to deter Soviet adventurism.[2]

## A Modified Version of Deterrence Theory: Less Is Often More, So Long as You Have Enough

The findings in this book strongly suggest the application of Mies van de Rohe's architectural dictum "Less is more" to another, quite different, domain. Teaching *rational* challengers deterrent lessons requires demonstrations of capability and will, as the traditional theory prescribes. But it is a particular kind of deterrent pedagogy that is called for. While it is essential to

---

2. This finding is consistent with both previous empirical and theoretical work on deterrence theory. See, for example, Lebow, *Between Peace and War*; George and Smoke, *Deterrence*; Achen and Snidal, "Rational Deterrence Theory"; and Paul Huth and Bruce Russett, "Testing Deterrence Theory: Rigor Makes a Difference," *World Politics*, 42, no. 4 (July 1990): 466–501.

have a substantial military force available to protect strategic interests, peripheral values are best protected through nonmilitary means. The defender gains a reputation for resolve and capacity by using its diplomatic, political, and economic resources. It need not use military force to make the challenger suffer losses.

Indeed, the trick is to do as little as is necessary to defeat the challenger. This is contrary to traditional deterrence logic that the defender should demonstrate as much capacity as possible in achieving its victories over the defender. But this logic is faulty. The more capacity the defender uses to achieve a victory, the *less* capable it appears to the challenger. If instead, the defender only uses a little capacity to achieve the same objective, the defender appears much more capable. The defender should impress its adversary with the apparent ease with which the defender is able to dispatch with any of the challenger's allies.

Moreover, employments of the military instrument positively degrade deterrent lessons. The challenger focuses so single-mindedly on what the defender is doing, it ignores the fact that regional actors are also uniting against it. Moreover, the defender's involvement in the overthrow of some ally of the challenger allows the latter to avoid coming to grips with the internal causes of its ally's ouster. This permits unwarranted optimism on the part of the challenger, and makes it feel the world is more receptive to adventurism than actually is the case.

But this does not at all imply that the defender can get away with doing nothing. Beyond the strategies in the periphery discussed above, the defender must have an obvious ability to defend its interests in strategic areas of the globe. The salience of absolute American military capabilities to Soviet calculations of American credibility cannot be overstated. But these were not calculations based on American use of these assets in third world arenas, but rather concerned the conventional and nuclear forces the United States had dedicated to the central front in Europe, Northeast Asia, and the Persian Gulf.

The defender can get away with doing nothing in one area. Deterrence theory needs to be expanded to capture the deterrent value in losses that affect the challenger, despite inaction on the part of the defender. Certainly, as we have seen, these losses figure in the challenger's calculations as to the value of future efforts at expansion in the periphery. While the addition of this class of cases would make deterrence theory more complete, it hardly completes the theory. A comprehensive theory would take into account many other feasible inputs into a challenger's decision-making calculus. These would include, but not be limited to domestic political incentives or disincentives to expand; economic rewards or punishments from expansionism; bureaucratic, institutional, and organizational imperatives either for or against expansionism; and pressure or restraint from one's allies elsewhere in the world to expand.

The above emendations of deterrence theory all assume a rational challenger. But the theory is inadequate if it cannot encompass the universe of possible challengers, though of course, the presumption must go to rationality. Regardless of who the challenger might be, it is critical to examine how that state is assessing the defender's credibility and the nature of regional dynamics in the Third World. Even if the challenger applies rational attribution processes, one must observe this to know for sure. If, however, the challenger uses bounded rationality and only operates with a limited menu of critical variables when assessing the world, it is crucial that the defender know what these variables are before designing a policy to teach this challenger the right set of lessons.

It is equally important to identify accurately a challenger operating with a peculiar belief system. As we know, there are four possible varieties to this challenger. It may be like the Marxist-Leninists of the Soviet Union, who believed that their ideology was universal, but that its propagation would be fiercely resisted by the imperialists. This required a modicum of deterrence, as noted above, but nothing like what was prescribed by deterrence theory. The ideology for which deterrence theory was designed is one that assumes both the universality of its own ideology and the inherent weakness of its opponent. This would be a very dangerous challenger, indeed, and would have required the strongest deterrent measures, had such a challenger existed. The final type of belief system assumes an irresolute adversary but believes its ideology is only applicable to some select subset of humanity. This challenger requires the strongest deterrent measures only if it occupies territories of strategic interest to the challenger.

A comprehensive theory of deterrence cannot get away with simply *assuming* what kind of opponent the defender is facing. A defender cannot deter unless it discovers what kinds of deterrent instruments are most respected by the challenger—indeed, if any are either necessary or effective.

The findings of this book look both back and ahead. The traditional version of deterrence theory provided a fundamentally misguided basis for American foreign policy in the Third World in the postwar years. It prescribed that the United States take unnecessary and extremely costly actions, such as fighting the Vietnam War. It ignored the deterrent power contained in nonmilitary assets, such as management of the Middle East through diplomatic intervention and economic and military aid. A revised theory for the future should recognize the strengths available to the defender and demand an accurate identification of the essential features of the challenger. A failure to abide by either one of these requirements will result in wasted lives and treasure.

# Appendixes

# Appendix A: The Salience of the Periphery and Its Relationship to Soviet Perceptions of U.S. Allied Behavior

In the first instance, Soviets had to have paid attention to the Third World for the assumptions of deterrence theory to be valid. Soviets must have analyzed events in the periphery when they made judgments about U.S. credibility, allied behavior, and regional dynamics. The evidence presented below demonstrates that in general the periphery had very little salience to Soviet observers in making judgments on these issues. Soviets primarily gauged U.S. credibility from Washington's policies on strategic arms control and detente with the Soviet bloc in general, from U.S. policy toward China, and from its level of military spending and force deployments. Soviets assessed the bandwagoning or balancing propensities of U.S. strategic allies in Europe and Japan by their attitudes toward the same issues: arms control, detente, relations with Eastern Europe and China, and levels of military effort. Only in the area of regional dynamics did Soviets predict the possibility of falling dominoes on the basis of events in the Third World.

Below I present evidence to support these general points. I provide quantitative data on the relative salience of the universe of cases, justifying my case selection in the process. I then provide support for the argument that deterrence theory has mistakenly assumed that the continued balancing of U.S. strategic allies against the Soviet Union is contingent on U.S. behavior in the periphery.[1]

## The Peripheral Salience of the Periphery

The Soviet assessment of U.S. credibility was derived primarily from strategic U.S. behavior, not from U.S. conduct in the Third World. This is not a counterintuitive finding since it is hard to imagine why the leaders of any country would pay more attention to the behavior of their main adversary in unimportant areas of the globe than in areas and on issues that are absolutely vital to the sovereignty, territorial integrity,

---

1. Strictly speaking, I am not testing the precise assumption of deterrence theory, since I am looking at *Soviet* perceptions of allied attitudes, not at the allied attitudes themselves. This does not violate the rules for testing deterrence theory. In fact, it is a more valid test in that what deterrence theory really implies is that the Soviet Union would have benefited from changes in allied behavior after U.S. losses. By determining whether in fact Soviets themselves perceived such advantageous situations we can submit the theory to a true test of its propositions.

and physical security of their country.[2] From 1973 to 1988, the Soviet observers made 786 assessments of U.S. credibility. They made half again as many inferences based on strategic U.S. behavior than on U.S. behavior in the Third World.[3]

Among the thirty-eight victories and defeats incurred by the Soviet Union since 1965, some of them had far greater salience to Soviet observers than others. In table A-1, I show this relative salience.

From 1965 to 1990, the forty-five Soviets used these thirty-eight cases 2,242 times when making inferences about the three components of deterrence theory.[4] As can be seen from the data in table A-1, several of the cases were far more important than others, and many had only negligible influence on Soviet perceptions. For example, the series of defeats the Soviets suffered in the Middle East in the Six Day War of 1967, the October War of 1973, and then the loss of its Egyptian ally constituted a highly salient event. Of the 1489 inferences made by Soviet observers from 1967 to 1985 about U.S. credibility, allied behavior, and regional dynamics, fully 40 percent of them were based on these Middle East cases.

There appears to be no correlation between the salience of the case and either the level of U.S. involvement or its status for the Soviet Union. The most salient set of cases for the Soviets were their losses in the Middle East. While their gains in Vietnam, Afghanistan, and Nicaragua were also influential, so too was their loss in the Dominican Republic. While direct U.S. involvement was highly salient in Vietnam and, to a much lesser extent, in the Dominican Republic, it had very little influence in Grenada. Indirect and no U.S. involvement were also randomly distributed along the salience continuum.

I based the case selection for this book on both the need to include variation in outcome and level of U.S. involvement, and the desirability of presenting the events that were most salient to Soviet observers. Hence, with a minor exception, I chose the most salient cases in each of the six circumstances. Vietnam, the Dominican Republic, and Grenada are included by default. Soviet gains in Angola, Ethiopia, and Afghanistan are the most influential cases with indirect U.S. involvement. Soviet losses in the Middle East are far and away the most salient cases with indirect U.S. actions. Iran and Nicaragua are the most salient cases of Soviet gains with no U.S. involvement.

---

2. Again, I want to stress that deterrence theory assumptions never were that a challenger would *ignore* these strategic indicators, but only that along with considering these, it would pay attention as well to the defender's behavior in unimportant areas of the world. It is this latter assumption that is undermined by the findings here.

3. Four hundred eighty-four (62 percent) of the total were based on strategic U.S. behavior; 317 (40 percent) were at least partially founded on U.S. behavior in the periphery. For a complete discussion of these figures, see Hopf, "Deterrence Theory."

4. I have examined every article and speech given by these forty-five Soviets that appear in *Letopis Zhurnalnykh Statei* and *Letopis Gazetnykh Statei* for the years from 1965 to 1990. These references are the two main indices of the Soviet press and cover hundreds of Soviet newspapers and journals. In the several thousand speeches and articles that I have read, these forty-five Soviet observers wrote or spoke of lessons from the thirty-eight events in this study a total of 2,242 times. What this means in practice is they mentioned the event and then went on to evaluate U.S. credibility, allied behavior, or regional dynamics based, at least in part, on their interpretation of this event.

**TABLE A-1.** The Relative Salience of Soviet Victories and Defeats in the Third World, 1965–90

| Loss or Gain for Soviets | Cases | % of Total Inferences | N | Level of U.S. Involvement |
|---|---|---|---|---|
| Loss | Middle East | 40 | 1,489 | Indirect |
| Gain | Vietnam | 39 | 342 | Direct |
| Gain | Afghanistan | 19 | 1,368 | None-indirect |
| Gain-loss | Nicaragua | 19 | 753 | None-indirect |
| Loss | Dominican Republic | 13 | 373 | Direct |
| Gain | Angola | 12 | 1,710 | Indirect |
| Gain | Iran | 12 | 615 | None |
| Gain-loss | Chile | 9 | 874 | None-indirect |
| Loss | Mali | 9 | 532 | None |
| Gain | Ethiopia | 8 | 615 | None-indirect |
| Loss | Zimbabwe | 7 | 615 | Indirect |
| Gain-loss | Grenada | 7 | 374 | None-direct |
| Loss | El Salvador | 5 | 989 | Indirect |
| Gain-loss | Somalia | 5 | 615 | None-indirect |
| Loss | Ghana | 5 | 532 | None |
| Gain-loss | Mozambique | 3 | 1,331 | None-indirect |
| Gain-loss | Peru | 3 | 874 | None-none |
| Gain-loss | Sudan | 3 | 532 | None-none |
| Gain | Libya | 3 | 532 | None |
| Loss | Zaire | 2 | 615 | Indirect |
| Loss | Indonesia | 2 | 373 | None |
| Gain-loss | Bolivia | 1 | 874 | None-none |

My only deviation from the choice of the most salient examples is the case of Ghana as representative of a Soviet loss with no U.S. action. While Mali is more salient, too many of the inferences from that case were made by one Soviet observer. In the case of Ghana, a variety of Soviets learned lessons from Nkrumah's overthrow, and they continued doing so years after the coup. The effects of Mali on Soviet perceptions were far weaker.

## The Irrelevance of U.S. Policy in the Periphery to Soviet Perceptions of Allied Behavior

In order for deterrence theory's assumption about allied behavior to be accurate, Soviet observers should have assessed the balancing and bandwagoning propensities of U.S. allies according to the latter's attitudes toward U.S. actions in the Third World. Since Soviets did not base their views of U.S. allies on U.S. behavior in the periphery, this assumption of deterrence theory is disconfirmed. Instead Soviets estimated the probable future behavior of U.S. allies by looking at the latter's attitudes toward arms control, U.S. military programs, detente in Europe and globally, and relations with

China. For example, from 1975 to 1988, members of the Soviet party leadership and the military and foreign policy elite made 188 assessments of U.S. allied attitudes. This was a period that included lessons from the Middle East, Vietnam, Afghanistan, Nicaragua, Angola, and Iran, that is, a period that covered six of the seven most salient cases. Despite the fact that these were the third world events of greatest influence on Soviet perceptions, in only 16 of these 188 lessons did Soviets link U.S. behavior in a case to allied attitudes toward the United States.[5]

Furthermore, in the 16 cases in which Soviet observers did connect U.S. behavior in the periphery to allied attitudes, the lessons they inferred were precisely contrary to those predicted by deterrence theory. If these assumptions were accurate, then after Soviet gains, Soviets should have seen U.S. allies as predisposed to bandwagon; after Soviet losses, they should have described U.S. allies as balancers. The lessons Soviets actually did infer were not consistent with these predictions. After Soviet losses, such as in Grenada in 1983, Soviets discussed allied opposition to the intervention and to any future repetitions of such actions by Washington.[6] After Soviet gains, such as in Angola and Ethiopia, Soviets noted how European members of NATO had recommitted themselves to prevent further revolutionary change in Africa, citing the two interventions in Zaire in 1977 and 1978, and the 1979 Lancaster House agreements on majority rule for Zimbabwe as examples of such balancing behavior.[7] Soviets noted similar allied balancing by China, European NATO members, Saudi Arabia, Egypt, and others after their intervention in Afghanistan.[8]

## Summary

The evidence in this appendix shows that deterrence theory's assumptions about the role of the periphery in generating lessons for Soviet observers are greatly misguided. Deterrence theory greatly exaggerates the role of the periphery in generating a challenger's perception of the defender's resolve and capabilities and the probable behavior of the defender's allies. Since Soviets paid much less attention to U.S. behavior in the Third World than in strategic areas when inferring lessons about U.S. credibility, U.S. efforts to teach Soviets lessons through dealing them defeats in the periphery were largely irrelevant to the task of deterrence. Similarly, deterrence theory's assumption about the connection between U.S. behavior in the Third World and Soviet perceptions of the attitudes of U.S. allies is also wrong. Soviets either did not infer lessons about U.S. allies or inferred lessons that contradicted the predictions of the theory.

---

5. For a detailed discussion of Soviet assessments of U.S. allied attitudes after each of the thirty-eight cases, see Hopf, "Deterrence Theory."

6. For example, see Aleksandr Yakovlev, "U.S. Policy of Intervention: A Challenge to UN Principles," *IA*, February 1984, 26–34. For further evidence regarding the lessons of Grenada, see Hopf, "Deterrence Theory," chap. 3.

7. For example, see Brezhnev's speech at the Sixteenth Trade Union Congress, *Pravda* March 22, 1977, 1–3. For additional lessons from Angola and Ethiopia that diametrically contradict deterrence theory, see Hopf, "Deterrence Theory," chap. 6.

8. See, for example, Ustinov, "Nemerknushchii Podvig" (Immortal Feat), *Pravda*, September 2, 1980, 3–4. For further evidence contrary to deterrence theory derived from the Afghanistan case, see Hopf, "Deterrence Theory," chap. 6.

# Appendix B: Representative Examples of Soviet Lessons

Under each heading below, I offer examples of each type of Soviet lesson. In doing so, I hope to show the reader how I assessed and coded the articles and speeches made by the forty-eight Soviets I analyzed for this study. Even these examples are not fully satisfactory, as the reader should read the entire speech or article to get a sense of the overall argument being made, and the context in which the lessons appear. I understandably do not offer reproductions of complete articles and speeches.

## High U.S. Credibility

Despite the recognition of the principles of peaceful coexistence . . . , American ruling circles continue to see military force as a most important foundation of their foreign policy. Moreover, one can see that the events of 1975, in particular the collapse of the puppet Saigon regime, led even to a certain increase in the militaristic sentiments and tendencies in the thinking of certain circles influencing American foreign policy. (Genrikh Trofimenko, "Evoliutsiya Voenno-Politicheskoi Strategii SShA Posle Vtoroi Mirovoi Voiny" [The Evolution of American Military-Political Strategy Since World War II], *VI*, March 1976, 64–65, 80–90)

There is now an inclination to see military power as the path to the resolution of international problems. American foreign policy failures, particularly in Southeast Asia, are causing a reversion to cold war thinking. . . . They cause some circles, especially those associated with the military-industrial complex, to call for the United States to take responsibility "for maintaining world order" by "containing" the Soviet Union. (Georgii Arbatov, "O Sovetsko-Amerikanskikh Otnosheniyakh" [On Soviet-American Relations], *Pravda*, April 2, 1976, 4–5)

[There are two approaches in American foreign policy toward the Third World]: direct subordination to broad anti-Soviet goals or the more flexible tactic with substantial bourgeois-reformist content, oriented at sustaining capitalist relations. The Reagan administration has chosen the first approach. According to its calculations, such an approach . . . allows an expansion in the front of the anti-Soviet, antisocialist campaign and guarantees an expedient cover for neo-colonialism and unties the hands of the United States with respect to regimes it does not like. An example of this tactic was the invasion of Grenada, realized with the accompaniment of false propaganda about the alleged conversion of this island into a Cuban-Soviet base. (Karen Brutents, "Osvobodivshiesya Strany v Nachale 80-x Godov" [Liberated Countries at the Beginning of the 1980s], *Kommunist*, 1984, no. 3, 103–13)

It must be borne in mind that the American president is vested with well-nigh monarchical powers. What can Congress do? Essentially, it can only withhold appropriations. You might say that this is a great deal. I do not agree. The invasion of Grenada showed that the president can start a war and present Congress with a fait accompli. Recall how Hitler engineered a border incident in Poland in 1939, accused Poland of aggression and started the war. What can Congress do if it is faced with the alternatives of voicing no confidence in the president or voting for a war already underway? You must not forget that Congress does not consist only of honest, upright humanists who respect international law. There is more likely to be a paucity of these. (Sergo Mikoyan, "Latin America: New Upsurge," *New Times*, 1985, no. 16, 18–21)

Even today, Washington leaders have peculiar interpretations of history. The failures of Truman and Dulles, the defeats in Vietnam, Iran, Central America, and Africa are explained by "inconsistency" in the use of American power to achieve overwhelming military superiority, by the "absence of resolve" to go to the limit, right up to using nuclear weapons. . . . Speaking a year ago, Reagan said he would have no lack of resolve. . . . At the time, the sense of these words were not very well grasped by Americans themselves. . . . But one must assume they are now. (Valentin Falin, "Politicheskoe Bezdorozhe" [Political Impasse], *Pravda*, January 20, 1982, 4)

[In response to the loss of the shah, the United States has] begun to openly declare a readiness to resort even to direct armed interference with the aim of maintaining the status quo. Both Brown and Brzezinski have made it known recently that the United States will take measures, including the use of its armed forces, to defend its interests in Saudi Arabia. . . . It is obvious that we are speaking of the . . . return of the United States to . . . direct methods of colonialism, of a rebirth of gunboat diplomacy. (Evgenii Primakov, "Blizhnii Vostok: Dalneishaya Militarizatsiya Politiki SShA" [The Middle East: The Further Militarization of U.S. Policy], *Kommunist*, 1980, no. 9, 105–15)

The eminent public opinion researchers, Yankelovich and Kagan, interpret Reagan's victory as a mandate from the American electorate to pursue a hard-line policy, right up to the use of force with the aim of "raising American prestige abroad." (Genrikh Trofimenko, "Osnovnye Postulaty Vneshnei Politiki SShA i Sudby Razryadki" [The Main Postulates of U.S. Foreign Policy and the Fate of Detente], *SShA*, July 1981, 3–14)

## Low U.S. Credibility

In conditions of a new upsurge of the anti-imperialist, revolutionary liberation movement on the [Latin American] continent, the United States did not opt to openly interfere in the political struggle in Chile and recognized the Allende government. (Irina Zorina, "Kharakhter i Perspektivy Revoliutsionnovo Protsessa v Chile" [The Character and Prospects of the Revolutionary Process in Chile], *MEIMO*, December 1971, 54–63)

American imperialists are striving, with the assistance of their political agents and social partners, to prevent developing countries from making any changes that might threaten their interests. That such a policy is historically foredoomed, even if it can make some headway for awhile, is quite obvious. Somoza's dictatorial regime . . . seemed unshakable to its American patrons, but it was swept away by a national uprising in a matter of months. (Vladimir Iordansky, "The Policy of Neocolonialism in Action," *IA*, June 1981, 85–90)

## Supportive Global Allies

For example, a year after the MPLA gained power in Angola, Brezhnev spoke of how American NATO allies "had interfered in the internal affairs of Zaire" and launched a "slanderous campaign" against Angola (Speech at Sixteenth Trade Union Congress, *Pravda*, March 22, 1977, 3–4). Primakov also saw balancing by American allies in Zaire. ("Neocolonialism: Essence, Forms, Limits," *IA*, November 1978, 66–71).

Chernenko saw Chinese participation with the United States in the war against the MPLA as evidence that the PRC had become a "reserve of imperialist forces in their attacks on socialism" ("Leninist Strategy of Peace in Action," *IA*, May 1976, 3–12).

Soon after the Soviet victory on the Horn, Brezhnev again remarked on NATO's "bloody interference" in support of the Mobutu government's response to the second Shaba uprising in Zaire (speech at a dinner with General Secretary Husak in Prague, *Pravda*, June 1, 1978). See also his speech at a dinner for the president of Madagascar, Didier Ratsiraka, *Pravda*, June 30, 1978). See also Brutents, "Neokolonializm na Poroge 80-x Godov: 'Modernizatsiya' Strategii" (Neocolonialism on the Eve of the 1980s: Modernization of Strategy), part 2, *MEIMO*, July 1979, 81–94.

Ustinov wrote of Chinese balancing with the United States against the Soviet intervention in Afghanistan ("Nemerknushchii Podvig" [Unfading Feat], *Pravda*, September 2, 1980, 3–4).

Ulyanvosky saw British, West German, Saudi, and Chinese support for the mujahideen ("Razvitie Revoliutsionnovo Protsessa v Afganistane" [Development of Revolutionary Process in Afghanistan], *MEIMO*, August 1983, 16–31).

Ogarkov wrote of NATO governments supporting American policy against Nicaragua, even as the citizens of these countries were increasingly opposed to American support for the Contras ("Nemerknushchaya Slava Sovetskovo Oruzhiya" [Unfading Glory of Soviet Armaments], *KVS*, 1984, no. 21, 22–26).

## Unreliable Global Allies

There is a growing tendency among many American allies to keep out of the adventures of American militarists which threaten to aggravate the international situation. (Andrei Kokoshin, "Naval Power in U.S. Strategic Plans," *IA*, April 1973, 56–62) '

The United States has found itself in total isolation. Its policies have been condemned even by the representatives of some major Western countries and NATO allies who have expressed indignation at the American aggression against Grenada. (Aleksandr Yakovlev, "U.S. Policy of Intervention: A Challenge to UN Principles," *IA*, February 1984, 26–34)

West Germany's justified fear of being left without oil for a long time compelled even the closest American ally in NATO to refuse to let the United States use its airports for transferring arms to Israel [during the October 1973 war]. Moreover, these European allies protested against [the American nuclear alert.] (Rostislav Ulyanovsky, "Energeticheskii Krizis i Borba Osvobodivshikhsya Stran za Ekonomicheskoe Ravnopravie" [The Energy Crisis and the Struggle of Liberated Countries for Economic Justice], *NAIA*, 1976, no. 2, 19–32)

## Regional Balancing

Latin American Christian Democracy in the end of the 1970s, possibly for the first time, took progressive, democratic positions when it, in general, supported the struggle of the Nicaraguan people against the Somoza dictatorship. However, victory in Nicaragua and the direction in which its people chose to develop the revolution have put Christian Democrats on their guard, especially their right-conservative wing. And already Christian Democrats have responded differently to events in El Salvador than to events in Nicaragua, every way possible hindering the development of the solidarity movement with the Salvadorans. (Iurii Korolev, "Revoliutsionnye Protsessy i Voprosy Sotsialno-Politicheskovo Razvitiya v Latin-skoi Amerike" [Revolutionary Processes and Questions of Socio-Political Development in Latin America], *LA*, April 1981, 59–64)

Through financial and economic integration with imperialism, they [Gulf oil exporters] hope to prevent a social explosion . . . as well as to suppress or corrupt the national liberation movement. . . . Iran indicates, however, that this model of social development is not as reliable or effective as its architects think. However, it would be wrong to underestimate the possibilities that the energy crisis of the early '70s and the ensuing numerous oil price increases gave to some oil-exporting countries in terms of these possibilities. (Nodari Simoniya, "Newly-Free Countries: Problems of Development," *IA*, May 1982, 83–91)

I recently was in Kuwait and met with leaders of this state. They, in particular, said that if Iranian forces cross the Iraqi border . . . —and Iranian soldiers may aspire for this in order to justify the sacrifices they made during their military operations—then a situation will be created wherein some Gulf countries may appeal to the United States for "aid." If this happens, Americans, "on a legal basis," can send the RDF [Rapid Deployment Force] to the Gulf. . . . It is not impossible that the next step will be an American miltary presence in the Gulf. (Evgenii Primakov, "Kogda Voinu Nazyvaiut Mirom" [When They Call War Peace], *LG*, July 7, 1982, 14)

## Regional Dominoes

While trying to "roll back the communist wave" in Asia, American imperialism . . . caused a colossal growth in anti-Americanism in the region, the expresssion of which is the collapse of SEATO and increasing criticisms of the actions of Washington by India, Sri Lanka, Burma, the Phillipines, Thailand, Australia, and others. The defeat . . . in fact did lead to a "chain reaction" in the sense that Southeast Asian countries and then countries in the entire region began to increasingly energetically raise doubts about the expediency of maintaining close military ties with the United States and are leaning toward pursuing policies independent of Washington. (Trofimenko, "Evoliutsiya Voenno-Politicheskoi")

That which is happening in Iran means not only the fall of an antipopular regime. At the same time this is a most serious defeat for neocolonialism. . . . One can say that this is a collapse of precisely the model of development that imperialism insistently tries to impose on liberated states. In fact, in many respects, Iran was a kind of "proving ground" on which neocolonialist strategy was tested. There, dependent capitalism was affirmed; foreign monopolies got almost unlimited freedom; an authoritarian dictatorship dominated. A policy of a close military-political alliance with imperialism was pursued. The regime assumed the role of subimperialist center and gendarme in the region of the Near East and Persian Gulf. . . . Already now there is every reason to think that the lessons of Iranian events foretell gloomy prospects for contemporary neocolonialism. These events show just how vulnerable is the neocolonialist structure. (Karen Brutents, "Neo-kolonializm")

# Bibliography

I have divided the bibliography into three sections. The first section contains works on international relations and deterrence theory and its critics. The second section comprises works on various psychological theories. The third, and by far largest, section consists of primary Soviet sources.

In this third section, I provide entries only for articles in journals and newspapers, not speeches in daily newspapers. For the latter, I provide the range of dates for the newspapers consulted for each Soviet author.

## International Relations and Deterrence Theory

Achen, Christopher H., and Duncan Snidal. "Rational Deterrence Theory and Comparative Case Studies." *World Politics* 41, no. 2 (January 1989): 143–69.

Allison, Graham T. *Essence of Decision: Explaining the Cuban Missile Crisis*. Boston: Little, Brown, and Co., 1971.

Blum, Douglas W. "The Soviet Foreign Policy Belief System: Beliefs, Politics, and Foreign Policy Outcomes." *International Studies Quarterly* 37, no. 1 (December 1993): 373–94.

Bueno de Mesquita, Bruce. *The War Trap*. New Haven: Yale University Press, 1981.

Checkel, Jeff. "Ideas, Institutions, and the Gorbachev Foreign Policy Revolution." *World Politics* 45 (January 1993): 271–300

Davis, Robert H. Review of Grimsted, "Archives and Manuscript Repositories in the USSR, Ukraine, and Moldavia." *Slavic and East European Journal* 34 (Winter 1990): 520–22.

Eckstein, Harry. "Case Study and Theory in Political Science." In *Handbook of Political Science*, vol. 7, ed. Fred Greenstein and Nelson W. Polsby, 80–121. Reading, MA: Addison-Wesley Publishing Co., 1975.

Evangelista, Matthew. "Transnational Alliances and Soviet Demilitarization." Paper prepared for the Council on Economic Priorities Project on Military Expenditure and Economic Priorities, October 1990.

———. "Economic Constraints on Soviet Grand Strategy: When Do They Constrain?" 1991. Typescript.

Fearon, James D. "Deterrence and the Spiral Model: The Role of Costly Signals in Crisis Bargaining." Paper presented at the 1990 annual meeting of the American Political Science Association, San Francisco, August 30–September 2, 1990.

Gaddis, John. *Strategies of Containment*. New York: Oxford University Press, 1982.

George, Alexander L. *Propaganda Analysis: A Study of Inferences Made from Nazi Propaganda in World War II*. Westport, Conn.: Greenwood Press, 1973.

George, Alexander L., and Richard Smoke. *Deterrence in American Foreign Policy: Theory and Practice*. New York: Columbia University Press, 1974.

Grimsted, Patricia Kennedy. *A Handbook for Archival Research in the USSR*. New York: International Research and Exchange Board, 1989.

Hopf, Theodore G. "Deterrence Theory and Soviet Foreign Policy: Soviet Lessons from Their Victories and Defeats in the Third World." Ph.D. diss., Columbia University, 1990.

————. "Polarity, The Offense Defense Balance, and War." *American Political Science Review* 85, no. 2 (June 1991): 475–94.

Hosoya, Chihiro. "Miscalculations in Deterrent Policy: Japan-U.S. Relations, 1938-41." *Journal of Peace Research* 2 (1968): 97–115.

Huth, Paul. *Extended Deterrence and the Prevention of War*. New Haven: Yale University Press, 1988.

Huth, Paul, and Bruce M. Russett, "What Makes Deterrence Work." *World Politics* 35, no. 4 (July 1984): 496–526.

————. "Testing Deterrence Theory: Rigor Makes a Difference." *World Politics* 42, no. 4 (July 1990): 466–501.

Ikle, Fred Charles. *How Nations Negotiate*. New York: Harper and Row, 1964.

Jervis, Robert. *The Logic of Images in International Relations*. Princeton: Princeton University Press, 1970.

————. "Deterrence Theory Revisited." *World Politics* 31, no. 2 (January 1979): 289–324.

————. "Deterrence and Perception." *International Security* 7, no. 3 (Winter 1982/83): 1–34.

Jervis, Robert, Richard Ned Lebow, and Janice Gross Stein, eds. *Psychology and Deterrence*. Baltimore: Johns Hopkins University Press, 1985.

Jervis, Robert, and Jack Snyder, eds. *Dominoes and Bandwagons: Strategic Beliefs and Superpower Competition in the Eurasian Rimland*. New York: Oxford University Press, 1990.

Kahn, Herman. *On Thermonuclear War*. Princeton: Princeton University Press, 1960.

Kanwisher, Nancy. "Cognitive Heuristics and American Security Policy." *Journal of Conflict Resolution* 33, no. 4 (December 1989): 652–75.

Kennan, George F. *Memoirs, 1925-1950*. Boston: Little, Brown, and Co., 1967.

Khong, Yuen Foong. *Analogies at War: Korea, Munich, Dien Bien Phu, and the Vietnam Decisions of 1965*. Princeton: Princeton University Press, 1992.

Lebow, Richard Ned. *Between Peace and War*. Baltimore: Johns Hopkins University Press, 1981.

Machiavelli, Niccolo. *Discourses*. London: Routledge and Paul, 1950.

Maxwell, Stephen. *Rationality and Deterrence*. Adelphi paper no. 50. London: International Institute for Strategic Studies, 1969.

Mendelson, Sarah E. "Internal Battles and External Wars: Politics, Learning, and the Soviet Withdrawal from Afghanistan." *World Politics* 45, no. 3 (April 1993): 327–60.

Mercer, Jonathan L. "Attribution Error and the Credibility of Threat and Promise." Columbia University, March 1989. Typescript.

————. "Broken Promises and Unfulfilled Threats: Resolve, Reputation, and Deterrence Theory." Ph.D. diss., Columbia University, 1992.

Rivera, David R. "Ronald Reagan, Economic Decline, and the Collapse of the Soviet Empire: Testing Prominent Explanations of the Wane of Soviet Expansionism." University of Michigan, April 1994. Typescript.

Russett, Bruce B. "The Calculus of Deterrence." *Journal of Conflict Resolution* 7, no. 2 (March 1963): 97–109.

————. "Pearl Harbor: Deterrence Theory and Decision Theory." *Journal of Peace Research* 4, no. 2 (1967): 89–106.

Schelling, Thomas. *The Strategy of Conflict.* Cambridge: Harvard University Press, 1960.

————. *Arms and Influence.* New Haven: Yale University Press, 1966.

Snyder, Glenn. *Deterrence and Defense.* Princeton: Princeton University Press, 1961.

Snyder, Glenn, and Paul Diesing. *Conflict among Nations.* Princeton: Princeton University Press, 1977.

Snyder, Jack. *Myths of Empire: Domestic Politics and Strategic Ideology.* Ithaca, N.Y.: Cornell University Press, 1991.

Thucydides. *The Peloponnesian War.* The Crawley trans. rev., with an intro. by T. E. Wick. New York: The Modern Library, 1982.

Tsebelis, George. *Nested Games: Rational Choice in Comparative Politics.* Berkeley: University of California Press, 1990.

Walt, Stephen M. "Alliance Formation and the Balance of World Power." International Security 9, no. 4 (Spring 1985): 3–43.

————. *The Origins of Alliances.* Ithaca, N.Y.: Cornell University Press, 1987.

————. "Alliance Formation in South Asia." In *Dominoes and Bandwagons: Strategic Beliefs and Superpower Competition in the Eurasian Rimland,* ed. Robert Jervis and Jack Snyder. New York: Oxford University Press, 1990.

Wolfers, Arnold. *Discord and Collaboration.* Baltimore: Johns Hopkins University Press, 1962.

## Psychological Theories

Abelson, Robert P. "Psychological Implications." In *Theories of Cognitive Consistency,* ed. Robert P. Abelson, Elliot Aronson, William J. McGuire, Theodore M. Newcomb, Milton J. Rosenberg, and Percy H. Tannenbaum, 112–39. Chicago: Rand McNally, 1968.

Anderson, Craig A., and Eliza S. Sechler. "The Effects of Explanation and Counterexplanation on the Development and Use of Social Theories." *JPSP* 47 (January 1986): 22–34.

Aronson, Elliot. "Dissonance Theory: Progress and Problems." In *Theories of Cognitive Consistency,* ed. Robert P. Abelson, Elliot Aronson, William J. McGuire, Theodore M. Newcomb, Milton J. Rosenberg, and Percy H. Tannenbaum, 5–27. Chicago: Rand McNally, 1968.

Chaiken, Shelley, and Suzanne Yates. "Affective-Cognitive Consistency and the Effect of Salient Behavioral Information." *JPSP* 46 (1985): 1470–81.

Converse, Philip E. "The Nature of Belief Systems in Mass Publics." In *Ideology and Discontent,* ed. David E. Apter. New York: Free Press, 1964.

Cyert, Richard, and James March. *A Behavioral Theory of the Firm*. Englewood Cliffs, N.J.: Prentice-Hall, 1963.

Janis, Irving, and Leon Mann. *Decision Making: A Psychological Analysis of Conflict, Choice, and Commitment*. New York: Free Press, 1977.

Jones, Edward E., and Daniel McGillis. "Correspondent Inferences and the Attribution Cube." In *New Directions in Attribution Research*, ed. John H. Harvey, William John Ickes, and Robert F. Kidd, vol. 1. Hillsdale, N.J.: Erlbaum, 1976.

Kahneman, Daniel, and Amos Tversky. "On the Psychology of Prediction." *Psychology Review* 80, no. 4 (1973): 237–51.

———. "Subjective Probability: A Judgment of Representativeness." In *Judgment Under Uncertainty: Heuristics and Biases*, ed. Daniel Kahneman, Paul Slovic, and Amos Tversky. Cambridge: Cambridge University Press, 1982.

Kahneman, Daniel, Paul Slovic, and Amos Tversky, eds. *Judgment Under Uncertainty: Heuristics and Biases*. Cambridge: Cambridge University Press, 1982.

Kaplan, Bernard, and Walter H. Crockett. "A Developmental Analysis of Modes of Resolution." In *Theories of Cognitive Consistency*, ed. Robert P. Abelson, Elliot Aronson, William J. McGuire, Theodore M. Newcomb, Milton J. Rosenberg, and Percy H. Tannenbaum, 661–69. Chicago: Rand McNally, 1968.

Kelley, Harold H. "Processes of Causal Attribution." *American Psychologist* 28, no. 2 (February 1973): 107–28.

Lindblom, Charles. "The Science of Muddling Through." *Public Administration Review* 19, no. 2 (Spring 1959): 79–88.

McGuire, William J. "The Current Status of Cognitive Consistency Theories." In *Cognitive Consistency*, ed. Shel Feldman. New York: Academic Press, 1966.

Meyer, John P. "Causal Attributions for Success and Failure." *JPSP* 41, no. 5 (May 1980): 704–18.

Nisbett, Richard, and Lee Ross. *Human Inference: Strategies and Shortcomings of Social Judgment*. Englewood Cliffs, N.J.: Prentice-Hall, 1980.

Nisbett, Richard, and T. D. Wilson. "Telling More Than We Can Know: Verbal Reports on Mental Processes." *Psychological Review* 84 (1977): 231–59.

Ronis, David L., Ranald D. Hansen, and Virginia E. O'Leary. "Understanding the Meaning of Achievement Attributions." *JPSP* 44 (April 1983): 702–11.

Ross, Lee, and Craig A. Anderson. "Shortcomings in the Attribution Process: On the Origins and Maintenance of Erroneous Social Assessments." In *Judgment Under Uncertainty: Heuristics and Biases*, ed. Daniel Kahneman, Paul Slovic, and Amos Tversky. Cambridge: Cambridge University Press, 1982.

Slovic, Paul, and Douglas MacPhillamy. "Dimensional Commensurability and Cue Utilization in Comparative Judgment." *Organizational Behavior and Human Performance* 11, no. 2 (February 1974): 172–94.

Steinbruner, John. *The Cybernetic Theory of Decision*. Princeton: Princeton University Press, 1974.

Sweeney, Paul D., and Kathy L. Gruber. "Selective Exposure: Voter Information Preferences and the Watergate Affair." *JPSP* 45 (June 1984): 1208–21.

Taylor, Shelley E., and Susan T. Fiske. "Salience Attention and Attribution: Top of the Head Phenomena." In *Advances in Experimental Social Psychology*, ed. Leonard Berkowitz, vol. 11. New York: Academic Press, 1978.

Valle, Valerie A., and Irene H. Frieze. "The Stability of Causal Attributions as a Mediator in Changing Expectations for Success." *JPSP* 37 (May 1976): 579–87.

Weick, Karl E. "Processes of Ramification among Cognitive Links." In *Theories of Cognitive Consistency*, ed. Robert P. Abelson, Elliot Aronson, William J. McGuire, Theodore M. Newcomb, Milton J. Rosenberg, and Percy H. Tannenbaum, 512–19. Chicago: Rand McNally, 1968.

Weiner, Bernard. "Achievement Motivation as Conceptualized by an Attribution Theorist." In *Achievement Motivation and Attribution Theory*, ed. Bernard Weiner. Morristown, N.J.: General Learning, 1974.

Wicklund, Robert A., and Jack W. Brehm. *Perspectives on Cognitive Dissonance*. Hillsdale, N.J.: Erlbaum, 1976.

Wyer, Robert S. Jr., and Leonard L. Martin. "Person Memory: The Role of Traits, Group Stereotypes, and Specific Behaviors." *JPSP* 47 (April 1986): 661–75.

## Primary Soviet Sources

**Andropov, Iurii**. Speeches in *Pravda*, December 28, 1973, to January 25, 1984.

**Arbatov, Georgii**. "Administratsiya Nixona v Serediny Distantsii" (The Nixon Administration at the Midterm). *SShA*, August 1970, 3–16.

"'Doctrina Nixona': Deklaratsii i Realnost" (The Nixon Doctrine: Declarations and Reality). *SShA*, February 1971, 18–25, 41–48.

"Amerikanskii Imperializm i Novye Realnosti Mira" (American Imperialism and New Realities of the World). *Pravda*, May 4, 1971, 4–5.

"Voprosy, Trebuiushchie Prakticheskovo Otveta—K Planiruemoi Amerikansko-Kitaiskoi Vstreche v Verkhakh" (Questions that Demand a Practical Answer—Toward the Planned American-Chinese Summit). *Pravda*, August 10, 1971, 4–5.

"Shag, Otveshchaiushchii Interesam Mira" (A Step Which Answers the Interests of Peace). *SShA*, November 1971, 55–57.

"Diskusii v Baltimore" (Discussions in Baltimore). *Izvestiya*, January 13, 1972, 3–4.

"Perspektivy Razryadki Sovetsko-Amerikanskikh Otnoshenii" (Prospects for Detente in Soviet-American Relations). *SShA*, February 1972, 26–31.

"Sila Politika Realizma" (The Power of a Policy of Realism). *Izvestiya*, June 22, 1972, 3–4.

"Sobytie Vazhnovo Mezhdunarodnovo Znacheniya" (An Event of Important International Significance). *SShA*, August 1972, 3–12.

"O Sovetsko-Amerikanskikh Otnosheniyakh" (On Soviet-American Relations). *Kommunist*, 1973, no. 3, 101–13.

"Vremya Reshenii—O Sovetsko-Amerikanskikh Torgovo-Ekonomicheskikh Otnosheniyakh" (Time of Decision—On Soviet-American Trade and Economic Relations). Part 1, *Izvestiya*, May 5, 1973, 4. Part 2, *Izvestiya*, May 8, 1973, 4.

"Sovetsko-Amerikanskie Otnosheniya na Novom Etape" (Soviet-American Relations at a New Stage). *Pravda*, July 22, 1973, 4.

"Vneshnyaya Politika SShA v Nauchno-Tekhnicheskaya Revoliutsiya" (U.S. Foreign Policy in the Scientific-Technological Revolution). Part 1, *SShA*, October 1973, 3–11. Part 2, *SShA*, November 1973, 3–16.

"Sovetsko-Amerikanskie Otnosheniya v 70-e Gody" (Soviet-American Relations in the 1970s). *SShA*, May 1974, 26–40.

"Novye Rubezhi Sovetsko-Amerikanskikh Otnoshenii" (New Frontiers in Soviet-American Relations). *Izvestiya*, July 13, 1974, 3–4.

"Manevry Protivnikov Razryadki" (Maneuvers of the Foes of Detente). *Izvestiya*, September 4, 1975, 3–4.

"O Sovetsko-Amerikanskikh Otnosheniyakh" (On Soviet-American Relations). *Pravda*, April 2, 1976, 4–5.

"Sovetsko-Amerikanskie Otnosheniya Sevodnya" (Soviet-American Relations Today). *Pravda*, December 11, 1976, 4–5.

"Bolshaya Lozh Protivnikov Razryadki" (The Big Lie of Detente's Opponents). *Pravda*, February 5, 1977, 4–5.

"S Pozitsii Realizma: Zametki ob Odnoi Amerikanskoi Knige" (From a Position of Realism: Notes on One American Book). *Izvestiya*, March 13, 1977, 4.

"Sovetsko-Amerikanskie Otnosheniya Sevodnya" (Soviet-American Relations Today). *Pravda*, August 3, 1977, 4–5.

"Razvitie Sotsialnykh i Politicheskikh Protsessov v SShA na Sovremennom Etape" (The Development of Social and Political Processes in the U.S.A. at the Present Stage). *Vestnik, AN, SSSR*, February 1978, 29–41.

"Vremya Otvestvennykh Reshenii" (Time of Responsible Decisions). *Pravda*, March 28, 1978, 4–5.

"Na Poroge Novovo Desyatiletiya" (On the Threshold of a New Decade). *Pravda*, March 3, 1980, 6.

"Vneshnyaya Politika SShA na Poroge 80-x Godov" (U.S. Foreign Policy on the Eve of the 1980s). *SShA*, April 1980, 43–54.

"Trudnyi Vybor" (Hard Choice). *Pravda*, March 9, 1981, 6.

"Domogayas Krizisa" (Courting a Crisis). *Pravda*, January 1, 1982, 4.

"Amerikanskaya Politika v Mire Snov" (American Policy in the World Anew). *Pravda*, July 16, 1982, 4.

"Razmyshleniya po Povodu Iubileya" (Ruminations on the Occasion of the Jubilee). *SShA*, November 1983, 10–15.

"Politicheskii Dokument Ogromnovo Znacheniya" (A Political Document of Enormous Significance). *Izvestiya*, November 26, 1983, 4.

"Chto, Esli ne Mir?" (What, if not Peace?). *Pravda*, August 13, 1984, 6.

Interview. *Komsomolskaya Pravda*, March 7, 1985, 3.

"Ekonomicheskoe i Politicheskoe Polozhenie i Vybory 1984 Goda v SShA" (The Economic and Political Situation in the U.S.A. and the 1984 Elections). *Vestnik, AN, SSSR*, May 1985, 67–82.

"Perspektivy Sovetsko-Amerikanskikh Otnoshenii" (Prospects of Soviet-American Relations). *SShA*, June 1985, 40–44.

"Igra s Ognem" (Playing with Fire). *Pravda*, July 1, 1985, 6.

"Kto Komy Bolshe Nuzhen?" (Who Needs Whom More?). *Pravda*, September 13, 1986, 4.

"The Bulldozer Syndrome." *NT*, 1986, no. 36, 4–5.

"20 Dnei Spustya" (Twenty Days Later). *Pravda*, November 4, 1986, 4.

"Ne Ot Khoroshei Zhizni" (Not By Choice). *Pravda*, November 21, 1986, 5.

"Militarizm i Sovremennoe Obshchestvo" (Militarism and Contemporary Society). *Kommunist*, 1987, no. 2, 104–15.

"Tma Pered Rassvetom?" (The Darkness Before the Dawn?). *Pravda*, September 10, 1987, 4

"Perestroika Shatters Stereotypes." *NT*, 1987, no. 47, 3.

"Pered Vyborom" (Before a Choice). *Kommunist*, 1988, no. 5, 110–19.

"SSSR-SShA: Potentsial Torgovli" (USSR–U.S.: Trade Potential). *Izvestiya*, April 10, 1988, 5.

"Prodvizhenie k Realizmu" (Advancement Toward Realism). *Pravda*, June 10, 1988, 6.

"Glasnost, Peregovory, Razoruzhenie" (Glasnost, Negotiations, Disarmament). *Pravda*, October 17, 1988, 6.

"Answering Questions." *KZ*, December 31, 1988, 5.

**Belyaev, Igor**. "Krushenie Illiuzii" (Collapse of Illusions). *Pravda*, February 21, 1965, 5.

"Pered Vstrechei v Accra" (Before the Meeting in Accra). *Pravda*, October 19, 1965, 5.

Slovo Revoliutsionnoi Afriki" (The World of Revolutionary Africa). *Pravda*, November 4, 1966, 5.

"Verolomstvo" (Treachery). *Pravda*, June 10, 1967, 3.

"Otpor Avantiuristam" (A Rebuff to the Adventurists). *Pravda*, June 19, 1967, 1.

"Politicheskie Diversii Izrailya" (Political Diversions of Israel). *Pravda*, June 30, 1967, 5.

"Agressoru Pridetsya Ubratsya" (The Aggressor Must Clear Off). *Pravda*, July 17, 1967, 1.

"UAR: Narod i Revoliutsiya" (UAR: People and Revolution). *Pravda*, July 23, 1967, 5.

"Kak Izrail Nachal Agressiiu" (How Israel Began the Aggression). *Pravda*, July 27, 1967, 4.

"Tuchi Sgushchaiutsya" (Clouds Are Gathering). *Pravda*, July 29, 1967, 4.

"Trudnyi Chas" (Difficult Hour). *Pravda*, July 31, 1967, 4.

"Kogda Osela Pyl" (When the Dust Has Settled). *Pravda*, August 3, 1967, 4.

"Ot Tripoli do Khartouma" (From Tripoli to Khartoum). *Pravda*, August 6, 1967, 4.

"'Nash Drug—Sovetskii Soiuz!'" (Our Friend—the Soviet Union!). *Pravda*, August 9, 1967, 4.

"Posle Khartouma" (After Khartoum). *Pravda*, September 5, 1967, 4.

"Atmosfera Ochishchaetsya" (The Atmosphere Is Clearing). *Pravda*, September 6, 1967, 4.

"Situation in the Arab World." *NT*, 1967, no. 39, 8–11.

"Raschety na Peske" (Calculations on Sand). *Pravda*, November 19, 1967, 4.

"Politika Mira i Politika Agresii" (Policy of Peace and Policy of Aggression). *Pravda*, December 4, 1967, 1.

"'Pozharnye Mery' Protiv Zdravovo Smysla" (Fire Prevention Measures Against Good Sense). *Pravda*, December 25, 1967, 4.

"V Plenu Samoobmana-Kto Zatyagivaet Blizhnevostochnoi Krizis?" (A Prisoner of Self-Deception—Who is Prolonging the Middle East Crisis?). *Pravda*, February 2, 1968, 4.

"Lessons of the 1967 Middle East Crisis." *IA*, March 1968, 40–46.

"Snova Samoobman—Na Sbito Rasschityvaet Izrail" (Again Self-Deception—Israel Miscalculates). *Pravda*, March 8, 1968, 4.

"I Golova Uvyazla, I Khvost Uvyaz" (If You Grab the Head, the Tail Will Follow). *Pravda*, March 24, 1968, 1, 4.

"Sotsialnye Sily i Perspektivy 'Tretevo Mira'" (Social Forces and the Prospects of the Third World). *MEIMO*, May 1968, 90–102.

"Vzglyad Cherez Sinai" (Looking Across the Sinai). *Zhurnalist*, May 1968, 65–69.

"Kto Torpediruet Missiu Jarringa?" (Who is Torpedoing the Jarring Mission?). *Pravda*, June 3, 1968, 4.

"Provaliushchiesya Raschety" (Failed Calculations). *Pravda*, July 3, 1968, 4.

"Oplot Mira" (Bastion of Peace). *Pravda*, July 14, 1968, 4.

"Den Proshlyi i Nastoyashchii" (Day Past and Present). *Pravda*, July 23, 1968, 4.

"'Chernye Operatsii' TsRU" (Black Operations of the CIA). *Pravda*, August 19, 1968, 4.

"Ways of Ending the Middle East Crisis." *IA*, October 1968, 25–28, 34.

"Pod Znakom Pobed" (Under the Sign of Victories). *Pravda*, November 3, 1968, 4.

"Provaly Imperialisticheskoi Politiki" (Failures of Imperialist Policy). *Pravda*, December 8, 1968, 1, 4.

"Otpor Narodov Politike Avantiur" (People's Rebuff to the Policy of Adventures). *Pravda*, February 23, 1969, 1, 4.

"Middle East Powder Keg." *NT*, 1969, no. 11, 5–7.

"Washington's Asian Boomerang" *IA*, May 1969, 65–70.

"Neodolimaya Sila" (Invincible Force). *Pravda*, May 25, 1969, 4.

"Arabskii Yashchik Pandory" (Arab Pandora's Box). *AIAS*, July 1969, 31–33.

"UAR: Revoliutsiya Prodolzhaetsya" (UAR: The Revolution Continues). *Pravda*, July 23, 1969, 4.

"UAR: Na Vnutrennem Fronte" (UAR: On the Domestic Front). *Pravda*, August 27, 1969, 4.

"Dragged-Out Middle East Conflict: Who Stands to Gain?" *IA*, September 1969, 67–70.

"Velenie Vremeni" (Wave of the Times). *Pravda*, November 23, 1969, 1, 4.

"Vopreki Proiskam Imperializma" (Despite the Intrigues of Imperialism). *Pravda*, February 1, 1970, 1, 4.

"Middle East Crisis and Washington's Maneuvers" *IA*, April 1970, 30–35.

"Sily Soprotivoleniya Agressoru Rastut" (Forces of Resistance to the Aggressor Are Growing). *MEIMO*, May 1970, 73–78.

"Sotsializm—Reshaiushchaya Sila Sovremennosti" (Socialism—Decisive Force of Modern Times). *Pravda*, May 10, 1970, 4.

"Zharkoe Leto 70-vo" (The Hot Summer of 1970). *Pravda*, July 5, 1970, 4.

"Who Is Encouraging Whom?" *NT*, 1970, no. 29, 11.

"Iz-za Chuzhoi Spiny" (From Behind Someone Else's Back). *Pravda*, July 21, 1970, 5.

"Torzhestvo Revoliutsii" (Triumph of the Revolution). *Pravda*, July 23, 1970, 4.

"Downed Phantoms and Peace Prospects." *NT*, 1970, no. 32, 4–5.

"Who Is Obstructing a Middle East Settlement?" *IA*, November 1970, 86–89.

"Uverennaya Postup Svobodu" (Assured Step Toward Freedom). *KZ*, May 25, 1971, 3.

"S Chernovo Khoda, Dokumentalnaya Povest" (Through the Back Door, Documentary Record). Part 1, *Znamya*, September 1971, 58–108. Part 2, *Znamya*, October 1971, 185–204. Part 3, *Znamya*, November 1971, 91–123.

"Nasledie Prezidenta Nasera" (Legacy of President Nasser). *AIAS*, November 1971, 8–11.

"Sovremennoe Natsionalno-Osvoboditelnoe Dvizhenie" (The Contemporary National Liberation Movement). *Politicheskoe Samoobrazovanie*, January 1972, 93–99.

"Gamal Abdel Naser—Nekotorye Cherty Ideinoi Evoliutsii" (Gamal Abdel Naser—Certain Features of his Ideological Evolution). *NAIA*, 1972, no. 2, 73–89.

"Faktory Dolgosrochnovo Deistviya" (Factors of Long-term Effect). *Sovetskaya Rossiya*, May 12, 1972, 3.

"Conference in Bologna." *NT*, 1973, no. 21, 16–17.

"Slavnaya Godovshchina" (Glorious Anniversary). *Pravda*, July 23, 1973, 3.

"Krax 'Filosofii Sily'-Izrail: Chto Zhe Dalshe" (Collapse of Israel's Philosophy of Force: What Next). *LG*, December 12, 1973, 14.

"Prochnyi Mir Blizhnemu Vostoku" (A Stable Peace for the Middle East). *Izvestiya*, July 9, 1974, 4.

"Put k Spravedlivomu Miru" (Path to a Just Peace). *Izvestiya*, May 28, 1975, 4.

"Egipet: Etapy Revoliutsii" (Egypt: Stages of the Revolution). *AIAS*, July 1975, 3–4.

"SShA i Blizhnevostochnyi Krizis" (The U.S.A. and the Middle East Crisis). *SShA*, March 1976, 17–27.

"V Spiske 'Zapreshchennykh'" (On the "Banned" List). *LG*, August 30, 1978, 14.

"Saudovskaya Arabiya: Chto Zhe Dalshe?" (Saudi Arabia: What Next?). *LG*, January 31, 1979, 14.

"Na Razvalinakh Monarkhii" (On the Ruins of a Monarchy). *LG*, April 4, 1979, 14.

"Iran: 'Da!' Respublike" (Iran: "Yes!" to the Republic). *LG*, April 18, 1979, 14.

"Operatsiya 'Neftepromysly'" (Operation "Oilfields"). *LG*, November 14, 1979, 14.

"Ierusalim: Vozmozhen li Mir v 'Gorode Mira'?" (Jerusalem: Is Peace Possible in the "City of Peace"?). *LG*, December 19, 1979, 14.

"Islam i Politika" (Islam and Politics). *LG*, January 16, 1980, 14.

"Uzel Amerikano-Iranskikh Problem" (Knot of American-Iranian Problems). *SShA*, February 1980, 48–58.

"Kogda Chernoe Vydaetsya za Beloe" (When Black Is Passed Off as White). *LG*, March 12, 1980, 14.

"Kto zhe Ugrozhaet Saudovskoi Aravii?" (Who Threatens Saudi Arabia?). *LG*, July 9, 1980, 14.

"Kemp-Devid: Tysyacha i Odin Tupik" (Camp David: A Thousand and One Dead Ends). *LG*, September 10, 1980, 14.

"Kto Seet Kamni" (Who Is Sowing Stones). *LG*, February 4, 1981, 9, 14.

"Blizhnii Vostok: Vremya Reshat" (Middle East: Time to Decide). *LG*, May 27, 1981, 14.

"Yasir Arafat: Borba do Pobedu" (Yasir Arafat: Struggle to Victory). *LG*, October 21, 1981, 1, 14.

"Blizhnii Vostok: Bolshaya Voina? Poka Generalnaya Repetitsiya" (Middle East: Big War? Still a Dress Rehearsal). *LG*, November 18, 1981, 14.

"Izrail: Upovaya na Voinu Protiv Sovetskovo Soiuza" (Israel: Hoping for a War Against the Soviet Union). *LG*, December 16, 1981, 9, 14–15.

"V Yadernoi Katastrofe ne Vyzhivet Nikto" (No One Will Survive a Nuclear Catastrophe). *LG*, May 19, 1982, 14.

"Kogda Voinu Nazyvaiut Mirom" (When They Call War Peace). *LG*, July 7, 1982, 14.

"Egipet—Strana Chudes" (Egypt—Country of Wonders) Part 1, *LG*, January 12, 1983, 10–11. Part 2, *LG*, January 19, 1983, 10.

"Egipet '83: Inye Vremena?" (Egypt 1983: Different Times?). *AIAS*, July 1983, 20–23.

"V Tel-Aviv i Obratno" (To Tel-Aviv and Back). *LG*, July 20, 1983, 10.

"Kogda Mavr Sdelal Ix Delo . . ." (When the Moor has Done His Duty . . . ). *LG*, March 21, 1984, 9, 14.

"Chetki Ministra" (Beads of a Minister). *LG*, May 15, 1985, 14.

"Viza v Emiraty" (A Visa to the Emirates). *LG*, June 19, 1985, 14.

"Delo Protiv Livii" (Plot Against Libya). *LG*, June 18, 1986, 15.

"Eshche Est Shans!" (There's Still a Chance!). *LG*, December 24, 1986, 14.

"Ne Otkryvat 'Vtoroi Front' Vsemirnoi Katastrofy" (Don't Open a Second Front to Worldwide Catastrophe). *LG*, March 18, 1987, 14.

"'Irangate': Vzglyad Iznutri s Utochneniyami . . ." ("Irangate": A View from Within with Some Clarifications . . . ). *LG*, April 22, 1987, 14.

"Islam i Politika" (Islam and Politics). Part 1, *LG*, May 13, 1987, 13. Part 2, *LG*, May 20, 1987, 12.

"Blizhnii Vostok: Stoletnyaya Voina?" (Middle East: One Hundred Year War?). *LG*, June 17, 1987, 14.

"Za 'Glasnostiu' SOI-Lozh" (Behind the Glasnost of SDI Is a Lie). *LG*, August 19, 1987, 14.

"Tantsevat pod Druguiu Muzyku . . ." (To Dance to Different Music . . . ). *LG*, April 27, 1988, 14.

**Bragina, Elena**. "The Role of the State in Newly-Free Countries' Socioeconomic Development." *IA*, January 1975, 60–65.

"Bibliograficheskaya Zametka" (Bibliographical Note). *NAIA*, 1976, no. 1, 206.

"Promyshlennyi Eksport Indii" (Industrial Export of India). *AIAS*, August 1976, 63–64.

"Urbanizatsiya v 'Tretem Mire'" (Urbanization in the Third World). *AIAS*, May 1977, 63–64.

"Problemy Obrazovaniya v Strankakh Iuzhnoi i Iugo-Vostochnoi Azii" (Problems of Education in Countries of Southern and Southeastern Asia). *AIAS*, August 1977, 63.

"Indiiskie Avtory o Probleme Zanyatosti" (Indian Authors on the Problem of Employment). *AIAS*, July 1978, 64.

"Osnovnye Napravleniya Vnutrennei Ekonomicheskoi Politiki Indii" (Main Direction in Indian Domestic Economic Policy). *MEIMO*, February 1979, 135–39.

"Peremeschcenie Promyshlennykh Moshchnostei v Razvivaiushchiesya Strany" (The Relocation of Industry in Developing Countries). *NAIA*, 1979, no. 5, 91–95.

"Protivorechiya Promyshlennovo Razvitiya Columbii" (Contradictions in the Industrial Development of Colombia). *MEIMO*, November 1980, 156–57.

"Mezhdunarodnaya Strategiya Razvitiya na 80–e Gody" (International Strategy of Development in the 1980s). *MEIMO*, June 1981, 122–24.

"Po Voskhodyashchei Linii" (Along an Ascending Line). *MEIMO*, July 1981, 148–50.

"Bezrabotitsa, Zanyatost, Motivatsii Truda v Razvivaiushcheisya Ekonomike " (Unemployment, Employment, and Labor Motivation in a Developing Economy). *NAIA*, 1981, no. 4, 15–25.

"Promyshlennaya Politika Razvivaiushchikhsya Stran" (Industrial Policy of Developing Countries). *AIAS*, August 1981, 62.

"Problema Diversifikatsii Eksporta Razvivaiushchikhsya Stran" (Problem of Diversification of Exports in Developing Countries). *MEIMO*, January 1983, 151.

"Zhenskii Trud v Promyshlennosti Razvivaiushchikhsya Stran" (Women's Labor in the Industry of Developing Countries). *AIAS*, October 1984, 54–56.

**Brezhnev, Leonid**. Speeches in *Pravda* and *Izvestiya* May 9, 1965, to October 13, 1982.

*Report of the Central Committee at the Twenty-third Party Congress, CPSU*. Moscow: Novosti, 1966. 10–55.

"Pyatdesyat Let Velikikh Pobed Sotsializma" (Fifty Years of the Great Victories of Socialism). *Kommunist*, 1967, no. 16, 3–47.

*Twenty-fourth Congress of the CPSU*. Moscow: Novosti, 1971. 6–40.

"Message to the First Festival of Friendship of Soviet and Cuban Youth." *Komsomolskaya Pravda*, July 17, 1976, 1.

*Documents and Resolutions. The Twenty-sixth Congress of the Communist Party of the Soviet Union*. Moscow: Novosti, 1981. 5–103.

**Brutents, Karen**. "Voprosy Ideologii v Natsionalno-Osvoboditelnom Dvizhenii" (Questions of Ideology in the National Liberation Movement), *Kommunist*, 1966, no. 18, 37–50.

"The African Revolution: Gains and Problems." *IA*, January 1967, 20–28.

"Natsionalno-Osvoboditelnoe Dvizhenie Sevodnya" (The National Liberation Movement Today). *Pravda*, February 1, 1967, 4–5.

"Epokha Sotsializma i Natsionalnoe Osvobozhdenie Narodov" (Epoch of Socialist and the National Liberation of Peoples). *Kommunist*, 1967, no. 18, 91–102.

"O Revoliutsionnoi Demokratii" (On Revolutionary Democracy). Part 1, *MEIMO*, March 1968, 15–28. Part 2, *MEIMO*, April 1968, 24–35.

"Pravyashchaya Revoliutsionnaya Demokratiya: Nekotorye Cherty Prakticheskoi Deyatelnosti" (Ruling Revolutionary Democracy: Certain Features of Practical Activities). Part 1, *MEIMO*, November 1972, 104–17. Part 2, *MEIMO*, December 1972, 115–29.

"Razryadka Mezhdunarodnoi Napryazhennosti i Razvivaiushchiesya Strany" (Detente and Developing Countries). *Pravda*, August 30, 1973, 4–5.

"V. I. Lenin i Natsionalno–Osvvoboditelnoe Dvizhenie" (V. I. Lenin and the National Liberation Movement). Part 1, *AIAS*, April 1975, 4–5. Part 2, *AIAS*, May 1975, 5–7.

"Imperializm i Osvobodivshiesya Strany" (Imperialism and Liberated Countries). *Pravda*, February 10, 1978, 3–4.

"The Soviet Union and Newly-Independent Countries." *IA*, April 1979, 3–14.

"Neokolonializm na Poroge 80–x Godov: 'Modernizatsiya' Strategii" (Neocolonialism on the Eve of the 1980s: Modernization of a Strategy). Part 1, *MEIMO*, June 1979, 72–84. Part 2, *MEIMO*, July 1979, 81–94.

"A Great Force of Modern Times." *IA*, March 1981, 74–85.

"Sovetskii Soiuz i Osvobodivshchiesya Strany" (The Soviet Union and Liberated Countries). *Pravda*, February 2, 1982, 4–5.

"Livanskaya Tragediya" (Lebanese Tragedy). *SShA*, September 1982, 6–8.

"Konflikt v Iuzhnoi Atlantike: Nekotorye Posledstviya i Uroki" (Conflict in the Southern Atlantic: Some Consequences and Lessons). *SShA*, November 1982, 19–31.

"Mezhdunarodnaya Napryazhennost i Razvivaiushchiesya Strany" (International Tension and Developing Countries). *Pravda*, June 22, 1983, 4–5.

"Kto Prepyatstvuet Miru v Livane" (Who Is Preventing Peace in Lebanon). *Pravda*, February 4, 1984, 4.

"Osvobodivshiesya Strany v Nachale 80-x Godov" (Liberated Countries at the Beginning of the 1980s). *Kommunist*, 1984, no. 3, 103–13.

"Dvizhenie Neprisoedineniya v Sovremennom Mire" (The Non-Aligned Movement in the Contemporary World). *MEIMO*, May 1984, 30–41.

"Cooperation and Dialogue with Political Parties and Movements." *IA*, November 1988, 37–40.

**Butlitsky, Arkadii.** "Serye Cardinaly Belovo Doma" (Gray Cardinals of the White House). *LG*, June 30, 1966, 4.

"Za Kulisami 'Molchalivoi Sluzhby'" (Behind the Scenes at the "Silent Service"). *KZ*, August 7, 1966, 3.

"First Shots in the U.S. Presidential Campaign." *NT*, 1967, no. 41, 13–15.

"Afrikanskie Mirazhi Washingtona" (African Mirages of Washington). *Gudok*, March 25, 1970, 3.

"Zionist Secret Service." *NT*, 1970, no. 15, 29–31.

"Po Zakonam Dzhunglei" (By the Laws of the Jungle). *Neva*, May 1972, 166–72.

"South Africa in the Grip of the Broederbond." *NT*, 1973, no. 2, 30–31.

"Knot of Apartheid Contradictions." *IA*, February 1973, 80–86.

"Militaristskie Ambitsii Londona" (Militaristic Ambitions of London). *Gudok*, February 7, 1973, 3.

"Blind Alley of Apartheid." *NT*, 1974, no. 23, 21–23.

"Porochnyi Krug Apartkheida" (Vicious Circle of Apartheid). *MEIMO*, November 1974, 72–82.

"'Smena Karaula' v Bruderbonde" ("Changing of the Guard" in the Broederbond). *Zarya Vostoka*, December 1, 1974, 2

"African Monologue." *NT*, 1974, no. 50, 20–22.

"Manevry Iuzhnoafrikanskikh Rasistov" (Maneuvers of South African Racists). *MEIMO*, August 1975, 90–95.

"Zagovor Protiv Afriki" (Plot Against Africa). *AIAS*, April 1976, 10–12.

"Angola—Sryv Proiskov Imperialisticheskoi Reaktsii" (Angola—Thwarting the Intrigues of Imperialist Reaction). *MEIMO*, May 1976, 84–90.

"V Tiskakh Bruderbonda" (In the Clutches of the Broederbond). *Neva*, June 1976, 181–86.

"Behind the Intervention." *NT*, 1977, no. 20, 10–11.

"IuAR: Krizis Rasistskovo Rezhima" (RSA: Crisis of a Racist Regime). *AIAS*, September 1977, 18–21.

"In the Rhythm of Soweto." *NT*, 1977, no. 47, 14–15.

"Vokrug 'Zairskovo Piroga'" (Around the "Zairean Pie"). *MEIMO*, September 1978, 116–22.

"New Premier, Old Policy." *NT*, 1978, no. 45, 27.

"Britain-Rhodesia: Salisbury Lobby." *NT*, 1979, no. 49, 24–25.

"Pod Teniu Svastiki" (Under the Shadow of a Swastika). *KZ*, August 18, 1981, 3.

**Chernenko, Konstantin**. Speeches in *Pravda*, May 17, 1978, to March 2, 1985.

"Leninist Strategy of Peace in Action." *IA*, May 1976, 3–12.

"Trust and Cooperation Among Peoples—A Guarantee of Peace and Security." *IA*, September 1980, 5–11.

**Falin, Valentin**. "Voennaya Razryadka Vozmozhna—Otvet za Zapadom" (Military Detente is Possible—The Ball is in the West's Court). *Pravda*, September 19, 1979, 4.

"Budushchee Evropy—V Mirnom Sotrudnichestve" (The Future of Europe is in Peaceful Cooperation). *Izvestiya*, November 22, 1979, 5.

"Politicheskoe Bezdorozhe" (Political Impasse). *Pravda*, January 20, 1982, 4.

"Doktrin Yadernoi Voiny" (Doctrine of Nuclear War). *Izvestiya*, January 21, 1983, 5.

"Alkhimiya s 'Nulem'" (Alchemy with "Zero"). *Izvestiya*, February 4, 1983, 5.

"O Ravnovesii i Ravnopravii" (On Balance and Equity). *Izvestiya*, February 12, 1983, 5.

"Kogda Dvazhdy Dva-Pyat" (When Two Times Two Equals Five). *Izvestiya*, February 21, 1983, 3.

"FRG Pered Vyborom" (FRG Before a Choice). *Izvestiya*, February 25, 1983, 5.

"Posle Vyborov" (After the Elections). *Izvestiya*, March 17, 1983, 5.

"Igra v Varianty" (Playing with Variants). *Izvestiya*, March 30, 1983, 5.

"Rassudku Vopreki" (Contrary to Common Sense). *Izvestiya*, April 5, 1983, 5.

"Golos Sovesti" (Voice of Conscience). *Izvestiya*, April 14, 1983, 5.

"Mir Vashemu Domu" (The World is Your Home). *Izvestiya*, April 30, 1983, 4.

"Imperskaya Spes" (Imperial Arrogance). *Izvestiya*, June 19, 1983, 5.

"Dialektika Po-Washingtonski" (Dialectics Washington-Style). *Izvestiya*, July 10, 1983, 4–5.

"Prezhde Vsevo Sovladai s Soboi" (First of All Control Yourself). *Izvestiya*, August 14, 1983, 4–5.

"V Pautine Lzhi" (In the Web of Lies). *Izvestiya*, August 29, 1983, 5.

"Dvulichie v Politike" (Hypocrisy in Politics). *Izvestiya*, September 11, 1983, 4–5.

"Ne Roi Drugomu Yamu" (Don't Lay a Trap for Someone). *Izvestiya*, September 30, 1983, 5.

"Gde Koren Zla" (Where the Root of Evil Is). *Izvestiya*, October 21, 1983, 5.

"Washington Topchet Pravo i Moral" (Washington Tramples on Rights and Morality). *Izvestiya*, October 28, 1983, 5.

"Seiut Veter" (They Sow Wind). *Izvestiya*, November 25, 1983, 4.

"Washington v Dvukh Izmereniyakh" (Washington in Two Dimensions). *Izvestiya*, November 27, 1983, 4–5. ,

"Podvodya Itogi . . ." (Summing Up . . . ). *MEIMO*, December 1983, 3–15.

"Ob Antimirakh" (On Anti-Worlds). *Izvestiya*, December 4, 1983, 5.

"SShA v God Vyborov" (The U.S.A. in an Election Year). *Izvestiya*, January 8, 1984, 4–5.

"Kovo Obmanyvaiut?" (Whom are They Deceiving?). *Izvestiya*, February 26, 1984, 5.

"Raschety i Proschety" (Calculations and Miscalculations). *Izvestiya*, March 14, 1984, 5.

"'Den Zakonnosti'" ("Day of Legality"). *Izvestiya*, April 17, 1984, 5.

"Minonosnaya Demokratiya" (Torpedo-Boat Democracy). *Izvestiya*, April 20, 1984, 5.

"Vcherashnii Den v Sevodnyashnem Vashingtone" (Yesterday in Today's Washington). *Kommunist*, 1984, no. 8, 120–25.

"Reagan Ostaetsya Reaganom" (Reagan Remains Reagan). *Izvestiya*, July 12, 1984, 4–5.

"Dallasskie Otkroveniya" (Dallas Discoveries). *Izvestiya*, August 31, 1984, 5.

"Kosmicheskii Avantiurizm i Realnost" (Cosmic Adventurism and Reality). *Izvestiya*, September 9, 1984, 5.

"Predvybornye Farsy" (Pre-Election Farces). *Izvestiya*, October 4, 1984, 5.

"Dvoe v Odnoi Lodke" (Two in One Boat). *Izvestiya*, October 21, 1984, 4–5.

"Priznanie" (Recognition). *Izvestiya*, November 16, 1984, 5.

"Nikaragua—Vystradannaya Svoboda" (Nicaragua—Tortured Freedom). *Izvestiya*, December 3, 1984, 5.

"Anatomiya Ocherednoi Avantiuriy" (Anatomy of the Next Adventure). *Izvestiya*, February 3, 1985, 5.

"S Imperskoi Kolokolni" (From an Imperial View). *Izvestiya*, March 24, 1985, 4–5.

"Na Poroge XXI Veka" (On the Threshold of the Twenty-first Century). *MEIMO*, January 1986, 98–103.

"Kursom v Kamennyi Vek" (On a Course to the Stone Age). Part 1, *Izvestiya*, January 23, 1986, 5. Part 2, *Izvestiya*, January 24, 1986, 5.

"Otkroveniya C. Weinbergera" (Discoveries of C. Weinberger). *Izvestiya*, February 2, 1986, 4–5.

"Washington Blokiruet Dvizhenie" (Washington Blocks Movement). *Izvestiya*, February 12, 1986, 5.

"Otvechat Pridetsya po Sushchestvu" (It Must be Answered Substantively). *Izvestiya*, February 21, 1986, 4.

"The Age of Wars Past." *NT*, 1986, no. 36, 4.

"Otchevo Nedrugam Neimetsya" (Why Enemies are Itching to Do It). *Pravda*, October 6, 1986, 4.

"Reikyavik: Dve Nedeli Spustya" (Reykyavik: Two Weeks Later). *Izvestiya*, October 28, 1986, 5.

"The Role of Strength in Politics." *NT*, 1987, no. 23, 6–7.

"Reikyavik, God Spustya" (Reykyavki, a Year Later). *Pravda*, October 10, 1987, 4.

"Are 'Simple Solutions' All That Simple?" *NT*, 1988, no. 11, 16.

"Kto Razvyazal Kholodnuiu Voinu" (Who Unleashed the Cold War). *Pravda*, August 29, 1988, 6.

**Glinkin, Anatolii**. "Latinskaya Amerika i Mirovoi Istoricheskoi Protsess v 19–20 vv." (Latin America and the World Historical Process in the Nineteenth and Twentieth Centuries). *LA*, 1971, no. 3, 31–34.

"Tendentsii i Perspektivy Mezhgosudarstvennovo Antiimperialisticheskovo Sotrudnichestva" (Tendencies and Prospects of Interstate Anti-imperialist Cooperation). Part 1, *LA*, 1973, no. 5, 14–30. Part 2, *LA*, 1973, no. 6, 6–23.

"Changes in Latin America." *IA*, January 1975, 51–58.

"Ayacucho: Traditsii i Sovremennost" (Ayacucho: Traditions and Modern Times). *LA*, 1975, no. 1, 5–16.

"Latinskaya Amerika: Sovremennyi Etap Protivoborstva s Imperializmom" (Latin America: Contemporary Stage of Resistance with Imperialism). *MEIMO*, July 1976, 17–33.

"Velikii Oktyabr i Mezhdunarodnye Otnosheniya v Latinskoi Amerike" (Great October and International Relations with Latin America). *LA*, 1977, no. 5, 34–41.

"Administratsiya Cartera i Latinskaya Amerika" (The Carter Administration and Latin America). *LA*, 1979, no. 4, 101–6.

"Kuda Idet Braziliya?" (Where is Brazil Going?). *LA*, July 1980, 122–25.

"Sistemnyi Podkhod—Osnova Uglublennovo Analiza Vneshnepoliticheskoi Deyatelnosti Latinoamerikanskikh Gosudarstv" (Systems Approach—Basis of a Deepened Analysis of the Foreign Policy Activities of Latin American States). *LA*, August 1981, 47–53.

"Zakliuchitelnoe Slovo" (Concluding Word). *LA*, October 1981, 72–73.

"Gegemonizm SShA v Zapadnom Polusharii: Istoriya i Sovremennost" (U.S. Hegemony in the Western Hemisphere: History and Modern Times). *LA*, May 1982, 37–47.

"Formirovanie Voenno–Politechskoi Strategii Administratsii R. Reagana" (Formation of the Foreign Policy Strategy of the Reagan Administration). *SShA*, June 1982, 121.

"Latinskaya Amerika v Globalnoi Strategii Imperializma" (Latin America in the Global Strategy of Imperialism). *MEIMO*, October 1982, 65–82.

"Sovremennaya Strategiya Imperializma SShA v Latinskoi Amerike i Karibskom Basseine" (Contemporary Strategy of U.S. Imperialism in Latin America and the Caribbean Basin). *SShA*, June 1984, 16–28.

"Latinskaya Amerika v Mezhdunarodnykh Otnosheniyakh v XX v." (Latin America in International Relations in the Twentieth Century). *LA*, April 1986, 50–58.

"Ot Deli do Kharare" (From Delhi to Harare). *LA*, August 1987, 52.

"Otvetstvennost vo Vzaimozavisimom Mire" (Responsibility in an Interdependent World). *LA*, November 1987, 68–79.

**Gorbachev, Mikhail**. Speeches in *Pravda*, July 13, 1980, to December 27, 1988.

**Gorodnov, Valentin**. "Sovetskie Afrikanisty v Somali" (Soviet Africanists in Somalia). *Vestnik, AN, SSSR*, August 1972, 90–91.

"'Afrikan Komiunist' v 1974 g." ("African Communist" in 1974). *NAIA*, 1975, no. 3, 166–71.

"'Afrikan Komiunist' v 1975 Godu" ("African Communist" in 1975). *NAIA*, 1976, no. 3, 163–67.

"Kniga o Iuzhnoafrikanskom Revoliutsionere" (Book about a South African Revolutionary). *AIAS*, December 1976, 59–60.

"Iuzhno-Afrikanskaya Respublika: Uglublenie Krizisa i Obostrenie Borby" (Republic of South Africa: Deepening of Crisis and Aggravation of Struggle). *MEIMO*, April 1977, 123–28.

"Soueto—Gore i Gnev Iuzhnoi Afriki" (Soweto—Sorrow and Rage of Southern Africa). *AIAS*, June 1977, 21.

"Detribalizatsiya Afrikanskovo Gorodskovo Naseleniya RSA v Usloviyakh Apartkheida" (Detribalization of the African Urban Population of the RSA in Conditions of Apartheid). *NAIA*, 1980, no. 4, 11–19.

"Rabochie Vsegda Vperedi" (Workers are Always Ahead). *AIAS*, March 1982, 28–30.

"Vesna Osvobozhdeniya" (Spring of Liberation). *AIAS*, November 1982, 27–29.

**Gorshkov, Sergei**. "Vernyi Strazh Mira i Sotsializma" (Faithful Defense of Peace and Socialism). *Selskaya Zhizn*, February 23, 1965, 1.

"Vakhta na More" (Watch on the Ocean). *Sovetskaya Rossiya*, February 1, 1966, 2–3.

"Nash Moguchii Okeanskii Flot" (Our Mighty Ocean Fleet). *Pravda*, July 30, 1967, 2.

"Na Strazhe Zavoevanii Velikovo Oktyabrya" (On the Defense of the Gains of Great October). *Morskoi Sbornik*, October 1967, 3–15.

Interview. *Pravda*, February 14, 1968, 3.

"Den Pobedy" (Victory Day). *Ekonomicheskaya Gazeta*, 1968, no. 19, 9.

"Na Okeanskikh Rubezhakh" (On the Ocean Frontiers). *Pravda*, July 28,1968, 2.

"Bitvy na Moryakh" (Battles on the Seas). *Izvestiya*, February 27, 1970, 3

"Dalnie Plavaniya—Shkola Morskoi Vyuchki" (Distant Cruises—School of Naval Instruction). *KZ*, April 16, 1970, 2.

"Okeanskii Strazh Rodiny" (Ocean Defense of the Motherland). *Pravda*, July 26, 1970, 2.

"Na Moryakh i Okeanakh" (On Seas and Oceans). *Pravda*, July 30, 1972, 2.

"Na Okeanskoi Vakhte" (On the Ocean Watch). *Pravda*, July 29, 1973, 2.

"Podvig Naroda" (Feat of the People). *Trud*, May 9, 1974, 1.

"Morskaya Moshch Strany Sovetov" (Naval Strength of the Country of Soviets). *Pravda*, July 28, 1974, 2.

"Matrosskii Podvig" (Sailor's Feat). *Trud*, April 11, 1975, 4.

"Boevye Bympely Rodiny" (Military Pennants of the Motherland). *Izvestiya*, April 29, 1975, 5.

"Opyt Istorii i Sovremennost" (Experience of History and Modern Times). *VF*, May 1975, 33–38.

"Okeanskii Shchit Rodiny" (Ocean Shield of the Motherland). *KVS*, 1975, no. 14, 9–16.

"Pod Flagom Rodiny" (Under the Flag of the Motherland). *Pravda*, July 27, 1975, 2.

"Vstrechaya XXV Syezd KPSS" (Meeting the Twenty-fifth Congress of the CPSU). *Morskoi Sbornik*, February 1976, 8–13.

"Na Okeanskom Vakhte" (On the Ocean Watch). *KZ*, February 11, 1976, 2.

Speech in *Pravda*, July 25, 1976.

Interview. *KZ*, March 31, 1977, 3.

"Na Morskikh Rubezhakh" (On the Ocean Frontiers). *Pravda*, July 31, 1977, 2.

"Voenno-Morskoi Flot" (The Navy). *VIZ*, October 1977, 50–51.

"Morskaya Moshch Rodiny" (The Naval Power of the Motherland). *KVS*, 1978, no. 3, 9–13.

"Vsegda na Strazhe" (Always on the Defense). *KZ*, February 7, 1978, 2.

Interview. *Pravda*, July 30, 1978, 2.

"Na Okeanskikh Rubezhakh" (On the Ocean Frontiers). *Pravda*, July 29, 1979, 2.

"Slavnoe Detishche Sovetskovo Naroda" (Glorious Creation of the Soviet People). *Kommunist*, 1980, no. 3, 43–56.

"Na Okeanskom Vakhte" (On the Ocean Watch). *Pravda*, July 27, 1980, 2.

"Okeanskaya Vakhta Voennykh Moryakov" (Ocean Watch of Sailors). *KVS*, 1981, no. 2, 26–33.

"S Pozitsii Boegotovnosti" (From a Position of Military Preparedness). *KZ*, February 13, 1981, 2.

Interview. *Pravda*, July 26, 1981, 2.

"Strategicheskie Operatsii na Tikhookeanskom Teatre Voennykh Deistvii vo Vtoroi Mirovoi Voine" (Strategic Operations in the Pacific Theater of Military Operations in World War II). *VIZ*, August 1981, 65.

"Gordaya Slava Sevastopolya" (Proud Glory of Sevastopol). *Izvestiya*, October 30, 1981, 6.

"Okeanskaya Vakhta" (Ocean Watch). *Pravda*, July 25, 1982, 2.

"Bazy Agressii" (Bases of Aggression). *Pravda*, April 15, 1983, 4–5.

Interview. *Pravda*, July 31, 1983, 2.

"Amerikanskie Avianostsy—Orudie Ekspansii" (American Aircraft Carriers—Instrument of Expansion). *KZ*, October 14, 1983, 3.

"Bazy Agressii" (Bases of Aggression). *Izvestiya*, December 10, 1983, 5.

"Iiun Sorok Pervovo Ne Povtoritsya!" (June 1941 Will Not Be Repeated!). *Izvestiya*, June 22, 1984, 3.

"Okeanskii Shchit Rodiny" (Ocean Shield of the Motherland). *KZ*, July 7, 1984, 2.

"Okeanskii Shchit Rodiny" (Ocean Shield of the Motherland). *Pravda*, July 29, 1984, 2.

Interview. *LG*, May 1, 1985, 10.

Interview. *VIZ*, July 1985, 76–80.

Interview. *Pravda*, July 28, 1985, 2.

**Grechko, Andrei**. Speeches in *Krasnaya Zvezda* and *Pravda* May 8, 1965, to June 4, 1975.

"Velikii Podvig Naroda" (Great Feat of the People). *KZ*, May 8, 1965, 2.

"Boevoi Soiuz Bratskikh Narodov" (Militant Alliance of Fraternal Peoples). *Pravda*, May 13, 1965, 3.

"Armiya Velikovo Oktyabrya" (Army of Great October). *NINI*, 1967, no. 5, 3–16.

"Torzhestvo Leninskikh Idei o Zashchite Sotsialisticheskovo Otechestva" (Triumph of Leninist Ideas on the Defense of the Socialist Fatherland). *KVS*, 1967, no. 20, 31–39.

"Armiya Oktyabrya" (Army of October). *KZ*, November 3, 1967, 3.

"Pyatdesyat Let Sovetskikh Vooruzhenykh Sil" (Fifty Years of the Soviet Armed Forces). *VIZ*, February 1968, 3–14.

"V. I. Lenin i Stroitelstvo Sovetskikh Vooruzhenykh Sil" (V.I. Lenin and the Construction of the Soviet Armed Forces). *Kommunist*, 1969, no. 3, 15–26.

"Na Strazhe Mira i Sotsializma" (On the Defense of Peace and Socialism). *Kommunist*, 1970, no. 3, 62–64,

"Torzhestvo Leninskovo Ucheniya o Zashchite Zavoevanii Sotsializma" (The Triumph of Leninist Teaching on the Defense of the Gains of Socialism). *KZ*, April 18, 1970, 2.

"KPSS i Vooruzhenye Sily" (CPSU and the Armed Forces). *Kommunist*, 1971, no. 4, 38–48.

"Moguchii Strazh Mira i Sotsializma" (The Mighty Defense of Peace and Socialism). *KZ*, March 27, 1971, 2.

"Velikaya Pobeda" (Great Victory). *Pravda*, May 9, 1971, 2.

"Vospityvat Voinov v Dukhe Vysokoi Boevoi Gotovnosti" (Nurture Soldiers in the Spirit of High Military Readiness). *KVS*, 1971, no. 22, 3–14.

"Sovetskaya Molodezh v Oborone Strany" (Soviet Youth in Defense of the Country). *Molodaya Gvardiya*, February 1972, 4–13.

"Vooruzhenye Sily SSSR" (Armed Forces of the USSR). *Kommunist*, 1972, no. 3, 54–58.

"Nadezhnyi Strazh Sotsializma" (Reliable Defense of Socialism). *KZ*, February 23, 1972, 2.

"Pobedu Koval Narod" (People Forged the Victory). *Pravda*, May 9, 1972, 2.

"Istoricheskaya Pobeda" (Historic Victory). *Pravda*, February 2, 1973, 2.

"Na Strazhe Rodiny" (In Defense of the Motherland). *Pravda*, February 23, 1973, 2.

"Velikii Podvig" (Great Feat). *Pravda*, May 9, 1973, 2–3.

"Bitva za Kavkaz" (Battle for the Caucasus). *Pravda*, October 8, 1973, 2.

"V. I. Lenin i Vooruzhennye Sily Sovetskovo Gosudarstva" (V. I. Lenin and the Armed Forces of the Soviet State). *Kommunist*, 1974, no. 3, 15–24.

"Na Strazhe Mira i Sotsializma" (On the Defense of Peace and Socialism). *Pravda*, February 23, 1974, 2.

"Nauka i Iskusstvo Pobezhdat" (Science and the Art to Win). *Pravda*, February 19, 1975, 4.

"Vsemirno-Istoricheskaya Pobeda" (World-Historic Victory). *VIZ*, May 1975, 5–15.

**Gromyko, Andrei.** Speeches in *Pravda* and *Izvestiya*, January 22, 1965, to July 7, 1988.

Interview. *Ogonek*, 1970, no. 2, 1.

"Press Conference in Paris." *NT*, 1980, no. 19, 26–30.

"Razoruzhenie—Nasushchnaya Problema Sovremennosti" (Disarmament—Vital Problem of Our Times). *Kommunist*, 1980, no. 11, 6–23.

"Leninskaya Vneshnyaya Politika v Sovremennom Mire" (Leninist Foreign Policy in the Modern World). *Kommunist*, 1981, no. 1, 13–27.

"Radi Mira na Zemle" (For the Sake of Peace on Earth). *Kommunist*, 1982, no. 18, 19–30.

"V. I. Lenin i Vneshnyaya Politika Sovetskovo Gosudarstva" (V. I. Lenin and the Foreign Policy of the Soviet State). *Kommunist*, 1983, no. 6, 16–32.

**Iordansky, Vladimir**. "Problems of Rural Africa." *NT*, 1965, no. 28, 18–20.

"Pyat Let Politicheskoi Zakalki" (Five Years of Political Tempering). *AIAS*, August 1965, 20–22.

Book Review. *NAIA*, 1965, no. 5, 199–204.

"Afrika: Intelligentsiya na Putyakh Revoliutsii" (Africa: Intelligentsia on the Paths of Revolution). *AIAS*, February 1966, 22–25.

"Tropical Africa's Alarms." *IA*, December 1966, 27–32.

"Tropicheskaya Afrika: O Prirode Mezhetnicheskikh Konfliktov" (Tropical Africa: On the Nature of Interethnic Conflicts). Part 1, *MEIMO*, January 1967, 47–56. Part 2, *MEIMO*, February 1967, 41–50.

"Ghana: Power Crisis." *NT*, 1967, no. 25, 12–14.

"O Kharaktere Voennykh Diktatur v Tropicheskoi Afrike" (On the Character of Military Dictatorships in Tropical Africa). *NAIA*, 1967, no. 4, 22–37.

"Sotsialnye Sdvigi v Gorodakh Tropicheskoi Afriki" (Social Shifts in the Cities of Tropical Africa). *MEIMO*, October 1967, 68–83.

"Protivorechiya Nekapitalisticheskovo Razvitiya v Afrike" (Contradictions of Noncapitalist Development in Africa). *NAIA*, 1968, no. 3, 45–56.

"Tropicheskaya Afrika: Vnutriobshchinnye Protivorechiya" (Tropical Africa: Intracommunal Contradictions). *MEIMO*, September 1968, 49–59.

"Vozhdi i Narod" (Chiefs and the People). Part 1, *AIAS*, January 1969, 8–10. Part 3, *AIAS*, March 1969, 12–15.

"Rassloenie Afrikanskovo Krestyanstva" (The Differentiation of the African Peasantry). *MEIMO*, March 1969, 44–54.

"Tropicheskaya Afrika: Cherty Novovo Goroda" (Tropical Africa: Features of a New City). *NAIA*, 1969, no. 1, 16–27.

"Colonialism and Tropical Africa's National Problems." *IA*, October 1969, 19–24.

"Tropicheskaya Afrika: V Poiskakh Politicheskoi Stabilnosti" (Tropical Africa: In Search of Political Stability). *MEIMO*, January 1971, 44–55.

Book Review. *NAIA*, 1971, no. 1, 187–94.

"Neboskreby v Koltse Nishchety" (Skyscrapers in the Midsts of Misery). *RKISM*, January 1976, 121.

"Tropicheskaya Afrika: Protivorechiya Arkhaichnovo Soznaniya" (Tropical Africa: Contradictions of Archaic Consciousness). Part 2, *AIAS*, March 1976, 40–43.

"Novyi Trud Sovetskikh Uchenykh" (New Work of Soviet Scholars). *AIAS*, June 1976, 62–63.

"Retsenziya" (Review). *NAIA*, 1976, no. 4, 161.

"Spasaiut Rasistov: Manevry Amerikanskoi Diplomatii na Iuge Afriki" (They Are Saving the Racists: Maneuvers of American Diplomacy in Southern Africa). *KZ*, September 25, 1976, 3.

"Manevry Imperializma na Iuge Afriki" (Maneuvers of Imperialism in Southern Africa). *Pravda*, February 16, 1977, 4.

"Za Spinoi Narodov Afriki" (Behind the Back of the Peoples of Africa). *Pravda*, September 14, 1977, 4.

"Iuzhnaya Afrika: Potvorstvuiut Rasistam" (Southern Africa: They Are Pandering to Racists). *Pravda*, January 31, 1979, 4.

"Tropicheskaya Afrika: Dinamika Natsionalnovo Samosoznaniya" (Tropical Africa: Dynamics of National Self-Consciousness). *MEIMO*, January 1980, 111–21.

"RSA: Lavina Narodnovo Gneva" (RSA: Avalanche of Popular Rage). *Pravda*, August 8, 1980, 4.

"Afrika: Dvadtsat Trudnykh Shagov Vpered" (Africa: Twenty Difficult Steps Forward). *Pravda*, December 15, 1980, 6.

"The Policy of Neocolonialism in Action." *IA*, June 1981, 85–90.

"Apartheid on the Skids." *NT*, 1986, no. 28, 29–30.

"Bog-Smutyan v Mifologii Iorubov: Obshchestvennoe Soznanie i Narusheniya Izvechnovo Poryadka" (God–Trouble-Maker in the Mythology of the Yoruba: Social Consciousness and Violations of Eternal Order). *NAIA*, 1988, no. 2, 35–44.

**Khazanov, Anatolii**. "Pozornyi Soiuz—Zachem Caetanu Priletel v London" (Odious Alliance—Why did Caetanu Fly to London). *SR*, July 17, 1973, 3.

"Kolonialnoe Nasilie v Novykh Dekoratsiyakh" (Colonial Violence in New Decorations). *AIAS*, December 1973, 8–11.

"Peoples of Africa in Struggle Against Colonialists." *IA*, April 1974, 28–34.

"Trudnoe Nachalo" (Difficult Beginning). *AIAS*, May 1976, 13–16.

"Problema Mezhgosudarstvennykh Konfliktov v Afrike i Sobytiya na Afrikanskom Roge" (The Problem of Interstate Conflicts in Africa and Events on the African Horn). *AIAS*, July 1978, 21–22.

"Iug Afriki—Ochag Kolonializma i Rasizma" (Southern Africa—Hotbed of Colonialism and Racism). *AIAS*, June 1980, 62.

"The USSR in Support of Freedom and Independence." *IA*, May 1981, 24–31.

"Belyi Dom i Chernyi Kontinent" (The White House and the Black Continent). *AIAS*, September 1981, 14–16.

"TsRU Protiv Afriki" (The CIA Against Africa). *AIAS*, March 1983, 10–12.

"U.S. Ideological Expansion in Developing Countries." *IA*, November 1985, 106–12.

**Kim, Georgii**. "Lenin i Nekapitalisticheskii Put Razvitiya" (Lenin and the Noncapitalist Path of Development). *AIAS*, April 1965, 2–6.

"O Novom Etape Natsionalno-Osvoboditelnykh Revoliutsii" (On a New Stage of National Liberation Revolutions). *AIAS*, July 1966, 2–4.

"Proletarskii Internatsionalizm i Natsionalno-Osvoboditelnye Revoliutsii" (Proletarian Internationalism and National Liberation Revolutions). *Pravda*, September 14, 1966, 4.

"Dorogoi Internatsionalizma" (On the Road of Internationalism). *AIAS*, November 1967, 32–35.

"Non-Capitalist Development: Achievements and Difficulties." *IA*, December 1967, 70–76.

"Nekotorye Problemy Natsionalno-Osvoboditelnykh Revoliutsii v Svete Leninskikh Idei" (Some Problems of National Liberation Revolutions in Light of Leninist Ideas). *NAIA*, 1969, no. 5, 3–17.

Speech in *Kazakhstanskaya Pravda*, October 4, 1969, 2.

"Leninizm—Znamya Boriushchikhsya Narodov" (Leninism—Banner of Fighting Peoples). *AIAS*, December 1969, 42–43.

"Antikommunizm—Sredstvo Borby Protiv Natsionalno-Osvoboditelnovo Dvizheniya"

(Anticommunism—Means of Struggle Against the National Liberation Movement). *AIAS*, March 1970, 5–8.

"Leninskie Printsipy Soiuza Sotsializma s Natsionalno-Osvoboditelnym Dvizheniem" (Leninist Principles of the Alliance of Socialism with the National Liberation Movement). *NAIA*, 1970, no. 2, 3–13.

"'Vek Natsionalizma' . . . Tak Li Eto?" (Age of Nationalism . . . Or Is It Really?). *AIAS*, September 1971, 8–11.

"Ob Ideologicheskikh Techeniyakh v Stranakh 'Tretevo Mira'" (On Ideological Tendencies in Countries of the "Third World"). *NAIA*, 1972, no. 5, 39–49.

"Vo Imya Sotsialnovo Progressa—O Roli Srednykh Gorodskikh Sloev v Edinom Natsionalno-Demokraticheskom Fronte" (In the Name of Social Progress—On the Role of Intermediate Urban Strata in the United National Democratic Front). *AIAS*, November 1972, 26–27.

"Ideologiya Natsionalizma v Stranakh Azii i Afriki Na Sovremennom Etape" (The Ideology of Nationalism in Countries of Asia and Africa at the Contemporary Stage). *Vestnik, Moskovskovo Universiteta, Seriya XIV, Vostokovedenie*, 1973, no. 1, 3–9.

"Natsionalizm, Proletarskii Internatsionalizm i Revoliutsionnyi Protsess na Vostoke" (Nationalism, Proletarian Internationalism, and the Revolutionary Process in the East). *PDV*, 1973, no. 1, 74–83.

"Nekotorye Problemy Sovremennykh Natsionalno–Osvoboditelnykh Revoliutsii v Azii i Afrike" (Certain Problems of Contemporary National Liberation Revolutions in Asia and Africa). *VI*, August 1973, 73–85.

"Gorod i Proletariat v Afrike" (The City and Proletariat in Africa). *MEIMO*, Feburary 1974, 147–48.

"Solidarnost: Novyi Podyem" (A New Rise in Solidarity). *AIAS*, June 1974, 2–4.

"Natsionalno-Osvoboditelnoe Dvizhenie: Problemy i Perspektivy" (National Liberation Movement: Problems and Prospects). *AIAS*, December 1975, 2–6.

"Sotsialistichekaya Orientatsiya: Problemy i Perspektivy" (Socialist Orientation: Problems and Prospects). *AIAS*, January 1976, 2, 3, 18.

"XXV Syezd KPSS i Problemy Natsionalno-Osvoboditelnykh Revoliutsii" (The Twenty-Fifth Congress of the CPSU and Problems of National Liberation Revolutions). *NAIA*, 1976, no. 3, 3–15.

"World Socialism and Present-Day National Liberation Revolutions." *IA*, August 1977, 67–76.

"Razryadka i Razvivaiushchiesya Strany" (Detente and Developing Countries). *Pravda*, August 9, 1977, 4.

"Velikii Oktyabr i Natsionalno-Osvoboditelnoe Dvizhenie" (Great October and the National Liberation Movement). *AIAS*, November 1977, 2–5.

"Neocolonialism's Ideological Expansion." *IA*, November 1978, 76–80.

"Razryadka i Sotsialnyi Progress Stranakh Azii i Afriki" (Detente and the Social Progress of Countries of Asia and Africa). *AIAS*, November 1978, 3–6.

"The Successes of the National Liberation Movement and World Politics." *IA*, February 1979, 85–89.

"Social Development and Ideological Struggle in Developing Countries." *IA*, April 1980, 65–75.

"Osvobodivshiesya Strany na Rubezhe 70–x i 80–x Godov: Faktory Stabilizatsii i Destabilizatsii" (Liberated Countries on the Eve of the 1980s: Stabilizing and Destabilizing Factors). *AIAS*, June 1980, 3–5.

"Aktualnaya Problema Sovremennoi Afriki" (A Real Problem of Contermporary Africa). *MEIMO*, March 1981, 155–57.

"The National Liberation Movement Today." *IA*, April 1981, 27–37.

"Usilenie Sotsialno-Klassovoi Differentsiatsii" (The Strengthening of Socioclass Differentiation). *AIAS*, November 1981, 4–9.

"Sovetskii Soiuz i Natsionalno-Osvoboditelnoe Dvizhenie" (The Soviet Union and the National Liberation Movement). *MEIMO*, September 1982, 19–33.

"Sovetskii Soiuz i Voprosy Mira i Bezopasnosti v Azii" (The Soviet Union and Questions of Peace and Security in Asia). *AIAS*, September 1982, 2–6.

Book Review. *NAIA*, 1983, no. 5, 189–92.

"Gonka Vooruzhenii i Razvivaiushchiesya Strany" (The Arms Race and Developing Countries). *AIAS*, October 1984, 2–5.

"The National Liberation Movement: Topical Problems." *IA*, September 1984, 43–52.

"Azii-Mir i Sotrudnichestvo" (Peace and Coooperation for Asia). *Izvestiya*, December 6, 1985, 5.

"Tikhookeanskii Region v Strategii Imperializma" (Pacific Ocean Region in the Strategy of Imperialism). *AIAS*, January 1986, 5–8.

"Razvivaiushchiesya Strany v Sovremennom Mire" (Developing Countries in the Contemporary World). *MEIMO*, March 1986, 61–72.

"Osvobodivskhiesya Strany: Sovremennyi Etap" (Liberated Countries: The Contemporary Stage). *Pravda*, September 1, 1987, 4.

"Tretya Vsesoiuznaya Konferentsiya Vostokovedov" (The Third All-Union Conference of Orientologists). *NAIA*, 1988, no. 5, 8–19.

**Kislov, Aleksandr**. "Konek-'Chelovek v Sedle'" (Pony-Man in the Saddle). *KP*, June 20, 1965, 3.

"Ded Moroz v Armeiskikh Botinkakh" (Father Christmas in Army Boots). *Pravda*, January 3, 1969, 4.

"Journey to the Temple of Ammon." *NT*, 1969, no. 6, 28–29.

"Suez: Na Perednem Krae" (Suez: On the Front Line). *Kazakhstanskaya Pravda*, June 5, 1969, 4.

"New Life of New Valley." *NT*, 1969, no. 41, 28–30.

"Svet Aswana" (Light of Aswan). *LG*, January 7, 1970, 14.

"Stoikost i Muzhestvo Port-Saida" (Firmness and Valor of Port Said). *Sovetskaya Estonia*, February 20, 1970, 3.

"Abu-Zaabal—Simvol Stoikosti" (Abu-Zaabal—Symbol of Firmness). *LG*, February 25, 1970, 9.

"Blizhnevostochnoi Konflikt i Manevry Washingtona" (Middle East Conflict and Washington's Maneuvers). *SShA*, April 1971, 74–76.

"Zionisty na Sluzhbe Amerikanskovo Imperializma" (Zionists in the Service of American Imperialism). *Izvestiya*, January 20, 1972, 4.

"SShA v Sredizemnomorye: Novye Realnosti" (The U.S.A. in the Mediterranean: New Realities). *SShA*, April 1972, 32–39.

"Belyi Dom i Sionistskoe Lobbi" (The White House and the Zionist Lobby). *VI*, January 1973, 48–61.

"Antisovetskie Proiski Amerikanskikh Sionistov" (Anti-Soviet Intrigues of American Zionists). *SShA*, March 1973, 46–55.

"Arabskaya Neft, Izrail i Politika SShA" (Arab Oil, Israel, and U.S. Policy). *SShA*, November 1973, 46–50.

"Vokrug Blizhnevostochnovo Krizisa" (About the Middle East Crisis). *SShA*, January 1974, 20–27.

"Sovetsko-Amerikanskie Otnosheniya i Blizhnii Vostok" (Soviet-American Relations and the Middle East). *SShA*, September 1974, 63–68.

"Diplomatiya SShA i Blizhnevostochnoe Uregulirovanie" (U.S. Diplomacy and a Middle East Settlement). *SShA*, May 1975, 78–83.

"Obsuzhdenie Sinaiskovo Soglasheniya" (Discussion of the Sinai Agreement). *SShA*, December 1975, 71–77.

"Nasushchnye Problemy Blizhnevostochnovo Uregulirovaniya" (Vital Problems of a Middle East Settlement). *SShA*, July 1977, 22–33.

"Blizhnevostochnaya Stavka Vashingtona" (Washington's Middle East Headquarters). *Pravda*, September 21, 1977, 4.

"Posle Sovetsko-Amerikanskovo Zayavleniya po Blizhnemu Vostoku" (After the Soviet-American Statement on the Middle East). *SShA*, December 1977, 43–48.

"Blizhnevostochnaya Politika SShA: Starye Tseli, Podnovlennye Metody" (Middle East Policy of the U.S.: Old Goals, Renovated Methods). *AIAS*, June 1978, 11–14.

"The Arms Race in the Middle East." *IA*, July 1978, 88–93.

"Nyneshnii Etap Politiki SShA v Afrike" (Present Stage of U.S. Policy in Africa). *AIAS*, September 1978, 2–6.

"Sdelka v Kemp-Devide—'Illiuziya Uregulirovaniya'" (The Deal at Camp David—The Illusion of a Settlement). *SShA*, November 1978, 59–64.

"Blizhnii Vostok i SShA: 'Novyi Kurs' v Prezhnem Napravlenii" (The Middle East and the U.S.: "New Course" in the Previous Direction). *AIAS*, June 1980, 8–11.

"Blizhnii Vostok i Strategiya SShA" (The Middle East and U.S. Strategy). *SShA*, June 1980, 15–26.

"Washington i Irako-Iranskii Konflikt" (Washington and the Iraq-Iran Conflict). *SShA*, January 1981, 51–56.

"Blizhnii Vostok i Kemp-Devidskii Tupik" (Middle East and the Camp David Dead End). *SShA*, March 1982, 36–41.

"SShA i Blizhnii Vostok, god 1982" (The U.S.A. and the Middle East in 1982), *SShA*, January 1983, 18–28.

"Pentagon Adventurism in the Middle East." *IA*, April 1983, 100–107.

"Washington i Regionalnye Konflikty na Blizhnem Vostoke" (Washington and Regional Conflicts in the Middle East). *SShA*, July 1986, 27–38.

"Blizhnii Vostok i Pentagon" (The Middle East and the Pentagon). *SShA*, April 1987, 13–24.

"Novoe Politicheskoe Myshlenie i Regionalnye Konflikty" (New Political Thinking and Regional Conflicts). *MEIMO*, August 1988, 40–47.

"Novoe Myshlenie i Regionalnye Konflikty" (New Thinking and Regional Conflicts). *Pravda*, September 29, 1988, 4.

**Kokoshin, Andrei.** "Mirovoi Okean v Politike SShA" (The World Ocean in U.S. Policy). *SShA*, November 1971, 14–26.

"Naval Power in U.S. Strategic Plans." *IA*, April 1973, 56–62.

"American Foreign Policy Strategy for the 1970s." *IA*, October 1973, 67–73.

"Teplye Vetry Peremen" (Warm Winds of Changes). *Molodoi Kommunist*, October 1973, 97–103.

"SShA i Mezhdunarodhnye Otnosheniya v Poslednei Chetverti XX v." (The U.S.A. and International Relations in the Last Quarter of the Twentieth Century). *SShA*, February 1976, 56–66.

"'Vzaimozavisimost:' Realnosti, Kontseptsii i Politika" ("Interdependence": Realities, Concepts, and Policy). *SShA*, January 1977, 12–22.

"Evoliutsiya Noveishikh Amerikanskikh Kontseptsii Razvitiya Mezhdunarodnykh Otnoshenii" (Evolution of the Newest American Conceptions of the Development of International Relations). *VI*, November 1977, 99–118.

"Tendentsii Razvitiya Tikhookeanskovo Regiona i Politika SShA" (Tendencies in the Development of the Pacific Ocean Region in U.S. Policy). *SShA*, April 1978, 16–26.

"Problema 'Natsionalnykh Prioritetov' SShA na Poroge Vosmidesyatykh" (The Problem of the "National Priorities" of the U.S.A. on the Eve of the 1980s). *SShA*, October 1979, 3–14.

"Vnutrennie Prichiny Peremen vo Vneshnei Politike" (Domestic Causes of Changes in Foreign Policy). *SShA*, July 1980, 3–13.

"'Novyi Kontinentalizm' kak Variant Vneshnepoliticheskoi Doktriny SShA na 80-e Gody" ("New Continentalism" as a Variant of the Foreign Policy Doctrine of the U.S.A. in the 1980s). *SShA*, October 1980, 68–73.

Book Review. *SShA*, August 1981, 104–5.

"Gruppirovki Amerikanskoi Burzhuazii i Vneshnepoliticheskii Kurs SShA" (Groupings of the American Bourgeoisie and the Course of American Foreign Policy). *SShA*, October 1981, 3–14.

"Yadernyi 'Trezubets' Vykhodit v Okean" (Nuclear Tridents Take to the Ocean). *LG*, November 25, 1981, 14.

"Monopolii i Vlast" (Monopolies and Power). *Kommunist*, 1982, no. 5, 108–12.

Book Review. *VI*, April 1982, 160–62.

"Formirovanie Voenno-Politicheskoi Strategii Administratsii Reagana" (Formulation of the Military-Political Strategy of the Reagan Administration). *SShA*, May 1982, 120–22.

Speech in *KP*, May 21, 1982, 4.

"Tipy Protivorechii i Raznoglasii na Verkhnem Urovne Ispolnitelnoi Vlasti v Sfere 'Natsionalnoi Bezopasnosti'" (Types of Contradictions and Differences at the Highest Level of Executive Power in the Area of National Security). *SShA*, March 1983, 50–59.

"Debaty v SShA Vokrug Planov Sozdaniya Kosmicheskoi Protivoraketnoi Sistemy" (Debates in the U.S.A. on Plans for Creating a Space Anti-Missile System). *SShA*, November 1983, 36–46.

"Problemy Prezidentskoi Vlasti" (Problems of Presidential Power). *SShA*, December 1983, 112–13.

"Diskussii po Tsentralnym Voprosam Voennoi Politiki SShA" (Discussion on the Central Questions of U.S.A. Military Policy). *SShA*, February 1985, 3–14.

"Yadernoe Oruzhie i Dilemmy Mezhdunarodnoi Bezopasnosti" (Nuclear Arms and Dilemmas of International Security). *MEIMO*, April 1985, 33–43.

"Pogonya za Illiuziei" (Race for Illusions). *Pravda*, June 14, 1985, 4.

"'Plan Rodzhersa,' Alternativnye Kontseptsii Oborony i Bezopasnost v Evrope" (The "Rodgers Plan," Alternative Conceptions of Defense and Security in Europe). *SShA*, September 1985, 3–14.

"Voprosy Kontrolya i Ogranichenie Vooruzhenii v Sovetsko-Amerikanskikh Soglasheni-yakh" (Questions of Verification and Limitation of Weapons in Soviet-American Agreements). *SShA*, February 1986, 29–38.

"Problemy Bezopasnosti—Amerikanskie Varianty" (Problems of Security—American Versions). *SShA*, July 1986, 98–100.

"S Pozitsii Realizma" (From a Position of Realism). *Pravda*, July 11, 1986, 4.

"Asimmetrichnyi Otvet" (Asymmetrical Response). *SShA*, February 1987, 26–27.

"Stabilnost i Peremeny v Mezhdunarodnykh Otnosheniyakh (Razmyshleniya o Dok-lade Professora John Gaddis)" (Stability and Changes in International Relations. [Thoughts about the paper of John Gaddis]). *SShA*, July 1987, 6–13.

"Kurskaya Bitva v Svete Sovremennoi Oboronitelnoi Doktriny" (The Battle of Kursk in Light of Contemporary Defensive Doctrine). *MEIMO*, August 1987, 32–40.

"Sopostavlyaya Voennye Doktriny" (Comparing Military Doctrines). *Pravda*, August 21, 1987, 4.

"Yadernoe Oruzhie i Strategicheskaya Stabilnost" (Nuclear Weapons and Strategic Stability). Part 1, *SShA*, September 1987, 3–13.

"Razvitie Voennovo Dela i Sokrashchenie Vooruzhennykh Sil i Obychnykh Voo-ruzhenii" (Development of Military Affairs and the Reduction of Conventional Forces). *MEIMO*, January 1988, 20–32.

"Sokrashchenie Yadernykh Vooruzhenii i Strategicheskaya Stabilnost" (The Reduction of Nuclear Weapons and Strategic Stability). *SShA*, February 1988, 8–12.

"Protivostoyanie Sil Obshchevo Naznacheniya v Kontekste Obespecheniya Strategi-cheskoi Stabilnosti" (The Opposition of Conventional Forces in the Context of Maintaining Strategic Stability). *MEIMO*, June 1988, 23–31.

"What We Expect." *NT*, 1988, no. 22, 17.

"Defense Is Best for Stability." *NT*, 1988, no. 33, 18–19.

"Tri 'Kita' Stabilnosti" (Three Keys to Stability). *KZ*, September 16, 1988, 3.

"Otnosheniya USSR-SShA: Istoricheskii Analiz" (U.S.S.R.-U.S.A. Relations: An Historical Analysis). *SShA*, October 1988, 110–11.

"Voprosy Issledovaniya Mezhdunarodnykh Peregovorov" (Questions for Research in International Negotiations). *MEIMO*, October 1988, 23–33.

"Alexander Svechin: On War and Politics." *IA*, November 1988, 125–26.

"Chemu Uchat Sudby Velikikh Derzhav?" (What is Taught by the Fates of Great Powers?). *Kommunist*, 1988, no. 17, 115–21.

**Korolev, Iurii**. "Borba za Edinstvo Rabochego Klassa v Chili (1956-70)" (Struggle for Unity of Working Class in Chile). *VI*, January 1973, 43–56.

"Svobodu Corvalunu" (Freedom for Corvalan). *Trud*, October 5, 1973, 3.

"Tragediya Chile" (Tragedy of Chile). *Molodoi Kommunist*, December 1973, 85–90.

"Chili: Dni Predatelstva" (Chile: Days of Betrayal). *LA*, 1974, no. 1, 70–78.

"Aktualnost Chiliiskovo Opyta" (Reality of the Chilean Experience). *LA*, September 1980, 6–14.

"Anti-Popular Regimes in Latin America." *IA*, September 1980, 114–21.

"Junta Pinocheta: Plody Pravleniya" (Pinochet Junta: Fruits of Government). *LA*, November 1980, 52–68.

"Proletariat—Vedushchaya Sila Sotsialnovo Progressa v Latinskoi Amerike" (Proletariat —Leading Force of Social Progress in Latin America). *LA*, March 1981, 6–21.

"Revoliutsionnye Protsessy i Voprosy Sotsialno-Politicheskovo Razvitiya v Latinskoi Amerike" (Revolutionary Processes and Questions of Sociopolitical Development in Latin America). *LA*, April 1981, 59–64.

"El Salvador: The 'Hot Spot' in Latin America." *IA*, June 1981, 61–66.

"Samostoyatelnost i Zrelost Burzhuazii . . ." (Independence and Maturity of the Bourgeoisie . . . ). *LA*, October 1981, 63.

"Partiya Tvorcheskovo Marksizma—K 60-letiiu Kommunisticheskoi Partii Chile" (Party of Creative Marxism—Toward the Sixtieth Year of the Chile Communist Party). *LA*, January 1982, 36–44.

"Transnatsionalizatsiya Ekonomiki Razvivaiushchikhsya Stran: Prichiny, Osobennosti i Predely" (Transnationalization of Economies of Developing Countries: Causes, Peculiarities, and Limits). *LA*, August 1983, 26–30.

"Revoliutsionnyi Protsess v Stranakh Tsentralnoi Ameriki: Istoricheskaya Preemstvennost i Osobennosti" (Revolutionary Process in Central American Countries: Historical Continuity and Peculiarities). *LA*, April 1984, 5–19.

"Istoricheskii Opyt Perekhodnovo Perioda" (Historical Experience of the Transition Period). *LA*, June 1984, 9–22.

"Vremya Reshenii" (Time of Decisions). *LA*, October 1984, 9–10.

"Reckless Policy: How the United States Is 'Saving' Central America." *IA*, December 1984, 94–102.

"Latinskaya Amerika: Protivorechiya Novovo Etapa" (Latin America: Contradictions of a New Stage). *MEIMO*, August 1985, 96–100.

"Revoliutsionno-Demokraticheskaya Perspektiva: Nekotorye Aspekty Analiza Perexodnovo Perioda" (Revolutionary Democratic Prospects: Certain Aspects of an Analysis of the Transition Period). *LA*, March 1986, 7–13.

"The Great October Socialist Revolution and Latin America." *IA*, August 1987, 76–82.

"Metamorfozy Vzaimozavisimosti: Regionalnyi Aspekt" (Metamorphoses of Interdependence: The Regional Aspect). *LA*, January 1988, 21–26.

"Chile: Sumerki Diktatury" (Chile: Twilight of a Dictatorship). *LA*, April 1988, 6–13.

"Zachem Chiliiskoi Diktature Plebistsit?" (Why a Plebiscite under the Chilean Dictatorship?). *LA*, June 1988, 30, 34, 36–37.

"Ne Demontazh i ne Rekonstruktsiya" (Neither Dismantling Nor Reconstruction). *LA*, July 1988, 56–59.

"Adekvatnost Proekta ili Novaya Levaya" (Adequacy of the Program or the New Left). *LA*, November 1988, 32–39.

"Latinskaya Amerika: Revoliutsii v Noveishee Vremya" (Latin America: Revolutions in Present Times). *LA*, November 1988, 125.

**Kosygin, Alexei**. Speeches in *Pravda* and *Izvestiya*, February 9, 1965, to June 18, 1980.

**Kremeniuk, Viktor**. "'Doktrina Nixona': Deklaratsii i Realnost" (The "Nixon Doctrine": Declarations and Reality). *SShA*, February 1971, 43–44.

"Indostan—Ot Konflikta k Uregulirovaniiu" (Hindustan—From Conflict to Settlement). *AIAS*, May 1972, 35–37.

"Prezidentskie Vybory i Blizhnii Vostok" (Presidential Elections and the Middle East). *SShA*, January 1973, 71–77.

"Strategiya SShA v Zone Indiiskovo Okeana" (U.S. Strategy in the Indian Ocean Region). *SShA*, May 1973, 6–17.

"Conflicts in Developing Countries and Imperialist Policy." *IA*, January 1974, 61–65.

"Regionalnye Napravleniya vo Vneshnei Politike SShA" (Regional Directions in U.S. Foreign Policy). *SShA*, May 1974, 44–51.

"Eshche Odna Popytka Pereosmysleniya Vneshnei Politiki" (Yet Another Try to Rethink Foreign Policy). *SShA*, April 1975, 91.

"Neokolonializm i Afrika" (Neocolonialism and Africa). *SShA*, July 1976, 97–99.

"Oktyabr, Natsionalno-Osvoboditelnoe Dvizhenie i Politika SShA" (October, the National Liberation Movement, and U.S. Policy). *SShA*, November 1977, 52–58.

"Aziatskaya Politika SShA: Proshloe i Nastoyashchee" (U.S. Asian Policy: Past and Present). *AIAS*, December 1977, 20–24.

"Washington i Razvivaiushchiesya Strany: Rol Kontseptsii 'Politicheskovo Razvitiya'" (Washington and Developing Countries: The Role of the Concept of "Political Development"). *SShA*, January 1979, 9–21.

"Nauchno-Tekhnicheskii Neokolonializm" (Scientific-Technical Neocolonialism). *MEIMO*, August 1979, 144–45.

"Razvivaiushchiesya Strany i SShA: Usilenie Protivoborstva" (Developing Countries and the U.S.: Increasing Antagonism). *SShA*, February 1981, 5–14.

"Po Staromu Stsenariiu Interventsionizma" (According to the Old Scenario of Interventionism). *SShA*, May 1981, 52–57.

"Orudie Agresivnoi Politiki" (Instrument of Aggressive Policy). *MEIMO*, July 1981, 143.

Book Review. *SShA*, October 1981, 99–100.

"Sovetsko-Amerikanskie Otnosheniya i Nekotorye Problemy Osvobodivshchikhsya Gosudarstv" (Soviet-American Relations and Certain Problems of Liberated States). *SShA*, June 1982, 7–18.

Book Review. *NAIA*, 1982, no. 6, 193–94.

"SShA-Afganistan: Proiski Prodolzhaiutsya" (U.S.A.-Afghanistan: The Intrigues Continue). *SShA*, January 1983, 56–59.

"Strategiya Ugroz i Agressii" (Strategy of Threats and Aggression). *KZ*, March 26, 1983, 5.

"Imperializm i Razvivaiushchiesya Strany: Evoliutsiya Vzaimootnoshenii" (Imperialism and Developing Countries: The Evolution of Relations). *AIAS*, December 1983, 4–7.

"'Doktrina Reigana'—Kurs na Eskalatsiiu Vmeshatelstvo" (The "Reagan Doctrine"—A Course of Escalating Interference). *SShA*, November 1985, 63–67.

"SShA v Regionalnykh Konfliktakh" (U.S.A. in Regional Conflicts). *SShA*, June 1986, 23–33.

"'Strategiya Sotrudnichestva' v Teorii Igr" ("Cooperation Strategy" in Game Theory). *SShA*, September 1986, 102–3.

"Voprosy Issledovaniya Mezhdunarodnykh Peregorov" (Questions of Investigating International Negotiations). *MEIMO*, October 1988, 23–33.

**Landa, Robert**. "Palestinskie Fidai" (Palestinian Fedayeen). *AIAS*, March 1971, 47–49.

"V Universitetakh Alzhira" (In the Universities of Algiers). *AIAS*, April 1974, 53–54.

"Osvoboditelnaya Borba Arabov Palestiny" (Liberation Struggle of Palestinian Arabs). *NAIA*, 1976, no. 1, 18–31.

"Palestinskii Vopros: Sotsialno-Politicheskii Aspekt" (Palestinian Question: Sociopolitical Aspect). *AIAS*, March 1976, 6–8.

"Iz Istorii Palestinskovo Dvizheniya Soprotivleniya (1967-1971 gg.)" (From the History of the Palestinian Resistance Movement). *NAIA*, 1976, no. 4, 29–31.

"Sovremennyi Etap Borby Palestinskovo Dvizheniya Soprotivleniya (1971-1976)" (Contemporary Stage of the Struggle of the Palestinian Resistance Movement). *NAIA*, 1976, no. 5, 15–29.

"U Alzhirskikh Krestyan" (Among Algerian Peasants). *AIAS*, January 1977, 33–35.

"Marokkanskie Vstrechi" (Moroccan Meetings). *AIAS*, February 1981, 40–43.

"Algeria: Progressive Development." *IA*, August 1981, 95–102.

"'Demokraticheskii Kapital' na Vostoke" ("Democratic Capital" in the East). *AIAS*, August 1982, 20–23.

"Rol Gosudarstvennovo Menedzhmenta v Sotsialnoi Evoliutsii Afro-Aziatskikh Stran Kapitalisticheskoi Orientatsii" (Role of State Management in the Social Evolution of Afro-Asian Countries of Capitalist Orientation). *NAIA*, 1985, no. 4, 35–38.

"Natsionalnoe i Sotsialnoe Soderzhanie Osvoboditelnykh Revoliutsii" (National and Social Content of Liberation Revolutions). *AIAS*, November 1985, 2–4.

"Vazhnyi Faktor Mirovovo Revoliutsionnovo Protsessa" (Important Factor of the World Revolutionary Process). *AIAS*, September 1987, 9–12.

"K Izucheniiu Sotsialnoi Struktury Afro-Aziatskovo Mira" (Toward the Study of the Social Structure of the Afro-Asian World). *NAIA*, 1988, no. 3, 54–64.

**Mikoyan, Sergo**. "Boriushchiisya Kontinent" (Fighting Continent). *SR*, August 1, 1972, 3.

"Razryadka Mezhdunarodnoi Napryazhennosti i Borba za Mir v Latinskoi Amerike" (Detente and Struggle for Peace in Latin America). *LA*, 1973, no. 5, 214–16.

"Vstrecha Storonnikov Mira v Paname" (Meeting of Peace Advocates in Panama). *LA*, 1975, no. 1, 213–16.

"Peru Posle 5 Febralya" (Peru After February 5). *LA*, 1975, no. 3, 221–24.

"Mezhdunarodnaya Politika Partii" (The Party's International Policy). *LA*, 1976, no. 4, 7–12.

"Torzhestvo Leninskoi Politiki Mira" (Triumph of Leninist Peace Policy). *LA*, 1977, no. 3, 7–9.

"Armiya i Politika v Sovremennoi Latinskoi Amerike" (Army and Politics in Contemporary Latin America). *LA*, 1977, no. 4, 142–45.

"Vremya Velikikh Peremen" (A Time of Great Changes). *LA*, 1978, no. 1, 8.

"Latin America: Winds of Change." *NT*, 1979, no. 3, 4–5.

"Administratsiya Cartera i Latinskaya Amerika" (Carter Administration and Latin America). *LA*, 1979, no. 4, 159–60.

"Globalnye Problemy i Razvitie" (Global Problems and Development). *LA*, 1979, no. 4, 60–62.

"Revoliutsionnoe Tvorchestvo Prokladyvaet Put k Pobede" (Revolutionary Creativity Clears Path to Victory). *LA*, February 1980, 5–8.

"Ob Osobennostyakh Revoliutsii v Nikaragua i ee Urokakh s Tochki Zreniya Teorii i Praktiki Osvoboditelnovo Dvizheniya" (On Peculiarities of the Revolution in Nicaragua and its Lessons from the Viewpoint of the Theory and Practice of the Liberation Movement). *LA*, March 1980, 35–44.

" 'Nyet'—Junte!" ("No" to the Junta!). *Pravda*, August 4, 1980, 6.

"Venezuela: Vneshnyaya Politika, Nekotorye Predposylki i Osobennosti Formirovaniya" (Venezuela: Foreign Policy and Some Preconditions and Peculiarities of its Formulation). *LA*, December 1980, 8–11.

"Storm and Stress." *NT*, 1981, no. 13, 18–20.

"Brazil: Problems and Preoccupations." *NT*, 1983, no. 50, 23–25.

"Politika Bezrassudstva" (Policy of Recklessness). *Pravda*, June 9, 1984, 4.

"Latin America: New Upsurge." *NT*, 1985, no. 16, 18–21.

"Debt Bondage." *NT*, 1985, no. 20, 24–25.

"Grenada: Naked Brigandism." *NT*, 1985, no. 47, 10–11.

"Braziliya v Sovremennom Mire" (Brazil in the Modern World). *LA*, April 1987, 6–13.

"The 'Volcanic Continent.' " *NT*, special supplement, *The October Revolution and the World*, November 1987, 29.

**Mirsky, Georgi.** "Klassy i Klassovaya Borba v Razvivaiushchikhsya Stranakh" (Classes and Class Struggle in Developing Countries). Part 2, *MEIMO*, March 1966, 57–69.

"Israeli Aggression and Arab Unity." *NT*, 1967, no. 28, 4–6.

"Armiya i Politika v 'Tretem Mire,' " (The Army and Politics in the "Third World"). *LG*, August 9, 1967, 14.

"Arab East: Moment of Truth." *NT*, 1967, nos. 46–47, 27–29.

"Hashimitskoe Korolevstvo Iordanii" (Hashemite Kingdom of Jordan). *MEIMO*, January 1968, 139–41.

"Arabskie Narody Prodolzhaiut Borbu" (Arabs Continue the Struggle). *MEIMO*, March 1968, 120–25.

"Israeli Aggression: One Year Later." *NT*, 1968, no. 22, 12–14.

"Rebirth of the Arab World." *NT*, 1968, no. 25, 10–12.

"Israel: Illusions and Miscalculations." *NT*, 1968, no. 39, 6–8.

"O Kharaktere Sotsialnykh Sil v Azii i Afrike" (On the Character of Social Forces in Asia and Africa). *Kommunist*, 1968, no. 17, 89–102.

"Politicheskaya Rol Armii v Stranakh Azii i Afrike" (Political Role of the Army in Asian and African Countries). *NAIA*, 1968, no. 6, 3–14.

"UAR: Home Front." *NT*, 1968, no. 50, 8–10.

"Third World: Illusions and Realities" *NT*, 1969, no. 1, 10–12.

"'Novaya Revoliutsiya' v Egipte" ("New Revolution" in Egypt). *MEIMO*, January 1969, 38–48.

"Suez: Na Perednem Krae" (Suez: On the Front Line). *Kazakhstanskaya Pravda*, June 5, 1969, 4.

"Changes in the Third World." *NT*, 1969, no. 39, 4–6.

"Developing Countries: Army and Society." *NT*, 1969, no. 48, 15–17.

"O Nekotorykh Osobennostyakh Evoliutsii Armii Latinoamerikanskovo Kontinenta" (On Certain Peculiarities of the Evolution of the Army on the Latin American Continent). *LA*, 1971, no. 4, 42–54.

"Tendencies in the National Liberation Movement Today." *IA*, August 1971, 18–20.

"The Path of the Egyptian Revolution." *NT*, 1972, no. 30, 21–24.

"Natsionalizm i Nekapitalisticheskii Put Razvitiya" (Nationalism and the Noncapitalist Path of Development). *MEIMO*, October 1972, 121–23.

"Aktualnye Problemy Natsionalno-Osvoboditelnovo Dvizheniya" (Actual Problems of the National Liberation Movement). *MEIMO*, November 1972, 155–57.

"O Roli Gosudarstva i Gosudarstvennom Kapitalizme" (On the Role of the State and State Capitalism). *AIAS*, April 1973, 34–37.

"Middle East: New Factors." *NT*, 1973, no. 48, 18–19.

"Nekapitalisticheskoe Razvitie: Tendentsii i Perspektivy" (Noncapitalist Development: Tendencies and Prospects). *Molodoi Kommunist*, May 1975, 107–12.

"Nekotorye Aspekty Sotsialisticheskoi Orientatsii" (Certain Aspects of Socialist Orientation). *AIAS*, June 1975, 24–26.

"Neokolonializm v Afrike" (Neocolonialism in Africa). *MEIMO*, June 1975, 141–43.

"Rol Armii v Obshchestvennom Razvitii" (Role of the Army in Social Development). *AIAS*, January 1976, 16–17.

"Menyaiushchiisya Oblik 'Tretevo Mira'" (The Changing Cast of the Third World). *Kommunist*, 1976, no. 2, 107–15.

"Kapitalizm i Puti Preodoleniya Otstalosti Razvivaiushchiskhsya Stran" (Capitalism and Paths of Overcoming the Backwardness of Developing Countries). *AIAS*, March 1976, 62–63.

"Chto Proiskhodit v Livane" (What Is Happening in Lebanon). *LG*, March 24, 1976, 15.

"Razvivaiuschiesya Strany i Mirovoi Kapitalizm" (Developing Countries and World Capitalism). *MEIMO*, March 1976, 36–45.

"Razvivaushchiesya Strany v Sovremennom Mire" (Developing Countries in the Contemporary World). *MEIMO*, January 1977, 140–41.

"Armiya i Politika v Sovremennoi Latinskoi Amerike" (Army and Politics in Contemporary Latin America). *LA*, 1977, no. 3, 69–74, 79, 80.

"Blizhnii Vostok: Tri Desyatiletiya—Chetyre Voiny" (Middle East: Three Decades—Four Wars). *MEIMO*, July 1978, 150.

"Rol Armii v Sotsialnom Razvitii Stran Azii i Afriki" (Role of Army in Social Development of Asian and African Countries). *VF*, March 1979, 98–108.

"Sotsialnya Rol Melkoi Burzhuazii" (Social Role of the Petite Bourgeoisie). *MEIMO*, May 1979, 140–41.

Book Review. *NAIA*, 1979, no. 4, 211–15.

"Biurokraticheskaya Burzhuaziya, Biurokraticheskii Kapital, Gossektor i Goskapitalizm" (Bureaucratic Bourgeoisie, Bureaucratic Capital, the State Sector, and State Capitalism). *NAIA*, 1979, no. 5, 204–8.

"Natsionalno-Osvoboditelnaya Borba: Sovremennyi Etap" (National Liberation Struggle: Modern Stage). *MEIMO*, June 1981, 17–30.

"Osobennosti Revoliutsionnovo Protsessa v Azii i Afrike" (Peculiarities of Revolutionary Process in Asia and Africa). *MEIMO*, June 1983, 147–49.

"O Perspektivakh Kapitalizma v Razvivaiushchemsya Mire" (On Prospects of Capitalism in Developing World). *NAIA*, 1985, no. 1, 81–82, 93–94.

"Razvivaiushchiesya Strany: Ekonomicheskii Rost i Sotsialnyi Progress" (Developing Countries: Economic Growth and Social Progress). *NAIA*, 1985, no. 5, 172–74.

"Konets 'Chernoi Epokhi'" (End of the "Black Age"). *AIAS*, January 1986, 27–31.

"Osvobodivshiesya Gosudarstva: Puti Razvitiya" (Liberated States: Paths of Development). *AIAS*, March 1987, 26–29.

"K Voprosu o Vybore Puti i Orientatsii Razvivaiushchikhsya Stran" (On the Question of Choice of Path and Orientation of Developing Countries). *MEIMO*, May 1987, 70–81.

"Sotsialisticeskaya Orientatsiya v Svete Novovo Politicheskovo Myshleniya" (Socialist Orientation in Light of New Political Thinking). *AIAS*, August 1987, 26–32.

"'Tretii Mir': Armiya i Vlast" (Third World: Army and Power). *Izvestiya*, March 4, 1988, 5.

"Ekstremizm, Terrorizm i Vnutrennie Konflikty v 'Tretem Mire'" (Extremism, Terrorism, and Domestic Conflicts in the Third World). *MEIMO*, August 1988, 69–74.

"Svet i Teni Nashevo 'Tretyemirovedeniya'" (Light and Darkness of Our Third World Studies). *MEIMO*, November 1988, 135–37.

**Ogarkov, Nikolai.** Speeches in *KZ*, June 5, 1980, to January 7, 1981.

"Stoim na Strazhe" (We Stand in Defense). *Izvestiya*, July 20, 1967, 3.

"Velikii Podvig Naroda" (Great Feat of the People). *Uchitelskaya Gazeta*, May 9, 1969, 1.

Answering Questions. *KZ*, July 10, 1973, 3.

"Velikaya, Otechestvennaya" (Great, Fatherland). *SR*, May 8, 1975, 2.

"Voennaya Nauka i Zashchita Sotsialisticheskovo Otechestva" (Military Science and Defense of the Socialist Fatherland). *KVS*, 1978, no. 7, 110–21.

"Velikii Podvig Sovetskovo Naroda" (Great Feat of the Soviet People). *Izvestiya*, May 9, 1978, 3.

"Sotsializm Umeet Zashchishchatsya" (Socialism Can Defend Itself). *KZ*, February 23, 1979, 2–3.

"Zavetam Lenina Verny" (True to Lenin's Precepts). *Izvestiya*, February 24, 1980, 2.

"Podvig vo Imya Mira" (Feat in the Name of Peace). *KP*, May 9, 1980, 2.

"Uroki Istorii" (Lessons of History). *KZ*, May 9, 1981, 2.

Na Strazhe Mirnovo Truda" (In Defense of Peaceful Labor). *Kommunist*, 1981, no. 11, 80–91.

Vo Imya Mira i Progressa" (In the Name of Peace and Progress). *Izvestiya*, May 9, 1982, 1–2.

"Tvorcheskaya Mysl Polkovoditsa" (Creative Idea of the Commander). *Pravda*, October 2, 1982, 3.

"Nadezhnyi Oplot Sotsializma i Mira" (Reliable Bastion of Socialism and Peace). *KZ*, February 23, 1983, 1–2.

"Pobeda i Sovremennost" (Victory and Today). *Izvestiya*, May 9, 1983, 2.

"Miru-Nadezhnuiu Zashchitu" (Reliable Defense of Peace). *Izvestiya*, September 23, 1983, 4–5.

Press Conference. *Pravda*, December 6, 1983, 4.

"Nemerknushchaya Slava Sovetskovo Oruzhiya" (Unfading Glory of Soviet Armaments). *KVS*, 1984, no. 21, 22–26.

**Podgorny, Nikolai**. Speeches in *Pravda* and *Izvestiya*, May 9, 1965, to May 5, 1977.

"Pyatdesyatoe-Letie Soiuza SSSR-Edinovo Mnogonatsionalnovo Gosudarstva" (Fifty Years of the U.S.S.R.-United Multinational State). *Kommunist*, 1972, no. 8, 19–20.

**Ponomarev, Boris**. Speeches in *Pravda*, June 3, 1966, to April 18, 1987.

"Istoricheskie Uroki VII Kongressa Kominterna i Sovremennost" (Historical Lessons of the Seventh Comintern Congress and Today). *Kommunist*, 1965, no. 16, 14–32.

"Moscow-International Symposium." *NT*, 1967, no. 50, 3–11.

"Istoricheskoe Znachenie Kominterna" (Historical Significance of the Comintern). *Kommunist*, 1969, no. 5, 11–28.

"V. I. Lenin—Great Leader of the Revolutionary Epoch." *IA*, April 1970, 3–12.

"Aktualnye Problemy Teorii Mirovovo Revoliutsionnovo Protsessa" (Actual Problems of the Theory of the World Revolutionary Process). *Kommunist*, 1971, no. 15, 37–71.

"Aktualnaya Zadacha Ideino-Politicheskoi Borby—Trotskizm—Orudie Antikommunizma" (Actual Task of Ideological-Political Struggle—Trotskyism—Instrument of Anticommunism). *Kommunist*, 1971, no. 18, 14–34.

"Ideinoe Nasledie G. Dimitrova i Sovremennost" (Ideological Legacy of G. Dimitrov and Today). *Kommunist*, 1972, no. 9, 18–37.

"Za Sotrudnichestvo v Borbe Protiv Gonki Vooruzhenii, za Razoruzhenie" (For Cooperation in Struggle Against Arms Race and For Disarmament). *Kommunist*, 1978, no. 7, 40–50.

"Imperializm i Osvobodivshiesya Strany" (Imperialism and Liberated Countries). *AIAS*, January 1980, 5–9, 15.

"Sovremennaya Obstanovka i Rol Demokraticheskoi Pechati" (The Contemporary Situation and the Role of the Democratic Press). *Kommunist*, 1983, no. 17, 3–19.

"Uroki Velikoi Otechestvennoi Voiny i Borba SSSR za Mir" (Lessons of the Great Patriotic War and the Struggle of the USSR for Peace). *Kommunist*, 1986, no. 11, 104–13.

"Borba Protiv Militarizma i Gonki Vooruzhenii v Sovremennom Mire" (Struggle Against Militarism and the Arms Race in the Contemporary World). *NINI*, February 1987, 3–12.

"Istoricheskoe Znachenie Sovetsko-Amerikanskovo Dogovora ot 8 Dekabrya 1987 g."
    (The Historical Significance of the Soviet-American Treaty of December 8,
    1987). *NINI*, February 1988, 17.

**Primakov, Evgenii**. "Krepit Edinstvo Sil, Boriushchikhsya Protiv Kolonializma"
    (Strengthen the Unity of Forces Fighting Against Colonialism). *Pravda*, June 12,
    1965, 4–5.

"Kair v Eti Dni" (Cairo in These Days). *Pravda*, June 11, 1967, 4.

"Izrail Igraet s Ognem" (Israel Is Playing with Fire). *Pravda*, June 12, 1967, 4.

"Narod na Zashchite Svoikh Zavoevanii" (People on the Defense of Their Triumphs).
    *Pravda*, June 13, 1967, 3.

"Vragi Arabskikh Narodov Proschitalis" (Enemies of Arab Peoples Miscalculated).
    *Pravda*, June 14, 1967, 5.

"Pozhinaiut Buriu" (They are Reaping a Whirlwind). *Pravda*, June 18, 1967, 5.

"Podozritelnaya Voznya" (Suspicious Bother). *Pravda*, June 19, 1967, 5.

"Hour of Ordeal." *NT*, 1967, no. 26, 7–9.

"Kair v Eti Dni" (Cairo in These Days). *Ogonek*, 1967, no. 26, 4–5.

"Behind the Scenes of the Israeli Gamble" *IA*, July 1967, 58–61.

"UAR: Revoliutsiya Budet Prodolzhena" (UAR: The Revolution Will Be Continued).
    *Pravda*, July 25, 1967, 4.

"Yemen: Reaction on the Offensive." *NT*, 1968, no. 3, 18–20.

"Vopreki Proiskam" (Despite Intrigues). *Pravda*, January 19, 1968, 4.

"Cairo Conspiracy Trial." *NT*, 1968, no. 7, 15–16.

"Dlya Razvitiya Revoliutsii" (For the Development of the Revolution). *Pravda*, March
    1, 1968, 5.

"The March 30 Programme." *NT*, 1968, no. 17, 5–7.

"Sevodnya v Caire" (Today in Cairo). *Pravda*, April 26, 1968, 4.

"UAR: Put k Budushchemu" (UAR: Path Toward the Future). *Pravda*, April 28, 1968,
    4.

"Kto Sryvaet Uregulirovanie" (Who Thwarts a Settlement). *Pravda*, May 20, 1968, 5.

"Politika, Vedushchaya v Tupik" (Policy Leading to a Dead-End). *Pravda*, June 21,
    1968, 4.

"Kuda Tyanut Izrailskie Praviteli?" What Are Israeli Rulers Longing For?). *Pravda*,
    October 13, 1968, 5.

"Eskalatsiya Naglosti" (Escalation of Impudence). *Pravda*, December 31, 1968, 5.

"Podderzhka Spravedlivoi Borby" (Support for a Just Struggle). *Pravda*, January 31,
    1969, 5.

"Peace Prospects in the Middle East." *IA*, February 1969, 49–50.

"Borba v Puti" (Struggle Under Way). *Pravda*, May 7, 1969, 4.

"Pochti Dva Goda Spustya" (Almost Two Years Later). *Pravda*, May 13, 1969, 4.

"Lestnitsa Vedushchaya Vniz" (Stairway Leading Down). *Pravda*, May 16, 1969, 4.

"Two Years After." *NT*, 1969, no. 24, 10–12.

"Novye Dni Sudana" (New Days for the Sudan). *Pravda*, June 28, 1969, 4.

"Borba Protiv Feodalnykh Ustoev" (Struggle Against Feudal Foundations). *Pravda*,
    August 20, 1969, 5.

"Irakskie Gorizonty" (Iraqi Horizons). *Pravda*, September 18, 1969, 4.

"Kto Meshaet Uregulirovaniiu" (Who Is Preventing a Settlement). *Pravda*, January 14, 1970, 4.

"Tel-Aviv: Na Stsene i za Kulisami" (Tel-Aviv: On Stage and Behind the Scenes). *Pravda*, February 5, 1970, 5.

"Po Puti Avantiurizma" (On the Path of Adventurism). *Selskaya Zhizn*, June 7, 1970, 3.

"Blizhnevostochnaya Politika SShA: Istoki, Perspektivy" (U.S. Middle East Policy: Sources and Prospects). *SShA*, September 1970, 3–13.

"Put k Spravedlivomu Miru" (Path to a Just Peace). *Pravda*, October 15, 1970, 4.

"Manevry SShA na Blizhnem Vostoke" (U.S. Maneuvers in the Middle East). *Pravda*, June 5, 1971, 4.

"Blizhnemu Vostoku-Spravdelivyi i Prochnyi Mir" (A Just and Lasting Peace for the Middle East). *Pravda*, January 5, 1972, 4.

"Economic Aspects of the Middle East Crisis." *IA*, June 1972, 37–42.

"Neblagovidnye Manevry Tel-Aviva" (Unseemly Maneuvers of Tel-Aviv). *Pravda*, February 15, 1973, 5.

"Vesna v Iraqe" (Spring in Iraq). *Pravda*, March 10, 1973, 4.

"Iraq: Novye Gorizonty" (Iraq: New Horizons). *Pravda*, July 12, 1973, 5.

"Nekotorye Voprosy Energeticheskovo Krizisa i evo Vliyaniya na Sovremennyi Mir" (Certain Questions of the Energy Crisis and Its Influence on the Contemporary World). *MEIMO*, February 1974, 66–72.

"V Nogu s Zaprosami Vremeni—Obzor Zhurnala 'Mezhdunarodnaya Zhizn,'" (In Step with the Demands of the Times—Survey of the Journal *International Life*). *Kommunist*, 1974, no. 11, 119–24.

"Pruzhiny Blizhnevostochnoi Politiki SShA" (Mainsprings of U.S. Middle East Policy). *SSHA*, November 1976, 3–15.

"'Sbalansirovannyi Kurs' na Blizhnem Vostoke ili Staraya Politika Inymi Sredstvami?" ("Balanced Course" in the Middle East or Old Policy by Other Means?). Part 1, *MEIMO*, December 1976, 38–51. Part 2, *MEIMO*, January 1977, 51–60.

"Sionizm i Izrail Protiv Arabskovo Naroda Palestiny" (Zionism and Israel Against the Arab People of Palestine). Part 1, *AIAS*, March 1977, 11–12. Part 2, *AIAS*, April 1977, 10–12.

"Blizhnevostochnyi Tupik: V Chem Prichina?" (Middle East Dead End: Who's to Blame?). *Pravda*, July 26, 1978, 4.

"Nekotorye Problemy Razvivaiushchikhsya Stran" (Certain Problems of Developing Countries). *Kommunist*, 1978, no. 11, 81–91.

"Neocolonialism: Essence, Forms, Limits." *IA*, November 1978, 66–71.

"Tsena Separatnoi Sdelki" (The Price of a Separate Deal). *Pravda*, December 15, 1978, 4.

"A Dead-End Middle East Settlement." *IA*, February 1979, 38–46.

"Osnovnye Tendentsii Razvitiya Mezhdunarodnoi Obstanovki v Aziatsko-Tikhookeanskom Regione" (Main Tendencies in the Development of the International Situation in the Asian-Pacific Ocean Region). *MEIMO*, November 1979, 51–60.

"Kogda Chernoe Vydaetsya za Beloe" (When Black Is Passed Off as White). *LG*, March 12, 1980, 14.

"Blizhnii Vostok: Dalneishaya Militarizatsiya Politiki SShA" (The Middle East: The Further Militarization of U.S. Policy). *Kommunist*, 1980, no. 9, 105–15.

"Islam i Protsessy Obshchestvennovo Razvitiya Stran Zarubezhnovo Vostoka" (Islam and Processes of Social Development in Countries of the Foreign East). *VF*, August 1980, 60–71.

"Osvobodivshiesya Strany: Problemy Obshchnosti" (Liberated Countries: Problems of Community). *NAIA*, 1980, no. 5, 16–28.

"Zakon Neravnomernosti Razvitiya i Istoricheskie Sudby Osvobodivshikhsya Stran" (The Law of Unequal Development and the Historical Fates of Liberated Countries). *MEIMO*, December 1980, 28–47.

Speech. *NAIA*, 1981, no. 1, 11–13.

"The Soviet Peace Program and International Development." *IA*, March 1981, 5–6.

"Strany Sotsialisticheskoi Orientatsii: Trudnyi, no Realnyi Perkhod k Sotsializmu" (Countries of Socialist Orientation: Difficult, but Real, Transition to Socialism). *MEIMO*, July 1981, 3–16.

"Mesto Osvobodivshikhsya Stran v Mirovoi Ekonomike" (The Place of Liberated Countries in the World Economy). *MEIMO*, March 1982, 16–33.

"Osvobodivshiesya Strany v Mezhdunarodnykh Otnosheniyakh" (Liberated Countries in International Relations). *MEIMO*, May 1982, 14–29.

"Kogda Voinu Nazyvaiut Mirom" (When They Call War Peace). *LG*, July 7, 1982, 14.

"Strany Vostoka v Sovremennom Mire" (Countries of the East in the Contemporary World). *Pravda*, August 11, 1982, 4–5.

"Aziya: Aktualnye Voprosy Obshchestvenno-Politicheskovo Razvitiya" (Asia: Actual Questions of Sociopolitical Development). *AIAS*, October 1982, 8.

"'Imperiya Dollara' v Proshlom i Nastoyashchem" ("Empire of the Dollar" in the Past and the Present). *MEIMO*, May 1983, 134–36.

"Aktualnye Zadachi Sovetskovo Vostokovedeniya" (Actual Tasks of Soviet Orientology). *NAIA*, 1983, no. 5, 3–15.

"Ne Teryat Vremeni!" (Don't Waste Time!). *LG*, August 17, 1983, 10.

"U.S.A.: Policy of Destabilization in the Middle East" *IA*, March 1984, 39–47.

"Kursom Diktata i Agressii" (On a Course of Diktat and Aggression). *Izvestiya*, July 20, 1984, 5.

"Volna 'Islamskovo Fundamentalizma': Problemy i Uroki" (The Wave of Islamic Fundamentalism: Problems and Lessons). *VF*, June 1985, 63–73.

"Put v Budushchee" (Path toward the Future). *Pravda*, January 22, 1986, 4.

"U Poroga Tretevo Tysyacheletiya" (On the Threshold of the Third Millenium). *LG*, February 5, 1986, 14.

"Filosofiya Bezopasnosti" (Philosophy of Security). *Pravda*, March 17, 1986, 6.

"Breeding Local Conflicts." *NT*, 1986, no. 21, 2, 18–19.

"Universalnost Moratoriya" (Universality of a Moratorium). *Pravda*, September 11, 1986, 4.

"Krupnyi Shag Vpered" (Big Step Forward). *Pravda*, January 5, 1987, 4.

Speech in *Pravda*, April 18, 1987.

"Novaya Filosofiya Vneshnei Politiki" (A New Philosophy of Foreign Policy). *Pravda*, July 10, 1987, 4.

"Novye Protivorechiya Katpitalisticheskoi Ekonomiki" (New Contradictions of Cap-italist Economics). *Pravda*, September 15, 1987, 4.

"Vzglyad v Proshloe i Budushchee" (A Look into the Past and the Future). *Pravda*, January 8, 1988, 4.

Interview. *MEIMO*, February 1988, 4–7.

"Facing the East Without Turning Our Back on the West" *NT*, 1988, no. 19, 10–11.

"USSR Policy on Regional Conflicts." *IA*, June 1988, 3–9.

Interview. *Pravda*, October 8, 1988, 4.

**Sheinis, Viktor**. "Neocolonialism as a Threat to Social Progress." *IA*, October 1973, 45–51.

"Izmeneniya v Ekonomike Kapitalizma i Nekotorye Osobennosti Neocolonializma 70-x Godov" (Changes in the Economy of Capitalism and Certain Peculiarities of Neocolonialism in the 1970s). *Ekonomicheskie Nauki*, January 1974, 58–70.

"Aktualnye Problemy Stran Azii i Afriki" (Actual Problems of African and Asian Countries). *NAIA*, 1975, no. 3, 37–52.

"Sotsialno-Ekonomicheskaya Differentsiatsiya i Problemy Tipologii Razvivaiush-chikhsya Stran" (Socioeconomic Differentiation and Problems of Typologizing Developing Countries). *MEIMO*, August 1978, 94–107.

"Srednerazvityi Kapitalizm: Realnost Latinskoi Ameriki" (Middle-Developed Capital-ism: The Reality of Latin America). Part 1, *LA*, 1979, no. 1, 65–73. Part 2, *LA*, 1979, no. 2, 130.

"Differentsiatsiya Razvivaiushchikhsya Stran: Ochertaniya i Masshtaby" (Differentia-tion of Developing Countries: Outlines and Scales). *AIAS*, January 1980, 32–36.

Book Review. *NAIA*, 1981, no. 4, 194–201.

"O Kriteriyakh Sotsialnovo Progressa v Razvivaiushchikhsya Stranakh" (On Criteria of Social Progress in Developing Countries). *NAIA*, 1981, no. 5, 64–80.

"O Spetsifike Sotsialnykh Protsessov v Razvivaiushchikhsya Stranakh" (On the Spe-cifics of Social Processes in Developing Countries). Part 1, *AIAS*, October 1981, 27–29. Part 2, *AIAS*, November 1981, 26–30.

"Razvivaiushchiesya Strany: Osobennosti Poslevoennovo Ekonomicheskovo Rosta" (Developing Countries: Peculiarities of Postwar Economic Growth). *MEIMO*, December 1981, 57–69.

"Razvivaiushchiesya Strany v 80-e Gody: Itogi i Perspektivy Sotsialno-Ekonomicheskoi Perestroiki" (Developing Countries in the 1980s: Results and Prospects of Socio-economic Restructuring). *AIAS*, September 1982, 28–32.

"Ekonomicheskie i Sotsialnye Problemy Razvivaiushchikhsya Stran Vostoka" (Eco-nomic and Social Problems of Developing Countries of the East). *MEIMO*, De-cember 1982, 115–23.

Book Review. *NAIA*, 1982, no. 6, 158–63.

"Sotsialnye Izmeneniya v Razvivaiushchikhsya Stranakh" (Social Changes in Devel-oping Countries). *AIAS*, March 1983, 25–27, 31.

Book Review. *NAIA*, 1983, no. 2, 178–84.

"MNCs i 'Subimperialisticheskie' Tendentsii v Latinskoi Amerike" (MNCs and "Sub-imperialist" Tendencies in Latin America). *LA*, October 1983, 63–69.

"Problemy Transformatsii Sotsialno-Ekonomicheskikh Struktur Razvivaiushchikhsya

Stran" (Problems in the Transformation of Socioeconomic Structures of Developing Countries). *NAIA*, 1983, no. 4, 21.

"Latinskaya Amerika: Protivorechiya Novovo Etapa" (Latin America: Contradictions
of a New Stage). *MEIMO*, May 1985, 118–23.

"Differentsiatsiya Razvivaiushchikhsya Stran: Novye Tendentsii" (Differentiation of
Developing Countries: New Tendencies). *AIAS*, August 1985, 22–26.

"Osobennosti i Problemy Kapitalizma v Razvivaiushchikhsya Stranakh" (Peculiarities
and Problems of Capitalism in Developing Countries). *MEIMO*, December 1986,
50–66.

"Razvivaiushchiesya Strany i Novoe Politicheskoe Myshlenie" (Developing Countries
and New Political Thinking). *RKISM*, 1987, no. 4, 77–90.

"Braziliya i Argentina v Sovremennom Mire" (Brazil and Argentina in the Contemporary World). *MEIMO*, August 1987, 71–77.

"Urovni i Varianty Stanovleniya Kapitalisticheskovo Sposoba Proizvodstva v Razvivaiushchikhsya Stranakh" (Levels and Variants of Establishing Capitalist
Means of Production in Developing Countries). *NAIA*, 1988, no. 1, 13–26.

"Kapitalizm, Sotsializm i Ekonomicheskii Mekhanizm Sovremennovo Proizvodstva"
(Capitalism, Socialism, and the Economic Mechanism of Contemporary Production). *MEIMO*, September 1988, 6–24.

"Strukturnye Sdvigi v Ekonomike Kapitalizma i Perspektivy Razvivaiushchikhsya
Stran" (Structural Shifts in the Economy of Capitalism and the Prospects of
Developing Countries). *AIAS*, November 1988, 20–23, 27.

"Sovremennyi Kapitalizm i Razvivaiushchiisya Mir: Kharakter i Perspektivy
Vzaimootnsohenii" (Modern Capitalism and the Developing World: The Character and Prospects of Relations). *NAIA*, 1988, no. 5, 126–29.

**Shevardnadze, Edvard**. Speeches in *Pravda* and *Izvestiya*, June 3, 1979, to December 21, 1988.

**Shirokov, Glerii**. "Razvivaiushchiesya Strany: Strategiya Industrializatsii" (Developing Countries: Strategy of Industrialization). *AIAS*, April 1976, 30–31.

"Industrializatsiya i Tekhnicheskoe Pereosnashchenie Narodnovo Khozyaistva Stran
Azii" (Industrialization and Technical Reequipment of the Economies of Asian
Countries). *AIAS*, December 1976, 26–29.

"Nauchno-Tekhnicheskaya Revoliutsiya i 'Tretii Mir'" (The Scientific-Technical Revolution and the "Third World"). *AIAS*, February 1977, 26.

"Tipologiya Nesotsialisticheskikh Stran" (A Typology of Nonsocialist Countries).
*AIAS*, July 1977, 24.

"Opyt Industrializatsii SSSR i evo Zhachenie dlya Stran Vostoka" (The Experience of
Soviet Industrialization and its Significance for Eastern Countries). *AIAS*, October 1977, 7–8.

"Sovetskii Soiuz i Natsionalno-Osvoboditelnoe Dvizhenie" (The Soviet Union and
National Liberation Movement). *NAIA*, 1978, no. 1, 6–12.

"Choosing a Road of Economic Development." *IA*, June 1978, 57–64.

"Promyshlennyi Perevorot v Stranakh Vostoka" (Industrial Revolution in Eastern
Countries). *AIAS*, August 1978, 25.

"Mezhukladnoe Vzaimodeistvie v Razvivaiushchikhsya Stranakh Vostoka" (Intersectoral Interaction in Eastern Developing Countries). *NAIA*, 1979, no. 4, 113–21.

Book Review. *SShA*, May 1981, 111.

"Razvivaiushchiesya Strany v Borbe za Novyi Mezhdunarodnyi Ekonomicheskoi Poryadok" (Developing Countries in Struggle for A New International Economic Order). *LA*, October 1981, 52–56.

"Sotsialno-Ekonomicheskie Izmeneniya v Stranakh Vostoka" (Socioeconomic Changes in Eastern Countries). *AIAS*, February 1982, 6–9.

"Problemy Zavisimosti Stran Vostoka" (Problems of the Dependence of Eastern Countries). *NAIA*, 1982, no. 3, 8 13.

"Sovremennye Transnatsionalnye Korporatsii" (Modern Transnational Corporations). *AIAS*, September 1982, 11.

"Ekspansiya Monopolii" (Expansion of Monopolies). *AIAS*, July 1983, 62–63.

"Razvivaiushchiesya Strany i Syrevoe Kapitalisticheskoe Khozyaistvo" (Developing Countries and Raw Material Capitalist Economy). *AIAS*, December 1984, 35–38.

"Preodolevaya Stoletiya" (Overcoming Centuries). *Izvestiya*, January 26, 1985, 5.

Osvobodivshiesya Strany v 80-e Gody" (Liberated Countries in the 1980s). *AIAS*, May 1987, 27–30.

**Shulgovsky, Anatolii**. "Anketa LA-69" (Questionnaire LA-69). *LA*, 1970, no. 1, 139–43.

"Leninskaya Teoriya Pererastaniya Demokraticheskoi Revoliutsii v Sotsialisticheskovo i Latinskaya Amerika" (Leninist Theory of the Growing Over of Democratic Revolutions into Socialist Revolutions and Latin America). *LA*, 1970, no. 2, 55–80.

"Latinskaya Amerika i Opyt Respublik Sovetskovo Vostoka" (Latin America and the Experience of Soviet Eastern Republics). *LA*, 1970, no. 3, 82–89.

"Latinskaya Amerika: Armiya i Politika" (Latin America: Army and Politics). *LA*, 1971, no. 4, 7–41.

Report. *LA*, 1972, no. 3, 199–203.

"Levoradikalnye Kontseptsii Revoliutsionnovo, Antiimperialisticheskovo i Demokraticheskovo Protsessov [*sic*]" (Left Radical Conceptions of Revolutionary, Antiimperialist, and Democratic Processes). *LA*, 1972, no. 4, 59–78.

"Opyt Resheniya Natsionalnovo Voprosa v SSSR i Ideologicheskaya Borba v Latinskoi Amerike" (Experience of Resolving the National Question in the USSR and Ideological Struggle in Latin America). *LA*, 1972, no. 6, 13–34.

"Kritika Nekotorykh Melkoburzhuaznykh Kontseptsii o Roli Armii" (Critique of Certain Petit Bourgeois Conceptions of the Role of the Army). *LA*, 1973, no. 5, 61–80.

"Aktualnye Voprosy Izucheniya Kommunisticheskovo i Rabochevo Dvizheniya" (Actual Questions of the Study of the Communist and Workers' Movement). *LA*, 1974, no. 3, 50–64.

"Vooruzhennye Sily Chili: Ot 'Apolitichnosti' k Kontrrevoliutsii" (Armed Forces of Chile: From Being "Apolitical" to Counterrevolution). *LA*, 1974, no. 6, 31–51.

"Ideologicheskie i Teoreticheskie Aspekty Revoliutsionnovo Protsessa v Peru" (Ideological and Theoretical Aspects of the Revolutionary Process in Peru). *LA*, 1975, no. 4, 10–28.

Book Review. *LA*, 1975, no. 6, 200–203.

"Polozhenie v Chili: Mify i Realnost" (Situation in Chile: Myths and Reality). *LA*, 1976, no. 5, 73–75.

"Rabochii Klass Latinskoi Ameriki: Politicheskie i Ideologicheskie Problemy Borby" (Working Class of Latin America: Political and Ideological Problems of the Struggle). *LA*, 1976, no. 6, 6–23.

"Armiya i Politika v Sovremennoi Latinskoi Amerike" (Army and Politics in Contemporary Latin America). Part 2, *LA*, 1977, no. 4, 146–49.

"Mezhdunarodnaya Sotsial-Demokratiya i Latinskaya Amerika" (International Social Democracy and Latin America). *LA*, 1978, no. 4, 100–103.

"Administratsiya Cartera i Latinskaya Amerika" (The Carter Administration and Latin America). *LA*, 1979, no. 4, 120–22.

"Social and Political Development in Latin America" *IA*, November 1979, 55–61.

"Eksperiment Bolshoi Istoricheskoi Vazhnosti" (An Experiment of Great Historical Importance). *LA*, March 1980, 6–12.

"Chile Sevodnya: Dobilas li Contrrevoliutsiya Svoikh Tselei?" (Chile Today: Has the Counterrevolution Achieved Its Aims?). *LA*, January 1981, 77–83.

"Neobkhodim Konkretno-Istoricheskii, Sotsialno-Klassovyi Analiz Sushchnosti Vneshnei Politiki" (A Concrete-Historical, Socioclass Analysis Is Needed of the Essence of Foreign Policy). *LA*, August 1981, 61–68.

"Kuda Idet Latinoamerikanskaya Xristianskaya Demokratiya?" (Where Is Latin American Christian Democracy Going?). *LA*, January 1982, 59.

"Gosudarstvo i Borba za Demokratiiu" (State and the Struggle for Democracy). *LA*, April 1983, 5–21.

"Sovremennye Otsenki Deyatelnosti MNC v Stranakh Latinskoi Ameriki" (Contemporary Evaluations of the Actions of MNCs in Latin American Countries). *LA*, August 1983, 36–39.

"Latinskaya Amerika: Protivorechiya Novovo Etapa" (Latin America: Contradictions of a New Stage). *MEIMO*, August 1985, 101–4.

"Na Puti k Edinstvu: Gruz i Tsennost Traditsii" (On the Road to Unity: Burden and Value of Traditions). *LA*, November 1988, 39–46.

**Simoniya, Nodari**. "Nekapitalisticheskii Put Razvitiya-Put Progressa" (Noncapitalist Path of Development—Path of Progress). *Kommunist*, 1965, no. 9, 121–24.

"O Kharaktere Natsionalno-Osvoboditelnykh Revoliutsii" (On the Character of National Liberation Revolutions). *NAIA*, 1966, no. 6, 3–21.

"O Roli 'Natsionalnykh Sotsializmov' v Revoliutsiyakh Vostoka" (On the Role of "National Socialisms" in Revolutions of the East). *VI*, April 1967, 47–58.

"Put Indoneziiskoi Revoliutsii" (Path of the Indonesian Revolution). *AIAS*, June 1967, 214–17.

"Revoliutsionnaya Demokratiya i Nekapitalisticheskii Put" (Revolutionary Democracy and the Noncapitalist Path). *AIAS*, September 1967, 2–4.

"Leniniskaya Ideya Revoliutsionno-Demokraticheskoi Diktatury i Nekapitalisticheskii Put Razvitiya" (The Leninist Idea of the Revolutionary Democratic Dictatorship and the Noncapitalist Development Path). *NAIA*, 1968, no. 2, 3–14.

"Po Povodu Monografii *Klassy i Klassovaya Borba v Razvivaiushchikhsya Stranakh*"

(On the Monograph *Classes and Class Struggle in Developing Countries*). Part 1, *NAIA*, 1969, no. 1, 44–53. Part 2, *NAIA*, 1969, no. 3, 49–54.

"Avantiuristicheskaya Liniya Pekina v Natsionalno-Osvoboditelnom Dvizhenii" (Adventurist Line of Peking in the National Liberation Movement). *Kommunist*, 1969, no. 12, 86–97.

"Za Aktivizatsiiu Antiimperialisticheskoi Borby" (For the Invigoration of the Anti-imperialist Struggle). *AIAS*, October 1971, 13–15.

"Natsionalizm i Politicheskaya Borba v Osvobodivshikhsya Stranakh" (Nationalism and Political Struggle in Liberated Countries). *MEIMO*, January 1972, 91–101.

"Ob Ekonomicheskom Soderzhanii 'Neekvivalentovovo Obmena'" (On the Economic Content of "Nonequivalent Exchange"). *NAIA*, 1972, no. 1, 22–36.

"Novoyavlennye 'Teoritiki' ili Podgoloski Pekinga" (Latter-Day "Theorists" or Yes-Men of Peking). *AIAS*, March 1972, 24–25.

"Moguchee Oruzhie Osvoboditelnoi Borby" (Mighty Weapon of Liberation Struggle). *Pravda*, October 5, 1972, 4.

"Natsionalnyi Vopros v Stranakh Sotsialisticheskoi Orientatsii" (National Question in Countries of Socialist Orientation). *MEIMO*, July 1973, 104–13.

"Nauchno-Tekhnicheskaya Revoliutsiya i Osvobodivshiesya Strany" (Scientific-Technical Revolution and Liberated Countries). *AIAS*, February 1974, 18.

"Kontseptsiya Edinovo Fronta i Problema Edinstva Antiimperialisticheskikh Sil" (Concept of United Front and Problem of Unity of Anti-imperialist Forces). *AIAS*, January 1975. 30–32.

"K Voprosu o Kharaktere Revoliutsionno-Demokraticheskikh Rezhimov i ix Sotsialnoi Baze" (On the Question of the Character of Revolutionary Democratic Regimes and Their Social Base). *AIAS*, January 1976, 7, 8, 14–15.

"Osvobodivshiesya Strany i Mirovoe Razvitie" (Liberated Countries and World Development). *AIAS*, January 1978, 4–8.

"Mezhdunarodnaya Sotsial-Demokratiya i Latinskaya Amerika" (International Social Democracy and Latin America). *LA*, 1978, no. 4, 119.

"K Voprosu o Sudbakh Kapitalizma v Stranakh Azii" (On the Question of the Fate of Capitalism in Asian Countries). *AIAS*, February 1979, 18–21.

"Dvizhenie Neprisoedineniya Nabiraet Silu" (The Non-Aligned Movement Gathers Strength). *AIAS*, August 1979, 3–6.

"Biurokraticheskaya Burzhuaziya, Biurokraticheskii Kapital, Gossektor i Goskapitalizm" (Bureaucratic Bourgeoisie, Bureaucratic Capital, the State Sector, and State Capitalism). *NAIA*, 1979, no. 5, 199–202.

Book Review. *NAIA*, 1979, no. 6, 196–99.

"The October Revolution and National Liberation Movements." *IA*, December 1979, 61–67.

"Imperializm i Osvobodivshiesya Strany" (Imperialism and Liberated Countries). *AIAS*, January 1980, 5–9, 15.

"Dvizhenie Neprisoedineniya na Novom Etape" (The Non-Aligned Movement at a New Stage). *AIAS*, March 1980, 6–8, 21.

"'Aid'in the Strategy of Neocolonialism." *IA*, August 1980, 30–37.

"The Mighty Tide of National Liberation." *NT*, 1980, no. 50, 22–23.

"Sovremennyi Etap Osvoboditelnoi Borby" (Modern Stage of Liberation Struggle). *AIAS*, May 1981, 15–17.

"Newly-Free Countries: Problems of Development." *IA*, May 1982, 83–91.

"Statistika Protiv Neokolonializma" (Statistics Against Neocolonialism). *AIAS*, November 1982, 10–14.

"Natsionalno-Gosudarstvennaya Konsolidatsiya i Politicheskaya Differentsiatsiya Razvivaiushchikhsya Stran Vostoka" (National State Consolidation and the Political Differentiation of Eastern Developing Countries). *MEIMO*, January 1983, 85–96.

"Voprosy Formatsionnovo Perekhoda v Antagonisticheskikh Obshchestvakh Vostoka v Sovremennuiu Epokhu" (Questions of the Formation of Transition in Antagonistic Eastern Societies into the Modern Epoch). *NAIA*, 1983, no. 2, 60–66.

"Gonka Vooruzhenii i Razvivaiushchiesya Strany" (Arms Race and Developing Countries). *AIAS*, January 1984, 2–5.

"The Struggle for National and Social Liberation: People's Inalienable Right." *IA*, March 1984, 107–14.

"O Perspektivakh Kapitalizma v Razvivaiushchemsya Mire" (On Prospects of Capitalism in the Developing World). *NAIA*, 1985, no. 1, 84–85.

"Dialektika Vazimosvyazei" (Dialectic of Interaction). *MEIMO*, March 1985, 125–33.

"Traditsionnye Faktory i Sotsialnoi Progress" (Traditional Factors and Social Progress). *AIAS*, October 1985, 25–29.

"The Charter of Freedom and Independence." *IA*, January 1986, 51–58.

"Na Puti Samostoyatelnovo Istoricheskovo Tvorchestva" (On the Path of Independent Historical Creation). *AIAS*, May 1986, 2–6.

"Leninskaya Kontseptsiya Perekhoda k Sotsializmu i Strany Vostoka" (Leninist Conception of Transition to Socialism and Eastern Countries). *AIAS*, April 1988, 2–5.

"Chestno Vesti Nauchnuiu Diskussiiu!" (Conduct a Scientific Discussion Honestly!). *AIAS*, June 1988, 16–18.

"Sovremennyi Kapitalizm i Razvivaiushchiisya Mir: Kharakter i Perspektivy Vzaimootnoshenii" (Modern Capitalism and Developing World: Character and Prospects of Interactions). *NAIA*, 1988, no. 5, 124–26.

**Sokolov, Sergei.** Speeches in *Pravda*, June 17, 1985, to March 2, 1986.

"Na Strazhe Mira i Sotsializma" (In the Defense of Peace and Socialism). *Izvestiya*, February 23, 1973, 1, 3.

"Nemerknushchee Velichie Nashei Pobedy" (Unfading Grandeur of Our Victory). *Selskaya Zhizn*, May 9, 1973, 3.

"Vsegda Na Strazhe, v Boevoi Gotovnosti" (Always on the Defense and in Military Readiness). *KZ*, February 23, 1974, 2.

"Vo Imya Mira na Zemle" (In the Name of Peace on Earth). *SR*, May 9, 1974, 2.

"Vernye Boevym Traditsiyam" (True to Militant Traditions). *SR*, February 22, 1975, 2.

"Vernost Zavetam Otsov" (Fidelity to the Precepts of our Fathers). *KP*, May 8, 1975, 2.

"Na Strazhe Mira" (In the Defense of Peace). *Pravda*, February 23, 1976, 2.

"Velikii Podvig Naroda" (Great Feat of the People). *SR*, May 9, 1976, 2.

"Nadezhnyi Strazh Otchizny" (Reliable Defense of the Fatherland). *KP*, February 23, 1977, 2.

"Moguchii Strazh Sotsialisticheskikh Zavoevanii" (Powerful Defense of Socialist Gains). *KZ*, February 22, 1978, 2.

"Nepobedimaya i Legendarnaya" (Invincible and Legendary). *Izvestiya*, February 23, 1979, 3.

"Surovyi Urok Istorii" (Severe Lesson of History). *KZ*, May 9, 1979, 2.

"Pod Rukovodstvom Partii, Vmeste s Narodom" (Under the Leadership of the Party and Together with the People). *Kommunist*, 1981, no. 3, 21–30.

"Nadezhnyi Shchit Rodiny" (Reliable Shield of Motherland). *KZ*, February 22, 1981, 2.

"Zakliuchitelnoe Slovo" (Concluding Word). *KVS*, 1981, no. 10, 57–58.

"Opyt i Uroki Istorii: K Vykhodu v Svet 12–vo Toma 'Istorii Vtoroi Mirovoi Voiny 1939–45'" (Experience and Lessons of History: On the Appearance of the Twelfth Volume of the "History of the Second World War, 1939-45"). *Pravda*, April 2, 1983, 3.

"Vsegda v Gotovnosti, Vsegda Nacheku" (Always Prepared, Always Alert). *KZ*, February 23, 1984, 2–3.

"Na Strazhe Zavoevanii Sotsializma" (In Defense of the Gains of Socialism). *KZ*, August 28, 1984, 2.

"Traditsiyam Verny" (True to Traditions). *Pravda*, February 22, 1985, 3.

Answers to TASS Correspondent. *KZ*, May 5, 1985, 1, 3.

Answers to TASS Correspondent. *Pravda*, May 6, 1985, 4.

"Sokhranit Dostignutoe v Oblasti Ogranicheniya Strategicheskikh Vooruzhenii" (Maintain What has Been Achieved in Limiting Strategic Weapons). *Pravda*, November 6, 1985, 4.

"Reshaiushchii Istochnik Boevoi Moshchi" (Decisive Source of Military Power). *Pravda*, February 23, 1986, 2.

"Pobeda, Obrashchennaya v Nastoyashchee i Budushchee" (A Victory Addressed to the Present and the Future). *Pravda*, May 9, 1986, 2.

"Bezopasnost: Problemy i Vozmozhnosti" (Security: Problems and Possibilities). *KZ*, January 22, 1987, 3.

"Na Strazhe Mira i Bezopasnost Rodiny" (On Defense of Peace and Security of the Motherland). *Pravda*, February 23, 1987, 2.

"Pobeda vo Imya Mira" (Victory in Name of Peace). *Pravda*, May 9, 1987, 2.

**Suslov, Mikhail**. Speeches in *Pravda*, June 5, 1965, to October 15, 1981.

**Trofimenko, Genrikh**. "Anti-Communism and Imperialism's Foreign Policy" *IA*, January 1971, 49–54.

" 'Doctrina Nixona': Deklaratsii i Realnost" (The "Nixon Doctrine": Declarations and Reality). *SShA*, February 1971, 30–32.

"Vazhnaya Problema" (Important Problem). *Pravda*, June 5, 1973, 4.

"Po Puti Mira i Bezopasnosti" (On the Path of Peace and Security). *KZ*, July 24, 1973, 3.

"SSSR-SShA: Mirnoe Sosushchestvovanie kak Norma Vzaimootnoshenii" (USSR–

U.S.A: Peaceful Coexistence as a Norm of Interrelations). *SShA*, February 1974, 9–17.

"Voprosy Ukrepleniya Mira i Bezopasnosti v Sovetsko-Amerikanskikh Otnosheniyakh" (On the Questions of Enhancing Peace and Security in Soviet-American Relations). *SShA*, September 1974, 8–18.

"Na Sterzhnevom Napravlenii" (In a Pivotal Direction). *MEIMO*, February 1975, 6–11.

"Uroki Vietnama" (Lessons of Vietnam). *SShA*, June 1975, 76–80.

"VPK: Novoe Issledovanie" (MIC: New Research). *SShA*, August 1975, 103–4.

"From Confrontation to Coexistence." *IA*, October 1975, 35–41.

"Evoliutsiya Voenno-Politicheskoi Strategii SShA Posle Vtoroi Mirovoi Voiny" (The Evolution of American Military-Political Strategy Since World War II). *VI*, March 1976, 64–65, 80–90.

"Traditsiya Realizmae i Borba Vokrug Razryadki" (Tradition of Realism and the Struggle Around Detente). *SShA*, July 1976, 26–28.

"Vneshnyaya Politika SShA v 70-e Gody: Deklaratsii i Praktika" (U.S. Foreign Policy in the 1970s: Declarations and Practice). *SShA*, December 1976, 17–28.

"Tekushchie Problemy Voennoi Politiki SShA" (Current Problems of U.S. Military Policy). *SShA*, March 1977, 92–98.

"Amerikanskii Podkhod k Mirnomu Sosushchestvovaniiu s Sovetskim Soiuzom" (American Approach to Peaceful Coexistence with the Soviet Union). Part 1, *SShA*, June 1978, 29–31. Part 2, *SShA*, July 1978, 38–53.

"Sredstva i Metody Vneshnei Politiki SShA" (Means and Methods of U.S. Foreign Policy). *VI*, May 1979, 63–77.

"Svidetelstva i Samoopravdaniya Ex-Prezidenta" (Testimony and Self-Justification of an Ex-President). *MEIMO*, June 1979, 136–44.

"Politika bez Perspektivy" (Policy without a Future). *MEIMO*, March 1980, 17–27.

"Washington: Kurs na Napryazhennost" (Washington: Course toward Tension). *SShA*, June 1980, 3–14.

"Pod Vyveskoi 'Sderzhivaniya'" (Under the Mask of "Deterrence"). *KZ*, May 23, 1981, 3.

"Osnovnye Postulaty Vneshnei Politiki SShA i Sudby Razryadki" (The Main Postulates of American Foreign Policy and the Fate of Detente). *SShA*, July 1981, 3–14.

"Aziatskaya Politika Washingtona" (Washington's Asian Policy). *AIAS*, November 1981, 9–11, 62.

"Formirovanie Voenno-Politicheskoi Strategii Administratsii Reagana" (Formation of the Military-Political Strategy of the Reagan Administration). *SShA*, May 1982, 124–25.

"Strategiya 'Pryamovo Protivoborstva'" (Strategy of "Direct Resistance"). *KZ*, June 2, 1982, 3.

"Ekonomicheskaya Agressiya Amerikanskovo Imperializma" (Economic Aggression of American Imperialism). *SShA*, May 1983, 99–106.

Book Review. *SShA*, November 1983, 120–21.

"Uroki Mirnovo Sosushchestvovaniya" (Lessons of Peaceful Coexistence). *VI*, November 1983, 18–27.

"Voennaya Strategiya SShA: Orudie Agressivnoi Politiki" (U.S. Military Strategy: Instrument of an Aggressive Policy). *SShA*, January 1985, 12.

Answering Questions. *KP*, February 16, 1985, 3.

"O Tikhookeanskoi Strategii Washingtona" (On the Pacific Ocean Strategy of Washington). *SShA*, October 1985, 3–14.

"Osmyslenie Opyta Razryadki" (Making Sense of the Detente Experience). *SShA*, September 1986, 93–99.

"Novye Realnosti i Novoe Myshlenie" (New Realities and New Thinking). *SShA*, February 1987, 4–15.

"O Statye J. Azrael i S. Sestanovich" (On the Article of J. Azrael and S. Sestanovich). *SShA*, August 1988, 41–50.

**Ulyanovsky, Rostislav.** "Nekotorye Voprosy Nekapitalisticheskovo Razvitiya Osvobodivshchikhsya Stran" (Certain Questions of the Noncapitalist Development of Liberated Countries). *Kommunist*, 1966, no. 1, 109–20.

"Sotsializm i Natsionalno-Osvoboditelnaya Borba—O Nekapitalisticheskom Puti Razvitiya" (Socialism and the National Liberation Struggle—On the Noncapitalist Development Path). *Pravda*, April 15, 1966, 4.

"Pod Devizom Solidarnosti—Posle Vstrech v Nicosi i Beirut" (Under the Motto of Solidarity—After Meetings in Nicosia and Beirut). *Pravda*, May 22, 1967, 4.

"O Nekotorykh Chertakh Sovremennovo Etapa Natsionalno-Osvoboditelnovo Dvizheniya" (On Certain Features of the Contemporary Stage of the National Liberation Movement). *NAIA*, 1967, no. 5, 21–36.

"Na Novykh Rubezhakh—O Nekotorykh Chertakh Sovremennovo Etapa Natsionalno-Osvoboditelnovo Dvizheniya" (On New Frontiers—On Certain Features of the Contemporary Stage of the National Liberation Movement). *Pravda*, January 3, 1968, 4–5.

"Nauchnii Sotsializm i Osvobodivshietsya Strany" (Scientific Socialism and Liberated Countries). *Kommunist*, 1968, no. 4, 96–104.

"K. Marx i Problemy Natsionalno-Osvoboditelnovo Dvizheniya" (K. Marx and Problems of the National Liberation Movement). *NAIA*, 1968, no. 5, 17–19.

"O Edinstve Sil Sotsializma i Natsionalno-Osvoboditelnovo Dvizheniya" (On the Unity of the Forces of Socialism and the National Liberation Movement). *Pravda*, October 14, 1968, 4–5.

"Krepit Edinstvo Natsionalno-Osvoboditelnykh Sil" (Strengthen the Unity of National Liberation Forces). *Pravda*, March 20, 1969, 4–5.

"Borba Cominterna za Leninskuiu Strategiiu i Taktiku v Natsionalno-Osvoboditelnom Dvizhenii" (The Struggle of the Comintern for Leninist Strategy and Tactics in the National Liberation Movement). *NAIA*, 1969, no. 3, 3–16.

"Osvoboditelnaya Borba Narodov Afriki" (Liberation Struggle of Peoples of Africa). *Kommunist*, 1969, no. 11, 39–42.

"Aktualnye Problemy Natsionalno-Osvoboditelnovo Dvizheniya" (Actual Problems of the National Liberation Movement). *NAIA*, 1969, no. 4, 3–14.

"Leninizm—Znamya Svobody i Progressa" (Leninism—Banner of Freedom and Progress). *Pravda*, October 25, 1969, 4.

"Natsionalno-Osvoboditelnoe Dvizhenie—Primety XX Stoletiya" (The National Liberation Movement—Signs of the Twentieth Century). *Izvestiya*, February 12, 1970, 2–3.

"Leninskaya Kontseptsiya Nekapitalisticheskovo Razvitiya i Sovremennost" (The Leninist Conception of Noncapitalist Development and Modern Times). *VI*, April 1970, 118–34.

"Lenin and the National Liberation Movement." *NT*, 1970, no. 16, 8–11.

"Dekolonizatsiya: Itogi i Perspektivy" (Decolonization: Results and Prospects). *Pravda*, November 12, 1970, 4.

"Nekotorye Voprosy Nekapitalisticheskovo Razvitiya" (Certain Questions of Noncapitalist Development). *Kommunist*, 1971, no. 4, 103–12.

"Dvadtsat Chetvertyi Syezd i Mirovoi Revoliutsionnyi Protsess—Kogda Sbrosheny Tsepi" (The Twenty-fourth Congress and the World Revolutionary Process—When the Chains Will Be Cast Off). *Izvestiya*, April 28, 1971, 2–3.

"Sovremennyi Etap Natsionalno-Osvoboditelnovo Dvizheniya i Krestianstvo" (The Contemporary Stage of the National Liberation Movement and the Peasantry). Part 1, *MEIMO*, May 1971, 91–104. Part 2, *MEIMO*, June 1971, 75–88.

" 'The Third World'—Problems of Socialist Orientation." *IA*, September 1971, 26–35.

"Burma's New Path." *IA*, May 1972, 16–22.

"Sotsialno-Ekonomicheskie Problemy Osvobodivshikhsya Stran" (Socioeconomic Problems of Liberated Countries). *Kommunist*, 1972, no. 8, 87–98.

"O Edinom Antiimperialsticheskom Fronte Progressivnykh Sil v Osvobodivshikhsya Stranakh" (On a Single Anti-imperialist Front of Progressive Forces in Liberated Countries). *MEIMO*, September 1972, 76–86.

"A Living Example." *NT*, 1972, no. 52, 4–7.

"Razryadka Mezhdunarodnoi" (International Detente). *Pravda*, August 30, 1973, 4–5.

"Razryadka Mezhdunarodnoi Napryazhennosti i Razvivaiushchiesya Strany" (Detente and Developing Countries). *NAIA*, 1973, no. 6, 4–13.

"Mezhdunarodnoe Znachenie Opyta Resheniya Natsionalnogo Voprosa v SSSR dlya Osbovodivshikhsya Stran" (The International Significance of the Experience of Solving the National Question in the USSR for Liberated Countries). *NAIA*, 1974, no. 6, 6–20.

"Indiya: Po Puti Progressa" (India: On the Path of Progress). *Pravda*, August 15, 1975, 4.

"Energeticheskii Krizis i Borba Osvobodivshikhsya Stran za Ekonomicheskoe Ravnopravie" (The Energy Crisis and the Struggle of Liberated Countries for Economic Equity). Part 1, *NAIA*, 1976, no. 2, 19–32. Part 2, *NAIA*, 1976, no. 3, 23–30.

"Natsionalno-Osvoboditelnoe Dvizhenie v Borbe za Ekonomicheskiuiu Nezavisimost" (The National Liberation Movement in Struggle for Economic Independence). *Kommunist*, 1976, no. 14, 116.

"Idei Velikovo Oktyabrya i Sovremennye Problemy Natsionalno-Osvoboditelnovo Dvizheniya" (Ideas of Great October and Contemporary Problems of the National Liberation Movement). *NINI*, March 1977, 3–25.

"Velikii Oktyabr i Natsionalno-Osvoboditelnaya Borba" (Great October and the National Liberation Struggle). *Pravda*, March 10, 1977, 4–5.

"Paths and Prospects of National Democracy." *NT*, 1978, no. 14, 19–20.

"Nauchnyi Sotsializm i Franz Fanon" (Scientific Socialism and Franz Fanon). *AIAS*, May 1978, 21–22.

"Ekonomicheskii Front Borby Protiv Neokolonializma" (Economic Front of Struggle Against Neocolonialism). *NAIA*, 1978, no. 4, 4–17.

"Nauchnyi Sotsializm i Kwame Nkrumah" (Scientific Socialism and Kwame Nkrumah). *AIAS*, February 1979, 24–28.

"O Stranakh Sotsialisticheskoi Orientatsii" (On Countries of Socialist Orientation). *Kommunist*, 1979, no. 11, 115–23.

"K Voprosu o Spetsifike Razvitiya Stran Vostoka" (On the Question of the Specifics of the Development of Eastern Countries). *NAIA*, 1979, no. 5, 58–74.

"Dvadtsatyi Vek i Natsionalno-Osvoboditelnoe Dvizhenie" (The Twentieth Century and the National Liberation Movement). *NAIA*, 1980, no. 2, 4–9.

"O Natsionalnom Osvobozhedenii i Natsionalizme" (On National Liberation and Nationalism). *AIAS*, October 1980, 4–6.

"Ograblenie Pod Maskoi 'Vzaimozavisimosti'" (Plunder Behind the Mask of "Interdependence"). *Kommunist*, 1981, no. 16, 76–87.

"Politicheskii Portret: Agostino Neto" (Political Portrait: Agostino Neto). *AIAS*, February 1982, 25–26.

"Politicheskii Portret: Marien Ngouabi" (Political Portrait: Marien Ngouabi). *AIAS*, May 1982, 40–41.

"Iranskaya Revoliutsiya i ee Osobennosti" (The Iranian Revolution and its Peculiarities). *Kommunist*, 1982, no. 10, 106–16.

"Sovetskaya Sotsialisticheskaya Federatsiya i Osvobodivshiesya Strany" (The Soviet Socialist Federation and Liberated Countries). *NAIA*, 1982, no. 6, 17.

"Razvitie Revoliutsionnovo Protsessa v Afganistane" (Development of Revolutionary Process in Afghanistan). *MEIMO*, August 1983, 16–31.

"Pod Pritselom Washingtona" (In the Gun Sights of Washington). *Pravda*, September 27, 1983, 4.

"O Natsionalnoi i Revoliutsionoi [*sic*] Demokratii: Puti Evoliutsii" (On National and Revolutionary Democracy: Paths of Evolution). *NAIA*, 1984, no. 2, 9–18.

"Sudby Iranskoi Revoliutsii" (The Fate of the Iranian Revolution). *Kommunist*, 1985, no. 8, 104–10.

"Aktualnye Problemy Natsionalno-Osvoboditelnovo Dvizheniya i Sotsialisticheskoi Orientatsii" (Actual Problems of the National Liberation Movement and Socialist Orientation). *NAIA*, 1986, no. 6, 3–13.

"K Kharakteristike Sovremennovo Neokolonializma" (Toward Characterizing Contemporary Neocolonialism). *NAIA*, 1987, no. 4, 86–92.

"O Roli Velikoi Oktyabrskoi Sotsialisticheskoi Revoliutsii v Noveishei Istorii Narodov Azii i Afriki" (On the Role of the Great October Socialist Revolution in the Most Recent History of Afro-Asian Peoples). *NAIA*, 1987, no. 5, 6–9.

"K Voprosu o Sotsialisticheskoi Orientatsii Osvobodivshikhsya Stran" (On the Question of the Socialist Orientation of Liberated Countries). *AIAS*, May 1988, 19–23.

**Ustinov, Dmitrii**. Speeches in *Pravda* and *Krasnaya Zvezda*, April 21, 1973, to August 29, 1984.

"Strazh Mirnovo Truda, Oplot Vseobshchevo Mira" (Defense of Peaceful Labor, Bastion of General Peace). *Kommunist*, 1977, no. 3, 12–22.

"Na Strazhe Zavoevanii Velikovo Oktyabrya" (In Defense of the Gains of Great October). *Pravda*, February 23, 1977, 2.

Order of the Day. *Pravda*, February 23, 1977, 1.

Order of the Day. *Pravda*, May 9, 1977, 1.

"Velikaya Pobeda" (Great Victory). *Pravda*, May 9, 1977, 2.

"Na Strazhe Revoliutsionnykh Zavovevanii" (In Defense of Revolutionary Gains). *KVS*, 1977, no. 21, 5–18.

Order of the Day. *Pravda*, May 9, 1978, 1.

"Pobeda vo Imya Mira" (Victory in the Name of Peace). *Pravda*, May 9, 1978, 2.

Order of the Day. *Pravda*, February 23, 1979, 1.

Order of the Day. *Pravda*, May 9, 1979, 2.

"Vysokii Rubezh Istorii" (High Frontier of History). *Pravda*, May 9, 1979, 2.

"Voennaya Razryadka—Velenie Vremeni" (Military Detente—Wave of the Times). *Pravda*, October 25, 1979, 4–5.

"Istochnik Velikoi Sily" (Source of Great Power). *Pravda*, February 22, 1980, 2–3.

"Narod—Geroi, Narod—Bogatyr" (People—Hero, People—Bogatyr). *Pravda*, May 9, 1980, 2.

Order of the Day. *Pravda*, May 9, 1980, 2.

"Nemerknushchii Podvig" (Unfading Feat). *Pravda*, September 2, 1980, 3–4.

"Delu Partii Verny" (True to the Cause of the Party). *Pravda*, February 21, 1981, 2.

"True to the Party's Cause." *IA*, May 1981, 20–23.

Order of the Day. *Pravda*, May 9, 1981, 1.

"Uroki Velikoi Pobedy" (Lessons of the Great Victory). *Pravda*, May 9, 1981, 2.

"Otstoyat Mir" (Defend Peace). *Pravda*, June 22, 1981, 2–3.

"Protiv Gonki Vooruzhenii i Ugrozy Voiny" (Against the Arms Race and the Threat of War). *Pravda*, July 25, 1981, 4.

"Armiya Druzhby Narodov" (Army of Friendship of Peoples). *Pravda*, February 23, 1982, 2.

Order of the Day. *Pravda*, February 23, 1982, 1.

Order of the Day. *Pravda*, May 9, 1982, 1.

"Osvoboditelnyi Podvig" (Liberating Feat). *Pravda*, May 9, 1982, 2.

Speech. *KVS*, 1982, no. 11, 8–14.

"Otvesti Ugrozu Yadernoi Voiny" (To Avert the Threat of Nuclear War). *Pravda*, July 12, 1982, 4.

Answering Questions. *Pravda*, August 20, 1982, 1.

"Istoricheskii Podvig" (Historic Feat). *Kommunist*, 1982, no. 16, 24–31.

Answering Questions. *Pravda*, December 7, 1982, 4.

"Moguchii Faktor Mira i Bezopasnosti Narodov" (Mighty Factor for Peace and Security of Peoples). *Pravda*, February 23, 1983, 2.

Order of the Day. *Pravda*, February 23, 1983, 1.

"Bessmertnyi Podvig" (Immortal Feat). *Pravda*, May 9, 1983, 2.

Order of the Day. *Pravda*, May 9, 1983, 1.

Answering Questions. *Pravda*, July 31, 1983, 4.
"Borotsya za Mir, Ukreplyat Oboronosposobnost" (Fight for Peace and Increase Defense Capabilities). *Pravda*, November 19, 1983, 4.
"Nesokrushimaya i Legendarnaya . . ." (Invincible and Legendary . . . ). *Pravda*, February 23, 1984, 2.
Order of the Day. *Pravda*, February 23, 1984, 1.
Order of the Day. *Pravda*, May 9, 1984, 1.
"Pobeda, Razveyavshaya Mify i Illiuzii" (The Victory that Shattered Myths and Illusions). *Pravda*, May 9, 1984, 2.
Answering Questions. *Pravda*, May 21, 1984, 4.
**Yakovlev, Aleksandr**. Interview. *KP*, December 25, 1983, 1, 3.
"Rakovaya Opukhol Imperskikh Ambitsii v Yadernyi Vek [*sic*]" (Cancerous Tumor of Imperial Ambitions in the Nuclear Age). *MEIMO*, January 1984, 3–17.
"U.S. Policy of Intervention: A Challenge to UN Principles." *IA*, February 1984, 26–34.
"Imperializm: Sopernichestvo i Protivorechiya" (Imperialism: Competition and Contradictions). *Pravda*, March 23, 1984, 3–4.
"Borba za Novyi Mezhdunarodnyi Ekonomicheskii Poryadok: Itogi Desyatiletiya" (Struggle for New International Economic Order: Results of a Decade). *MEIMO*, July 1984, 101.
"Protiv Militarizma i Revanshizma" (Against Militarism and Revanchism). *MEIMO*, December 1984, 106–10.
"Istoki Ugrozy i Obshchestvennoe Mnenie" (Sources of Threat and Public Opinion). *MEIMO*, March 1985, 3–17.
Commentary. *Vestnik, AN, SSSR*, May 1985, 82.
"Mezhdunarodnoe Znachenie Varshavskovo Dogovora" (International Significance of the Warsaw Pact). *MEIMO*, July 1985, 14–25.
"Opasnaya Os Amerikano–Zapadnogermanskovo Militarizma" (Dangerous Axis of American–West German Militarism). *SShA*, July 1985, 3–15.
"Say and Hear the Truth." *NT*, 1988, no. 41, 13–14.
**Yakovlev, Petr**. "Mezhdunarodny Monopolii Protiv Narodnovo Edinstva" (International Monopolies Against Popular Unity). *LA*, 1976, no. 3, 125–38.
Book Review. *LA*, 1976, no. 4, 201–2.
"Dvizhushchaya Sila Imperialisticheskoi Ekspansii" (The Moving Force of Imperialist Expansion). *LA*, 1976, no. 5, 49–66.
"Latinoamerikanskii Kurs Washingtona" (Washington's Latin American Course). *SShA*, December 1978, 15–27.
"O Burzhyaznykh Kontseptsiyakh Radryadki" (On Bourgeois Conceptions of Detente). *LA*, 1979, no. 3, 38–45.
"Administratsiya Cartera i Latinskaya Amerika" (The Carter Administration and Latin America). *LA*, 1979, no. 4, 136–37.
"Novyi Etap v Amerikano-Brazilskikh Otnosheniyakh" (New Stage in American-Brazilian Relations). *SShA*, April 1980, 55–63.
"Washington and the Militarization of Latin America." *IA*, August 1981, 74–79.
"Mnimye Paradoksy i Realnye Zakonmernosti" (Imaginary Paradoxes and Real Laws). *LA*, September 1981, 57–59.

"Rabochii Klass i Vneshnyaya Politika" (The Working Class and Foreign Policy). *LA*, February 1982, 17–19.

"Ot Dekreta o Mire k Programme Mira" (From the Decree on Peace to the Peace Program). *LA*, December 1982, 40–53.

"Dva Kursa v Mirovoi Politike i Latinskaya Amerika" (Two Courses in World Politics and Latin America). *LA*, March 1984, 6–16.

"American Neocolonialism's Testing Range in the Caribbean." *IA*, February 1985, 70–76.

"Tri Goda Pravleniya Radikalov" (Three Years of Radical Government). *LA*, February 1987, 14–23.

**Yazov, Dmitrii**. Speeches in *Pravda*, July 29, 1987, to July 13, 1988.

"Perestroika v Rabote Voennykh Kadrov" (Restructuring the Work of Military Cadres). *VIZ*, July 1987, 4–12.

"Voennaya Doktrina Varshavskovo Dogovora—Doktrina Zashchity Mira i Sotsializma" (Military Doctrine of the Warsaw Pact—Doctrine of the Defense of Peace and Socialism). *Pravda*, July 27, 1987, 5.

"O Voennom Balance Sil i Raketno-Yadernom Paritete" (On the Military Balance and Nuclear Parity). *Pravda*, February 8, 1988, 5.

Press Conference. *Pravda*, March 18, 1988, 4.

"The Military Balance of Strength and Nuclear Missile Parity." *IA*, April 1988, 18–22.

Order of the Day. *Pravda*, May 9, 1988, 1.

"Podvig vo Imya Zhizni" (Feat in the Name of Life). *Pravda*, May 9, 1988, 2.

"Kachestvennye Parametry Oboronnovo Stroitelstva" (Qualitative Parameters of Defense Construction). *KZ*, August 9, 1988, 1, 2.

"Vozmozhna li Evropa bez Yadernovo Oruzhiya?" (Is a Nuclear-Free Europe Possible?). *Trud*, August 9, 1988, 3.

**Zorina, Irina**. "Chile: Komu Prinadlezhit Vremya" (Chile: To Whom Does Time Belong). *MEIMO*, August 1969, 121–27.

"Paradoksy Latinoamerikanskovo Reformizma" (Paradoxes of Latin American Reformism). *MEIMO*, January 1970, 37–47.

"Chile: Pobeda Narodnovo Edinstva" (Chile: Victory of Popular Unity). *MEIMO*, November 1970, 82–86.

"Chile: Novyi Etap Istorii" (Chile: New Stage of History). *LA*, 1971, no. 1, 6–22.

"Kharakter i Perspektivy Revoliutsionnovo Protsessa v Chile" (Character and Prospects of Revolutionary Process in Chile). *MEIMO*, December 1971, 54–63.

Book Review. *LA*, 1972, no. 4, 169–75.

"Chiliiskii Narod Podtverdil Svoi Vybor" (Chilean People Have Reaffirmed Their Choice). *MEIMO*, May 1973, 75–82.

"Katoliki i Revoliutsiya" (Catholics and Revolution). *MEIMO*, August 1973, 154–57.

Book Review. *LA*, 1973, no. 5, 161–64.

Book Review. *LA*, 1975, no. 6, 197–200.

"Politik, Pisatel, Chelovek—K 60-letiiu V. Teitelboim" (Politician, Writer, Man—On the Sixtieth Birthday of V. Teitelboim). *LA*, 1976, no. 2, 173–74.

Book Review. *LA*, 1977, no. 5, 207–9.

"Razvivaiushchiesya Strany v Politicheskoi Strukture Sovremennovo Mira" (Developing Countries in the Political Structure of the Contemporary World). *MEIMO*, August 1982, 80–91.

"'Subimperialisticheskie' Tendentsii: Mezhdunarodno-Politicheskii Aspekt" ("Subimperialist" Tendencies: International Political Aspect). *LA*, October 1983, 70–75.

"Argentina na Istoricheskom Povorote" (Argentina at a Historic Turning Point). *MEIMO*, May 1984, 57.

"Na Stremnine Ideinovo Protivoborstva" (In the Rapids of Ideological Resistance). *MEIMO*, December 1984, 138.

"Latinskaya Amerika: Protivorechiya Novovo Etapa" (Latin America: Contradictions of a New Stage). *MEIMO*, August 1985, 107–11.

"Meksika, God 1985–i . . ." (Mexico, 1985 . . . ). *MEIMO*, November 1985, 103–4.

"Braziliya i Argentina v Sovremennom Mire" (Brazil and Argentina in the Contemporary World). *MEIMO*, August 1987, 71–77.

"Razoruzhenie dlya Razvitiya ili Vooruzhenie za shet Razvitiya?" (Disarmament for Development or Arming at the Expense of Development?). *LA*, August 1987, 58–62, 73–75.

"Kontseptsiya Vseobshchei Bezopasnosti i Razvivaiushchiesya Strany" (Conception of General Security and Developing Countries). *LA*, November 1987, 99–101.

# Index